FILM FESTIVALS

FILM FESTIVALS

Culture, People, and Power
on the Global Screen

CINDY HING-YUK WONG

RUTGERS UNIVERSITY PRESS
New Brunswick, New Jersey, and London

Library of Congress Cataloging-in-Publication Data

Wong, Cindy H., 1961–
  Film festivals : culture, people, and power on the global screen /
Cindy Hing-Yuk Wong.
      p. cm.
  Includes bibliographical references and index.
  Includes filmography.
  ISBN 978–0–8135–5065–7 (hardcover : alk. paper) — 978-0-8135-5121-0 (pbk. : alk. paper)
  1. Film festivals.   2. Motion pictures.   3. Motion picture industry.   I. Title.
  PN1993.4.W66   2011
  791.43079—dc22
                                                                    2010045438

A British Cataloging-in-Publication record for this book is available from the British Library.

Visit our Web site: http://rutgerspress.rutgers.edu

Manufactured in the United States of America

For Gary and our kids, Larissa and Graciela

Contents

Acknowledgments

Since this project began many years ago, I have had the opportunity to learn and discuss with many festival participants and organizers as well as to share with my colleagues in studies of media at the College of Staten Island and Graduate Center–City University of New York. CUNY, PSC-CUNY, and the College of Staten Island have provided funding, time, and support for pieces of this work, including the acquisition of images for the final text. The work was also supported through my year as a Fulbright Fellow in Hong Kong (2006–2007), including ties to both City University of Hong Kong and Hong Kong University.

Indeed, many of those who inspired, interrogated, and supported this project are linked to Hong Kong. These include film professionals such as Fruit Chan, Norman Wang, Yeung Fan, and Alan Fong as well as many people associated with the Hong Kong Film Festival: Li Cheuk To, Law Kar, Roger Garcia, Peter Tsi, and my brother, Jacob Wong. Others have proved gracious and supportive global colleagues, including Gina Marchetti at HKU and Nancy Tong, formerly affiliated with City University of Hong Kong. My student Ma Ran also provided important contributions from her work on urban-generation filmmakers. Other friends and family in Hong Kong who have shared my labors and conversations must include the late Wong Yuen Ling, Zhang Xiaowen, Shirley Wong, Katie Yip, Kevin Chuc, and many other friends.

In addition, I certainly have received support and commentary from colleagues and students in New York, including a wider family at CSI that includes Cynthia Chris, Jeanine Corbet, Kristie Falco, David Gerstner, Steve Hager, Michael Mandiberg, Edward Miller, Sherry Miller, Ella Shohat, Jason Simon, Matthew Solomon, Norie Taniguchi, Valerie Tevere, Ying Zhu, and the late George Custen. Janet Manfredonia and Rosemary Neuner-Fabiano have also provided constant help in myriad ways. Beyond the department of Media Cultures, friends and colleagues such as Ann Helm, Wilma Jones, Kathryn Talarico, Francisco Soto, and David Podell have offered invaluable support. Roberta Pearson continues to be a friend and advisor. Mirella and Charles Affron have been mentors, scholarly companions, and rare friends whose relationships have now grown across generations.

Ethnography in multiple field sites also has left me indebted to countless organizers and participants in many festivals. In particular, I would like to thank Ulrich and Erika Gregor, Milena Gregor, John Biaggi, Kanako Hayashi, Richard Peña, Oscar Cardenas, Ruby Rich, Sarah Schulman, Jim Hubbard, Teresa

Calvina, Klaus Eder, Amos Gitai, Autero Ripstein, Paz Alicia Garciadiego, Roya Rastegar, Skadi Loist, and the staffs and others with whom I have worked at the Hong Kong International Film Festival, the Berlin Film Festival, the Locarno Film Festival, the San Sebastián Film Festival, Tokyo Filmex, the San Francisco International Lesbian and Gay Film Festival, MIX, Tribeca Film Festival, the New York Film Festival, the Philadelphia Film Festival, and other events. I also acknowledge the support of libraries and archives worldwide that have contributed data and films to this project over many years, including the New York Public Library, Charles Silver at the Museum of Modern Art, the Hong Kong University Library, the Hong Kong Film Archives, Cinémathèques in Toulouse and Paris, the Filmoteca in Barcelona, the Ludington Library in Bryn Mawr, the Bryn Mawr College Library, and the library at the College of Staten Island.

In the preparation and completion of the manuscript, I have received wonderful tutelage from Leslie Mitchner and her colleagues, Catherine Keeran and Marilyn Campbell, at Rutgers University Press. In addition, I want to acknowledge the input—and support—of my readers for the press, Wheeler Winston Dixon and the late Peter Brunette. I am also grateful to Derik Shelor, who has done a superb job copyediting the book with precision and patience.

Finally, of course, I am indebted to my family. My family of origin, including my brother, who has made the HKIFF part of our lives, my late mother, Chit Ming Leung, and my father, Yuen Ching Wong. And the next generation, Larissa Jiit-Wai McDonogh-Wong and Graciela Jiit-Heng McDonogh-Wong, who have grown up amid festivals and films, stacks of papers and last-minute deadlines, in Locarno and Hong Kong and other venues as well. As they find their own paths and write their own stories, I will add one more dedication to their collection. And Gary, whose support to everything I do has been unwavering. This project would not have been possible without the constant urging, discussions, meals, and travels we have shared for many, many years. Finally, he gets a dedication, too.

FILM FESTIVALS

Introduction

Film festivals attract widespread global attention as glittering showcases for films and people. Yet, they also constitute vital nodes for global film industries, businesses, institutions, and information. Festivals provide places in which multiple agents negotiate local, national, and supranational relations of culture, power, and identity. Ultimately, they are crucial centers for the development of film knowledge and film practices: festivals and the people who create and re-create them thus shape what films we as audiences and scholars will see, what films we respect or neglect, and often, how we read such cinematic works. Hence, the study of film festivals allows us to understand complex global relationships of film cultures through the historical development and contested hierarchy of films, filmmakers, film languages, themes, and places.[1]

Gilles Jacob, longtime director and president of the Cannes International Film Festival, explained to *Variety* that this festival serves

> to take the pulse of world cinema once a year. To gather the movers and shakers of the profession in one place so they can exchange ideas, show each other their movies, and do business. To discover new talents. . . . To spotlight new trends in filmmaking. . . . To promote a type of cinema that's both artistic and of wide appeal. To showcase striking and difficult works that wouldn't otherwise get the attention they deserve. To salute great filmmakers who will add to the festival's prestige. To give the people behind a film the chance to meet the world's press. To generate miles of free publicity for the films taking part, enough to stretch from Paris to Los Angeles. . . . And finally, to recharge filmmakers' and producers' batteries once a year so they have the courage to carry on—by showing them movies they'd have been proud to work on and produce.[2]

As this passage from the leader of what is arguably the premier world film festival insists, festivals go far beyond cinephilia, their prized auteurs, glamorous events and people, and global accolades. Film festivals deal with business, from production to distribution, including the very financing that ensures their own reproduction. Film festivals create and participate in public spheres of discussion through global media—identifying novelty and thriving on competition for the first, the best, the most daring, or the most significant films while catalyzing debates over issues ranging from technical achievements to human rights and sexual identities. Film festivals, though, seldom highlight blockbusters. Instead, festivals, as places where people go to "recharge batteries" and to envy or to argue with difficult films, represent places of creativity and conflict on a local and global scale. In short, film festivals provide a unique network through which all those involved in cinema may view the past, explore the present, and create the future. Festivals constitute a dynamic system where a specific cultural artifact—cinema—circulates and multiple actors continuously strive to redefine its meaning and place in its immediate environment, a wider film world, and larger socio-economic and political contexts.

Film festivals also celebrate place: the city that hosts them, the nation and national/regional industries that often underpin them, and the globalization of relations of production and film markets. Festivals define the very cultural capital that cities and nations embrace as brand-name events for cities of the creative class.[3] In the early histories of film festivals, up to the late 1960s, such gatherings made strong direct statements about statecraft as well. Venice embodied the cultural claims of Fascist Italy, while Cannes emerged from the strategies of its French opponent (with Hollywood allies). During the cold war, festivals in Berlin and Karlovy Vary (Czechoslovakia) glared at each other from opposite sides of the Iron Curtain. Today, while such geopolitical divisions are less apparent in Europe, festivals in Ouagadougou (Burkina Faso), Mar del Plata (Argentina), Pusan (South Korea), and Hong Kong all challenge "Western" hegemony in filmmaking, evaluation, and distribution while competing with each other as regional showcases.

Nonetheless, besides Sundance, which is a very recent "American" festival (1978), the differences in festival culture in the United States make a political, economic, and cultural statement as well. While American filmmakers have participated in global festival culture since the 1930s, for decades this participation was filtered through Hollywood's control of the domestic market and global perceptions of the products—Classical Hollywood films, stars, glamour—that these studios could bring to Cannes, Venice, and Berlin. Where Hollywood became one offering among many national traditions in these fora, film festivals in North America represented an alternative globalism where elite audiences could learn about European art cinema and its widening gaze. Hence, early American festivals often seem truncated by comparison to their European or Asian counterparts—less concerned with global discovery, production, or distribution than with representation of current trends: San Francisco (1957) and New York (1963) both emerged under strong European tutelage. Meanwhile, Toronto (founded in 1976) has become the most important North American world cinema market, while Montréal is the continent's only recognized "A"-level competition festival.

This does not mean the experience or importance of festivals today is completely different in the United States, either; we must be careful to interpret American structures and experiences without recourse to "exceptionalist" visions while noting local differences. Sundance, for example, is an important

"American" festival, devoted to recognition and support of American independent films—that is, films made in counterpoint to Hollywood as a national industry. Yet, it is equally clear that Sundance has become, for some of its successful veterans, a training ground for Hollywood-like or Hollywood-lite careers with larger-budget films for more mainstream audiences and multiplex box offices, especially in the United States.[4] Caroline Libresci, international programmer of Sundance, admits, "If you take your film to Rotterdam, you have all European eyes on you, and at Sundance, you have all American eyes on you—hopefully."[5] Despite its increasing interest in non-American filmmakers, Sundance remains primarily an American festival in content, audience, and business.

European festivals also have been known to showcase American independent works, as Rotterdam did in its early days.[6] Some of the very themes that Sundance and U.S. independents champion in terms of diverse experiences and voices of race, ethnicity, and class also appeal to global film festivals whose audiences still identify American society, for better or worse, with such issues. Sundance Grand Prize winner *Frozen River* (2008), for example, made it to European festivals like Hamburg, Geneva, and San Sebastián, where it won a prize distributed by the World Catholic Association for Communication as well as an acting award. *Precious* (2009) followed a similar trajectory, including Un Certain Regard at Cannes, San Sebastián, and theatrical distribution. Other "ethnic" Sundance prize-winning films dealing with the American Latino experiences (*Quinceañera* [2006] and the U.S.-Argentine *Sangre de mi sangre/Padre nuestro* [2007]) have gained less global festival traction. Meanwhile, in San Sebastián, the United States was strongly in evidence in 2008: director Jonathan Demme chaired the jury, while a Lifetime Achievement Award went to Meryl Streep. Woody Allen and the Coen brothers also won awards, and Ben Stiller's *Tropic Thunder* was in competition. The Golden Conch that year, however, went to the Turkish-French-German-Belgian coproduction *Pandora's Box* (*Pandoranin kutusu*).

Despite their global importance and publicity appeal, discussion of festivals has remained for the most part the domain of journalists and memoirs,[7] institutional practitioners and festival publications, supplemented by the rich materials provided in catalogs and Web sites.[8] Only recently has there emerged more systematic interest in film festival studies, with the increased presence of film festival panels in academic conferences. Skadi Loist and Marijke de Valck have developed the Film Festival Research Network (FFRN), which provides a detailed bibliography for film festival studies and a forum for researchers to exchange ideas.[9] Dina Iordanova has coedited two volumes of *Film Festival Yearbook*, with another to be published in 2011, and Richard Porton has edited *Dekalog 3: On Film Festivals*. Nonetheless, besides these anthologies, Marijke de Valck's *Film Festivals: From European Geopolitics to Global Cinephilia* is the only monograph on film festivals. I recognize the path-breaking importance of de Valck's work in terms of its recognition of history, function, and complexity of festivals and their participants, although it is important that this, like the other works cited, was published in Europe and concentrated on European festivals.[10] This is particularly important when we try to understand the power and distortion of the European gaze in film knowledge mediated through key festivals and the alternatives visible from other positions within the festival world.

Other scholars have applied the interdisciplinary cultural perspectives of film and media studies to incorporate film festivals and the questions they raise into studies of history, politics, and meaning.[11] This book adds further dimensions to this growing literature, paying serious attention to film festivals on a global scale as complex and contested arenas of social, cultural, economic, national, regional, and transnational practices. Building on seven years of ethnography, interviews, film analyses, and archival research within film festivals worldwide—especially Locarno, Berlin, San Sebastián, Hong Kong, and New York—this volume provides an interdisciplinary perspective on the organization, content, differences, and meanings of film festivals within a global festival context and their impact on what we see as film. It also underscores how film festivals are created by people: producers, directors, agents, stars, programmers, critics, and spectators who have shared their viewpoints and experiences with me. Synthesizing historical processes, textual analyses, participant observation, and personal interviews, I show that film festivals are not only important for what they offer on-screen, or for their claims about politics, culture, and identities, but also for their centrality to the networks, business, knowledge, and circulation that constitute global film today.

While covering the major established European festivals and the films they show, this book situates film festivals as truly global phenomena. It balances the best-known events and power of Cannes, Berlin, and Venice with the dynamics of other European festivals, such as Locarno (Switzerland), San Sebastián (Spain), and Rotterdam (Netherlands) and the complex roles of North American filmmaking and festivals within this system. It pays particular attention to the changing role of regional festivals and networks around the world, especially the Hong Kong International Film Festival (HKIFF) and the definition of Chinese, Asian, and global cinema. In addition, this work links smaller festivals defined by place, genre (silent film, animation, science fiction), or themes (gay, lesbian, bisexual, and transgender/transsexual films, human rights, Asian Americans, etc.) to this global system and discourses of film, underscoring festivals as places of cultural discussion and production. Through this, I reiterate the connections of programming, product, and criticism that unite multiple nodes of cinephilia and films themselves. Finally, throughout the book I highlight the multilayered relations of festivals and film industries, seen from the perspective of auteurs, critics, film funders, and even Hollywood. For films, filmmakers, and audiences, this system constitutes and reconstitutes a world of cinema and cinema culture represented or experienced in myriad, albeit fragmented ways.

places of cultural discussion and production

mass media coverage / annual calendar
parties / awards

Relations with Hollywood, in fact, prove especially illuminating for understanding festivals as a global system. Film festivals function as alternative sites for the production, distribution, and exhibition of independent films from all over the world: this is part of their global cachet. They are obviously not vertically integrated like the Classic Hollywood Studios; however, they form a complicated, competitive global network, spatially as well as temporally in an annual calendar that very much controls the lives of alternative, independent cinema. Hollywood stars, products, and glamour, however, also represent central elements of major festivals from Cannes to Sundance. Even for smaller festivals jockeying for place in a crowded calendar, a Hollywood celebrity or special event provides immediate endorsement and attention.

For most people, film festivals burst into mass media coverage as intense, albeit ephemeral events—a week or two of glitz, buzz, myriad screenings, and jumbled events. Whether we talk about the Big Three festivals—Cannes, Venice, Berlin—look at Sundance, Tribeca, and Toronto in North America, or examine other significant world festivals in Hong Kong, Pusan, Locarno, Rotterdam, San Sebastián, and Mar del Plata, the insistent global icons of all festivals are films, discoveries, auteurs, stars, parties, and awards. After the lights dim, festivals still embody competition among global cities, cultural and economic negotiations among filmmakers, industries, and festivals themselves, and more abstract struggles for the right to define film taste and knowledge. Let me separate some of these densely interwoven themes with regard to film itself, to the people involved, to the geographies of film festivals, and to the taste and knowledge constructed through them.

Reading Festivals: The Films, the People, the Places, and the Canon

Cinema can be approached from many perspectives—through films, people, places, and more abstract aspects of knowledge and culture. Festivals, obviously, are initially defined by the films themselves. These texts focus us as spectators and participants even if we talk about cinema from divergent perspectives, including aesthetics, meaning, production, distribution, and everything in between. Festival films, in one sense, are simply films that choose festivals as their first or primary exhibition sites; indeed, Peter Wollen defines the festival film simply by its exhibition venue rather than by any textual elements.[12] Some films actually remain cloistered in festival worlds, finding a life on the festival circuit and perhaps limited distribution through art house movie theaters, universities, and DVDs. A few others gain greater success, economically or aesthetically. Still others are films rediscovered or recast within festival worlds as classics or overlooked moments in cinematic development.

Beyond simple exhibition, however, widely shared patterns of film selection and evaluation have shaped festival films over time. Though festival selections have overlapped with "mainstream" cinema, festival films more often are distinguished from those in general distribution: they tend to be nonstudio produced, lower budget, serious movies—similar to what many people label "art house" or "art cinema."[13] Translated into a global context, this means festival films tend to be non-Hollywood, artistic, serious, and edgy. Still, these defining elements are also context dependent: Oliver Stone's *W* (2008), for example, released for general audiences in the United States, was reframed as a gala event for festival screening in Hong Kong, where it had no theatrical distribution. Hong Kong's swashbuckling *Swordsman II* (1992), by contrast, "became" a serious film for the Philadelphia Gay and Lesbian Film Festival, which focused on the sexual transformation of its villain from male to female. Spectacle, narrative, and even high production values have their place in festival catalogs and among prize winners.

Tracing practices of selection over time, especially with reference to Hollywood as an active participant in many early festivals, shows how "boundaries" of popular and art film have shifted as well. Hollywood films competed in the early years of Venice, and stars like Mae West, Gary Cooper, and Paul Muni were ready for the inaugural Cannes Festival of 1939, which was cancelled when Hitler invaded Poland. After World War II, as the festival world revived, the 1946 program at Locarno included Roberto Rossellini's *Rome, Open City (Roma, città aperta)* (1945), Sergei Eisenstein's *Ivan the Terrible* (1944), and the national film documentary *Typical Pictures of Swiss Life* (1946). Yet audiences, exhausted by years of enclosed neutrality, enjoyed Billy Wilder's *Double Indemnity* (1944), George Sidney's *Bathing Beauty*, starring Esther Williams (1944), and Henry King's *Song of Bernadette* (1943) as well. The prizewinner that year was the French director René Clair, but the film he was associated with was his production of *And Then There Were None* for Twentieth Century-Fox, while Jennifer Jones took home the best actress award for *Song of Bernadette*. In 1955, the gritty Hollywood production of *Marty* won both the Oscar for Best Picture and the Palme d'Or at Cannes. Later, as both Hollywood and festivals changed, major Hollywood films tended to be screened out of competition while American independents found new venues, support, and reputation in festivals. The prominence of Quentin Tarantino, Michael Moore, Sean Penn, and Natalie Portman among other contemporary "artistic" American celebrities at Cannes thus has a long and complicated heritage.

In large festivals with hundreds of screenings, films span different genres, formats, themes, and audiences. While fictional feature films gain the most attention in screening and publicity, documentaries, shorts, experimental films, avant-garde cinema, animation, student work, and even unfinished projects all have their places in major festivals as well as in different specialized festivals. The Panorama section in Berlin, for example, includes features, documentaries, and shorts. The Human Rights Watch International Film Festival, a multi-site festival, documents abuses around the world, from Chile to Tibet. The HKIFF screens work from each university film program in the metropolis and also

includes a Midnight Madness section whose choices range from punk to horror. Beyond the festivals, film markets and coproduction fora offer places for student essays, unfinished works, multimedia projects, and even pornography.

Nonetheless, while festivals program different kinds of films for multiple target audiences in a sometimes dizzying array of sections, the primary selections of the major festivals, through the years, have favored a special kind of film: dark, serious, challenging, and linked to classic or emergent auteurs. Musicals and even comedies prove less welcome on critical center stages. Do film festivals thus demand that their public see film as serious and artistic? Following Rick Altman's work on genre,[14] then, is there a "genre" of major festival films? And what does this mean for film knowledge? This is a question taken up in chapter 2.

As the festivals select and honor these films, they also add value to them.[15] Nearly all film festivals are about prestige, yet not all films have prestige, nor do they earn more through the festivals themselves. At the same time, festival programmers must seek to recognize and create taste, capturing the "best" films and "discovering" more. Hence, as major nominees and winners are announced each year, they chronicle the politics, fashions and geographies of film: *Diary of a Country Priest (Journal d'un curé de campagne*, Venice, 1951), *400 Blows (Les quatre cent coups*, Cannes, 1959), *La dolce vita* (Cannes, 1960), *Breathless (A bout de souffle*, Berlin, 1960), *La notte* (Berlin, 1961), *Taxi Driver* (Cannes, 1976), *Vagabond* (Venice, 1985), *City of Sadness* (Venice, 1989), *Pulp Fiction* (Cannes, 1994), *Taste of Cherry* (Cannes, 1997), *Fahrenheit 9/11* (Cannes, 2003), *Still Life (Sanxia hoaren*, Venice, 2007), *Frozen River* (Sundance, San Sebastián, 2008), and *Uncle Boonmee Who Can Recall His Past Lives* (Cannes, 2010). Other choices, however, may seem obscure or confusing—the Hollywood pacifistic *Friendly Persuasion* (1956) won at Cannes, for example, in a year when the same film lost the Oscar. And some festival winners have faded from view or distribution. For smaller films, new directors, or less popular genres (documentary or shorts), nonetheless, festival recognition may sustain and even create films and careers.

To understand how festivals play a central role in defining cinema, we must also look at their human actors and networks. This goes beyond filmmakers, stars, and business agents. Festivals include the programmers, the critics, the press, and the academics. Moreover, they depend on lay audiences who attend festivals, read coverage, or rent DVDs "endorsed" by festival recognition. Directors represent pivotal figures in these human webs. Many of the films we encounter at film festivals, for example, are classified as works of cinematic masters (auteurs). This category was defined by evaluations of iconic figures of film history such as Jean Renoir, Akira Kurosawa, Robert Bresson, Federico Fellini, Michelangelo Antonioni, Howard Hawks, and Satyajit Ray. Among mature contemporary filmmakers, recognized auteurs include Agnès Varda, Quentin Tarantino, Abbas Kiarostami, Emir Kusturica, Jane Campion, and Wong Kar Wai. Over decades, some of these figures have evolved from newcomers to

Figure 1. Auteurs are celebrated on the marquee of the Palais des Festivals at the Cannes Film Festival, 2010.
Source: "Festival Hall—Cannes Film Festival 2010," by Jamie Davies, http://www.flickr.com/photos/jamiejohn/4616022984/in/faves-52138611@N02, CC By 2.0.

revered teachers of master classes to objects of posthumous retrospectives. Yet, at the same time that they look backward, film festivals compete for discoveries. Few knew about Steven Soderbergh, Christopher Nolan, Samira Makhmalbaf, Fatih Akin, Jia Zhangke, or Apichatpong Weerasethakul until film festivals acknowledged them. In both retrospection and movement forward, festivals validate a global Who's Who of film. Film scholars still debate the concept of the auteur—is the author/director of cinema the sole creator of films? But auteurs themselves are undisputed "stars" of film festivals.[16]

Directors share the stage with other film figures in festivals who are more accustomed to the spotlight. For Cannes's sixtieth anniversary in 2007, for example, the festival invited global film talent to jump out at viewers from a composite poster. Directors Souleymane Cissé of Mali and Wong Kar Wai of Hong Kong featured prominently. Yet their visages were eclipsed by the instantly recognized global faces of Penelope Cruz, Samuel L. Jackson, Juliette Binoche, and Bruce Willis. Auteurs are central to film knowledge, but stars have glittered more brightly on the red carpets and in public relations events of major festivals since their origins, a role epitomized by the 1953 image of Brigitte Bardot (and subsequent less successful imitators) as a nineteen- year-old bikini-clad starlet on La Croissette, the Mediterranean beach of Cannes. In addition to offering

Competitions / programs

photo opportunities, stars promote products, arrange deals, and participate in juries and other formal institutional events of the festival. Sponsors demand stars who add value to large and small events—and some stars now expect remuneration for such professional services, depending on the venue.

Less recognizable but nonetheless significant faces of film festivals include producers and distributors. The Weinstein brothers or the art house giant Wild Bunch are names more associated with parties and business pages than red carpet photographs, but their semi-public roles underpin the business of film. While many festivals began as exhibition venues for the celebration of cinema, most now include distribution mechanisms as well. Cannes has the Marché, Berlin has the European Film Market, and Hong Kong has Filmart. These film markets are trade events, bringing investors, distributors, agents, and artists together. Producers and filmmakers want to sell the distribution rights of their projects so they can finish the movie they are making or to sell this movie so they can make the next one. Sales agents are middlemen who identify potentially profitable films and acquire the rights to sell them to distributors all over the world.

Money and opportunity bring people to festivals. In recent decades, many festivals have added multiple competitions to their programs, so that filmmakers can use prizes to secure either distribution or capital for production. In the last two decades, festivals themselves have entered the business of producing movies, providing funds, from the Hubert Bals Funds in Rotterdam to the Pusan Production Fund.[17] The people who constitute this circuit of production, distribution, and exhibition, in turn, shape alternative cinema and its subsequent reading and trajectories.

Further outside the spotlight, an even larger network of people circulates through the global festival circuit, moving from event to event, combining spectatorship with instrumental capacities of production, sales, distribution, urban and national politics, criticism, and journalism. Participants share venues, events, and environs but use the festival for very different reasons. People associated with specific films—producers, directors, actors, scriptwriters, publicists—promote their films while at the same time looking for new opportunities in which they may take different roles, keeping an eye on markets as much as prizes. Critics, festival programmers, and distributors busily seek the best films to write about, to acquire for exhibition, or to buy for regional distribution. Paparazzi want the best pictures of the hottest stars, and the press wants scoops and buzz, projecting yet another image of the festival to the world.

Others are less mobile actors on a global stage. Local politicians show up to shore up support for the festival, to brand the city or state, and perhaps to snare photo opportunities for their own careers. The armies of organizers, writers, programmers, staff, and volunteers who run the festival want to make sure that everything runs smoothly, from tickets to high-quality projection and sound. All these people have different relationships with film festivals as individual events and system: a programmer may be a frazzled organizer in one event but a consultant, critic, or spectator in others. It is this complex web of human interactions worldwide that continues to make film festivals the dynamic nodes that they are.

Finally, except for Cannes, which only allows film professionals, multiple audiences sustain the festivals. Nonetheless, among writings on festivals, audiences often have been overlooked or read simply as reliable sources of income and abstract statistics or groups to boost attendance numbers. While professionals watch films at festivals with varied agendas, many festival audiences see these exhibitions as exciting glimpses of art cinema and other worlds. My media students in Hong Kong awaited the HKIFF catalog with real excitement, while those in New York look to the New York Film Festival, Tribeca, or MIX for the same thrills. Indeed, film festivals are cultural institutions whose organizers see one of their priorities as nurturing a local educated cinemagoer. Thus in 2008–2009, the Hong Kong International Film Festival offered an Ingmar Bergman retrospective to commemorate the great director's death in 2007. Between summer screenings and another special section in the 2009 festival, the organizers made almost all his films available with extensive catalog commentary, including relevant documentaries and even obscure footage, such as his early television advertisements. At the same time, festival programmers are keenly aware of the changing tastes of their young audiences. The 2007 HKIFF opened with an artsy but accessible film, *I Am a Cyborg, but That's OK*, featuring the East Asian teen heartthrob Rain in a leading role in a Berlin-winning film by Korean auteur Park Chan-Wook. The festival also showcased contemporary Asian cult films in a section entitled "I See It My Way."

Through their participation, audiences supply money and spread publicity while participating in a local culture of cinema and wider validation of the festival/film canon and new trends worldwide. Audiences are important to sustain the culture of cinephilia and to demand that festivals serve as guardians of quality cinema, especially as festivals have changed in the last few decades to accommodate the business of cinema.

Audiences experience and reaffirm the sense of film festivals as events in real places as well.[18] As I will show throughout the book, while film festivals as a system embody complex global negotiations, individual festivals occupy concrete spaces, histories, and contexts. Benito Mussolini added a film festival in 1932 to the historical Venice Biennale to consolidate Venice as a cultural center of Italy while making claims about Europe and the world. For the Fascist state, film seemed to be an important addition that reinforced and reinterpreted claims about modernity, culture, and power. Cannes emerged in direct response to Italy: excluded from prizes and prestige, the French (and their film industry) felt that the nation needed its own festival.

Within the nation-state, festivals also mark rivalries like that which emerged between Biarritz on the Atlantic coast and Cannes on the French Riviera: hosting a glamorous film festival in a resort during the off-season was a sound business idea at the end of the Depression as well as a contribution to national glory. Cannes won, nearly leaving Biarritz to cinematic oblivion. However, with the intellectual support of Henri Langlois, founder of the Cinémathèque Française, Biarritz gained the short-lived but significant Festival du Film Maudit (1949–1950), linked to the important *Revue du cinéma*.[19] The city subsequently has added festivals for television, shorts, and Latin American films. The Palais in Cannes, meanwhile, although profoundly imbued by "the Festival," also hosts international gatherings of television distribution and advertising awards and less media-oriented events dealing with real estate, yachts, and cosmetic surgery.

Festivals expanded geographically after World War II, although their association with resort cities continued. Locarno, a Swiss resort, asserted its neutral position when postwar costs constrained Cannes and Venice. Karlovy Vary, a Bohemian spa city that began to host a festival for a newly independent postwar Czechoslovakia, became a showcase for the Eastern Bloc after Soviet occupation (eventually competing with Moscow and Prague).[20] The competition of spa cities and cultural capitals emerged thereafter in 1947 when Edinburgh began a festival specializing in documentary film. In 1951, Western occupation forces in Berlin established a festival as a major showcase for Western film and democracy as the cold war intensified. Nevertheless, businessmen organized a festival in the Spanish resort of San Sebastián in 1953 as isolation of the Fascist Franco regime began to thaw, escaping, perhaps, the connotations of the capital.

As Marijke de Valck rightly noted, film festivals were a European phenomenon first. Non-European festivals emerged slowly, as a sense of a festival world of networks and competitors took shape. Globalization incorporated both a wider selection of films and new festivals in Sydney, Australia (1954), San Francisco (1957), the resort city of Mar del Plata, Argentina (recognized 1959), New York City (1963), and other world settings. Still, global spaces have not been equal in either film or geopolitical position. Western Europe, with the Big Three festivals, remains the most dominant region for the film festival world, within which Cannes is the undisputed leader. Beyond this triumvirate, the International Federation of Film Producers Associations (FIAPF) has accredited nine other competitive feature festivals distributed worldwide: Mar del Plata, Locarno, Shanghai (China), Moscow (Russia), Karlovy Vary, Montreal, San Sebastián, Tokyo (Japan), and Cairo (Egypt).[21] These are generally labeled the "A" festivals, even if FIAPF officially only provides accreditation, not ranking. The "A" festival designation is widely used by all in the film festival circle to refer to a FIAPF-endorsed general competitive film festival where an international jury is constituted to give prizes, a hierarchy that took shape in the 1940s and 1950s. Half of these festivals are in Europe, although political and economic centers generally have eclipsed resorts. Interestingly, none is situated in a predominantly Anglophone setting.[22]

Meanwhile, other European festivals have established important niches defined by specializations and outreach. Rotterdam, for example, pioneered European interest in Asian cinema and films of the global South,[23] and it was also the first festival to promote global coproduction. Among European "A" festivals, San Sebastián specializes in global Spanish-language cinema (even though it takes place in Euzkadi, the Basque Autonomous Region), providing it with unique linkages to new production in Latin America as well as supporting diverse national industries within Spain.

Beyond Europe, though, "A"-level film festivals do not necessarily represent the best known or most vital of world festivals. Despite FIAPF's designation of Móntreal as an "A"-level festival, Toronto, Sundance,[24] and Lincoln Center's New York Film Festival have more clout and prestige. Tribeca, born out of the tragedy of 9/11 and backed by star power like that of Manhattanite Robert De Niro, provides a more conscious example of how film festivals have been used to bring vitality and visibility to specific places. The Academy of Motion Picture Arts and Sciences, that is, Hollywood, also supports U.S. film festivals, giving small grants to support New York, Telluride, and the Maine Jewish Film Festival.

Continent by continent, audience by audience, festivals weave together place and history, incorporating social, economic, and cultural change and competition in stories to which I will return throughout this book. Hong Kong, colonized by the British from 1841 to 1997, has become a cultural icon of the postcolonial city. In the twenty-first century, as I will show, it competes with Tokyo, Pusan, Singapore, Shanghai, and Bangkok as festival, marketplace, and funder of Asian films. In South America, the Havana Film Festival (founded in 1979) was once very important for Spanish-language cinema: the ultimate revolutionary, alternative public sphere. In 1986, it sponsored the "Largest Retrospective on African Film in the World," a showcase reciprocated in Ouagadougou the next year. Subsequently, Havana has surrendered its Latin American position to San Sebastián, in an interesting assertion of trans-Atlantic imperialism. Meanwhile, in the Middle East, Dubai (2004) and Abu Dhabi (2007) have inaugurated film festivals in their quests to become modern, global metropoles funded by oil money. These events echo a diadem of acquired global cultural institutions ranging from branches of the Louvre and the Guggenheim to the presence of New York University and the Sorbonne.

Besides these large international festivals that last a week or more, smaller local festivals recur in towns and cities all over the world. Some of them offer wide general programs despite the lack the star power and position of major world festivals: the Philadelphia Film Festival, for example, founded in 1991, now screens 300 films for 70,000 spectators over two weeks. It shares a local annual calendar with other festivals devoted to LGBTQ themes and a newer youth-oriented event on film and music as well as ethnic and thematic screenings.

Other small festivals are genre- or issue-oriented in ways interwoven with needs and issues of particular localities, epitomized in famous gay and lesbian international film festivals in San Francisco and New York. Meanwhile, for Japanese manga, the Tokyo International Anime Fair provides a primary outlet. Other festivals re-create place and meaning around different film formats, such as animation, for which Annecy in France, Zagreb in Croatia, and Ottawa in Canada are major festivals, sometimes with their own attached markets. None have been centers for the history or production of animated film any more than the provincial city of Foix has a unique relation to Cinema of Resistance or St. Petersburg has a unique claim on ecological films. The Pordenone Silent Film Festival, meanwhile, is a premier event that takes over a small Italian resort but prides itself on being scholarly and exclusive.

These festivals are vital parts of local filmic, artistic, and sociocultural worlds. They parallel (and sometimes participate in) other arts and music festivals that create cultural cachet for cities and states: the New York Film Festival is organized by the Lincoln Center Film Society, while the Hong Kong International Film Festival launches six weeks of metropolitan markets and expositions ranging from music to furniture (Edinburgh, by contrast, has recently separated its film festival from the heady calendar of August events that have affirmed the city as a cultural capital). Organizers argue that festivals boost cultural tourism, invite business, and improve quality of life for urbane populations. During their screenings, festivals often use venues from or seek affiliations with other arts and cultural institutions, such as museums, galleries, art centers, and universities. Panels in lecture halls, crowds in public spaces, and coffee in nearby cafes reinforce the familiarity of interested audiences, filmmakers, producers, distributors, and budding auteurs in the creation of a filmic public sphere.

Within larger cities, even smaller film festivals, lasting one or two days with a handful of nonpremiere films, celebrate social groups or causes (Jewish film, Asian American media, the environment), highlight the commercial production of different national cinemas (French, Peruvian, or Korean cinema), complement university-related programs, and offer films for particular audiences, such as animation for children. Such small-scale exhibitions crop up almost every week in the newspapers of metropolises like New York, Hong Kong, Sydney, and Barcelona, sheltered in university halls or tucked into the schedule of a multiplex. These events make film festivals everyday events, far from the scale, business, and stars of Cannes, Berlin, and Sundance. Their selection and discussion of films also validate the circuit of grand festivals as anchors and generators of a system that people glimpse by participation in these smaller festivals.[25]

Global festivals create an interlocking world, but this system is open to contradictions and conflicts over cultural power. Censorship, geopolitical barriers between "East" and "West," and money interrupt the flow of films and peoples across festival networks. Other contradictions emerge from strategies to promote filmmaking itself. In 2007, for example, the focus of "Berlinale Talent Campus . . . [was] on a current and burning theme addressed by world cinema: the search for cultural identity in a global—and globalized—film business."[26] Through this program, young filmmakers worldwide were brought to Berlin to learn their craft. In so doing, however, they bypassed apprenticeship in local, national, or even regional film festivals and worlds. Global festivals also have promoted openness to sexual and gender explorations that have generated conflicts in local settings worldwide; at the same time, one notes that the women on juries at major festivals are much more likely to be actresses than the handful of female directors (Lina Wertmuller, Jane Campion, Lucrecia Martel, Margarethe von Trotte, Samira Makhmalbaf, Agnès Varda, Sofia Coppola, Ann Hui) who have approached auteur status. In 2011, Cannes considered a record four females for the Palme d'Or.

Individual festivals and the links between them transcend art, awards, business, and public relations. They shape the lives and futures of film workers, the solvency of small film companies and large corporations, the prestige of cities, nations, and regions, and the construction of academic and public knowledge about film and video. These public meanings evolve from festival to festival because of politics, economics, technology, sociocultural changes, and aesthetics. Through these processes, festivals force us to consider how film knowledge takes shape within an imagined community of film, filmmakers, and audiences. Four key structural features within festivals, in fact, help this text ask what film knowledge is, who controls it, and how it changes over time.

First, festivals showcase a complex world of films, international, historical, and especially contemporary. It is easy to overlook this holistic claim in the quest for novelty and variety, but festival catalogs, their varied sections, retrospectives, and discussions, provide both wide viewing and scholarship to canonize individual films, auteurs, and national cinematic canons while at the same time asserting the importance of a growing, coherent canon of good and significant films, a world of knowledge in constant motion. The HKIFF in 2007, for example, showcased films of Romania and of Portuguese documentarian Pedro Costa; provided special programs on Taiwanese director Edward Yang, Hong Kong's Herman Yau, and historical Hong Kong films; and concluded with a retrospective on the late Italian master Luchino Visconti. Each event can be read as a programming choice or appeal to audiences, but each also has a wider resonance within a holistic vision of cinema and cinematic knowledge. Hong Kong programmers were excited that they had caught the first wave of global fascination with Romanian films that has subsequently been confirmed by festival awards, critical studies, and wider theatrical releases. Costa, despite his relatively narrow focus on immigrants in Portuguese society, was recognized at Cannes in 2002; his *Colossal Youth* (*Juventude en marcha,* 2006) was screened in Cannes, London, and Toronto. Visits to Berkeley, Harvard, and other universities and reviews in cinematic journals have reinforced his position in world film knowledge that the HKIFF draws upon and reinforces. Yang and Visconti are both acknowledged global auteurs; the former had lifelong ties to the HKIFF, while the latter enshrined European cinematic history in the festival. Yau, by contrast, has been regarded as a local cult favorite and colleague for whom a retrospective provides new recognition after twenty years making films like *Human Pork Chop* (*Bat sin fan dim ji yan yuk cha siu bau*, 1993). It is less clear if this recognition will be picked up by other festivals or critics, who have "admitted" John Woo, Ringo Lam, Wong Kar Wai, and other Hong Kong filmmakers to a global pantheon. Together, however, all these pieces evoke a global kaleidoscope of film itself for local audiences.

Second, film festivals actively cultivate new talents and works from all over the world through their scouting and selection, their film funds, and programs to train emerging filmmakers on a global scale, like the Berlin Talent Campus, Cannes's Cinéfondation, or the San Sebastián International Film School Meeting. Some may be local: South by Southwest (SXSW) Film Festival hosts the Texas High School Film Competition, where finalists' works are shown at the regular film festival, and the Sundance Institute has become active in initiatives ranging from indigenous filmmaking to social entrepreneurship to archival preservation.[27] In this tutelage, festivals actively expand the canon by bringing people up within the world of film and pushing at the edges. Circulation through the festival world then affirms these selections. Festivals constitute an interdependent system where training in one program may lead to funding through another festival and eventual screenings and recognition within a wider hierarchy.

Third, festivals intersect with other discourses and institutions in the wider construction of film as a field of knowledge. They emerged alongside the establishment of cinema clubs, art house cinemas, reviews, and serious studies of cinema from the likes of André Bazin and Andrew Sarris. If cinema were to be treated as art, it made sense for the Venice Film Festival to become part of the Venice Biennale. In the post–World War II years, with the dominance of Hollywood films all over the world, film festivals could be read as artistic responses to Hollywood's encroaching hegemony (and its more personalized knowledge of stars and glamour). By the 1960s, with well-established institutions like Cinémathèque Française and the British Film Institute and magazines like *Revue du cinéma*, *Cahiers du cinéma*, and *Sight and Sound*, cinema had become defined as worthy of "important" studies in the university, in libraries, and through museums as well as multilayered publications. Film festivals exist in the context of the establishment of cinema as a serious art that is worthy of academic pursuit as well as art patronage, be it from investors or from governments.

Finally, all these roles raise important questions of who defines what is good for whom and how, where art and value are never defined by undisputed or neutral criteria. Film festivals make cultural capital concrete in the shapes of Golden Palms, Bears, Lions, Leopards, and other gilded figurines that populate carousels of screening and appraisal. Of course, many films shown in these festivals never earn a prize, although all can claim on their DVD releases to have been "screened" or "selected." Nevertheless, prizes, even more industrial awards like the American Oscar, the Spanish Goya, the French César, or Taiwan's Golden Horse, have always seduced filmmakers and those who follow festivals. The Fédération Internationale de la Presse Cinématographique, International Federation of Film Critics (FIPRESCI) has awarded prizes since 1946 in Cannes; in the last count, more than twenty festivals worldwide now have FIPRESCI prizes. Yet, while the major festivals have always entailed competitive prizes and strictly delineated entry requirements that demand exclusive premieres, others, like Rotterdam or Hong Kong, did not have any competition until the 1990s and have showcased films that have been screened elsewhere. And others, from Locarno to Sundance, tout "audience awards" that reflect popularity more than critical judgment.

This last point demands more elaboration here. Knowledge entails process. The ranking of film festivals dictates the added prestige each film receives through different festivals and awards. In the last twenty years, for example, any director who has become a Cannes favorite, such as Wong Kar Wai, Steven Soderbergh, or the Dardenne brothers, seldom premieres subsequent works in other festivals, whether or not they win again at Cannes. A few might even manage the enviable position of Ken Loach, described as "a perennial Venice favorite"[28] and "a Cannes regular who has shown more than a dozen films at the festival."[29] Moreover, while films and festivals are specific cultural and, at times, national products, global film canons also tend to demand recognition gained through festivals outsides of one's country. Indeed, this book will grapple with if and how a film or filmmaker can be seen as "good" if he or she is not picked up and ratified by the major European festivals.

Individual prize works and auteurs form only part of the story of the constitution of a shared canon. However, festivals as an annual system demarcate trends and visibility, the shift of gaze that reshapes our reading of "cinema" over time. One after another, major film festivals celebrated works from Akira Kurosawa and Kenji Mizoguchi from Japan in the 1950s, focused on Federico Fellini and Michelangelo Antonioni from Italy and the French New Wave in the 1960s, and then turned to Robert Altman, Francis Ford Coppola, and Martin Scorsese from the United States in the 1970s. In the 1980s, Eastern European auteurs like Andrzej Wajda and Emir Kusturica surged into prominence. Iranian directors like Abbas Kiarostami and Mohsen Makhmalbaf gained global recognition in the 1990s before the turn to Romania and Eastern Europe in the new millennium. Festivals in the last decade also have highlighted the work of women, gay, and dissident filmmakers who face social limits in their own national cultures or national industries while looking for the next trends and schools to emerge.

Still, as I will show in many chapters, this social construction of film knowledge has profoundly unequal ramifications, as I have signaled in the case of female directors. African films have rarely won major festival prizes; even Latin American production has gained little cachet in the major "A"-level festivals. This book explores this imbalance over time through attention to the rise of Asians, especially global Chinese, as prizewinners, programmers, jury members, and canon, and the complex relationships among national cinema, auteurs, and film festivals linked to this evolution. In the 1980s, fifth-generation Chinese cinema was hardly known in China or the West, although Hong Kong provided glimpses into this world. Then, Chen Kaige's *Farewell My Concubine* (1993) and Zhang Yimou's *Red Sorghum* (1987) and *Ju dou* (1990) and others were picked up by Berlin, Venice, and Cannes for inclusion in their competition and many won prizes (resonating with other global Chinese works from Taiwan and Hong Kong). While many of their films were either banned or hardly known in China through the 1990s, these filmmakers enjoyed international recognition as well as art house distributions outside China. Indeed, insofar as these were selected for opposition to Chinese culture and politics (e.g., the emphasis on gay themes among Chinese festival films), charges of Orientalism have been leveled against these works and their readings.[30] Meanwhile, as Zhang has taken on more popular projects in a burgeoning global China, like the staging of the opening and closing ceremonies of the 2008 Beijing Summer Olympic games, his star has been eclipsed on the festival circuit.[31]

Issues of unequal global cultural exchange and power are pervasive and multifaceted. The "A"-level festivals have always been more powerful in economic foundations, cultural production, and star power. Many festival films from smaller countries are financed by joint global investments now sponsored in or through these festivals. Hence, it becomes difficult to define who is speaking what to whom. Is there a difference between films produced outside the West for Western audiences and others that are more "authentic" or are aimed at national or culturally distinct audiences in content and form? One might think here, for example, of the often uneasy relations of Bollywood and film festivals, which are uncertain how to analyze such a gigantic industry. Bollywood is an extremely successful national and diasporic cinema, yet not recognized by many as serious enough for major festival prizes. Most filmmakers are well aware of who their audiences are; the diverse expectations from these interested parties have a strong influence on the festival films and ultimately on film knowledge.

Form, content, or ideas in films also play their roles. These constitute global film knowledge. For their audiences and mediated publics, festival films often stimulate conversation on controversial topics. Cannes awarded Michael Moore a prize for his antiwar, anti-Bush documentary *Fahrenheit 9/11* a few months before the 2004 U.S. presidential election. Berlin has highlighted German Turkish immigrants and war in Bosnia, while Cannes has been preoccupied by its ties to the Maghreb. Nonetheless, festivals can also look far afield: Venice gave a Golden Lion to Jia Zhangke's *Still Life* (2006), a film depicting China's controversial Three Gorges Dam, while Rotterdam has promoted Malaysian films that have been banned by the Malaysian government. Apart from the major competitions, sidebar events are more innovative in form and content, screening more challenging and, at times, controversial films that resonate across hundreds of group- and issue-oriented film festivals that speak to smaller but highly motivated audiences. Festivals like the San Francisco International Gay and Lesbian Film Festival, the Human Rights Watch Film Festival, or Asian American and ecological film festivals create publics and public spheres in which films and audiences may have a more direct relation to film arguments than in the multilayered negotiations of art and business at Cannes or Hong Kong.

While film knowledge is constantly in process, all these fora nevertheless converge in an idea of holism—the sense that festivals embody distillations of a larger world of cinema as cinema. Controversies are balanced with classic or near-mainstream works, exotic newcomers are interwoven with screenings of more "reliable" French, Italian, and Japanese art films; small audience documentaries and shorts complete programs anchored by prestige galas; and topical festivals will mention if a work premiered at Venice or Toronto. While festivals focus, discuss, and change global film culture, they embody the idea of film as a field of knowledge, past, present, and future.

Literature, Theory, and Methods

Film festivals, like cinema, are not only about texts, but also about the institutions and people that produce, distribute, and exhibit these texts as well as the manner in which we as audiences receive them. All these questions mean that film festivals provide an important institutional framework for the study of issues of cinematic taste, power, industry, and postcolonial global relations. Despite their centrality to global film, however, I have noted that few monographs have specifically addressed the issues of the festivals. Besides de Valck's work, Emmanuel Ethis also produced a sociological study of the Cannes film festival, perhaps the most closely examined of any such global event.[32] Wu Chia-Chi has completed dissertation work on transnational Chinese-language cinema and reception in film festivals, and SooJeong Ahn has completed a dissertation on the Pusan International Film Festival.[33] Other academic articles treat aspects of specific festivals, including the Venice, Berlin, Toronto, Karlovy Vary, and Pusan festivals.[34] A few more scholars, including Rhyne Ragan, Roya Rastegar, and Skadi Loist, have been working on dissertations on different aspects of film festivals.

Others have provided important pieces of the puzzle within wider film studies contexts. Thomas Elsaesser was one of the first to discuss the impact of film festivals on German national cinema. Dina Iordanova also looked at Eastern European festivals in various contexts. Mette Hjort and Duncan Petrie underscore the importance of festivals for small national cinemas, and Richard Roud and Vanessa Schwartz have situated Cannes in wider French perspectives. Scholars of Iranian cinema have been especially illuminating on how festivals interact with political and cultural barriers, including Azadeh Farahmand's dissertation on the relationship between Iranian national cinema and film festivals.[35]

In addition to academic studies, film critics, journalists, and film personalities, as noted, have provided reports and memoirs on many festivals (especially Cannes and Sundance),[36] while how-to books explain film entries and judging. Both the daily festival reports from *Variety, Screen,* and *Hollywood Reporter* and less specialized press reports on festivals that are part of global media culture also have provided important resources. While trade periodicals detail films, deals, and connections, mainstream newspapers from the *New York Times* to the *South China Morning Post* have provided diverse perspectives on local and global events. Cinema Web sites, such as Senses of Cinema, Hors Champ, and the Internet Movie Database, also have provided invaluable resources.[37]

Finally, film festivals are themselves producers of knowledge. Every year, festivals produce elaborate catalogs and special publications that sell the films to their audiences. These volumes all go beyond commerce to establish the expertise and cachet of each festival. Hong Kong, for many years, for example, produced annual conference studies on histories and themes of Hong Kong film, ranging from early film to "Images of the City" to Cantonese melodrama. Film festivals, as contemporary institutions immersed in the business of media, are very media savvy. Most festivals use their Web sites to attract attention from their potential participants, filmmakers, audiences, other festivals, and sponsors. These Web sites are also places where festivals define themselves. Not only do they provide valuable information and data, they allow me to examine what the festivals themselves consider important and how they want the outside world and their competitors to see them. Many of these rich, multilingual Web sites have transferred their archives of film selections, prizes, and even journalism to public sites (e.g., www.festival-cannes.com, www.hkiff.org.hk, www.mardelplatafilmfest.com). Older festivals also have produced rich anniversary memoirs.[38] These primary materials from the festivals provide important information on films and place and allow for cross-readings of trends and comments.

Building on these data and immediate models, this book envisions film festivals as embracing many different social and cultural issues. Thus, it draws on methods and theories from cultural studies, urban studies, transnational and global studies, cinema and media studies, geography, and anthropology. For the films and their respective canonization, Pierre Bourdieu's concepts of cultural capital, distinction, and the construction of aesthetics is indispensable; I also have drawn on other elements of the French structuralist tradition, including the ur-model of Ferdinand de Saussure, to help frame this complex world as a system.[39] Traditions in media studies that have discussed the formation of taste, aesthetics, and the canon in film—as well as challenges posed in studies of third-world cinema or queer cinema—offer yet another prism to approach film festivals.[40] While some of these are textual, most are cultural studies works, in the sense defined by British cultural studies and to a lesser extent by the Frankfurt School.[41] All these approaches link text, production, reception, history, and lived experience as conflicted and holistic analysis of film festivals.

With regard to festivals as institutions, their use of space and their nurturing of diverse viewpoints, Jürgen Habermas, Nancy Fraser, and others have provided especially useful insights about the public sphere and alternative public sphere. These works have also shed light on the construction of the nation as an imagined community, resonating with work of Benedict Anderson as well as more directly national studies like those of Elsaesser, Iordanova, and Schwartz.[42] While Elsaesser and de Valck have made extensive use of network theories from Manuel Castells to Bruno Latour, this book instead reads the interconnections of film festivals as both a system and a dynamic process. Festivals depend on and compete with one another—a constantly contested system of institutions and peoples that relates to larger systems of cinema as well as local and global geopolitical, cultural, and economic forces.

Finally, understanding the audiences and the place and space of film festivals is integral to the understanding of film festivals as processes. Here, I rely on my training as an anthropologist as well as decades of work in cultural studies and reception theory.[43] Ethnography itself reinforces this sense of place while it enriches this textual, institutional, and cultural analysis. Ethnography, here, entails active participant observation as well as cultural analysis of venues and presentations. These experiences have been strongest in terms of decades of contact with the Hong Kong International Film Festival. Yet, I have developed personal, firsthand contacts and experiences of spaces, events, audiences, and encounters across a wider global stage encompassing Locarno, Berlin, and San Sebastián as well as smaller festivals in New York, Philadelphia, San Francisco, Dublin, Hong Kong, Macau, Lima, and other sites. Scrambling for tickets, waiting in museum lobbies, crowding the press office, attending parties, and rushing to get to screenings scattered across a city all constitute features of festivals, as do the varied reflections of those who generously have consented to be interviewed outside the festival time frame. Together these provide a level of analysis that a distant observer cannot attain, linking experience to abstract system.

All these approaches to festivals, finally, have been balanced and centered, inevitably, by films themselves as texts, commodities, and experiences. Indeed, these films constantly bring the project back full circle from social, business, or political analysis to the raison d'être of festivals and their centrality to media studies. Whether reviewing student films at San Sebastián, taking my children to premieres in Hong Kong, or spending seemingly endless nights chasing down past prizewinners of Cannes, Locarno, Berlin, and Venice in libraries and on DVDs, I have learned, remembered, and enjoyed the fact that festivals are about films. Quite apart from textual analyses, theories of authorship, business relations, or disparities of global power, these moments have affirmed the project and reminded me why festivals are neither arbitrary nor ephemeral, but in fact remain significant and exciting for so many of us around the world.

The chapters that follow look systematically at different aspects of festivals and festival worlds within this framing holistic vision. The first chapter introduces the history and structure of film festivals, balancing selected case studies with a synthetic historical and global vision. The next two chapters build on this foundation with a focus on films and filmmakers of the festivals. Chapter 2 looks at festival feature films as a "genre," their characteristics and range, culminating in a close reading of Cristian Mungiu's 2007 Cannes Palme d'Or film, *4 Months, 3 Weeks, and 2 Days* (*4 luni, 3 saptamâni, si 2 zile*).

Chapter 3 complements this analysis with extratextual elements of festival films, anchored by the construction of the festival auteur. Here again, the chapter concludes with close readings of two auteurs and their discursive contexts: Micheangelo Antonioni and his masterpiece *L'avventura* (*The Adventure*, 1961) and Abbas Kiarostami and his later masterwork, *Taste of Cherry* (*Ta'm-e guilass*, 1997).

Chapter 4 balances aesthetic concerns by an examination of different yet critical functions of festivals: their roles in the business of film. This includes not only sales and distribution but the recent active engagement of many festivals in the production of films themselves. Here, analysis of Chinese filmmaker Jia Zhangke again allows us to read abstract processes in the career of a single festival favorite.

Chapter 5 balances such behind-the-scenes negotiations with those in front of the screen: the meanings of audience and discussion in the construction of the filmic public sphere. This chapter focuses on two clusters of issues represented by human rights discussions and lesbian, gay, bisexual, transgender events, respectively, to understand the role of festivals in films and society.

Finally, chapter 6 brings together these issues through my case study of the Hong Kong International Film Festival and its evolution within Hong Kong as a place and Hong Kong and wider Asian film worlds. My conclusion reviews these materials and underscores future issues for festivals and their study. Before we move to these, however, let me present the parts and functions of the film festival as our shared field of study.

Calendars and Events: The Operation of the Festival

Whether a major film festivals with multiple sections or a smaller and focused one, the sections that are most important are those in which there are major competitions. The competitive festivals are so categorized by FIAPF because they are required to host competitions. Beyond such a major competition with substantial prizes, common features or interests in festivals include sidebars for younger filmmakers, shorts, some kind of a retrospective, special programs of the year (a national cinema, an auteur, or a film movement), a section of local/ national cinema of the hosting nation, if appropriate, some "open features" to attract crowds, and more recently, a section that includes productions from film schools. On the more business side, many festivals have markets, coproduction markets, and other fora that help filmmakers and distributors connect.

While Cannes obviously does not represent all festivals, it remains the one festival that all other festivals look to. Moreover, it has a multilingual Web site (www.festival-cannes.com) that provides more background on individual programs and history. Therefore I will primarily use Cannes to explain briefly how festivals tend to structure themselves. Since Cannes, except for "Cinéma de la Plage," is not open to the public, I will supplement this discussion with an explanation of how a more audience-centered festival like Hong Kong accommodates its local publics.

In Cannes, the official competition for a Palme d'Or receives the most press; to be included in Cannes competition is extremely important in the festival circuit. For years, the committee itself was anonymous except for the public directors of the festivals: "the Cannes selection committee is made up of a small number of film industry professionals and critics whose names are not publicized."[44] As part of a reorganization in 2004, the eight French representatives were made public (including the son of long-time eminence Gilles Jacob) as well as their wider international cohort, including "Joël Chapron (Central and Eastern Europe), Lorenzo Codelli (Italy), Mamad Haghigat (Iran), Christiane Peitz (Germany), Brice Pedroletti (Asia), Agnès Poirier and Simon Perry (Great Britain), Jose Maria Riba (Spain, Latin America), Ilda Santiago (Brazil), Magda Wassef (Mediterranean countries)."[45] Theoretically speaking, films can simply be submitted to the Cannes selection committee, and thousands are received and reviewed each year. However, Cannes alumni and important producers, sales agents, and distributors have many connections with Cannes that they can use to put their films in a more favorable light for the selection committee, who will decide on out-of-competition films as well as those showcased in Un Certain Regard. The selection committee is also charged with selection of the more public juries.

Cannes's selections are always highly anticipated among professionals as well as wider audiences. About one month before the start of the festival in mid-May, the festival director announces the lineup of the competition; films, however, can still be added after the initial announcement. In 2010, eighteen feature films were chosen, representing fourteen different countries; generally speaking, roughly twenty films compete annually. A similar number of films are screened out of competition. In this press conference, the festival director also announces the line up for shorts and sidebar events as well as the films to be shown out of competition, ranging from big American films at the Lumière theater to special screenings, such as a three-hour documentary on Nicolae Ceauşescu, the late Romanian dictator. While other festivals may not have the same cachet or secrecy, the announcements of the programs and competitions always focus news coverage and audience interests. For Cannes, the most important competitive sidebar event is entitled Un Certain Regard (a certain look), also controlled by a selection committee. Un Certain Regard was established in 1978 to encourage works by younger filmmakers and offers a prize of 30,000 euros.

Cannes, being an "A"-level festival, has to have an international jury. The heads of the jury always have been well-known international auteurs, actors, or film professionals—Tim Burton, Isabelle Huppert, Sean Penn, Stephen Frears, Wong Kar Wai, Emir Kusturica, Quentin Tarantino, Patrice Chereau, David Lynch, Liv Ullmann (note the gender distribution). The head works with about eight other jury members, including cinematographers, technical people, critics, and writers. If they are women, they are most likely to be actresses. There are also juries for Cinéfondation and Shorts, Un Certain Regard, and Camera d'Or. In 2010, Atom Egoyan was the jury president of Cinéfondation as well as short films; Claire Denis for Un Certain Regard, and Gael Garcia Bernal for Camera d'Or. While other festivals cannot garner the star power that Cannes can, they can have jury members from the festival world, like Marco Müller, an art film producer who has been running different top festivals for decades. Again, the jury is an important institution that adds prestige to a festival. Its members' prominence guarantees the quality of the prizes the festival presents and allows colleagues to get together to exchange ideas and socialize.[46]

Despite these opportunities and the quest for coverage of the film world, certain exclusions remain. As Monica Bartyzel noted on the Web site Cinematical in 2010:

> History also comes into play. As Movieline points out: "Since 2000, the Cannes Film Festival has screened two hundred and fourteen films in competition. Of those: Seventeen titles were directed by a total of fourteen women; two titles—Shrek and Persepolis—were co-directed by women; the last year to feature no women directors in competition was 2005 (and before that: 1999)." . . . the record number of women to compete in one year was three—last year's trio of Jane Campion, Isabel Coixet, and Andrea Arnold. In fact, there has only been one female filmmaker to ever win the prestigious Palme d'Or: Jane Campion for The Piano [1993].[47]

Of course, Sofia Coppola's Somewhere won the Golden Lion for best picture in Venice in 2010.

Another significant section of Cannes is Cinéfondation, established in 1998, which invites works from film schools all over the world. Monetary prizes range from 7,500 to 15,000 euros.[48] While other festivals often encourage student works, few festivals can afford the programs of Cannes, including professional mentoring (L'Atelier) and residential fellowships (Le Résidence). This foundation is supported by the National Cinema Center and the city of Paris as well.[49]

There is a competition for short films, where around ten films under fifteen minutes are chosen to compete. In addition, Cannes offers a prize, Camera d'Or, given to first works, oftentimes selections from the official selection, including Un Certain Regard; winners can also come from Directors' Fortnight or Critics' Week. Finally, the Critics' Week (La Semaine Internationale de la Critique) and noncompetitive Directors' Fortnight (Quinzaine des Réalisateurs) are separate but parallel events that were established in 1961 and 1969, respectively. The Critics' Week focuses attention on seven feature and short films, with prizes given by a vote of journalists.[50] Selections for the Quinzaine, sponsored by the French directors' guild, are made by their appointed representative and a consulting committee.[51] Today, the event is still noncompetitive and shows about twenty features and twelve shorts. Just as Cannes honors established auteurs, the Directors' Fortnight established the Carrosse d'Or in 2002, which is given to a single director. Past recipients include Jacques Rozier, Clint Eastwood, Nanni Moretti, Sembene Ousmane, David Cronenberg, Alain Cavalier, Jim Jarmusch, Naomi Kawasé, and Agnès Varda.

A few prizes are given in multiple festivals, including the FIPRESCI prize of the International Federation of Film Critics (www.fipresci.org), which is awarded in over twenty festivals around the world, including Cannes, Ankara, Hong Kong, Guadalajara, and Miami. Another major award is the SIGNIS Award, given by the World Catholic Association for Communication since 1947. Here, certain themes are clearly favored: Robert Bresson received this award at Cannes for *The Trial of Joan of Arc* in the early 1960s; American Paul Haggis received the accolade for his *In the Valley of Elah* at Venice in 2007, while in 2010 the French film *Des hommes et des dieux* added this praise at Cannes to its other festival prizes.[52]

Despite the rewards of competitions, many cinephiles and critics would argue that the sidebars are always more interesting because they are "fresher," with new talents doing innovative works, while the competitions tend to favor established auteurs. In a longer trajectory, one can sometimes see an auteur move from being accepted in the sidebars to the competition and prizes. Chris Marker, Bernardo Bertolucci, and Ken Loach were invited to the Critics' Week before they were famous. Theo Angelopoulos, Youssef Chahine, and Werner Herzog were all at Directors' Fortnight when their careers started.

Besides these competitive sections, Cannes has introduced Cannes Classics, World Cinema (Tous les cinemas du monde), and Cinema at the Beach (Cinéma de la Plage)—the only free-access event of the festival. Here the festival, like many others, fulfills two of its major roles. It validates the history of cinema by showing the best of the past, to acknowledge that the history of cinema is important and to consolidate the role of cinema in defining culture. The free screening, finally, represents the role cinema plays in entertaining the masses and shows the festival's responsibility to its local audiences.

Most festivals divide their sections to help audience members make their viewing selections. In Locarno, for example, films shown at the Piazza Grande are generally crowd pleasers. In Hong Kong, the Gala presentations are for popular works, while Master Classes and Auteurs include more established filmmakers and Indie Power is for newer independent works. In addition, festivals recognize local production: San Sebastián offers a Basque section; Locarno, a Swiss section, and Hong Kong, a Hong Kong section. In the last few years, more and more youth-oriented sections have been added to many festivals to attract and nurture a new generation of festival-goers.

In addition to these screenings, many festivals have markets; Cannes's Marché is devoted to the business of film, buying, selling, and finding distribution rights.[53] Markets are open to anyone who can pay the fee. At Cannes, there are different floors for the Marché: the higher one goes, the bigger the deals. Major film companies have their elaborate booths on the third floor, while small companies have their booth on the first floor, generally called the Bunker. In 2010, this marketplace had nearly 10,000 participants, including more than 600 exhibitors (and 900 festival programmers).[54]

In most festivals, there are press conferences, so that the press can interact with the filmmakers and actors and have more opportunities to take pictures. Cannes offers Photocall before the press conference, where the actors and directors simply pose for the cameras. Publicity is one of the major functions in film festivals. Festivals are able to get the word out so that a film or a filmmaker gets noticed, gets distributed, gets reviewed, and gets recognized and the festival, together with its branding effort, can also be spread around the world.

The most interesting aspect of a major festival press conference is its global dimension, with press as well as filmmakers from all over the world. Different languages are spoken and simultaneously translated in the booths above or behind. Nevertheless, English remains a dominant language in global film festivals. Even in Europe, where they will speak French in Cannes and German in Berlin, English is the immediate second language for most. Film festivals cannot be separated from international business, especially a film business where English-speaking (Hollywood) films dominate the global market.

Since Cannes is only for professionals, access entails a fairly straight hierarchy. Accredited professionals all have differently colored badges, and these badges in turn signal which screenings they have access to, and which one they do not. Film programmers for other festivals must see as many films as they can so that they can work on the programs for their own events. Producers sell their films, but oftentimes "bigger" films are represented by larger production companies that do the selling. Acquisitions people are looking for good or potentially

Figure 2. International Pavilion, Cannes Film Festival, 2010.
Source: Cannes Film Festival 2010, by Jamie Davies, http://www.flickr.com/photos/
jamiejohn/4615914777/in/faves-52138611@No2, CC By 2.0.

profitable films to buy. Aspiring filmmakers seek investors or buyers if they have finished products. The market badges at Cannes are the only badges that can be bought. Yet, if one makes a short film and submits it to the Short Film Corner of the market, one can get access to the festival too.[55]

Different countries also try to sell their cinematic goods at Cannes through the Village International, opened since 2000; in 2010, sixty countries participated in the Village, where nations have their own pavilions by the beach. In these pavilions, different countries seek to attract filmmakers to their locations through scenery and facilities as well as the many tax breaks the governments offer. They also promote their national industries. The bottom line is that Cannes is just as much about the business of cinema as it is about the art of cinema; democratically, it embodies an all-inclusive cinema.

Structures at festivals are complemented by place, ambience, and image. Cannes, for example, has long had its red carpet that showcases the stars and auteurs. Since the late 1990s, more and more festivals are relying on the red carpet to define themselves or at least expose themselves to the public. The red carpet, where stars greet the press and their fans and are photographed before they enter the cinema, has become the iconic image of film festivals in general. Often, this feature must be added to borrowed venues, although most newly built structures for film festivals, like the Palais des Festivals at Cannes, the

Berlinale Palast, or the soon-to-be-finished new Palazzo in Venice have been designed to showcase the red carpet, giving maximum exposure for the stars, not unlike the grand steps of opera houses. When the red carpet is not in use, one sees regular festival-goers taking pictures near the festival's logos, absorbing some of their allure and glamour. While the red carpet becomes a signifier for the festivals, festivals sell merchandise as well: bags, T-shirts, posters, umbrellas, and mugs with logos. These booths also sell festival publications for those who want to know more about the event and its special programs. Together, these commercial outreaches sustain efforts to brand the festival far beyond its site.

These items also connect to a more regular film festival audience who just want to see movies. Most festivals now have online ticket sales. Most of the tickets are in line with the regular ticket prices of local cinemas. However, for dedicated viewers, there are usually ways to buy a larger block of tickets, or passes, of different levels. In some festivals, the professionals who have the less prestigious badges, for example, have access to unsold tickets on the day of the screening or the day before the screening. At Berlin, for example, I joined long morning lines that allow cinephiles to take in as many movies as they can during the festival. Other festivals also arrange special prices for students and future audiences.

And finally there are the parties—just beyond the reach of mass audiences but intensely visible and discussed in daily gossip. Hundreds of parties take place during festival times. Again, like badges, some are more exclusive and some are more open. Many require invitations, and with the right connections, one can always find parties to go to. Since film festivals are events that allow people to meet face to face, parties are king/queen. They have also been important sites for my field research, where knowledge, connections, and gossip are shared. As producer Christine Vachon observes,

> When I showed my diaries of film festival life to an associate, he complained. "All that happens in them is that you go to parties and get drunk." I responded.
>
> "Don't you understand? That's what you do at festivals." That and schmooze and show your films to audiences that generally want to like it, and hold press conferences at which people ask questions like, "What was the budget?"[56]

Festivals host official parties for specific sections and special events. When I went in San Sebastián in 2008, the party for the film schools was intimate, with limited fancy food and drinks. The finale party for the whole festival was elaborate, with good food, unlimited drinks, and a grand setting. People, though, were genuinely enjoying themselves. Individual films, companies, and countries cater their own events, while the daily trade press publishes rankings (how many champagne glasses the party gained the night before). And then there are many casual business meetings all over in cafes and restaurants, or simply good talk among like minds to discuss the quality of the films. This construction of social ties connects multiple audiences as people run into each other in shuttle buses, start chatting with fellow passengers, find out that they both know someone, and begin great conversations. This reminds us that film festivals, no matter how business-minded they can be, are also very social events with a great deal of human interaction that is very difficult to quantify, yet vital to their goals. This perspective can become clearer as we turn to history and evolution.

1

History, Structure, and Practice in the Festival World

Film festivals represent the ultimate celebrations of cinema, not only as a mass medium, but also as collections of creative texts and engaged participants within a larger global framework. Together with institutions like film archives, film museums, cinémathèques, ciné clubs, film societies, and film classes in universities, they constitute a specific stratum of Miriam Hansen's "discursive horizons."[1] Hansen's ideas, which she applied to early cinema, situate the discourses of all cinematic practices within others that refract many processes and consequences of modernity as they participate in them. Film festivals, in turn, form one complex component of this set of discourses and resonate closely with others in social and cultural formations. Within this discursive horizon, film festivals brought cinema away from its roots as a mass medium and endowed it with the "distinction" of serious art.[2]

At the same time, it would be a mistake to think that film festivals ever have severed their deep connections to their mass roots or to film industries, especially that of Hollywood. In fact, film festivals are too diverse and multifaceted to be painted with a single brushstroke. Major competitive festivals depend on the glamour of stars and spectacles as well as cutting-edge art; thus, they occupy the peculiar role of bridging art and commercial cinemas (both of which in and of themselves have porous boundaries). At the same time, other festivals highlight or unify specific groups, publicize particular social causes, or showcase diverse forms of cinema, sometimes in calculated opposition to mainstream tastes. Festivals link the erudite discourses of archives and scholars with wider audiences but simultaneously facilitate the academization of the popular.

This chapter provides a general historical and sociocultural overview of film festivals, which begins with the many elements that made their emergence possible—the invention of cinema, the debate on what cinema should be, and the demarcation between cinema as a mass medium and cinema as an art form. It is important to understand that the many institutions that have been brought up with the invention of cinema played equally important roles in making the film festival a possible element in the larger film discourse. The magazines (from trade magazines to fan magazines to more high-brow art magazines), newspapers, and film critics who worked for these publications brought legitimacy to cinema beyond its mass origins, identifying cinema as art. Yet, film festivals are not just about art cinema, a distinction drawn in practice as well as form.

From here I look at the early engagement of film festivals with national and international politics, especially as these surrounded the birth of the best-known festivals of the present, including Venice, Cannes, Berlin, and Locarno, and the atmosphere before and after World War II. Here, I underscore the tensions of art and geopolitics played out in particular on a stage divided by dichotomous power blocks—Allied and Axis giving way to cold war East and West.[3]

After this, I follow more diffuse strains of globalization and aestheticization that opened up a wider range of festivals during and after the conflictive 1960s, even as established festivals developed important innovations like new sections that accommodate a more expansive definition of cinema—for example, Un Certain Regard at Cannes. I continue to show further changes in the 1980s and 1990s, including expansion and changing roles and demands on multilayered festivals and their multiple audiences in a post–cold war world.

Finally, as this history brings us into the contemporary world, in which festivals open somewhere, literally, every day of the year, I balance the continuing unifying roles of the festivals maintained by FIAPF—and more regularly by flows of critics, producers, organizers, and films that sustain a global and local forum for art cinema and mass appeal—as they face new challenges.[4]

This chapter (and to a great extent, this book) examines an emergent global institution—the film festival—which lacks a coherent body of governance or formal codes, yet which occupies a defining role in global cinema, film industries, human careers, and even cities and nations. Festivals encapsulate how cinema can be used to consolidate—to reproduce as well as to question—categorization, interpretation, and hierarchies of film, including its relationship to other media and society. We must begin, however, with the recognition that film emerged and thrived for decades before festivals came to exist.

Before Film Festivals

Film, as one of the first electric mass media, with its bourgeois "inventors," had its humble beginning among a largely unlettered populace, framed by the gaudy spectacle of vaudeville and the cheap thrills of nickelodeons. Its early history was one of constant invention, with new technologies and cultural products taking shape amid great social changes at the turn of the nineteenth and twentieth centuries. These innovations in product and distribution converged with rearticulations of urban spaces, gender, and immigration, as well as the formation of a modernist aesthetic and sensibility. The emergence of new groups into public spaces, the redefinition of public and private roles of gender, and the nature of cosmopolitan culture were all filtered through questions of who was making movies, where movies were shown, and to whom.[5]

Film festivals did not enter the cinematic field for nearly forty years after the Lumière brothers hosted their first public screening at the Indian Salon at the basement of the Grand Café in Boulevard des Capucines in 1895. In this time, movies matured as a system of production and distribution on national and international scales. There were few studios at the turn of the century. Around 1905, Pathé emerged as a major player in France that was also successful in Europe and the United States. In the United States, Edison, Biograph, and Vitagraph competed among themselves while actively resisting the dominance of Pathé.[6] It took no time before fierce competition arose between Edison and Biograph, which led to the creation of the Motion Picture Patents Company, the Big Three, and the Little Five.[7] In Europe, Italy had an industry close to the French in production, while Denmark carved out an astonishing global position as filmmaker and exporter.[8] Meanwhile, in Latin America and Asia, cinema arrived in metropolitan centers just a few months after Lumière and Edison had screened their products to their domestic audiences in 1896, and national as well as regional cinemas followed.[9]

Film productions soon became industrialized; however, spaces for small producers and minuscule budgets remained accessible to many. Moreover, this early, open ambience permitted opportunities for women as filmmakers, minority and working class voices, and small-scale global productions that would not be recaptured even in film festivals for decades.[10] This early character of open access in film production started to decline by the mid-1910s; by the 1920s and 1930s producers with limited resources were marginalized. Film festivals would thus also serve as one mechanism to address imbalances, creating a space for smaller and alternative productions and audiences.

The First World War interrupted European productions as well as the global flow of imports to the United States. The United States, with its largely autonomous market, not only became self-sustaining but also started to dominate the Latin American market. American producers would use this continued domestic market and production to position themselves strongly in the European and eventually the world market from the 1920s onward. This American dominance created a lopsided playing field in the global film business, with implications for form and aesthetics as well. Hollywood, its textual form, institutions, and commercial business practices, established itself as "the norm," which, at the same time, has prevented it from ever being the alternative, at least at its initial exhibition.[11] Nevertheless, the boundaries between commercial and its alternatives were never rigid; ample examples of Classical Hollywood Cinema have been "rescued" by critics and film festivals and raised to the status of art cinema. Similarly, film festivals are very much a response to this global Hollywood dominance, national as well as artistic, but this does not mean that film festivals have ever been anti-Hollywood.

This period coincides with Dudley Andrew's classification of the first stage, or the pre-academic period of film studies: "for half a century, filmmakers and aficionados engaged in zealous discussions in cineclubs and contributed to chic journals or produced mimeographed notes themselves."[12] This cinephilia or "proto-cinephilia,"[13] as a practice, crystallized a film culture that eventually would allow film festivals to both thrive and gain "legitimacy." As Pierre Bourdieu asserts, cinema belongs to the category of "middle-ground" arts.[14] Cinema's artistic status has always been contested. Thus, early voices paved the way for a diverse and conflictive discourse that has continued to seek to define cinema's role in the larger social and cultural hierarchy within its *habitus*—a "practice-unifying and practice-generating principle."[15] At the same time, since cinema is first and foremost a mass medium, different groups in society have projected varied concerns onto it.

When cinema was new, for example, social reformists as well as conservatives fretted over its power to indoctrinate the public. Films could be "bad" for weak women and naive children; of course, film also could be used to elevate the public. When cinema became more institutionalized, the industries started worrying more about film's low-brow status (and the economic consequences thereof) and wanted to elevate cinema to a middle-class pursuit.[16] Studios like Vitagraph and Triangle started building movie palaces, making films that would be considered high culture, and encouraging middle-class behavior from its audience, while simultaneously maintaining the lucrative mass audience base. This impetus established Hollywood, with directors like D. W. Griffith and Cecil B. DeMille, as a bastion of solid middle-brow entertainment, expensive and polished yet accessible to a large audience.

While Hollywood was exerting dominance around the world in the early twentieth century, different experimentations of cinema and audience took shape among global artists as well as national populations that had been pushed aside by Hollywood. Surrealist films, for example, were very much the product of their time as elite European artists played with this new medium with scant concerns for mass audience or profits.[17] In the Soviet Union, by contrast, cinema served revolutionary functions both in aesthetics and in distribution in service of collective goals.[18] Weimar Germany's major studio—UFA, although initially a commercial entity and only later a Nazi propagandizer—differentiated itself from Hollywood by making exportable expressionist films.[19] Back in the United States, meanwhile, Oscar Micheaux and others produced race films that used Hollywood narrative form, but did so with content—and actors—that Hollywood had shunned.[20]

Many films relied on their own national distribution systems, yet there were also alternative exhibition venues that dealt with films that crossed national boundaries or stood outside mass distribution systems. According to Haidee Wasson, in the 1920s, film societies abounded in France, Germany, and the United Kingdom, exemplified by Le Club des Amis du Septième Art, founded in 1920 in Paris. The social construction of this world embodied Andrew's elite vision of film as art: Richard Abel asserts that film societies in Paris consisted merely of "an identifiable network of critics, journals, cine club lectures, screenings, and specialized cinemas."[21] In New York, the New York Film Society and New York Film Forum emerged at the same time, although neither lasted more than half a year. In the United Kingdom, the London Film Society was formed in 1925; its cofounder was Iris Barry, who later headed the film library of the Museum of Modern Art in New York. Its initial members included playwright George Bernard Shaw, author and critic H. G. Wells, and documentarian Paul Rotha. One of its earliest efforts was to show its objection to the 1909 Cinematograph Censorship Law by screening uncensored films. It was also the meeting place for Alfred Hitchcock and his future wife, Alma.[22] In Brazil, the Chaplin Club was founded in 1928.[23] As David Andrews points out, these art house groups were far from "monolithic," but rather a "pluralist bazaar."[24] These places expanded the possibilities of cinema, but did not necessarily dictate a higher form of cinema; this arrangement resonates with similar manifestations of later film festivals.

Unlike the nickelodeons (which were neighborhood-based) and middle-brow movie palaces, both of which had a relatively impersonal relationship with their audience, these film societies nevertheless formed communities of like-minded cinephiles. Cinema, for those who created the film societies, was not escapist entertainment but an object to be studied and appreciated. Cinema crossed boundaries and challenged established orders: the London Film Society screened *Potemkin* while it was banned in regular theaters in England. Donald Spoto also asserts that because of the society's high-class membership, even the royal family became more interested in cinema.[25] These practitioners were projecting themselves as different from the mass working-class or immigrant audience associated with film in the United States as well as middle-brow culture. They wanted different films, different spaces to watch these films, and different social and cultural relationships with their fellow filmgoers (and filmmakers). These film societies even became film schools a sort, where budding filmmakers could learn the craft of other's works, a role still prominent in film festivals.

More specialized cinemas also functioned as differentiated spaces. The Théâtre du Vieux-Colombier, a successor of Club des Amis de Septième Art, opened in 1924, showing revivals like *The Cabinet of Dr. Caligari*. Studio 28 followed as an avant-garde cinema in 1928 in Montmartre, Paris; it screened the surrealist breakthroughs *L'Age d'Or* and *Un chien andalou*. Richard Roud says that Henri Langlois, who founded the Cinémathèque Française, was a frequent spectator; his visits inspired him to open his own ciné club.[26] The roots of the later Cineteca Italiana are found in Italian amateurs of the 1930s,[27] while in the United States, according to Haidee Wasson, nineteen small art theaters served various American cities in 1927, screening revivals, experimental works, and European art films. These were very much in the business of "nurturing specialized, intelligent audiences."[28]

In Japan, the little cinema movement of the 1920s was closely related to the leftist film movement; it also advocated an alternative cinema form that saw "cine-poems as alternatives."[29] Ultimately, a diffuse but global trend took shape, where some educated audiences were attracted to cinema beyond its mass media manifestations and demanded their own spaces as well as programming, with few commercial aspirations beyond the basic economics of survival and reproduction.

Yet, not all alternatives to Hollywood were art cinemas. Race films—casting ethnically marked actors for audiences who reflected this ethnicization—were screened across the United States, sometimes at racially segregated cinemas, sometimes at midnight shows in mainstream cinemas, and sometimes even in churches. These film practices of African Americans were very much divorced from activities advocated by ciné clubs or film societies. Alternatives also included the international movement of films among migrant communities, including Hong Kong products shipped to Chinatowns across the world or Italian films that found audiences in Italian immigrant communities in New York. One sees a similar separation between the two vaguely labeled alternatives to Hollywood today, one reified as art cinema, patronized by the educated classes, and the other a grassroots cinema of sorts created by a population structurally marginalized by mainstream society as a whole: Tyler Perry and his career spanning from church viewings to mainstream distribution comes to mind.

Another, more shadowy exhibition space of alternative early cinema was that of pornographic cinema. As Curt Moreck notes, as cited by Gertrud Koch, "In most cases, these sotadic films were screened in private societies or especially in men's clubs founded for this purpose. Tickets in Germany cost between 10 and 30 marks. Prostitutes, pimps, cafe waiters, barbers, and other persons in contact with the clientele handled the distribution of tickets and they earned a tidy profit through scalping. Since vendors usually knew their clientele and its inclinations, they seldom came into conflict with the police."[30] Indeed, the most popular places for such screenings were brothels. This cinema, and the later development of global pornographic circuits, would nevertheless intersect with festivals around issues of sexuality and censorship.

As a mass medium, cinema intersected with other mass media. As film critics in daily newspapers started writing on films, they brought together readers of the two media. Other publications created different albeit overlapping audiences in fan magazines such as *Girls' Cinema* or *Picture-Goers*, and glossy movie magazines like *Motion Picture Classic*. Trade publications—*Photoplay*, *La Cinématographie Française*, *Movie Maker*, *Experimental Film*, *Moving Picture World*, *Billboard*, *Views and Films Index*—expanded realms of global critical discourse, while more "distinctive" film writing became more prominent in the 1920s.[31] In France, Louia Delluc's *Cinéa* appeared from 1921 to 1923. The first British film journal was the idiosyncratic *Close Up* (1927–1933), but numerous newspapers, from the *Daily News* to the *Daily Mail*, already had dedicated writers for film writing and other criticism.[32] According to Laura Marcus, C. A. Lejeune, who wrote for the *Manchester Guardian*, and Iris Barry, who wrote for *The Spectator* before she moved to the *Daily Mail*, both promoted cinema as an equal to other art forms, adding that "a new art form" demands a new critical language.[33] More elite cultural publications like *The Spectator*, *Film-Kurier* in Germany, and *Revue du cinéma* (founded in 1929 and later parent to the distinguished *Cahiers du cinéma*)[34] elaborated a multinational critical discourse that museums and academic journals would later join. Within different societies in the early twentieth century, cinema was a much talked about cosmopolitan subject.

The content of discourse about cinema varied widely. Some sources offered apparently mundane readings, instructing the reader how to be a modern woman through multiple acts of consumption or reveling in the dream life of stars and exotic plots. Other writers examined social issues, discussing the themes or effects of cinema. Still others promoted investigation of the medium itself. Many elite discussions were about the art of the film, including film's relations to other arts, especially theater, photography, or the inherent ingredients of the moving image, movements, forms, and film's ability to transform time and space. In other words, writers began to study the formal elements of cinema to understand its potential as well as to compare cinema with the other established art forms. Some, like critic E. A. Baughan,[35] argued that cinematography is an art and that if cinema had been less dependent on narrative, filmmakers would have started theorizing the unique art of cinematography. Yet, these erudite approaches were cushioned by a wider mass interest in spectacle, stars, and entertainment.

With such growing interest in cinema as high culture, universities also started to offer classes in cinema. Dana Polan's masterful exploration of the study of cinema in the United States deftly illustrates that the different classes that were offered covered aesthetics, social scientific issues, and practical aspects of filmmaking and the film business.[36] As in festivals, different demands on the medium played out in the classrooms—was film art, a social and cultural practice that affected society, or an industrial product that invited cooperation between institutes of higher learning and the commercial entities? Polan's study ends in 1935, when the film library of the Museum of Modern Art opened, making it more possible for institutions to borrow films from a prestigious high-culture institution that also was interested in preservation, linking the infrastructures of art to films. The diverse demands on the study of film crystallized once again the inevitable multifaceted nature of this new medium—an all-encompassing cultural practice that relied on its mass appeal, yet demanded and sustained more "serious" inquiries from certain classes of people in society.

Museums and archives, in a sense, complete these discursive horizons by creating a permanent and ongoing place of history. While many films were made before 1930, there was little effort in preservation, although using film as a tool for preservation of historical record came slightly before the preservation of film itself. As early as 1919, the British Imperial War Museum started collecting moving images of the First World War. By 1923, trade magazines such as *Photoplay* argued that "the motion picture needs a museum. . . . The archives and relics of the early motion pictures . . . [are] scattered over all parts of America."[37] According to Roud, the French critic Leon Moussinac coined the word ciné-mathèque—a film library—in a 1921 issue of *Cinémagazine*.[38] By the 1930s, with the knowledge that nitrate films were unstable and that silent films would be lost with the advent of synchronized sound film, the idea of preserving films became more urgent.

In the 1930s, three major institutions for film preservation were founded on both sides of the Atlantic. The British Film Institute formed in 1933, and added an archival section in 1935. Henri Langlois and Paul-Auguste Harlé founded the Cinémathèque Française in 1936. On the other side of the Atlantic, the Museum of Modern Art established its film library in 1935 under Iris Barry. These three institutions together constituted the founding members of the Fédération Internationale des Archives du Film (FIAF) in 1938. Film and its discourses had been deemed valuable enough for curatorship and preservation.

A final, less erudite institution from this period that has come to play an important role in film festivals over time bears special mention. This is the International Federation of Film Producers Associations (FIAPF).[39] Founded in 1933 in Paris, its members comprised film producers' organizations from different countries. While it later came to regulate film festivals, FIAPF primarily seeks to protect producers on issues ranging from copyrights and technology standardization to media regulations. In terms of film festivals, the organization specifies its role as being "to facilitate the job of the producers, sales agents, and distributors in the management of their relationships with the festivals."[40] The general standards FIAPF expects are logistical and business oriented.[41]

Emergent film festivals, then, would fit within the network of these various institutions and discourses, constituted by and for an educated high-brow audience who demanded a more artistic and serious cinema in conjunction with smaller scale, grassroots institutions formed by these audiences, whether ciné clubs, small theaters, avant-garde cinema, or archives. The increased importance of writing on film in newspapers and the trade press as well as in high-brow art magazines also legitimized cinema as a serious medium. The introduction of university classes in cinema and the incorporation of cinema into established institutions of high culture further endorsed the practice of a more serious and respectable cinema. Ultimately, the first thirty years of motion pictures witnessed a maturation of the medium of film. On the one hand, Hollywood successfully completed its quest for global dominance; on the other hand, cinema became capable of absorbing diverse audiences, filmmakers, and eventually films that expressed themselves in very different manifestations. As institutions and groups crafted a niche for specialized audiences who demanded a more challenging cinema and in turn sought distinction in such practice, filmmakers and artists who wanted to produce a cinema that might not be very popular found themselves capable of making films. Serious films became sustainable because of the demand of a small but fairly loyal audience nurtured by institutions that provided the structures for such endeavors.

At the same time, film festivals do not replace these institutions; instead, they complement and work with many of them, linking them across cities and audiences. Ciné clubs continued to thrive in the 1940s, 1950s, and 1960s, giving rise to important journals like *Cahiers du cinéma* (founded 1951), which was instrumental in promoting the European art cinema of the 1960s, where film festivals became major players. Museums collect and curate films shown at film festivals; film festivals program retrospectives that bring attention to archives. Interest groups find space in the umbrella of film festival scheduling, while films and critics travel the world linking the discursive horizons of film as art (and as mass medium) in concrete, focused, and glamorous events. And film festivals negotiate audiences—larger and more diverse than those who read critical journals, join film clubs, or search out archival programs—thus sustaining these other places of discourse as well. Having laid forth the sociocultural formation of early film as mass medium, then, in dialectic with the construction of distinctive apparatus of high-brow culture, I turn to the film festivals themselves.

Film Festivals Create Histories in Nations and Cities: 1930–1960

The Origins: 1930s

While appropriating the aspirations of the cinephiles who were debating the art of the cinema and the other film enthusiasts, the first film festival came from a rather different source. The Mostra Cinematografica di Venezia, which began in 1932, was a creation of Benito Mussolini's Fascist regime, which saw cinema as "the most powerful weapon."[42] Italian Fascists used the rhetoric of film as art to glorify the nation-state and to further their goals, insisting that Italy as a film-producing nation could compete with Hollywood. They proclaimed cinema as a medium was an art to be respected alongside both Italy's glorious heritage and new constructions of civic architecture, education, and music.

To explore the Venice festival, one also has to understand film policies and production in Italy in the 1920s and 1930s. Before the First World War, Italy was one of the major film production nations for the world market, with epics like the spectacular and successful *Cabiria* (1914). A dynamic avant-garde Italy, however, saw a decline in its feature film output from 371 films in 1920 to only eight in 1930.[43] Without film production, Italy lost its international market share. The Fascist government not only needed to rescue Italian cinema, but also saw the potential of cinema as a manipulative tool. It was keen in using documentaries and newsreels to publicize Italian achievements while features entertained domestic and foreign audiences.

In 1926, L'Unione Cinematografica Educative (LUCE)—a state-sponsored documentary consortium—was founded, promoting Italian successes and fomenting the cult of personality around Benito Mussolini, Il Duce, who fully utilized the visual component of the medium. Not unlike the Nazis in Germany, the Fascist government formed the Ente Nazionale per la Cinematografia to oversee all operations of cinema production, distribution, and exhibition. Various auxiliary organizations to promote cinema were formed, including the Fascist Youth Cinema Club (Cine-GUF-Gioventù Universitaría fascista) in 1933 and a proto-film school, the Centro Sperimentale de Cinematografia, in 1935; the center also published a theory-oriented journal, *Bianco e nero* (beginning in 1937), as well as the more entertainment-oriented *Cinema* (established in 1936). The center became a formative laboratory for Roberto Rossellini, Michelangelo Antonioni, and Giuseppe De Santis. More importantly, Cinecittà, a massive studio, was built in Rome in 1937, providing the necessary hardware for the development of the Italian film industries.

Instead of artists, critics, and cinephiles promoting institutions to support art cinema as an alternative to the mainstream commercial cinema, the Fascist government formed parallel structures and discourses to support its version of a serious, glamorous, *and* nationalistic cinema. While cinephiles often opposed censorship, the Fascists formed the Direzione Generale per la Cinematografia to control foreign film exhibition in Italy, censoring Jean Renoir's 1937 *Grand Illusion* while funding other more militaristic films, such as *Scipio Africanus* (1937)—a film that glorified a Roman defeat of the Carthaginian Hannibal in the Second Punic War and thus resonated with Mussolini's African colonialism. By 1938, in a desperate measure to compete with Hollywood, the importation of American films was banned.[44]

The Venice Film Festival, an outgrowth of the established Venice Biennale arts festival, thus became one component of Fascist discourses of the Italian cinema and modernity before the Second World War. Unlike the early cinephiles described in the previous section, moreover, the Fascist government became heavily involved in the production of cinema. Identifying cinema as a useful tool to promote its agenda, with a belief that the viewing public would be seduced by the images on screen, the centralized government promoted the production of both fiction and nonfiction cinema by providing monetary resources and a first-rate studio to facilitate the production of desirable films and images. The festival reaffirmed these goals. As Pierre Sorlin states, "The annual Venice Festival, in 1932, was merely an attempt to lure a few European and American intellectuals in the peninsula. But, by 1935, with the institution of awards reserved for Italian films only, the festival was used to promote Italian films."[45] Still, betraying its initial fascination with Hollywood, Venice awarded Greta Garbo's *Anna Karenina* with the Mussolini Cup for best foreign film in 1935. Nonetheless, the festival highlighted Italian and German Nazi cinema: *Scipio Africanus* won the Mussolini Cup at the Venice Festival in 1937, and Leni Riefenstahl's *Olympia* shared the same cup with *Luciano Serra, pilota* in 1938.[46] The British and American jury members walked out of the festival before the Mussolini Cup was awarded to these two films: *Olympia*, as a nonfiction film, was not even eligible for the prize. The French participants, including the historian and functionary Philippe Erlanger, walked out over the festival authorities' veto of *The Grand Illusion*.

Given the blatant Fascist/Nazi sympathies of the Mostra Cinematograpica di Venezia, Cannes must first be read as a national as well as artistic response within this new arena of cinematic debate. Back in France, Erlanger initially wanted to start a Festival of the Free World (FIF). A 1938 FIF document averred, "The major American, English and French film companies would be happy not to return to Venice. . . . If, therefore, the Venice Festival should no longer have the same success and be replaced by a similar organization in another country, it would be desirable that France be called on to take advantage of this."[47] However, politics was not the only incentive for the establishment of the festival: the French film industry had also faced ups and downs after World War I and the Depression. The Cinémathèque Française, established in 1936, demanded special treatment for cinema in France. For Cannes, meanwhile, commerce and tourism were equally important. A festival in September could prolong the summer seasons of the resorts in France; hoteliers lobbied hard to bring the festival to Côte d'Azur, beating their Atlantic rival at Biarritz. To add historical legitimacy to the festival, Louis Lumière was selected as the honorary president of the festival. Cannes gained strong and immediate support from Britain and the United States. *The Hunchback of Notre Dame* premiered on the first and only day of the festival, September 1, 1939, the day Hitler invaded Poland.

Looking at the histories of these two initial film festivals, it is clear that while cinematic art was used to justify the existence of such events, other overwhelming desires propelled them in particular ways. The first was clearly geopolitical: Venice was Fascist and Cannes was anti-Fascist.[48] Another component was the festivals' desire to court Hollywood. Before Mussolini signed the Treaty of Friendship with Germany in 1936 and formed the "Rome-Berlin Axis," the Venice festival had sought to build international relationships with other major film-producing countries, and especially with Hollywood. The initial Festival of the Free World and subsequent Festival International du Film at Cannes could not have garnered the kind of support it had without the full support of Hollywood.

A third point is the issue of place. Cannes and Venice have been important modern tourist destinations rather than centers of film production or national power. Film festivals formed a welcome addition to the tourist industries, especially when situated in times of low use and when utilizing existing facilities (hotels, cinemas). Inadvertently, with these early locations, film festivals did not need to be spatially linked to film production centers and thus became free to consider other geographic concerns. Cinema, after all, is an art form that can be mechanically reproduced, and therefore is portable. These three objectives seem far from the desire and discourse of the cinephiles; however, they converged in elevating the status of cinema and facilitated the connection of discourses of criticism, art, and preservation.

Postwar Rebirth and Expansion: 1940s and 1950s

The "Peacetime Remake"[49] of the festival at Cannes marked the trajectory of festival away from pure politics in a postwar Europe toward serious art. Erlanger invited Robert Favre Le Bret to become the head of the festival. Favre Le Bret was a journalist and director of the Paris Opera; the festival was thus immediately linked with the stature of high art. Nevertheless, there was a great deal of semi-diplomatic maneuvering across the Atlantic even at the early days of the first French festival to make sure mass/middle-brow film was not absent. Hollywood actually did not commit itself to the 1946 festival until it knew that the Blun-Byrnes Accord would be signed in May 1946, opening French cinema to U.S. films every week except one per month in exchange for a partial erasure of French war debt to the United States. Hollywood still did not send any stars except Maria Montez, hardly a major name compared to the group Hollywood had intended to send over in 1939. Despite these diplomatic issues, Hollywood films had quite a strong presence at Cannes. The number of films invited was related to the number of films produced by each country; hence, Hollywood always had the right to select a substantial presence, both in films and in stars.

Venice returned in 1947, with the Golden Lion of St. Mark replacing the Mussolini Cup (and the transitional Grand International Prize of Venice) in 1949. It proved more open to newly socialist influences, awarding its first postwar prize to the Czech film *The Strike* (*Siréna*) as that country tilted toward the coalescing Soviet bloc.

The new Locarno International Film Festival was actually the first international film festival held after the end of the Second World War, slightly before Cannes. Since Switzerland was neutral during the war, there had been sporadic small festivals held in different parts of the country during the war. The Basel film club, Le Bon Film, had organized the Semaine Internationale du Film in 1939. In Lugano, it held the first and second Rassegna del Film Italiano with the backing of a tourist-centered Pro Lugano in 1941 and 1942. In 1944, to make the Rassegna more international, the "Italiano" was dropped and the organizers included films like John Huston's *Across the Pacific* (1942). The second Rassegna Internazionale du Film in 1945 invited Disney's *The Three Caballeros* (1944) and Robert Bresson's *Angels of the Street* (*Les Anges du péché*, 1943). In the meantime, Henri Langlois had organized Images du Cinéma Français at the Musée Cantonal des Beaux-Arts in Lausanne, which eventually led to the founding of Lausanne Ciné Club, which in 1949 became the Cinémathèque Suisse in Basel.

Organizers for Rassegna continued to search for a permanent home; the city of Lugano did not support the project. Next door in the lake resort of Locarno, some private individuals—local cinema owners, film distributors, tourist groups, and members of Club del Buon Film, later the Circolo del Cinema and Circolo deglo Arti—took over the festival. The first Locarno International Film Festival was inaugurated on August 22, 1946.

Despite Locarno's history of neutrality, just as early festivals divided between Axis and Allies, the rebirth of film festivals in the post–World War II era faced the escalation of the cold war across film as a cultural battlefield. The Soviet Union, for example, complained that the United States had many entries in Cannes while the USSR was only invited to present one film in 1949. Thus it declined the invitation from Cannes and went to Venice instead. Cannes continued to have an uneasy relationship with the Soviet Union for years, marked by the sporadic presence of Soviet films. When they were shown, some turned out to be too propagandistic: in 1951, the festival refused to show *Liberated China* even after the Soviet filmmaker reedited the film and renamed it *New China*.[50]

This struggle shaped the formation of new festivals as well. Postwar Czechoslovakia offered small film festivals in Mariánské Lázně and Karlovy Vary, showing a few films in a few days as the country struggled to remain a bridge between East and West. When the communists consolidated their power in 1948, the Karlovy Vary festival grew into an event that followed the party line of the communist East. In its official history, the Web site states that "the program was put together with an awareness of the propagandistic strength of film and the importance of this medium as a tool in the ideological struggle against the West."[51] Nonetheless, William Wyler won best director there for *The Best Years of Our Lives* in 1948.

While the festival was primarily a showcase for films from the Eastern Bloc, Western films were included if they were considered "progressive." Not unlike the Venice festival when it was under Mussolini, where Fascist and Nazi films won prizes, socialist films would always garner one of the many prizes at Karlovy Vary. The festival inaugurated an international jury in 1951: except for Umberto Barbaro, an Italian film critic who had translated works by Vsevolod Pudovkin and Sergei Eisenstein, and Georges Sadoul, a French film historian and communist, all the other jury members came from Czechoslovakia, the Soviet Union, China, Poland, Hungary, and East Germany.

Proliferation also demanded more organization. The International Federation of Film Societies (IFFS) set up in 1947 at Cannes to coordinate interests and events. Together with FIAPF, these two organizations have formed part of a loose-knit network of coordination and legitimization of festivals as a unity as well as diverse group. Karlovy Vary was granted the "A" status by FIAPF the same year Berlin received such designation in 1956. This reflects how FIAPF tried to make sure that the Eastern Bloc was represented in global film circles. However, with the establishment of the Moscow film festivals, FIAPF mandated that there should only be one "A" festival in the Eastern Bloc each year. From 1959 to 1993, Karlovy Vary and Moscow hosted the festival in alternate years.

The height of cold war cinematic confrontation was reached in Berlin. The Berlin festival was initially an American initiative. Oscar Martay, a film officer of the Information Service Branch of the American High Commissioner for Germany in Berlin, came up with the idea of a film festival in 1950 just after the travails of the Soviet blockade of the city and the dramatic Allied airlift. Newly divided West Berlin formed an outpost of "free" West Germany surrounded by communist East Germany; a film festival, heavily supported by the "West," would show the oppressed "East" the values of the democratic, capitalist society. Martay called for a meeting in October that included government cultural and tourism officials, journalists, film distributors and producers, representatives of the German film industries, and Martay's British counterpart.[52]

According to Heide Fehrenbach, the newly born Bonn government also was interested in supporting cinema as mass culture. Federal funds had been distributed to different cities, and festivals in Mannheim and Oberhausen became aligned with the politics of the city governments. Both cities differentiated their programs from regular commercial cinema and strived to promote Kulturfilm. Berlin was different in that its initial establishment was highly political on a global scale; it was also the first major festival to move beyond a resort location. The festival was established with the help of the city government and of other local Berlin interests who wanted to revive the past glory of Berlin as a cultural center and as the birthplace of German cinema. Yet, its repercussions went far beyond the nation.

While festivals were made possible because films had been promoted to be considered serious art, Martay insisted that the Berlin film festival should not be part of a larger cultural festival week (Festepielwoche).[53] From an American point of view, films should remain a mass medium and not be exclusive. The first director of the festival, Alfred Bauer, was an adept administrator and historian of the new art of cinema. He had worked for UFA at the end of its Third Reich existence, was the author of *Feature Film Almanac,* and was a consultant on film for the British. The Berlin International Film Festival was to show the world as well as West Berlin's immediate neighbor, East Berlin, the films as well as ways of life of the democratic West.

At the very first meeting that Martay called in October 1950, the committee had already decided to have three films each from the United States and England, and two each from France, Italy, Austria, and Germany. An additional film would be included from the Netherlands, Denmark, Sweden, Finland, Israel, Egypt, India, Mexico, and Australia. The omission was obvious: there were seven negative votes to reject admission of films from the Eastern Bloc.[54] The festival was nonetheless very keen on attracting audiences from the East; it sponsored outdoor screenings at Potsdamerplatz, the border between East and West Berlin, to attract an audience in the East who could see the films from East Berlin.

East Germany reacted quickly to the establishment of the Berlin festival by proposing the World Youth Festival, organized by FDJ, the official East German youth organization, in the summer of 1951. In July 1951, the Festwoche des Volkdemokratischen Films was held in East Berlin. Six films participated, representing Poland, Czechoslovakia, Rumania, Hungary, Bulgaria, and the People's Republic of China.

While dealing with the political cold war with the Eastern Bloc, the (West) Berlin organizers also had to work with France and Italy to solicit their participation in the first festival. However, both France and Italy refused official participation unless Berlin omitted a competition. Berlin in the end had a German jury, rather than an international jury as in FIAPF-recognized "A" festivals, which at that point were only Venice and Cannes. Unofficially, the producers' associations of the two countries sent films on their behalf to the festival.

The first Berlin festival opened on June 6, 1951. The opening film was Alfred Hitchcock's 1940 *Rebecca,* and its star, Joan Fontaine, attended. While the festival yearned for more international glamour, there was not an impressive international presence. However, there was a great parade of German stars, including Hans Söhnker and Dorothea Wieck. Mayor Ernst Reuter called Berlin an "oasis of liberty and independence, surrounded by a system of violence and oppression, which uses art for the purpose of propaganda . . . [showing] Berlin to be a bastion which the totalitarian powers storm in vain."[55] His comment was contested, however, by the East German *Tägliche Rundschau* newspaper, which designated the festival as "West Berlin's decadent film façade" and added that "West Berlin Films have given clear proof of the state of affairs of film production in capitalistic countries, especially of the situation in a country occupied by Americans; decadent in content, with petit-bourgeois and placating sentimentality, monstrously dollied-up kitsch, anti-Soviet tendencies and warmongering, nihilistic emptiness and pathological excesses."[56]

Embroiled in the ideological struggle between East and West, the Berlin festival also sought a broader European—if not international—recognition for its aesthetic vision. Even before FIAPF rewarded it with "A" status in 1956, the festival, also known as Berlinale, polled the public for best picture for each category, including the three levels of audience-selected "bears" (Gold, Silver, and Bronze) for fiction and documentary films. Audience members were given entrance tickets to rate the film as "very good," "good," "average," or "poor." In 1954, for example, David Lean's comic *Hobson's Choice* won the audience vote for Golden Bear. The festival also used this audience poll to further consolidate its democratic credentials. This audience-centered award can also trace its lineage to the United States' insistence that the festival remain relevant to the masses. However, the festival organizers yearned for official recognition, so that Berlin could share the international stage with Venice and Cannes: Europe, as we see, defined the cultural world.

After Berlin and Karlovy Vary, Locarno gained this recognition from FIAPF in 1958. Oddly, it followed San Sebastián, which was recognized by FIAPF in 1957, while festivals in Brussels, London, Edinburgh, Melbourne, San Francisco, Vancouver, and Leningrad did not get approved.

One striking outlier to this systematization was the 1949 Festival Independent du Film Maudit (Independent Festival of Accursed Film) in Biarritz, France, with a jury led by writer and filmmaker Jean Cocteau. Cocteau himself declared, "The time has come to honour the masterpieces of film art which have been buried alive, and to sound the alarm. Cinema must free itself from slavery just like the many courageous people who are currently striving to achieve their freedom. Art which is inaccessible to young people will never be art."[57] This festival had been created by the organizer of the Paris Cine Club Objectif 49, a forum of New Criticism whose members included Cocteau, Henri Langlois, Raymond Queneau, and André Bazin; these highly literary figures took "Maudit" from poet Stephane Mallarmé's term *poètes maudits*. The term *film maudit* (accursed film) and Cocteau's use of words like "buried alive" and "slavery" evoked the idea that the cinema was suffering in chains. Only Film Maudit would free cinema, a quest that could be achieved by "courageous" and "young" people. The first and only festival, in July 1949, was to compete with Cannes. Antonie de Baecque and Serge Toubiana, in their biography of François Truffaut, describe the teenager's correspondence with his friends about the festival, which opened with Marcello Pagliero's *Roma città libera* (1946).[58] Truffaut also saw Jean Vigo's 1934 *L'Atalante*, Orson Welles's 1947 *The Lady from Shanghai*, and Jean Renoir's *The Southerner* (1945). Other young French cinephiles, including Jean-Luc Godard, Jacques Rivette, Claude Chabrol, and Eric Rohmer were all there, ill-suited to the elegance of its setting at the Biarritz casino. While this festival was never repeated, its organizers and the Young Turks who attended later became responsible for the development of *Cahiers du cinéma*, the Nouvelle Critique, and eventually the Nouvelle Vague. Cocteau himself would later head the jury at Cannes (1953, 1954), while Truffaut and Godard would force important changes in the festival in the 1960s.

The FIAPF applications from festivals in London, Toronto, Sydney, and Vancouver underscore the continuing globalization of the idea and practices of the film festival alongside experimentation. The Edinburgh Film Festival, for example, was actually one of the world's first documentary festivals. Founded in 1947, it was part of the Edinburgh International Festival, an art festival aimed at reviving the cultural scene of Scotland after the Second World War. The film festival was championed by John Grierson, the famed British documentarian.

Like Lugano's Rassegna del Film Italiano, many film festivals also have emerged as national entities, in the sense that they primarily have shown films from their own country and yet have tried to promote global connections. The Thessaloniki International Film Festival started in 1960 as the Week of Greek Cinema, and became international only in 1992.

The first American festival began in 1957 in San Francisco. It was founded by Irving Levin, a Bay Area theater owner who had visited many European film festivals and wanted to create an event to attract more audience to his theaters. Small theaters like the Vogue, Bridge, and Clay played foreign films to a small audience.[59] Levin helped organized an Italian film festival in 1956, and the First San Francisco Film Festival was launched in 1957: the best film went to Satyajit Ray's *Pather panchali,* incongruously awarded by Shirley Temple Black. The San Francisco festival has undergone many changes since then, but it has very much remained a festival important to the local audiences as well as the city of San Francisco, which offers a wide variety of cultural activities and institutions. Aesthetics also intersected with globalization in the New York Film Festival, founded in 1963 by Amos Vogel and Richard Roud, who had been involved in the Cinémathèque of Paris.[60] For its first decade, New York was almost the twin of the London festival. The festival started in a time when European art cinema was at its apex, but in New York the venue, the audience, and associated publicity have always been more important than innovation or cinematic prestige.

These festivals established a common American pattern that I referred to in the introduction. Even for a global location like New York, a selection of twenty films can showcase very innovative art films for a fairly sophisticated audience at a prestige location, the Lincoln Center. In 1972, the festival was able to host the world premiere of Bernardo Bertolucci's *Last Tango in Paris* because of the friendship between Roud and Bertolucci. However, in general, the New York festival is not a festival for international premieres. The films presented at the New York festival often have been discovered and discussed elsewhere. Even after film scholar Richard Peña replaced Roud in 1988, the present New York Film Festival remains an audience festival. Publicists have told me that the New York festival is an important launching pad for U.S. distribution (even though deals may already have been negotiated at Cannes or Toronto). Today, A. O. Scott of the *New York Times* calls the event "A Film Festival with a Penchant for Making Taste, Not Deals."[61] Most deals have been made before films get to the festival screen, and most of the films shown already have U.S. distribution, so they can be seen in art house cinemas not long after the festival and its intense press coverage. The 2009 edition, for example, included Cannes winner *White Ribbon,* Oscar contender *Precious,* American independent documentary *Sweetgrass,* Polish master Andrzej Wajda's *Sweet Rush,* and *Ghost Town,* a Chinese documentary by Zhao Dayong, which actually premiered at the festival.

By the 1960s, then, a global festival circuit had clearly emerged, dominated by Europe and the global North, although looking beyond this production. While festivals were sites of competitive government investment and sponsorship as well as aesthetic competitions, they were established as places of repeated contact, creative knowledge, and discussion of the past, present, and future of film. The decades ahead would see expansion and even challenges to this framework, with an ever-widening global inclusion of peoples, places, and products in webs that are artistic, commercial, and political.

Globalization and Controversy since the 1960s

Revolution and Extension: The Long 1960s

While it is easy to characterize the 1960s as a decade of global change, this is nonetheless an important observation to apply to film festival history. This decade had already seen the consolidation of a global network of major events. Film debate, to refer again to Dudley Andrew's scenario, had entered its golden age, from the classroom to major publications of theory and history.[62] But other extra-cinematic currents also swirled around the institution as well. While Cannes in 1968 was, according to one newspaper, "dozing in the sunshine, far from the barricades,"[63] the riots of Paris students and workers spilled over into protests that included the young filmmakers who would redefine French film. The festival committee had already withdrawn Peter Brook's controversial *Tell Me Lies* in 1968—before the shutdown—not because of its anti–Vietnam War message but because of the sensitivities of negotiations between the United States and Vietnam in Paris.[64] Yet as screenings began, Louis Malle, François Truffaut, Jean-Luc Godard, Roman Polanski, Milos Forman, and others collaborated with director Carlos Saura and his wife, actress Geraldine Chaplin, to block the screening of Saura's own *Peppermint Frappé*. The festival closed on May 19; apparently, some of the exhibitors from the Marché found refuge in Rome.[65] Its films were only screened at Cannes forty years later, in the 2008 classic section.

These protests led to changes in the function of Cannes as well. The more open and noncompetitive Directors' Fortnight emerged in response to May 1968. Young filmmakers, including Truffaut and Godard, founded the Société des Réalisateurs de Films (SRF), which has been responsible for the Fortnight since its inception in 1969. That year, it showed over sixty feature films: every film submitted was shown.

Locarno evolved in more peaceful ways, but also promoted breaks with the established model. It extended aesthetics into history, a process that many festivals now share with other discursive horizons of criticism, academic scholarships, and museums. In the late 1950s, for example, it tried to launch a retrospective on Jacques Tati, but the rental agent prevented this. Other programs, nevertheless, paid homage to Humphrey Bogart and Ingmar Bergman. In the early 1960s, Locarno held retrospectives on Fritz Lang, Georges Meliès,

Figure 3. Protest at the 1968 Cannes Film Festival.
Source: © Mirkine/Sygma/Corbis.

Jean Vigo, and King Vidor. While some other retrospectives treat genres, themes, or national/regional origins, most retrospectives still focus on—and reinforce the meaning of—specific auteurs. For example, Egyptian director Youssef Chahine was given a major retrospective in Locarno in 1996. He then received the Lifetime Achievement Award at Cannes in 1997, and in 1998 the New York Film Festival also presented a retrospective on him.

Locarno established an important record for extending aesthetic boundaries and debates in other regards as well. In 1963, Lina Wertmuller's *The Basilisks* (*I basilischi*) won the Silver Sail, making Wertmuller one of the first women and the only female director honored by a festival recognized by FIAPF (Riefenstahl had been honored at Venice in 1938). In that decade, some Locarno juries were composed entirely of film directors, showing the festival's respect for the auteurs as it welcomed challenging new works of Pier Paolo Pasolini and Paulo Rocha.

FIAPF, in 1969, also gave Locarno the designation of a festival for First Films, which meant that Locarno could only hold competitions involving a director's premiere work. The festival had hoped to host competitions for films from the third world; nonetheless, this designation recognized Locarno's place in the aesthetic vanguard. Locarno screened Spike Lee's *Joe's Bed-Stuy Barbershop: We Cut Heads* in 1983, which won a Bronze Leopard and earned Lee his first trip to Europe. Locarno also became one of the first film festivals to investigate and screen Chinese films: in 1985, it showed Chen Kaige's *Yellow Earth* as well as Hou Hsiao-hsien's *Summer at Grandpa's* (*Dong dong de jia qi*), paving the road for the subsequent success of Chinese-language cinema in Western festivals. The festival pioneered Korean and Iranian cinema on European screens as well. When Marco Müller became the festival director in 1992, after working in Turin, Rotterdam, and Pesaro, he had close contact with Hong Kong programmers and brought even more Asian cinema to the festival. Locarno also published materials dealing with Asian American cinema and Bollywood, among other vanguard areas.

Locarno today is hardly unique in its presentation of different auteurs and national cinemas; however, its development points to how the aesthetic aspects of cinema were used to promote the prestige and connections of the festival through globalization. This is even more evident in one of the first global festivals to transcend national ambitions: Rotterdam, founded by Hubert Bals in 1972. Bals was an enthusiast for "Third World, political, underground, and independent cinema as well as documentary, experimentalism, and avant-garde filmmaking."[66] After his untimely death in 1988, the Hubert Bals Fund was established to support young global filmmakers and has emerged as a major creative force in this regard, while reinforcing the program and position of the festival even though it has never sought FAIPF accreditation. Over the years, Rotterdam has continued to be a very forward-looking festival and has nurtured a great number of global auteurs, among them Chen Kaige, Moufida Tlatli, Zhang Yuan, and Cristian Miugui.

North American festivals took on new forms after the 1960s that pointed to the diverse strains of change in this time of post-national festivals. Toronto, for example, began in 1976 as a "Festival of Festivals" anthologizing prizewinners from the established network.[67] The festival has been a promoter of Canadian cinema since its inception; Liz Czach's work on film festival programming at the Toronto Film Festival makes a cogent argument that the festival programmers provide critical cultural capital to Canadian cinema and also addresses the issue of what constitutes Canadian cinema, which is at least bicultural, making national cinema a complicated category. Czach shows that a "festival such as Toronto provides a context in which Canadian films are positioned on an international stage."[68] This practice links the national to the international: Toronto serves as a platform to showcase a national cinema that does not have a large audience so as to attract national and international attention from the press as well as the film festival circuit. On its Web site, the festival is billed as the "leading public film festival in the world, screening more than three hundred films from more than sixty countries every September. It is the launching pad for the best of Hollywood and international cinema, enjoyed by half a million enthusiastic film fans each year."[69]

Toronto has also become a center for business, especially the negotiations of North American distribution—and a precursor for autumnal Oscar buzz. Here, it lays claim to being more than a national festival with regard to an important market and provides a gateway for global films to enter the United States. In 2009, publicized attendees included not only Matt Damon and Mary J. Blige but also Bill Clinton. But perhaps most reflective of the festival's deep transnational roots was the debate over the showcasing of Tel Aviv in the festival's City to City Program. Here, protests against this admitted attempt to rebrand Israel after Gaza included Alice Walker, Ken Loach, Noam Chomsky, Julie Christie, Danny Glover, and Israeli filmmaker Udi Aloni. Meanwhile, others who signed petitions against the protest as a form of censorship included Jerry Seinfeld, Sacha Baron Cohen, and Natalie Portman. The presence not only of Hollywood but of a larger U.S. debate was striking. The *Guardian* underscored this point by linking the controversy to Jane Fonda, who stayed out of it, despite her previous involvement in political debate over Vietnam and Iraq.[70]

Meanwhile, the United States Film Festival began in Salt Lake City in 1978 as a way of attracting filmmakers to Utah. In 1980 it moved away from the city to the ski resort of Park City, and in 1985, under the guidance of Robert Redford and his Sundance Institute, it became the Sundance Film Festival, focused on the promotion of American independent film. As many commentators have pointed out, Sundance has come to epitomize an anti-Hollywood forum within American filmmaking. Despite continual (American) media hype, it remains the least international of all major film festivals because of its heavy Americanness. Non-U.S. programmers and publicists have expressed the view that Sundance is simply "too American" and see few advantages at Sundance for smaller films from the rest of the world. The Sundance Film Festival did not even add an international audience prize until 1999 or world cinema jury prizes until 2005.[71]

After three decades, Sundance now faces considerable pressure because of its role as a market for independent films and because of the complexity of distribution networks that may lead to larger projects (more Hollywood than Cannes). *Variety* critic Robert Koehler excoriated the festival in a 2010 article:

> Sundance has become, quite simply, a horror show for cinema: a place where more bad films can be seen under awful viewing conditions than any other festival, and yet which also paradoxically goes the extra mile to bother with a usually fascinating through small section for experimental and non (or semi-) narrative film titled "New Frontier" which is then secluded in such a manner

to ensure that as few people as possible will see it. The largest and most famous American film "festival" has quite possibly damaged the cinema it was specifically designed to support—American indie film—more than any cluster of neglectful studios ever have, because it rejects cinephilia with cool (and in bad years, freezing) disinterest.[72]

Nonetheless, Sundance has a high visibility across the United States. It has integrated itself into American filmmaking schools and even other popular media through the Sundance Channel, a joint cable television project of Redford and the Institute, Universal (NBC), and Showtime (CBS) begun in 1996. This channel was sold to Cablevision in 2008.[73]

While film and festivals evolved in Europe and North America, other festivals spread far beyond the producers and audiences of the global North, making diverse claims about nation-states and worlds. The Tehran film festival, for example, began in 1972 under the shah of Iran. Dictatorial regimes have often had a deep but ambivalent relationship with such international showcases, as is evident in these top-down festivals' evolution over time: as film historian Peter Cowie observed, "Millions of dollars are spent around the world each year by governments—and even dictators—seeking to buy acceptance in intellectual, glitzy, and diplomatic circles."[74] The Fajr International Film Festival replaced Tehran in 1982 after the Iranian revolution of 1979. To reinforce the idea of a new Iran, the Fajr ("sunrise" in Persian) festival is held in late January to commemorate the anniversary of the revolution. Given the religious government of Iran, the Fajr festival follows a clear party line based in a particular Shia Muslim worldview and practices; however, the festival has allowed Iranians to see international cinema, including works by Andrei Tarkovsky, Yasujiro Ozu, and Theo Angelopoulos. It has been extremely important to Iranian cinematic culture: local audiences wait in long lines and few Iranian filmmakers want to be screened globally until they have premiered at the festival.

Medhi Abdollahzadeh, a contributor to *Gozaar*, a forum on human rights and democracy in Iran, argues that the festival changed as the political climate in Iran moved from liberalization to hard-line conservatism.[75] In 2010, with the unstable political climate in Iran, the Fajr festival again became a space for political contestation, including boycotts by both local and international filmmakers.[76] Nevertheless, "Javad Shamaghdari, cinematic deputy of culture and Islamic guidance minister, issued a message for the 28th Fajr International Film Festival and said 'We want a cinema for the 70 million Iranian audience. . . . We are proud that we are Muslim. So we struggle to have a cinema under the Islamic culture and knowing relying on Islamic belief and faith. . . . Cinema is art.'"[77]

Manila provides an interesting contrast in global political history. Although the Metro Manila Film Festival showcasing Filipino films began in 1975, Imelda Marcos envisioned a grander world event as the Philippines suffered under corruption and martial law. A palatial center was built for the first Manila International Film Festival in 1982, with construction problems causing the deaths of scores of workers and making it a symbol of the failure of that regime for years afterward (a point still underscored by guides when I visited the site in 1996). Meanwhile, the festival in Mar del Plata, which had begun in 1954, became a victim of Argentina's dictatorial regimes and did not return to the world stage until the 1990s.

Other festivals developed stages for non-European films that connected with wider festival circuits in different ways. The PanAfrican Film and Television Festival of Ouagadougou (Festival panafricain du cinéma et de la télévision de Ouagadougou, or FESPACO) began in Burkina Faso in 1969 with seven nations (five African) and twenty-three films but has evolved over decades into a show-case for films often neglected in wider international competitions.[78] The Hong Kong International Film Festival began in 1977. The Havana Film Festival began as a showcase for Latin American films under the Castro regime in 1979. All have fostered different patterns of local and global growth and connection within a larger system.

In this period, then, we see multiple expansions of the festival world in terms of location, filmic interests in the past and present, and even generations. While it would be tempting to read the message of May 1968 or even Sundance as one of independence and democracy, we note that older and European festivals have maintained their hegemony while others have jockeyed for position within particular regional or commercial contexts (e.g., the impact of Hollywood on North American festivals). At the same time, this period marked a proliferation of smaller festivals around genres and interests that have enriched the festival world to the present as well.

Since the 1980s: Diversities of Theme and Place

The best-known festivals are those of large scale and international prestige that include not only systematic screenings of core prestige products (films in compe-tition) but also multiple entries and arrangements that include sections for new cinema makers, retrospectives, sections devoted to particular lengths or genres, and other options aimed at different audiences and markets. By sheer volume and variety, Cannes, Berlin, and others have continued to claim center stage within the festival world through systematic attention to multiple audiences and professional expertise in situating these festivals within a larger calendar. The same person may not attend an outdoor screening of a crowd-pleasing film like *Ali-G Indahouse*, starring Sacha Baron Cohen (which I saw with my children in 2002 in the plaza in Locarno), and a nearly deserted presentation of a video doc-umentary on human rights or a panorama of student shorts. The large festivals incorporate these alternatives not only to build audiences but also to continue flows of new films and positions of power: today's student may be tomorrow's auteur . . . and perhaps decades beyond that, the subject of an honorific presentation or retrospective. Connections with cinematographers, institutions, business people, and funders in emergent national industries in Iran, Romania, and Malaysia may ensure prestige films years later. And publicity reinforces power, as Cannes has shown well in its history.

Nevertheless, since the 1980s, the primary changes in the festival world have come from the many smaller festivals that have taken shape with more limited goals in mind. Many American cities, for example, host festivals whose programs set up along ethnic lines, whether Chinese, African American, American Indian, Jewish, or other showcases of transnational or intranational connections. A Chinese cinema festival is not the same as a Chinese American film festival, although they both may program some cross-cutting international offerings in order to appeal to wider audiences. Other national or regional specializations (Brazilian, French, European, Asian, African, etc.) may go beyond heritage issues, although meanings can become ambivalent: a French film festival is more likely to invoke the global prestige of French culture and film, while a Latin American film festival in the United States or Europe seems, almost inevitably, to coordinate with local immigrant and heritage organizations. Once again, international politics impinge, at least indirectly, on the meaning of the festival.

Similarly, thematic festivals focus on particular subject matters or areas of debate: human rights, women's rights, LGBTQ issues, or ecology. Even this range suggests an array of audiences and involvements ranging from those who have political concerns with particular issues to those who identify with films and plots as well as issues and organizations. This interplay, in fact, is discussed at greater length in the examination of film festivals and the public sphere in chapter 5.

Still other thematic festivals develop less specific group interests associated with dedicated segments of audience as much as politics: festivals devoted to mountain films, to musicals, or to bad (albeit not *maudit*) films. This book will spend less time on the vast range of these different kinds of festivals than on more complex "A"-level and major regional festivals; however, it recognizes that these festivals constitute part of the fabric of a complicated film festival world. However small or broad, they are connected to other festivals in terms of the circulation of films, texts, and film knowledge. Sometimes they may share personnel if the festivals have the financial means, and they certainly overlap in potential audiences. And even the smallest festival keeps the idea of a festival world present and alive.

Many smaller festivals support the circulations of selected festival films on a smaller scale as well. Gay, lesbian, bi-, and transgendered filmmakers have established international connections through the London Lesbian and Gay Film Festival, the Turin International Gay and Lesbian Festival, the San Francisco International Lesbian and Gay Film Festival, Los Angeles's Outfest, and other outlets in Chicago, Philadelphia, Hamburg, Lisbon, Dublin, Austin, Tampa,

Melbourne, and Mumbai.[79] These, in turn, have reinforced institutions found in larger festivals and circuits, exemplified by San Francisco's creation of Frameline, the umbrella organization of the San Francisco International LGBT Film Festival, which supports distribution of LGBTQ films, and, since 1990, also includes production funds.[80] They also connect to other discursive horizons of LGBTQ discourse, including scholarship and preservation.

While these thematic film festivals negotiate film in relation to particular audiences, issues, and imagined communities, others choose to present film in its many textual dimensions. Again, most festivals show feature-length fiction films even though they have sections on documentaries, animation, and short films that are often novel and newsworthy even if limited in commercial distribution. There are, however, festivals that are devoted to specific formats and genres other than the features—animation, documentary, shorts, fantasy, ethnography, or children's films. These more specialized festivals attract dedicated followings, both in terms of audience and producers, yet may not begin with the same localization or identification that we see in metropolitan gay festivals or an Asian American film festival in Los Angeles. Some of them mirror other mainstream festivals in their structures, while others do not.

The International Animation Film Festival at Annecy, France, for example, celebrated its fiftieth anniversary in 2010. While a charming medieval and renaissance city with both lakes and mountains that act as backdrops for films— and a candidate to host the Winter Olympics in 2018—Annecy lacks strong historic association of production or distribution. Instead, the festival reinforces urban culture and branding. Other prominent animation festivals include Zagreb (1972), Hiroshima (1985), and Ottawa (1975). These festivals are international in scope and have sections for different formats, from features to shorts, films to television to digital works. Just as many festivals are accredited by FIAPF, animation festivals are sponsored by the Association International du Film d'Animation (or ASIFA). Annecy, indeed, is very similar to larger conventional film festivals; it has its market, conferences, sponsors, stars (Tim Burton), and everything that parallels the major festivals. Thus, Annecy is not a "small" festival at all; the primary difference is that it focuses on animation to the exclusion of other, more publicized genres.

The Pordenone Silent Film Festival (Le Giornate del Cinema Muto), however, represents a different kind of festival. Pordenone is the most established silent film festival; created in 1982 by the local film archives and film club, the festival devotes its energy to the first thirty years of cinema history. It is not competitive, but it provides a Jean Mitry Award to scholars and archivists working on the specific period. The festival has proven to be very important in the rediscovery and preservation of early cinema as well as in the nurturing of the study of early cinema. The festival is global, showing works from all different parts of the world, and helping to discover and popularize lost prints that exhibit the global reach of early cinema, while reframing other films with restored prints and new orchestrations. For example, Josef von Sternberg's film *The Case of Lena Smith* (1929) was found in Japan and shown in Pordenone in 2003,[81] while 2009 saw Erich von Stroheim's *Merry Widow* enhanced with a new orchestral score and accompaniment.[82] Pordenone, then, is more like an academic conference than a conventional film festival. Films are never premiered at Pordenone, but they are "new" because they are orphaned films that have been newly rediscovered or restored. The films Pordenone shows rarely have much market value; therefore, there is hardly any business interest in this festival. However, the festival attracts serious scholars, preservationists, musicians, archivists, and dedicated early cinema cinephiles. The 2005 presentation of Russian silent cinema from before the creation of the Soviet Union in 1917 pushed the boundaries on the study of Russian cinema, while in 2009 a new section, "The Canon Revisited," offered the festival as a platform through which to rethink knowledge of established classics. And more than a thousand people attend every October while its organizers and fans network with other silent film festival organizers from Bologna (Il Cinema Ritrovato, founded 1986), San Francisco (1992), London (1998), and Bristol (2005). Many associated with these silent film festivals also take part in the activities of film archives and museums.

We might also read this diversity of festivals in terms of locality and audience. Every festival has some audience; films simply need to be seen. Except for Cannes, whose formal screenings are restricted to film professionals who are actually audiences, all festivals invite more general publics as ticket buyers, in seminars and events, and as gawkers beside the red carpet. The general audience is very important in the success of film festivals, not only financially but also in their role in creating an atmosphere to ensure the success of the festivals. Yet these "civilians" seldom occupy an important role in the organization of film festivals, nor do they participate in programming decisions. Nonetheless, the local audiences are oftentimes the most consistent contributors because they attend the festivals in their communities from year to year while programs and even programmers change.

At the same time, festivals are also seen as aspects of global urban branding, tourist attractions as well as local services.[83] Some cinephiles roam from festival to festival, while other spectators travel to specific festivals. And the idea of a festival may indicate the general culture of a city rather than merely selling tickets and hotel rooms at a specific destination. The spectacular festivals, in fact, may be off-putting to locals, while the most audience-friendly festivals are those that are smaller, less business-oriented, and local whose objectives are showing good films to an appreciative audience.

Marijke de Valck's study of the cinephiles at Rotterdam stresses the importance of audience in Rotterdam, which has recorded over 350,000 visits in a single year.[84] She credits this to the festival's lack of red carpet and to its openness; she also highlights the festival venue, a downtown multiplex that allows the festival to program different types of films in the same cinemas to attract more viewers with diverse tastes. Here one notes the festival's effort to keep the audience in mind when putting its programs together, both in terms of diversity and in basic logistical advantages in selling tickets. This emphasis on audience, not unlike the practices I will discuss in Hong Kong, provides space for the festivals to program both more avant-garde alternative works and more accessible art house releases. On the one hand, different cinema screens may reify the separation between the more esoteric works and middle-brow fare, but on the other hand, a multiplex-like creative programming (in spaces between blockbusters) allows the possibility of crossing those boundaries with the mixing of audiences.

More audience-centered festivals often lack film markets and formal competitions even though they are vital elements of the cultural lives of San Francisco, New York, Philadelphia, Chicago, and other cities. Another major audience-centered U.S. festival is Telluride, which began in 1973. This, however, is located in a remote mining town in Colorado that requires extra effort just to get there. The festival does not sell individual tickets, but only passes, ranging from $390 to $3,900, and makes a point that the filmmakers accompany their films at the festival. It only shows twenty films a year and there is no award. Since the third festival, the programmers no longer announce the line-up until the very beginning of the festival. In 1975, when Jeanne Moreau, Chuck Jones, and King Vidor were invited to the festival and Moreau cancelled because of medical reasons, the local press printed "Moreau Cancelled" rather highlighting the presence of Chuck Jones or Vidor.[85] Bill Pence, one of the founders and organizers, believes that not publicizing the program removes the "hypes" on the films. Telluride shows films that are American and more accessible, including *Brokeback Mountain, Juno,* and *Vincere.* It has also invited prominent noncinema professionals to be guest directors of the festival: past guest directors include Laurie Anderson, Salman Rushdie, Edith Kramer, Don Delillo, Stephen Sondheim, and Slavoj Žižek. These people curate a series of films and introduce them to the audience, shaping a particular experience of the filmic public sphere. The inclusion of famous artists provides more legitimacy to the festival; at the same time, Telluride is introducing another level of celebrity into the festival, even though it is a high-brow crowd that reaffirms film as a cultured art.

Telluride has evolved over the years. Originally, it was a very small event, where Pence asserts that "everyone had the same experiences." In a town with only three blocks, people did bump into each other. This festival has hardly any local participation; neither the organizers nor the audience live in Telluride. Some of the cinemas are even temporary, making the location only meaningful in a limited temporal plane. Therefore, the "small towniness" of the festival is very much a constructed and ephemeral experience. As the festival became more popular, its very early intention of not directly doing business has shifted.

In 2009, both Sony Pictures Classics and IFC acquisition teams were in Telluride and held rather lavish dinners at the same restaurant. These are the major art film distributors today in the United States. Telluride is also covered by glossy magazines like *W*, where an interview with IFC president Jonathan Sehring put Telluride in the league of Toronto and New York in terms of art house acquisitions.[86] This is part of the trend of increased industrial infiltration in film festivals in this new millennium.

Telluride is also translocal in site as well as audience: it offers small satellite festivals in New England, where Pence lives. In these festivals, only six films are chosen and they are fairly accessible films that would normally receive art house distribution in the United States but might arrive more slowly in New Hampshire. Other festivals also have such tentacular events, whether summer sessions for the HKIFF, coordinated programs for New York's MIX in Brazil, or Locarno's screening of selected films across the border in Milan.

Truly audience-inclusive / responsive festivals may, in fact, have only a few films for a small audience, with limited press coverage and few aesthetic assertions or business ambitions. The Festival de Cinema Independent de Barcelona, for example, has a section called "Pantalla Hall" (Hall Screen) which does not charge any admission and creates a relatively open forum in a downtown museum-exhibition center, the Centre de Cultura Contemporània (CCCB). It offers noncommercial cinema in different formats, including shorts, animation, documentary, and fiction, while the audience can mingle freely with the filmmakers. As Stefan Berger, from the International Federation of Film Societies, sums it up: "The central meeting point, the Pantalla Hall of CCCB, was well chosen. Here you could enjoy a series of additional short films, animation, and documentaries for free. Here an Indian evening with live dance performance was held as the 'pièce de resistance' of the festival. Here you could exchange thoughts in a warm, constraintless environment."[87]

What does local environment have to do with it? All of these festivals have evolved over time with film practices and cultures of their locales—whether dominating the city as in the case of Cannes (or Park City) or fitting into a larger range of cosmopolitan activities. This includes knowledge of local tastes (more Japanese and fewer Latin American films in Hong Kong), a set of venues, and other aspects of operation and organization discussed in the final section here. It also involves local support, whether from the government (at multiple levels, including the state), private donors, corporate sponsors, or a regular base of moviegoers who will buy tickets and attend events. Local authorities and businesses, in turn, look for recompense through money spent or more intangible values of place identity.

Despite the need for local support, though, nearly all film festivals are in some way tourist festivals—festivals that try to bring people into the cities and towns. Certainly, this applies to specialty festivals like Annecy, Pordenone, or

Telluride. Even for more general events, though, tourism is linked to a desire to sell the local and to a larger extent the regional. It is not surprising that venues such as Venice, Cannes, Karlovy Vary, Locarno, San Sebastián, and Mar del Plata are all resorts, heavily dependent on tourism. Archival images of these festivals are full of images of beaches, or other forms of friendly water, be it the spa in Karlovy Vary or the lake in Locarno. Indeed, aquatic attractions sold the festivals for local organizers (especially since festivals do not take place in competition with other prime tourist uses). Even the "alternative" to Cannes, the celebration of films maudits, would occupy the casino at Biarritz, and yet another French resort, Deauville, has become a major center for third-world film.

Film festivals occupy an interestingly contradictory position in representing the local. Images of sun and fun, scantily clad starlets, and established stars are juxtaposed with the representation of the more reified leisure of high art. Nevertheless, even though the films can be high, middle, or even low brow, film festivals demand time for an audience to see film, having a good time in its many manifestations, be it escapism or study or frontal encounter with the darkest impulses of human activities.

As they have escaped as well as continued their resort origins, film festivals often connect to other art institutions and cultural attractions, sharing spaces and collections as well as discourse. This is apparent in the link of the very first festival in Venice with the Venice Biennale. The Edinburgh festival is a component of the vast panoply of the Edinburgh Art Festivals; in 2007, the Hong Kong International Film Festival became ensconced in a two-month celebration of both arts and commercial activities in design, music, and film itself. The use of Lincoln Center for New York, the Brooklyn Art Museum's own cinemaFEST, New York University's First Run Film Festival for student films, all link museums, universities, and even corporate sponsorship to festivals in a wider local arts scene. Meanwhile, institutions like the British Film Institute, the Hong Kong Film Archive, and the Paris Cinemathèque connect cities and spaces to events beyond the limited festival calendar.

Julian Stringer, among others, has explored the relationships between global cities and the film festival economy.[88] In most festivals, local government officials are present in ceremonial events, giving legitimacy to the festivals and the city's stamp of approval, oftentimes with financial assistance. Most festivals are too small to substantially benefit or hurt the city by their absence or presence, yet together with other cultural events, from other art festivals of one kind or another, concerts, theaters, and museums, film festivals contribute to the cultural mosaic global cities want to portray. Hence, a vital audience may not even stay for the films. During the gala opening of the First Asian Film Awards in Hong Kong in 2007, for example, an array of government officials were seated in the first rows of the Convention Center Hall. They included many Mr. Wongs, who served as directors of the Hong Kong International Film Festival Society, the Hong Kong Trade and Development Council, and the secretary of commerce of the Hong Kong Special Administrative Region; these men gave prepared speeches (not always the most lively ones) for a good part of the pre-award ceremony to an audience eager to see the Korean pop star Rain later in the event. Even Cannes is supported by the French Ministry of Culture, the province, and the city, with a budget of 20 million euros in 2007. Therefore, while many government officials leave the festivals themselves to the festival boards and staffs, they always show up for the photo ops. However, when sensitive cultural and political issues erupt, sponsors may play different roles.

Local festivals thus are loci of competition among cities. While Cannes holds global primacy, it has competitors across France (Biarritz, Deauville, Nancy, Annecy). And the city of Paris itself, a force in Cannes's Cinéfondation, has taken an active role in preservation as well as screening. The July Paris International Film Festival, founded in 2002, is imbued with the spaces and audiences of the city, from outdoor screenings at city hall to all-night screenings with coffee and croissants. While this festival channels premieres from Cannes to a metropolitan audience, it has added other accouterments of larger and competitive festivals, including retrospectives, star attractions, and the Paris Project, which supports global filmmakers in assembling French coproductions. Tensions between cities as political capitals and their claims as cinematic capitals have occurred in other settings, national and regional. In Rome's first film festival in 2006, for example, then-Mayor Walter Veltroni was the force behind the establishment of the event, with a venue designed by star architect Renzo Piano and a budget (24 million euros) outstripping Venice. It was even held just one month after Venice, in October. One German programmer told me in 2007 that it would be impossible to have two big film festivals in the same country within two months; he believed that the old festival would eventually prevail. Veltroni's unsuccessful bid to defeat Silvio Berlusconi led to changes: by 2008, the budget had been cut to 15 million euros and its codirectors had departed, although the 2009 festival boasted Meryl Streep and scenes from *Twilight*.[89] As I will show later, tensions among Hong Kong, Shanghai, and other competitors for Chinese films also play out against a regional tapestry in which Pusan, Bangkok, Sydney, and Tokyo have also asserted claims through film festivals that go beyond audience and tourism.[90]

Perhaps the most striking convergence of place, festival, audience, and urban agendas has been Tribeca, in New York. While I have already mentioned the role of the venerable New York Film Festival, Tribeca's Web site notes that "Robert De Niro, Jane Rosenthal, and Craig Hatkoff founded the Tribeca Film Festival in 2001 following the attacks on the World Trade Center to spur the economic and cultural revitalization of lower Manhattan through an annual celebration of film, music and culture. The Festival's mission focuses on assisting filmmakers to reach the broadest possible audience, enabling the international film community and general public to experience the power of cinema and promoting New York

City as a major filmmaking center."⁹¹ Tribeca is also one of the very few festivals that is run by a for-profit company, Tribeca Enterprises, which may explain why the festival goal is to reach the "broadest possible audience" and its openness to many business ventures. Over the past decade, this initial effort at regeneration has expanded into its own cinema, year-round programming, and a branch festival in Doha, Qatar, that began in 2009. However, in recent years, the trade press has been lukewarm to the festival and sometimes has complained that it lacks any distinctive directions and identity.⁹²

These demands for audiences and sponsors might lead to more conflicts if global competition did not have some loose agreements: festivals compete for auteurs and works, but cannot afford to compete on schedules. Hence, major festivals have to adhere to a calendar that allows them to craft the year into appropriate segments. Berlin, for example, did not see the cold weather as a problem and moved the festival from June/July to February in 1978 to be in a better position in this global festival calendar. This decision was very much based on a business model where Berlin saw the late winter as "a period of meager trade and few festivals."⁹³ Thus, Berlin would capitalize on showing films produced since Venice and be ahead of Cannes, which has eyed the fall spot of Venice (with encouragement from Hollywood distributors, whose fall prestige releases usually are not ready in time for the Cannes festival in the spring). However, individual cities may simply find the right time for the festival for that specific city. Hong Kong holds its festival in April because of the Easter holiday, so that people are off from their work and have time to go see movies, paying the bills for the festival. HKIFF also uses the Chinese New Year's holiday as another moveable landmark for completion and distribution of the catalog. Similarly, Paris in July has become a capital for tourists before residents leave for their own vacations: a perfect transitional month for a festival after Cannes.

Situated within a multilayered network, small festivals and multiple audiences remind us of the impassioned interests that established cinephilia around ciné clubs, isolated art houses, or college film series. Ironically, many of these institutions have become victims of technological change in the cinematic world, as video, DVDs, television, and the Internet have made once exotic or alternative films available to individual spectators worldwide. Here, film festivals have survived as both collective and sanctioning experiences and as gateways to distribution for films and filmmakers. Other horizons of discourse—journalism, museums, and universities—have survived as well, although continually facing new demands of audience, interpretation, and knowledge for the future, just as film festivals do.⁹⁴

Festival Worlds Today

The variety of interests and themes of these smaller festivals and the sections they intersect within festival sidebars and marketplaces in Cannes, Toronto,

Hong Kong, and other sites underscore the dialectic of film as a mass medium and the packaging that highlights specific interests and appeals across the festival world. Despite these differences, however, many contemporary festivals share some general issues of organization and function that we should review before moving onward. While national, group, or thematic intentions have been paramount for many festivals at different times, festival organizers and programmers, nevertheless, also see themselves as the guardians of quality cinema that transcends national industries and their demands. By the late 1990s, new film festivals became closely aligned with their host cities and communities, with film festivals serving as another venue to add to wider global cultural offerings. While many festivals, especially the major international festivals, bridge periods and interests through multiple sections, all these film festivals participate in global flows defined by the aesthetics of films rather than simply its industries. Except for some very specific local festivals that only showcase their national or regional cinema, like the Guadalajara Mexican Film Festival or Fuokoka Asian Film Festival, the majority of film festivals today have global palettes and global ambitions.

As these festivals bring world cinema to their local audiences, they also compete in an international arena to gain stature within the film festival world. Therefore, while major festivals like Cannes, Venice, Berlin, San Sebastián, Pusan, Mar del Plata, and Toronto have their own local and national contexts, even they seek to identify, attract, and dominate cutting-edge cinema from around the world. This very internationalist flow of film festivals makes it necessary that they maintain loose global networks, from the more formal arrangements of FIAPF, to the informal but very real festival calendar that all international festivals respect with caution, to consultancies and friendships among programmers and critics.

The crux of this globalization is continuous exchange and communication; however, these exchanges are not equal. This global aspect of film festivals also confirms the inevitable, arbitrary, and rarely mutable hierarchy of different festivals. The prestige of major festivals rests on the films they program, especially for their world premieres, and the people / guests and press they can attract to their festivals, primarily directors and stars. Cannes now undeniably stands at the top of the pack, followed by Venice and Berlin, all old European festivals. This does not mean that the films that have premiered in these festivals or have won prizes there are necessarily box office successes, but within the loose film festivals community, these films garner the most prestige and circulate through subsequent festivals as an affirmation of primacy by the other festivals that add the Golden Lion or Palm designation to their catalog copy.

Here, Western European festivals claim hierarchical distinction so that their prizes and even screenings bring global prestige, making these festivals the ultimate cinematic taste makers. This also suggests that films from other countries can only be recognized if they manage recognition from these European festivals, reinstating colonial relations of power and taste that are uneasily read by filmmakers and diplomats. In subsequent chapters on Hong Kong and on the public sphere, this book will discuss in more details these complex relationships between the West and the non-West and its many contradictory implications.

The global aspect of film festivals again creates a peculiar relationship with the United States and Hollywood. Stars and directors from the United States are often heavily coveted by the European festivals; Hollywood images and glamour are global even if many works by these stars would seldom be screened in festivals. Since the concept of the *"premiere"* allows for the first screening in each festival's home country, Hollywood films can also negotiate openings, publicity, and presence around the festival cycle. Yet the international qualities of many of these festivals must balance the inclusion of Hollywood and independent American films with traditional powerhouse industries of art cinema (France, Germany, Italy, Japan) and choice selections from other countries. Cannes today, as it has been for decades, is international not only because it presents the best of French and European cinema, but also because it extensively covers the world; except for Africa (a blatant area of neglect), all continents are well represented each year. Different negotiations of local industry and global vision play out in Hong Kong, Rotterdam, and Mar del Plata.

At the same time, the global reach of festivals brings them into more concrete international political relations, manifested in censorship and boycotts—in other words, which countries will provide their films and which countries will withhold them. Festivals must grapple with political issues as well as personal ones, as invited filmmakers are occasionally barred from attending either by their own countries or by the festivals' host countries. This was already a public problem when festivals were caught between Western and Eastern blocs, in Europe and in Asia. However, it continued after the fall of the Berlin Wall. In 1997, the United States did not provide a visa for Iranian director Abbas Kiarostami to attend the New York Film Festival (leading the Finnish director Aki Kiarosmaki to boycott that event as well). Meanwhile, in 2009, the Iranian government prevented director Jafar Panahi from attending the Berlinale, then put him in prison when he was invited to sit on the jury at Cannes in 2010. The chapters on the public sphere will discuss this theme, as will my notes on the Hong Kong International Film Festival and that festival's complex relations with the People's Republic of China in terms of censorship and withholding of films from the colonial times to the present.

As the late twentieth century started to spread a neoliberal corporate business model into cultural institutions, film festivals became more embroiled in the implementation of cultural tourism as well as cultural investment. If film festivals are sponsored by different public, local, regional, and national organizations, the organizers who have to apply for funds must show the relevance of the festivals to the development of their region. Some film festivals seem almost to be reflexes of the local tourist industry. The annual Wine Country Film Festival, for example, was established in 1986 in California wine country, in Napa and Sonoma. On its Web site, its founder/director Stephen Ashton compares the *terroir* (the characteristics of the land) for wine production to that of the film festival, "the terroir of cinema." He also links films to wine and cuisine in their deep cultural roots. Not unlike the programmers of other festivals, Wine Country's organizers stress that they "choose to celebrate our differences rather than fear them."[95] The festival has an international program; in 2009, it included works from all over the world, assembling a program of films of many different genres. Most films selected have not had wide release, but they can be considered second-tier festival films that have traveled in different smaller festivals or the sidebars of major festivals. The promotional video of the festival, however, sells the space of the festival, where the audience will be in the beautiful vineyards of California wine country, savoring good wine and food in outdoor cinemas.[96]

Yet most major festivals also have corporate sponsors. The Cannes Web site, for example, displays logos as diverse as Chopard, L'Oréal, Renault, and HP. L'Oréal and BMW appear as sponsors for Berlin, while the ubiquitous cosmetic company shares billing with Lancia, Person, Canon, and Kodak among others at Venice. For smaller festivals, public-private negotiations may mean a more agonizing quest for corporate funding as public resources run dry. Corporate sponsors may respect serious cinema, but they are nevertheless responsible to their shareholders, and sponsorship is about the bottom line. Film festivals bring cultural prestige to corporations, and they particularly like stars and red carpet. With extensive press coverage, the public sees the corporations as civic partners within their respective communities; the customers see the glamour associated with famous actors. With these different elements, sponsoring corporations hope to cultivate their brands and create sophisticated and responsible images.

The latest incarnation of festivals as online events mediated through the Internet challenges any ties of place and audience. Up to this point, traditional festivals are not sacrificing their concrete space and place, but only adding virtual dimensions to them. Tribeca 2010, for example, hosted a distinct virtual section, where for $45 one could watch eight features and eighteen shorts at home as well as participate virtually in other events of the festival. Hardly any completely online festivals exist, except for the likes of Babelgum or Con-Can, both run by commercial media companies.[97] When festivals are completely removed from specific spatial and temporal elements, they challenge nearly all aspects of film festival existence and relations among filmmakers, programmers, and audiences. So far, however, online film festivals have not proven to be a threat to traditional film festivals.

Any new technology that has been nurtured and accepted by many poses challenging dimensions to how film festivals are organized and used by their different constituents. It would be naive to simply see new virtual technologies as liberating and opening new venues for all. It would be equally naive to see that the virtual world will take away the aura of physical festivals. A similar argument might have been made for television or DVDs, but both ultimately became part of the transformation and lives of festivals.

The politics of global flows, differentiation, and politics in these events, nonetheless, are sustained by a universalist discourse of art and aesthetics that transcends the festival or the nation. There is no film festival that does not see itself as devoting its energy and effort to the preservation and development of the art of cinema. Even festivals that are overtly politically oriented, like the Human Rights Watch Film Festival, or community-based, like MIX, use the art of cinema to achieve their specific goals. The term *aesthetics* encompasses diverse aspects of seeing cinema as expressions of human creativity, including multiple schools of thought (realism, neorealism, expressionism, avant-garde), questions about the formal elements of cinema, and breaking new grounds to promote artistic practices worthy of attention by those who decide artistic standards. In this regard, too, many film festivals and programmers see themselves as offering a cinema that is different from the commercial cinema people encounter every day in their neighborhoods, even though few festivals truly avoid the glamour and allure of Hollywood, or its local equivalents. Yet aesthetic considerations also need to find their place among other concerns of the global festival. The next two chapters will discuss the different discourses on aesthetics within film festivals, from the idea of a festival film to the construction of the auteur, including voices of the critics and theorists, and the relationship between film festivals and film canons. Here, I am simply suggesting that these universal discourses are formed in different ways by festivals as they negotiate film as a global medium and an aesthetic product. This negotiation is scaled down, in fact, in interesting ways if we turn from the larger multisectional programs of Cannes, Hong Kong, or Toronto to smaller-scale, thematic festivals and audiences worldwide.

Conclusion

This chapter provides a general historical and structural overview of film festivals, which explains the many elements that have made film festivals possible and meaningful: the invention of cinema, the debate on what cinema should be, the demarcation between cinema as a mass medium versus cinema having the wherewithal to be an art form, and the development of differentiated audiences and networks. Through these, the chapter examines the discursive horizon cinema has occupied at different periods to contextualize what film festivals mean in different contexts.

As we have seen, film festivals took shape in the larger world of cinematic discourse. Ciné clubs, art houses, and museums also have provided different spaces for cinema. Media and institutions continue to converge with film festivals today, in a world where festivals and films also maintain Web sites for a constant virtual presence, enhancing the specific and localized festival event.

At the same time, these histories and sociologies of festivals insist that film festivals are not just about art cinema or cinema as art. From their very inception, film festival organizers and sponsors courted the glamour of Hollywood and the money of those studios as well as other national producers. More importantly, a well-rounded and nuanced understanding of cinema, both as a medium and a social practice, demands that analysts understand the constant negotiations to define cinema as both art and mass consumption.

While we can separate these themes analytically, we must remember that they constantly intersect in the creation, meaning, and experience of film festivals. Global connections cannot be appreciated without the local contexts, nor national industries without recognition of international canons and aesthetics. Larger questions on the relationships between festivals and their diverse communities as well as on the construction of film knowledge—looking backward at history and forward to new filmmakers—also warrant further considerations. By outlining the diversity that exists within film festivals, I have shown that festivals come in different forms and shapes; some share similar elements, while others set themselves apart by power, specialization, or genre. Nonetheless, through all these events and among almost all their agents, films remain the center. Films as texts are still the talk of the festival professionals as well as larger communities. Hence, as we move ahead, the next two chapters will address festival films and their meanings.

2 The Films of the Festivals

While festivals bring together multiple, divergent structures of art, business, politics, spectatorship, and space, their primary building blocks remain simple and constant: films themselves. Films constitute the raison d'être of the festivals, although they are linked in special ways to the filmmaker, who is identified as the primary artist/creator within this world. In fact, festivals have solidified a special relationship between directors and films; within the festival context, it is difficult to separate the films from the auteur. With concerted efforts, auteurs and festivals have developed in a symbiotic relationship embodied by film, mediated by business concerns. New directors create films that festivals discover so that, over time, festivals and these maturing directors can rely on each other for support, recognition, and canonization; this complementarity underpins the reproduction of both film festivals and filmmakers. While each festival presents an array of new works every year mapping the breadth of world cinema, these films come from specific directors, film movements, and national traditions that provide continuity and control of festival exchanges year to year. This chapter addresses the textual elements of festival films, with some reference to the auteurs associated with these works, while the following chapter situates the auteur in the context of other extratextual elements, from reception to formation of a film canon. While "separating" films and filmmakers into two complementary chapters, in fact, I will show how deeply intertwined these building blocks have become in the creation of a global festival world.

In this chapter, I use a few carefully selected films to answer the general question: Are there specific films that fit the label "festival films"? On a pragmatic level, of course, all films shown in film festivals are festival films, solely based on exhibition practices. Thousands of films are screened in hundreds of festivals over the year; they range from the lyrical evocations of *Tropical Malady* (Weerasethakul, 2004, Cannes) to the "reflexive" comedy of *Tropic Thunder* (Stiller, 2008, San Sebastián), embracing the tense and sensual wartime thriller *Lust, Caution* (Lee, 2007, Venice) and the studied tale of mother and son that is *Alexandra* (Sokurov, 2007, Cannes). This array of feature films is stylistically and thematically diverse, and as we have seen, many festivals systematically showcase different kinds of films: shorts, avant-garde, experimental, student/ grassroots efforts, documentaries. Moreover, some films screen in competition, some outside, some in retrospectives, and some only at the markets or at auxiliary events.

Despite such diversity, in Peter Wollen's conversation with Brazilian artist and video maker Artur Omar, Omar still posits "a whole new genre of films—the festival film genre," with its own "rules and traditions in order to win prizes at festivals."[1] This reminds me of a more cynical conversation cited by a programmer dealing with videographers from Nigeria's burgeoning Nollywood DVD market who was told, "Just tell us what kinds of films you want for the festival and we will make them." Winning prizes at festivals might be the ultimate goal (for both art and business), but there are few well-known film festivals and not that many prizes or even openings to spread around. For most filmmakers, to be included in a festival and to move into gradually more exclusive festivals and realms of competition is a long-term process that takes place over many films (again, the auteur as career binds films over time).

This elusive quest for such a category of works entails the analysis of textual and formal strategies of festival films that, in turn, reshape film production, festival selection, and film knowledge and valuation. This is also a "genre" in constant flux: as of now, festivals have not been receptive to Nollywood film—sensual melodramas that are very popular in Anglophone Africa and its diaspora, or most popular fares, consumed primarily by the local or regional populations all around the world. Yet festivals have also welcomed some more generic films, like gangster flicks from Hong Kong, even if these are attached to an auteur, like Johnnie To.

At the same time, most films in the world do not screen at festivals. Jonathan Rosenbaum tells us that festival film is "mainly a pejorative term in the film business, especially in North America. It generally refers to a film destined to be seen by professionals, specialists, or cultists but not the general public because some of these professionals decide it won't or can't be sufficiently profitable to warrant distribution." While *Around the World in 80 Days* played at Cannes to coincide with the festival and *Robin Hood* (2010) was screened in Cannes out of competition, these screenings represent different strategies of marketing and meaning for such mainstream films, even if few of this genre would attempt such ploys. Similarly, as Dudley Andrew notes in his foreword to a recent collection on global art cinema:

> Every other year FESPACO (Festival du Cinema Panafricain) screens about 100 films from Francophone African countries, both sub-Saharan and Maghrebian, as well as an increasing number of titles from Senegal, Mali, and Burkina Faso whose work is funded in Europe and who expect to be screened on several continents, then distributed on DVD through the Parisian outlet Cine3mondes. Only one Nigerian film, however, has ever been showcased at FESPACO or treated to the chance, despite the fact that Nigeria produces an estimated 1,500 videofilms annually. *Ezra*, which took top prize at that festival in 2007, was, as you might suspect, an exception to Nollywood, financed as it was mainly outside Nigeria (by ARTE), with screenings in Paris and

a brief run in New York. Otherwise Nollywood has been an antiglobal phenomenon of stupendous proportions.

Festival films, therefore, also can be defined by what they are not.[2] This chapter cannot survey all films shown at film festivals, much less those not selected. Instead, I have chosen certain kinds of films that represent major trends within dynamic choices of film festival programmers. I focus on feature films both because they receive more attention in the festival and festival press and because they are more likely to be known and accessible to readers who may want to screen them on their own. Oftentimes, shorts represent the most innovative works and newest voices; they are also launching pads for the directors' future feature presentations. Shorts later may be rediscovered in retrospectives as training grounds for established feature film directors, just as Ingmar Bergman's television commercials have been rediscovered for a festival and DVD market. Yet, their general inaccessibility makes them of less interest here as a focus of shared reading and analysis.

Similar issues emerge with regard to animated films, nonfiction, and avant-garde films. Documentaries represent a mainstay of festivals, especially Sundance, and occasionally prove to be competitors and winners on larger stages (e.g., *Fahrenheit 9/11* at Cannes in 2004). Yet more often, they stand apart because of their concrete themes, including those documentaries that deal with the making of feature films or with their auteurs. All these genres also have important independent festivals that celebrate their special characteristics, creators, audience, and funding—Sundance for documentaries and shorts, the international festivals at Clermont-Ferrand and Oberhausen for short films, Annecy for animation, or the Margaret Mead Festival of ethnographic films. Documentaries, ethnographic, and activist nonfiction films also have specific meanings to which I will return in my discussion of the public sphere.

My selection of works privileges films that have been deemed "successful" as well. This means that the films have gained wide circulation, at least in terms of the film festival circuit, and that they have been reviewed and critiqued a great deal. Thus, films and filmmakers become canonical, influential in their own right with regard to future films. This approach favors films shown at top-tier festivals, especially at Cannes, because these showcases remain the measure of success. In many ways, because Cannes constitutes the accepted standard of success in the festival circuit and to some extent the larger art house circuit, the very infrastructure Cannes has built over the years further consolidates the significance of certain films and auteurs who may have been discovered elsewhere and whose works at Cannes are picked up by other festivals. A mutual reinforcement exists among films (and auteurs) at Cannes, wider festival communities, and film studies scholars and audiences to propagate this success. Even so, this does not mean that there is a recipe for "festival success." Often, judgment on how "good" a film is has as much to do with access, connection, taste, and luck as with essential artistic qualities. In following chapters, I will elucidate the business and cultural processes involved in securing success in the festival circuit and beyond to art houses, limited mainstream distribution, DVD, and video on demand.[3]

Within this delineation of the festival film by "successful" features, I begin the chapter with an evocation of what festival films are *not* before returning to the relation of festival and mainstream films that permeates this text as a whole. Here, crossover films and filmmakers as well as general questions of genre establish rough boundaries within which I turn to some basic characteristics of festival films: their seriousness / minimalism in vision and sound; their open and demanding narrative structures; their intertextuality (including their use of "stars"); and, finally, their subject matter, including controversy as well as freedom. Having established both limits and a paradigm, I then grapple with another almost contradictory demand of the film festival as a renewable event: the search for novelty, for discovery which challenges but confirms the meaning of festival films. I end with a detailed analysis of one recent festival success, the 2007 Romanian film *4 Months, 3 Weeks, and 2 Days*, directed by Cristian Mungiu, as a concrete example of all these points.

As I noted, the characteristics of individual films, yearly panoramas, and innovations demand an awareness of the continuity created by auteurs. Auteurs, over time, guarantee the availability of films for the festival and transmute novelty and controversy into a canon, both moving forward and retrospectively. Film festivals also use auteurs to promote themselves; if Locarno boasts that it "discovered" Kiarostami, Rotterdam takes credit for the success of Cristian Mungiu because it funded *4 Months* . . . , even though both directors had had success in local and regional festivals before these European festivals. This chapter uses works by a few select auteurs as anchors, beginning with Robert Bresson (French, 1901–1999) for long-term association with classic festivals. Gus Van Sant (American, b. 1952), Aleksandr Sokurov (Russian, b. 1951), and the Dardenne brothers (Belgian, Jean Pierre b. 1951 and Luc b. 1954) exemplify currently established filmmakers who have screened multiple works in major competitions. Finally, Cristian Mungiu (Romanian, b. 1968), Lucrecia Martel (Argentine, b. 1966), and Apichatpong Weerasethakul (Thai, b. 1970) exemplify emergent global auteurs on the festival circuit. These case studies complement more detailed analyses of the auteur as social / discursive construct in the next chapter, with a particular focus on Michelangelo Antonioni (Italian, 1912–2007) and Abbas Kiarostami (Iranian, b. 1940) and the words and images they have created.

Outside the Mainstream: What Festival Films Are Not

The opening of *Godzilla* at Cannes (1998) certainly earned more media coverage and bigger box office receipts than the lyrical and reflective Palme d'Or prizewinner that year, *Eternity and a Day* by Theo Angelopoulos. Similarly, the screenings at the Piazza Grande at Locarno always have larger audiences than films in competition for the Golden Leopard—the piazza's capacity endorses the programmer's placement of more "accessible" films in this central open urban space, works that merit an audience popularity award. However, in the larger, yet exclusive, festival world, which sees itself as only tangentially related to the mainstream commercial cinema, the defining works that garner the most critical and programming attention are the features in the main competition or select side events (e.g., Un Certain Regard or Directors' Fortnight at Cannes), perhaps one hundred out of the thousands of films screened each year. As *Time* reporters Richard and Mary Corliss asserted about Michael Haneke's Palme-winning film *The White Ribbon* (Cannes, 2009), "This is a pure art film, daunting and demanding, spare and unsparing, making no concession to the prevailing popular taste—except, perhaps, film-festival taste."[4]

What, by contrast, is a mainstream film? In the weeks after Cannes closed in 2010, for example, multiplex cinemas worldwide were slow to book its oneiric discovery prize-winner, *Uncle Boonmee Who Can Recall His Past Lives* by Thai filmmaker Weerasethakul, even though the film proffers magic and monkey ghosts. Instead, mainstream publicity (even more than audiences) focused on *Shrek Forever After*, *Sex in the City 2*, and *Prince of Persia*. These Hollywood products offered clear, undemanding plots, established stars, rich decor, special effects, seemingly predictable audiences, and short titles that audiences and headline writers could wrap themselves around. Two were sequels with highly identifiable characters, one linked as well to a long-running television series; the third was based on a video game. The first had tie-ins at McDonald's for family audiences driven by children's demands.[5] The second purported to connect to boutiques and fashionistas, gay and straight, and its director appeared on Jon Stewart's *The Daily Show*. *Prince of Persia*, diametrically different from the Iranian films of the festival circuit even in its casting of an American Hollywood star as the hero, offered to an adolescent male mass audience many things that blow up. Whether they succeeded or failed, predictability, ease of understanding, mass intertexts, and high-budget effects were all part of the mainstream cinema that were inimical to the festival film.

Cannes prizewinners may have stars, but they lack complementary products at McDonald's (Quikburger, Café de Coral). In general, they also lack sequels, unless one really wants to compare *Shrek* 1, 2, 3, and 4 to Antonioni's *L'avventura*, *La notte*, *L'eclisse* (*The Eclipse*) and *Il deserto rosso* (*Red Desert*). The issue of budget will be treated later; yet, so far, CGI and similar expensive effects have been less common on the festival screen than in the multiplex. Emotions blow up more than buildings. And neat Hollywood endings are far from the enigmatic closures that often spark discussions of festival films after the lights go up.

The role of audience and discussion underscores contrasts between festival films and Hollywood and national film industries, whether the Italian Cinecittà,

Mumbai-based Bollywood, or Lagos's Nollywood. Festival films simply do not try to reach a mass audience. This is an issue of both scale and exclusivity, bound by circularity. That is, because these films do not need (and cannot reach) a mass popular audience, textually these films can choose not to follow the conventions commercial cinema deems necessary within a viable commercial model in specific historical and geographical junctures—from attractive romance to sagas of massive explosions. At the same time, because of these choices, such films do not appeal to mass audiences. Thus, festival films consciously complement mainstream cinema, marking the different possibilities of the medium and their respective distinctiveness vis-à-vis one another.

Festival/art films have a more critical dialectic relationship with Classical Hollywood cinema with regard to "truth." As many scholars have shown, mainstream Hollywood cinema, because of its spatial and temporal coherence, comprehensive narrative structure, signifying practices, and textual conventions, presents a world that does not invite inquiries. It presents a status quo that is natural, acceptable, and logical. Mainstream narrative cinema then becomes the Althusserian ideological state apparatus, or at least embodies the logic of Roland Barthes's "myth on the right," smug and unquestioned.[6] Alternatives to Hollywood, for over a hundred years, have championed a cinema that is more "unsettling," films that question the formal textual properties, characterization, narrative, and subject matter of the mainstream narrative cinema epitomized by Hollywood. Festivals provide fora where the discourses of filmmakers, critics, and film scholars come to life, from the Italian critics who advocated neorealism for the film magazine *Cinema* in the 1940s, through advocates of auteurs at *Cahiers du cinéma*, to the German directors who signed the 1962 "Oberhausen Manifesto."[7] Godard's counter-cinema or Lars von Trier's "Dogma 95—The Vow of Chastity" also represent strategies for serious, alternative, "truthful" filmmaking. These directors claim their films are more truthful because they are not dreams manufactured by the "factories." Truth, though, does not mean an unproblematic, transparent representation of what one sees in the world, but a reworking of a world where a truth can come out, often through the manipulation of the artists free of perceived immediate commercial interest.

Nevertheless, not all alternatives to Hollywood are oppositional, even if festival films oftentimes claim this aura. Festival-oriented cinema must appeal to other kinds of audiences: the festival cinephiles, the festival professionals, and the festival critical apparatus. As the previous chapter has suggested, film festivals are more complicated than the earlier version of film societies, but like these cinemas they offer products for viewing and discussion. Steve Neale stresses that art cinema is still a commodity, even though it circulates in a different circle.[8] Such lack of accessibility to the mass audience itself becomes a claim of prestige for the film festival, producer, director, and audience—a position mainstream films sometimes parody.

Still, distinctions are not so absolute as ideologues might portray them. While festivals pride themselves in differentiation from Classical Hollywood cinema (and other mainstream traditions), they also screen crossover films. Among American productions, for example, *Pulp Fiction* (1994), *Magnolia* (1999), *Brokeback Mountain* (2005), and *The Wrestler* (2008) all have shared the laurels of the "A"-level festivals, including competition, with the stage at the Golden Globes and the Oscars.[9] Many of these are American "independent" movies—the ostensible American answer to Hollywood. They are generally lower budget in comparison with regular Hollywood pictures (ranging in budget from $6 million for *The Wrestler* to $8 million for *Pulp Fiction* to $14 million for *Brokeback Mountain* to $37 million for *Magnolia*). While these works have captured major prizes in festival competitions, they also have major global distribution, including U.S. national distribution beyond the art house circuit and limited DVD distribution. Ang Lee's *Brokeback Mountain*, for example, which won the Golden Lion in Venice as well as a Golden Globe in the United States, grossed $178 million worldwide; *The Wrestler*, which also received accolades at Venice, the Golden Globes, and the Academy Awards, earned $43 million; *Pulp Fiction* earned $213 million internationally, and *Magnolia*, $48 million. While these are obviously not blockbusters, they are very profitable films. Despite their alternative qualities, these films are in English and are tied into the massive distribution and promotional network of Hollywood; their financial successes do not simply spring from the films' intrinsic qualities.

Crossover films tend to be offer good conventional narratives. *Pulp Fiction* and *Magnolia* are formally more interesting, with difficult characters, transgressive plotlines, and some play with temporality; *Magnolia* (1999, Berlin), for example, has a complicated plot where seemingly disparate events link together within a twenty-four-hour time frame. Yet, it is also classical in the sense that the movie ties up all the loose ends, providing explanations to the audience to orient them in terms of space and time. All of these movies also have very strong psychologically credible characters; they may be quirky or odd, but they are credible, at least in an intertextual generic sense. For Hollywood (or major American studios and distributors), these are "quality" products, not blockbusters. In fact, as I will continue to argue, they "represent" America well to a festival world conditioned to think of the United States through/in opposition to Hollywood.

These crossover films are also critical of mainstream ideologies, a significant extratextual contribution to their international reception. *M*A*S*H* (1970, Cannes) similarly lacked a tight plot, unfurling as a sequence of episodes that gradually ensconced us in the complexities of a military medical unit in Korea. This film established Robert Altman as an auteur with his use of overlapping sound and dialogue, an anticlassical device. *Apocalypse Now* responded to the Vietnam War, while Ang Lee's film reread an essentially American genre, the western, through gay men, an attractive entry for the festival with its reinterpretation of a genre and gender. *Pulp Fiction* (1994, Cannes) self-consciously twisted genre movies and popular culture icons, a refreshing entry for the 1990s. But many of its actors returned comfortably to Hollywood products thereafter, their reputations enhanced. *The Wrestler* is not formally innovative; however, its subject matter—aging people at the margins of urban life—fits the demand of seriousness for festivals.

These films also have stars. Hollywood stars are ipso facto international stars because of Hollywood's distribution muscle, yet they, too, can alter their images through independent films. Robert Altman's *Prairie Home Companion* (2006, Berlin) offered Meryl Streep and Lindsey Lohan; Taratino's *Inglourious Basterds* (2009, Cannes) had Brad Pitt and Cannes/Oscar winner Christoph Waltz; and Steven Soderbergh's *Che* (2008, Cannes) won an acting award for Benicio del Toro. The list goes on and on, which in many ways suggests that U.S. entries to these "A" festivals are set apart from movies from the rest of the world for their ability to straddle both the more mainstream serious cinema arena and the more exclusive art film circuit.

Mainstream values are not solely the purview of Hollywood, however. One should not forget the Palme d'Or winner of 1963, Luchino Visconti's *Leopard* (*Il gattopardo*). This, too was a lavish period court drama, co-financed by Fox, which insisted that a "star" be used for the role of Prince Salina. Fox and Titanus, the Italian production company, recruited Burt Lancaster, without Visconti's consent, although this turned out to be a memorable collaboration. *The Leopard*, too, is a linear narrative, with a sweeping story: the Risorgimento, nobility, rebellion. It has big sets—the forty-plus-minute ballroom scene—and major stars—Lancaster, Alain Delon, and Claudia Cardinale. The version that was screened at Cannes ran 205 minutes in Italian, yet the English version released by Fox was cut to 106 minutes, for which Visconti claimed "no paternity."[10] This is obviously an interesting interplay between a festival film and its mass release version.

Looking at these few films, we see that festivals are not averse to fairly conventional narrative cinema and definitely welcome stars who will show up at post-screening events. These crossover films come closer to the Oscars' use of "quality" to describe winning works, but do not necessarily lack formal challenges or twists of gender, language, and outcome associated with festivals. But no one really confused *Brokeback Mountain* and *Shrek*, either, even if they might overlap on public relations junkets or billboards. And the publicity campaigns and mass media readings of such works emphasize this divergence, as do the ratings that construct audiences within the mainstream: festival films can be NC-17 or R, not necessarily G or PG. Most, if released in the United States theatrically, are not rated.

Festival films, finally, differ from mass Hollywood productions in that they are often works identified with specific directors, and, sometimes, with specific schools, groups, or countries more than genres, stars, or stories. Even the four crossover films mentioned above are all considered to be products of America auteurs—Quentin Tarantino, Ang Lee, Paul Thomas Anderson, and Darren Aronofsky. If festivals films are closer to art (which itself has its complicated logic to commodification) than to a mass market commodity, the long history of Western art demands that the art has a creator, be it a painter, a writer, or in terms of film, a director. This was the position taken by authors at *Cahiers du cinéma* more than half a century ago to be the *politique des auteurs*. Despite André Bazin's disagreement, François Truffaut asserted that Alfred Hitchcock and Howard Hawks were both auteurs who left their signatures in a highly industrialized system. Most festival films' directors, working in a less restrictive environment, would be more self-conscious candidates to become auteurs through film festivals. In smaller, non-studio-produced films, the director, while not autonomous, has more control over her work than their commercial counterparts, but she still is not an "isolated" creator like Michelangelo, Beethoven, or Virginia Woolf. "Sometimes, the distinction of auteur and non-auteur is subtle and grasped only in the viewing," as Liz Wrenn, of the British distributor Electric Pictures, suggests: "A film by Wong Kar Wai, say, you know it's immediately by him; or Jaco van Dormael's 'The Eighth Day,' it's clear it's by the maker of 'Toto the Hero.' But, fine director though he is, you couldn't identify, for example, a film by Michael Winterbottom if you chopped the credits off."[11]

At the same time, the creators of many of these festival films have shared a formation and a subjectivity itself informed by the film festival world. They themselves have become imbued with the discourse of auteur. They are aware of intertextualities in form, allusion, and meanings that are heightened in the intense discourse of the festival, where films are often "about" or at least speaking to other films. Intertextuality, of course, informs production as well as reception, and it extends beyond the auteur to "schools of cinema": *Life and Nothing More* is not only a Kiarostami film, but also an Iranian film and a festival film. This self-conscious awareness of intertextuality as a textual strategy underpins and legitimates the search for family resemblances among festival films.

Festival films often are identified with art cinema. Yet, are festival films and art cinema interchangeable terms? David Bordwell's classic 1979 article defined European art cinema as an alternative to Hollywood cinema in its handling of "realism, authorship, ambiguity," which speaks to festival films as well.[12] Both art and festival films share difficulty and academic respect and a sense of critical interest that situates them in the film canon, from cineclubs to universities. Steve Neale, furthermore, has traced the development of art cinema in Europe and states squarely that international film festivals uphold art cinema's "status as 'Art.'" This status is then reproduced and regenerated "through the existence of prizes and awards."[13]

Yet, we may also be cautious here with regard to nuances. It is also important to recognize smaller, less immediately obvious distinctions between feature festival films and avant-garde / art / experimental films. The latter screen predominantly in museums or galleries, and few museum films and video pieces face limitations on running time. They are also juxtaposed to other kinds of installations and works of art in these settings that establish new connections but alter conditions and practices of spectatorship.[14]

Another difference between these two art cinemas is their relationship to film as a medium and to its audiences. As Peter Wollen asserted in the 1970s, there are "The Two Avant-Gardes": the first being works that primarily question the medium of film, the other "an avant-garde within the feature film format."[15] While many film festivals have sections on the avant-garde, it remains on the fringe of film festivals, rather than becoming a *pièce de résistance*. Often, these are films that invite study beyond the labored enjoyment of a compelling festival feature. Major festivals offer no golden animal / plant award for the experimental avant-garde.

The distinction may be hazy still within the range of a particular filmmaker: Andrew Pulver of the *Guardian*, for example, commented on Abbas Kiarostami's film *Shirin* (2008), when shown at Venice, writing, "The truth is that Kiarostami's film-making has become more and more pared down over the years, and he has in recent times acted more like an installation artist than a feature film-maker. *Shirin* might be happier sitting on a video monitor in the Pompidou Centre on 24-hour loop."[16] Similarly, Ronnie Scheib at *Variety* described other Kiarostami works as his "mainstream oeuvre"—a stretch of anyone's concept of mainstream. Kiarostami's most recent work, *Certified Copy*, does bring the auteur back to the mainstream of European art cinema at least.

Finally, the difference between museum art films and festival screenings is an issue of institutional function within complementary discursive horizons. Museums build and hold collections and analyze art over time in permanent spaces; visitors to a museum have more control over how they view the selections. Most museum selections are not time-bound, even cinema. Film festivals, even those with permanent homes, do not have their space year-round, nor do they amass permanent collections. Festival audience visits are concentrated; they have been trained and expect to see serious, innovative films, but do not demand recursive examination or multiple intertexts screening alongside them. Even so, this remains a more ambiguous distinction than that dividing mainstream cinema and festival films, to whose defining characteristics we now turn.

Serious Film: Defining the Festival Film

While Rick Altman's image of genrification is valuable as a tool in the analysis of festival films,[17] festival films do not constitute an established genre, even when we include all the questions posted about film genre as evolving processes. Instead, my objective is to look for patterns and to deal with exceptions so as to approximate a set of features, a family of resemblances that have proven to attract festival programmers at different points in history. This entails textual dispositions and extratextual features that make certain films attractive for those who program festivals. Yet this "category" is constantly evolving due to social and cultural changes, historical and geographical differences, and the lack of any stable institution that arbitrates any specific standard. Moving through this dynamic and ever changing ambience, we can grasp certain tendencies that epitomize festival films before turning to the equally important balance of novelty and change. Here, then, I begin with tone (seriousness).

Tone: Seriousness, Austerity, and Minimalism

One clear hallmark of many festival films is their serious demeanor. This is often embodied by an austerity of sight and sound as well as a sobriety of themes and actions. Pain, death, loss, and questions are the stuff of festival films, even if skewered by a more mainstream auteurist comedy like Woody Allen's *Love and Death* (1975). Laughter and music may provide relief or ambience, but they rarely drive the festival film *comedy*.

As a corollary, film festivals also tend to avoid big, expensive productions in favor of stark minimalism. Their films are small movies—in budget, in scale, in sets, and in special effects. As I will show in chapter 4, this smallness also allows film festivals to take on a supporting role in production and distribution of these films.

Austerity imbues the motion of the film as well. Shots and camera movements, while often carefully executed, are rarely elaborate. Shots vary, of course, but festival film directors are not shy about using shots that are far away from the subject, and the durations are often long. Handheld roughness may be a mark of immediacy and truth, even if constructed with this meaning in mainstream films as well.

Sets are modest; many festival films are shot on locations that, in turn, comprise everyday homes, offices, or other readily accessible spaces. Set designs can be meticulous, but seldom baroque.[18] Oftentimes, the quotidian is emphasized in festival films: the set is the site where deep human issues arise. These films are crafted without the bells and whistles that characterize the Hollywood blockbuster.

Yet, austerity is not simply absence or denial. Many of these movies demand concerted effort from the audience to actively seek the meaning that texts imply. Often, the filmmakers seem to beckon the audience to work with them to find meaning for themselves. Again, we see a symbiosis between film and audiences of critics and cinephiles who want more than relatively passive engagement for two hours.

The Son (2002, Dardenne), which was nominated for the Palme d'Or and won nine other awards in different festivals, exemplifies many of these points. It is a stark film about relationships bound by a past tragedy that remains an open

Figure 4. The everydayness of *The Son* (*Le fils*) (Jean-Pierre and Luc Dardenne, 2002).

wound. As the film opens, a handheld Steadicam follows the everyday movements of the main character, the bespectacled Olivier, a carpenter. There is no traditional establishing shot, but only multiple medium shots of Olivier, wearing blue overalls, in his workshop, following him through his work and interaction with other workers. Since the camera is handheld, the shots are very fluid. They reveal Olivier's face, different parts of his body, his back, and his movements. This fragmented shooting style carries the whole movie. The audience only discovers that Olivier is some kind of instructor by witnessing him teaching other young men. The workplace set is equally basic with its tools, materials, and workbenches and bare corridors and stairs through which Olivier moves around the building.

The story is spare and elliptical. A woman, whom we later see working at an office in the workshop, asks Olivier if he can take on another young man; the camera lingers on Oliver reading the file, but he says he already has four working for him. The camera follows Oliver, from the back, a bit restless, lighting a cigarette, walking downstairs to look into the office where the woman works. He then gets into his car, goes home, opens canned food, and listens to his phone messages. His home is bare, with nothing on the white walls. The doorbell rings and a woman enters. The two characters obviously know one another although their initial silent interaction is awkward. The audience slowly finds out that she is getting remarried soon, and that she is pregnant. Olivier goes back to his workshop and asks to take on the new apprentice, Francis. He follows him, observes him, and teaches him carpentry. Olivier then goes to the gas station where his ex-wife, the woman who is pregnant, works. He tells her that Francis, the youth who killed their son, has been released from prison. This moment of revelation—to the audience—is hardly exceptional; all is done in a quiet, controlled, and powerful manner.

The first hour of *The Son* exemplifies minimalist filmmaking. Information about characters and situations are presented to the audience without comments. Obviously the mise-en-scène—handheld camera, camera movements, basic bare sets, and the medium shots—entails choices made by the filmmakers to present Olivier as a character who is not at ease, but is doing what he is supposed to do without knowing why. This kind of observational cinema invites the spectator to explore for himself or herself the fairly mundane lives of an ordinary working man. One can argue that meeting the killer of one's son is dramatic, yet this is presented in such an off-handed way that it does not carry much narrative weight.

The rest of the movie follows Olivier trying to figure out who Francis is and to see if Francis feels any remorse. He finally tells Francis that he is the father of the child Francis killed. This is done through a few spare scenes, on the street, in an interaction where the two try to figure out, literally, the distance between point A and B, and on the final trip in the movie where Olivier takes Francis out to the lumber yard to learn about the different kinds of wood.

This austerity resonates with other festival intertexts: a festival genre builds on references as well as practices. For example, in Robert Bresson's *L'argent* (*Money*), which won the Palme d'Or in 1983, when Yvon is introduced, the audience sees him at work through a sequence of only three shots without his face, showing him disconnecting the hose, putting it back on the truck, opening the door, and walking away to a full shot of him handing the bill for oil to Lucien, the crucial exchange where he receives counterfeit money. This is not a moment of forced drama so much as one whose very unmarked quality makes the film resonate with wider experiences. Later, in the final murder scene, no direct killing is seen on screen—nor is Yvon even visible above the waist, resonating with the early introduction of him. Instead, we see only fragmented images: the ax, the frantic dog, Yvon's movement in entering the house, going upstairs, downstairs, his encountering the woman in her room, his asking her, "Where is the money?" a swing of the ax that knocks down the lamp, and splattering of blood on the wall. The ax drops into the water, which then turns red.

In both films, the audience comes to know the character by observing what he does, not by identifying with him or feeling the way he does. In no part of either of these two movies does Olivier or Yvon invite empathy from the audience. There is never any extreme emotion, even with extreme actions of a mass murderer. Since the audience is never told why characters do what they do, the audience has to look for the information within the careful yet austere presentation of "facts." Images are there not to shock the viewers with graphic violence or overblown emotions. Instead, using few shots, the scenes demand that the viewer understand what has been presented to her (all meticulously shot, staged, and edited) and to find meanings herself.

Focus: Small Moments, Shots, and Sounds

Works by many of the great festival directors present small moments dissected in detail. In Aleksandr Sokurov's *Mother and Son* (1997), there are few shots. The film presents a son's care for his dying mother in her last days. The movie is an ode to Romantic painting where every shot is long and slow, covering the sparse landscape of the village where the two spend their last moments together. The austerity comes from the painterly landscape, shot with special filters and lenses, the sky, the leaves, and the wind. Though the landscape is distorted, it merges with the characters to form a complete picture that harmonizes the people and their surroundings.

In Apichatpong Weerasethakul's *Syndromes and a Century*, by contrast, a film funded by the New Crowned Hope festival in Vienna in celebration of Mozart's 250th anniversary, the austerity is such that very little happens. Weerasethakul saw this film as a meditation on his parents' experiences as doctors, with the first part taking place in a rural hospital and the latter in an urban hospital in a fairly big city. There are no close-ups in the film's 105 minutes. Most of the shots are extremely long; the closest shots are medium shots from the waist up. The shots themselves are also very long, temporally, with static or very controlled slow camera movements. There are recognizable characters, but no forced encounters between audience and characters. This is a demanding movie because the text forces the audience to pay attention to subtle changes in the movie. It is also enigmatic, in that some events seem to happen twice, yet with some variations. The dreamlike tone of this film becomes part of Weerasethakul's auteurist signature.

Austerity extends to sight as well as sound. Sound has always been an important component in cinema. Hollywood blockbusters have "big" sounds that guide and heighten our responses; festival films have quieter sounds. The Dardenne brothers provide no music or background sounds in their films. The sound of rain builds a powerful ambience in Lucrecia Martel's *The Swamp* (*La ciénaga*), while in most Tsai Ming-liang films, the sound is only diegetic. In *The Hole* (1998), for example, the dripping noises become incessant and oppressive throughout the film and assume the power of a character in their own right. Similarly, the wind, the raking of leaves, and the dog barking all play important roles in *Diary of a Country Priest* (Bresson, 1951), creating an environment that explains the characters and their context.

One can also see the intersection between the use of sound and the stylistic hallmarks of an auteur. Antonioni, as pointed out by Peter Brunette, for example, always uses the sound of leaves in the wind. This is both an auteurist signature and a device that again asks the audience to pay attention to a sound that is fairly ordinary. Its meaning can be about nature, commenting on the state of affairs of the specific scenes, but it also creates spaces for the audience to interpret and reflect upon certain moments of the film or their relations to other scenes.

However, there are exceptions. Emir Kusturica's works, from *When Father Was Away on Business* (1985) to *Underground* (1995), are "big" and "loud." Both have fairly high production values, especially by contemporary Yugoslavian or Croatian standards. Nevertheless, because of his subject matter and control, as well as associations with the turmoil of the late twentieth-century Balkans, Kusturica could be read as a truth teller from a land unlike those of the silences of Belgium, Scandinavia, or spiritual France.

Open Narratives

Festival films often confront classical ideas about narrative, whether in connections, temporality, order, or outcome. As Richard Maltby describes narrative in cinema, "every picture . . . needs a story to be constructed around it, to place it in a temporal context and provide it with a before and after."[19] In Hollywood, these temporal clues are coherent: there must be causality between the act before and the act that follows. Festival films, by contrast, privilege the suggestive, evocative, spare, and nonlinear. Coherence must be constructed, not found. This does not necessarily mean that festival films are not narrative, only that they do not adhere to the straight "classical" mode.

This opposition has to be understood in relation to the dominant mode of cinematic language as practiced by Hollywood and most popular cinemas in the world. Alternatives to established Hollywood aesthetics have been present since the Hollywood style consolidated its global dominance in the late 1910s— whether Eisenstein's montage, German expressionism, or Luis Buñuel's surrealist works. Both ideological and pragmatic grounds intersect in this opposition. Mainstream narratives, through repeated established textual conventions, explain the world as it is, as natural, spatially and temporarily consistent, something that can be grasped and understood. Revolutionary and avant-garde cinema, on the other hand, forces the viewers to question the status quo, with the hope of arousing them to ask more questions about their everyday lives. The German studio UFA, which made works like *The Cabinet of Dr. Caligari* (1920), understood that it needed to offer a product that could be differentiated from the films coming from the United States and hence challenged Hollywood's naturalistic style. Thus, UFA consolidated its reputation as makers of art films, and successfully transported *The Cabinet of Dr. Caligari* to the United States, making it different primarily through its use of expressionist sets. It became art.[20]

This point echoes Peter Wollen's observation about Jean-Luc Godard's counter-cinema in *Wind from the East* (*Le vent d'est*), as an embodiment of "narrative transitivity versus narrative intransitivity."[21] Psychological motivations that help to explain series of events in classic narrative films are simply absent in many festival films. For example, in *The Son*, the audience has to guess what is going on with Olivier's life. The first half hour of the film simply shows what Olivier does, thus giving time for the audience to know him. There is no background, no histories, no psychological profile of why he does what he does. We simply see him working, eating, doing the most mundane tasks. By eschewing any linear sequence, many films become episodic, which again requires the viewer to link the different episodes in the film instead of following a straight causality. As in the case of sets, shots, and sounds, the reader must work to build the text, which becomes part of the festival experience.

Direct causality is avoided while ellipses are common. In *Pickpocket* and *L'argent* the audience eventually gets to know the characters, but not because Bresson tells us why they are who they are. We encounter Michel in *Pickpocket* and Yvon in *L'argent* in the present, Bresson gives us no explanation as to why the two characters became who they are. Bresson presents a step by step development of the fall of Yvon, but the film text provides no connection from one scene to another. Yvon loses his job because of the forged money; Yvon does not want to ask for the job back; Yvon is involved in a criminal act; Yvon is caught; Yvon is sentenced to go to jail. . . . While one event follows another, the latter does not necessarily explain the former and the motivation, and choices made of and by the characters are never explained. It is very hard to be empathetic to the characters. This technique, of course, brings us back to Brechtian theater, which asks the audience to disengage and is antithetical to Classical Hollywood Cinema.

The use of ellipse forces the viewer to fill in the gaps of the narrative. In Bresson's *Diary of a Country Priest,* the priest goes to visit the village aristocrat, but the next shot is one of the priest saying goodbye to the aristocrat. No information is provided as to the content of the talk between the two, except their facial expression after the conversation. This suggests a note of discord that eventually foreshadows the rejection of the priest by the rural gentry community.

Besides ellipse, oftentimes, the diegetic reality is not relevant. In Lucrecia Martel's *The Headless Woman* (*La mujer sin cabeza,* 2008), the protagonist, Vero, thinks that she has run over someone while driving home. The film never explains what exactly happens at that moment when the car has two jolts. The audience sees Vero being distracted by the sound of the cell phone; there is a great deal of audio information, including the car hitting something. Vero knows that she has hit something and contemplates going out of the car to find out, but in the end she decides to just drive ahead. By withholding the information that would explain exactly what has happened, Martel deliberately leaves that fact open, thereby taking away its significance. Facts do not always need to be explicated, because what is important is how the characters create scenarios depending on their perceptions and for the audience to figure out why, not in a casual way, but in a deeper understanding of human relations. What is relevant is that Vero decides not to stay at the scene of the incident, and that this decision eventually leads to subsequent actions by her and her friends and relatives, who may or may not have covered up the accident that may or may not have happened. Vero and her people belong to the bourgeoisie, while the boy who might have been hit or not is working class. The refusal to explain what transpired forces the audience not only to be forever unsure of the event, but also to infer, from the different actions the characters undertake, how class relations express themselves in Vero's world, and to a larger extent in Argentine society.

Narratives are also disrupted: the use of Super 8 footage in Gus Van Sant's *Paranoid Park* adds nothing to the narrative progression of the main plot line of what happens to the security guard—a plot line introduced about ten minutes into the film. This footage, however, adds to the feel of the place, the world of the teenage skateboarders and their angst. Weerasethakul, in *Syndrome and a Century*, inserts long shots of people and doctors walking along the corridor of the hospital that add no narrative details to the already scant storyline but complete its aesthetic installation.

Nevertheless, in most of Bresson's films, time, while not always connected, does move forward. In more recent works like those of Apichatpong Weerasethakul, linear time itself is challenged. For example, in *Syndrome and a Century*, it would make no difference in terms of narrative if the two parts were switched. Very similar scenes take place in both hospitals, with the same characters, engaging in the same activities. Time, therefore, is not there to explain causality, time is there to be experienced. If time moves slowly, it gives time to the audience to pay attention to different aspects of the mise-en-scène, information that may not advance the plot but adds to the feelings, atmosphere of the films.

In Aleksandr Sokurov's *Father and Son* (2003), the film opens with the father consoling the son after his nightmare. It ends with another dream, with the father, contented, alone on the rooftop in the snow. Formally, this is a tight structure with dramatic and sober images. The opening scene, without image, in black after the title, starts with a reassuring voice saying, "It's over; it's over," followed by heavy breathing. It then fades into a close shot of two male bodies struggling, with hands holding down the wrists. Three close shots of the body struggling, with the same voice saying "easy" and "it's over," are followed by the close-up, wide-angle shot of a mouth opening wide, and then a wider shot than the first three that introduces the faces of the two. The two then continue in this dreamlike state, where the father (the audience at this point would not know that they are father and son) asks where the son is now in the dream, and the son responds by saying he is alone in the rain, with a shot of him in a field with a tree, savoring the rain, running happily. The father asks if he himself is there, the son says no. Later the father says he is there too and the son says, "Yes, now I see you," but the scene cuts back to their embrace in the room.

The dream that ends the movie has both men dressed and going to sleep in their respective beds. Parallel editing shows the two going to bed, with the same camera angles and scales of the same act of sitting on the bed, lying down, and falling asleep with successively closer shots. After close-ups of the father and the son falling asleep, it then cuts to the hillside and the tree the audience first sees at the beginning of the film, but with no one, then the son, naked, asleep in bed, then the father walking out of the window in the snow, intercut with another shot of one hand touching the other's body. Just like with the first dream, father and son carry on a conversation: the son asks if he is there, the father says, smiling, "I am alone here." We hear the sound of windows being shut and then a shot of the closed window. The camera follows the father in a wide shot, where it shows the back of the father next to the dome where father and son have played, now covered with snow, and it fades out. These intensely spare parallel shots, in the end, defy any real sense of beginning or end as dream time and real time merge and separate. The use of different state of mind, subjective reality, has been a fairly usual device in art cinema, exemplified by ancestral films like Ingmar Bergman's *Wild Strawberries*.[22]

For film festivals, films relying on anticlassical narrative distinguish themselves from the mass cinema and elevate the status of all concerned, from producers, directors, and programmers to audience as people who are not afraid of demanding and difficult films. At the same time, the work does not lead to a single, conclusive reading. Festival films are both spare and open-ended, stimuli and vehicles for discussion of meaning rather than stories with undemanding mass appeal. If we look back at *The Son*, after Olivier tells Frances that he is the father of the murdered boy, the film simply ends with Francis coming back to Olivier and offering to help load the timber into the car. A small gesture of help concludes the movie, but the spectator is required to bring an ending to it. In Kiarostami's *Taste of Cherry*, does the man succeed in committing suicide? Why does he want to kill himself? The film ends with video documentary footage of the filming of the film, with actors and crew on location. The audience again has to decide whether the main character has indeed avoided death because he heard the meaning of the taste of cherry, or if he indeed succeeds in his original quest. Even the final insertion of documentary footage makes explicit the films as artifact, breaking the diagetic coherence of the film.

Everydayness: Nonprofessional Actors and Stars

While press coverage of film festivals are all about movie stars (and some auteur stars), the films in competitions do not always have stars or even professional actors. Using nonprofessional actors is hardly a rule, but many filmmakers at festivals have embraced it. This is very much another aspect of minimalism and of distinction from the studio system and values of Hollywood and other mainstream national cinemas. Many filmmakers, not unlike the Italian neorealists, believe that stars have too much baggage. They are known; they embody sometimes-unwelcome intertextuality. Nonprofessional actors are ipso facto unknown and can offer a blank slate to the viewer.

Figure 5. Last scene of *Taste of Cherry* (*Ta'm-e guilass*) (Abbas Kiarostami, 1997), with the camera crew.

Robert Bresson, for example, goes to the extreme of calling his actors models. This converged with his ideas of minimalist filmmaking in that the actors should not embrace big, expressive acting as dictated by mainstream cinema. While some of Bresson's lead actors have gone on to have acting careers, most of his leads are first timers. Claude Laydu was cast after Bresson rejected all nonbelievers to play the role of the priest.[23] Nadine Nortier of *Mouchette* was an unknown until the film received critical responses.

The 2010 Palme d'Or winner, Apichatpong Weerasethakul's *Uncle Boonmee Who Can Recall His Past Lives*, also uses nonprofessional actors. Not only were the majority of his actors amateurs, they were from the specific area of northeast Thailand where the film took place and where a specific northeastern dialect is spoken. In the film press kit, Weerasethakul asserts that "to me, Boonmee is anonymous. So I could not use professional actors who have many public identities. I think the amateurishness is precious when you are aiming for early cinema's acting style. So I cast people from all walks of life. We ended up having a roof welder and a singer to play Boonmee and Huay."[24] The use of nonprofessional actors is then imbued with authenticity. Here, Weerasethakul seems to equate cinema with a special kind of everydayness, a complexly mediated truth.[25]

Festival films also transform actors, deconstructing stardom and yet incorporating its allures. When Theo Angelopoulos cast Harvey Keitel in *Ulysses' Gaze* or Jane Campion used him in *The Piano*, Keitel was building his reputation as a serious actor. Antonioni always used famous actors—Marcello Mastroianni, Monica Vitti, Alain Delon, Vanessa Redgrave, and Jack Nicholson—while Bergman had almost a repertory company of familiar, powerful stars—Max Von Sydow, Harriet Andersson, Ingrid Thulin, Liv Ullmann. Many American Palme d'Or winners feature international stars, like Robert De Niro in *Taxi Driver*. Indeed, De Niro's acting, as Travis Bickle, in many ways became the focus of the film, very different from the priest, the pickpocket, or the delivery man in Bresson works (again, expectations vis-à-vis Hollywood differ). More recently, Lars von Trier of the Dogma group has played with the public personas of Björk, Catherine Deneuve, and Nicole Kidman in his films while Juliette Binoche has appeared in works by André Téchiné, Krzysztof Kieslowski, Chantal Ackerman, Hou Hsiao-hsien, Abbas Kiarostami, and Jia Zhangke, negotiating prizes at Venice and Cannes as well as Oscars and Césars. Such stars definitely command more attention when they are on screen, and the films themselves lend more space to their star power as festival readings transform them.

The stars that interest "A"-level European festivals are also Hollywood and European stars; regional stardom has a very different meaning, even if it represents the internationalness of the films as well as of their actors. Hong Kong's Maggie Cheung exemplifies the conflicts of stardom and recognition facing the actor as well as the filmmaker. Early on in her career, she received a Golden Bear for her work as an actress in Stanley Kwan's *Yuen Ling-yuk* (1992). Her global fame grew with regular starring roles in Wong Kar Wai's films through the 1990s, but Cannes only recognized her with a best actress award for the unglamorous but transnational role of Emily Wang in Olivier Assayas's 2004 *Clean*. Cheung had been married to tastemaker Assayas from 1998 to 2001, and was living in France. Cheung, like other actresses and actors, has served on juries in Berlin, Venice, and Cannes—ironically, an accolade not generally given to the nonactors of festival films. Bollywood and Nollywood stars, for example, are generally absent on juries.

Furthermore, as some festival auteurs evolve, especially non-Western directors, they attract internationally known professional actors and stars. In his early career, Wong Kar Wai always cast local Hong Kong stars; however, as he became more established in the festival world, he turned to Rob Lowe, Rachel Weisz, and singer Norah Jones in *My Blueberry Nights*. His subsequent project, *The Lady from Shanghai*, was rumored to star Rachel Weisz, after Nicole Kidman and Hugh Jackman turned down roles. In the end, the project never materialized.

The collaborations between established auteurs and actors underline the contributions festivals and festival films make over time to actors, directors, and producers, who obviously value such endeavors with their willingness to invest. Unknown directors have little access to established actors and actresses. Once these auteurs have established their names through exposure at major film festivals, actors may aspire to work with them for different experiences. Acting for a festival auteur may not pay a great deal, but it puts the actors into a category very far from the mass media heartthrob and adds gravitas to the actors' reputations.

Directors also may be trying something quite new. Even if the director is not the one who always controls casting, the director, weighing different options, has to agree to casting choices in the end. Abbas Kiarostami started using professional Iranian actresses in *Shirin*. When asked why he would use professionals, he replied, "It was an ethical debt which I felt I owed to Iran's professional actresses, since I had never put them before my camera. It was a debt I owed to myself, too! I had denied myself two important and appealing aspects of cinema: not just beauty, but also the complexity that you find in women. Actually, I still don't know whether those actresses were giving a performance or if we did elicit a genuine reaction from them."[26] The reporter continued to ask why he cast Juliette Binoche in *Shirin*, and Kiarostami simply described the situation as one where Binoche was a guest in his house when the film was shot. She generously offered to play one of the 114 actresses in that film and he accepted. Kiarostami explained that Binoche wore no makeup and was not paid.[27] As Kiarostami and Binoche became friends, she starred in his first film shot outside of Iran (in French, English, and Italian). This, in turn, won her a best actress award at Cannes in 2010.

Nonprofessional actors, nonetheless, tend to provide the festival films more legitimate claim to authenticity, to substantiate the claim that a serious filmmaker does not want the audience to be distracted by the glamour of the familiar faces of the actors. In a way, the director is saying, "Do not look at the actors and actresses, look at how I am constructing my film." For some, the actors are of no more importance than the props; they are there to construct the film. On the other hand, established auteurs have had many more opportunities to work with established actors and actresses. This, of course, has to be supported by willing investors who see the value of these festival films and welcome the addition of recognizable actors and actresses to increase their potential to reach a larger audience than those of the festival cinephiles.

Genres/Anti-Genres and Themes

Not surprisingly, the rejection of narrative often leads to a rejection of specific conventions of reading that define particular mass genres and audience expectations.[28] Comedies and musicals simply seem to violate the serious tone of the festival forum: at most, one can live with the ironies of Pedro Almodóvar or the surrealism of Luis Buñuel: Woody Allen, by contrast, however distinctive an auteur and frequent a festival pick, has never been a festival favorite.[29] Again, festivals may differ in this, quite apart from those that are genre-specific (science fiction, animation—although nothing on this scale exists for popular genres such as Westerns, romance, or police/thrillers). Berlin, though it has recognized comic sensibilities on occasion with films like *The Wedding Banquet* (Ang Lee, 1993), could justify this film since it also brought gay issues into Chinese cinema. Berlin also presented its 2002 award to Hayao Miyazaki's bittersweet animated family story *Spirited Away.* Gilles Jacob, in a 1996 interview, seemed almost wistful on this absence:

> There are comedies that have the qualities of auteur films—intelligence, wit, humor, liveliness, characters, and structure. I don't want to single out a particular film from the Cannes selection this year, but take the examples of Ernst Lubitsch and Billy Wilder. Maybe in their time they were looked down on, but they're both immortals in the history of cinema—and they made comedies.
>
> So, let's look around us to see if there are any Ernsts or Billys nowadays and, if there aren't, let's help the industry so that more of them can make films.[30]

To some extent, the discovery of the darkly comic sensibilities of post-communist Romanian cinema may have answered this need.

Musicals prove problematic as well. Berlin selected Gene Kelly's *Invitation to the Dance* for a 1956 award; it is striking here that MGM actually had delayed the release of the film for four years out of justified concerns for its box office potential as an overly artistic dance film. And Berlin returned to an operatic musical with *U-Carmen e-Khayelitsha* from South Africa in 2005, the first and only sub-Saharan film to win such a major award. Cannes, meanwhile, has awarded the Golden Palm to two musicals—Jacques Demy's *Parapluies de Cherbourg* (1964), which took the genre to the extreme of excluding nonmusical interludes in a story of love and loss, and Bob Fosse's *All that Jazz,* which again turned the musical into a Felliniesque saga of self-destruction and mortality. Locarno and Venice have not smiled on such efforts, and even a handful of such awards scarcely balance the scores of "serious" dramas that have been selected instead; *All that Jazz,* for example, was actually part of an unlikely tie with Kurosawa's *Kagemusha.*

Darker genres like Westerns, science fiction, horror, or thrillers have only tended to gain recognition if so reflexive that they rupture expectations of the genre itself. Godard's blend of politics, sci-fi, and noir, *Alphaville,* won the Golden Bear in Berlin in 1965; Robert Altman blew up the Western for another Golden Bear in 1976 with *Buffalo Bill and the Indians, or Sitting Bull's History Lesson;* and Ang Lee's *Brokeback Mountain* subverted the bonds of cowboys for the gaze of Venice forty years later. Again, the presence and career of the auteur insists that these are not "merely" genre films.

Genre crossing and hybridization can also make a film more novel, difficult, and acceptable. As mentioned earlier, Emir Kusturica's films are not particularly minimalist, but *Underground* is a good example of a mixed genre film. It combines comical farce, melodrama, politics, and war to create a dystopian vision. The films are self-reflective: characters speak directly to the audience, with a film and theater within the film, inserting documentary footage into the narrative, and commenting on different levels of reality and allegory. *Underground* is loud, full of distinctive characters, both humans and animals, which complement Kusturica's vision of Yugoslavia and Milosevic's modern Balkans. *Underground* is far from austere, but it is extremely complex, weaving different levels of film forms and references to Kusturica's sense of history.

If a director becomes a master of a particular, self-reflective genre, his works are accepted as auteurial products, whether the surreal humor of the later Buñuel or even a reflexive, intertextual noir: Hong Kong director Johnnie To has had four films in competition at Cannes, although they are all generic thrillers. But this in itself invokes a kind of intertextuality with generations of Hong Kong films that established these conventions—John Woo, Ringo Lam—as they entered an earlier festival scene without prizes. Since many genres are considered to be popular and commercial, however, they are not the most welcome additions to film festivals.

Despite the limited appeal of some genres, festival films still cover all kinds of subject matter. There are grand period pieces, like Visconti's *The Leopard* (*Il gattopardo*, 1963), Sofia Coppola's *Marie Antoinette* (2006), or skewering portraits of the intellectuals and upper class of Fellini or Antonioni. There are the working classes of the Dardenne brothers and Paoli and Vittorio Taviani or Mike Leigh, the War on Terror in Michael Moore's *Fahrenheit 9/11* (2004), gangster films like Quentin Tarantino's *Pulp Fiction* or Johnnie To's *Vengeance* (2009), and films discussing the plight of educating women in Kurdistan in Samira Makhmalbaf's *Blackboards* (2000).

Given this diversity, it is hard to say that festivals prefer specific subject matter so much as that there is a tendency to include movies about issues that mainstream cinema normally avoids, again, a dialectic as much as an essence. Popular cinema avoids films where "nothing much happens": given the need for strong narrative structures, popular movies cannot simply be about a slice of everyday life which is not "exciting." Yet, in film festivals the everyday is elevated to a much higher ground, with winners like Nanni Moretti's *The Son's Room* (2001, Cannes) and Wang Quanan's *Tuya's Marriage* (2006, Berlin). Both are about ordinary people, one Italian middle class, and the other Mongolian Chinese. The former lost a son and the film describes how the family copes with the loss; the latter is about a woman's quest to find a new husband so she can take care of her old husband.

Mainstream cinema tends to stay away from controversy, while festivals invite and savor films that tackle controversial subject matters. Many festival films from outside Western Europe tackle taboo social and political issues—especially if these are issues that are less problematic within a Western audience framework. Here, there is a clear negotiation of the gaze across space as well as form and subject—although we must be wary of questions of a colonial gaze that are raised around this selection. One even sees this in the turn to Eastern Europe following the fall of communism, where festivals have focused on the problems of this regime and its aftermath. Emir Kusturica's *When Father Was Away on Business* (1995) portrayed the old communist rule in Yugoslavia in the 1950s. His second Palme d'Or winner, *Underground (Once Upon a Time There Was a Country*, 1995), was about the villainy of a later Balkan War; in the same year, Theo Angelopoulos's *Ulysses' Gaze* (1995) was also made in the Balkan war zone. *Underground* was hailed as a courageous piece on the Balkan war, yet many Bosnians saw it as pro-Serbian.[31] More recently, another Eastern European film from Romania, *4 Months, 3 Weeks and 2 Days*, has presented the brutal experience of a woman seeking an abortion in the last days of Nicolae Ceauçescu.

Festivals also can leave history behind. One notes a rise and fall in interest in Spanish film around the end of the Franco regime—Buñuel's searing *Viridiana* was smuggled out to win at Cannes in 1961, although it cost him new exile from Spain. Berlin, in particular, celebrated the transition in Spain with awards to José Luis García Sanchez (*The Trouts [Las truchas]* 1978), Tomás Muñoz (*The Elevator [El ascensor]*, 1978), Emilio Martínez Lázaro (*What Max Said*, 1978), Carlos Saura (*Fast, Fast [Deprisa, deprisa]* 1981), and Mario Camus (*The Hive [La colmena]*, 1983). Yet as Spain has become more European, interest in its films has waned, despite the auteurial popularity of Pedro Almodóvar (whose entire cast won the best actress award at Cannes 2006 for *Volver*). This presents a striking contrast to the enduring presence of Ireland and its civil wars among prize films across Europe, including *In the Name of the Father* (Jim Sheridan, Berlin, 1994), *Michael Collins* (Neil Jordan, Venice, 1996), *Bloody Sunday* (Paul Greengrass, Berlin, 2002), and *The Wind that Shakes the Barley* (Ken Loach, Cannes, 2006). In a similar vein, the Golden Lion in Venice went to *The Magdalene Sisters* in 2002. There is a niche for countries that are somewhat less "European" than the powerful European North, where the Balkans, Spain, and Ireland can be seen with a domestic inter-regional orientalist gaze.

Looking further afield, festivals, especially the dominant Western festivals, have always been fascinated with movies coming from "oppressive" regimes. The early wave of Chinese cinema that arrived at festivals, including Zhang Yimou's *Red Sorghum* and Chen Kaige's *Farewell My Concubine* were fairly exotic. While magnificent films, they fit squarely with the expectation of the West, with overtones of Orientalism in terms of cultural values and gender. These works echo earlier Japanese films, such as *Rashômon* (1950), *Tale of Genji (Genji mono-gatari*, 1952), *Gate of Hell* (1953), and *The Crucified Lovers (Chikamatsu monogatari)* (1954), all of which conformed to certain Western views about the Far East—set in the distant past on court lives, with lavish costumes or colorful samurai. Hou Hsiao-hsien's *City of Sadness* (1989) was one of the first movies that foregrounded the silent subject of the 228 massacre, where many native Taiwanese people were killed by the KMT (Nationalist Party from the mainland).

Such a gaze has consequences. After Zhang Yuan's *East Palace, West Palace* (1996) was invited to be shown at Cannes's Un Certain Regard, the Chinese government confiscated his passport so he could not attend the screening. In discussing the issue of gay films in China, Chris Berry suggested that "I suspect Zhang Yuan would have enjoyed the little performance Cannes put on to address the Chinese government's actions. By placing an empty chair on the stage to symbolize his absence, they simultaneously made both him and his absence present to the audience."[32] The work of another Chinese director, Lou Ye's *Summer Palace* (2006), takes place in 1989 during the Tiananmen Incident, with graphic depictions of the brutality at Tiananmen as well as explicit sex scenes, including full-frontal nudity. The film was initially invited to compete for the Golden Palm, but was withdrawn after the Chinese censor rejected it. His 2009 Cannes entry, *Spring Fever*, about a gay triangle, also created controversy on how Lou worked clandestinely in China. Though Chinese in content, the film is registered as produced in Hong Kong and France.

Many American films that win the Palme d'Or, as I have suggested, are in one way or another critical of the United States. Yet, they may also be limited in voice and dialogue. Spike Lee's *Do the Right Thing*, for example, generated quite a bit of buzz as a window on American racism, but Lee has never won a major festival prize. Nor has any other African American- or Latino-directed film gained top prizes at the major festivals.

Western European art films remain more about interior struggle, even though most are embedded within a veiled critique, generally, of capitalism. Neither Bresson's *L'argent*, Antonioni's *L'eclisse*, nor the Dardenne brothers' *Rosetta* is didactic, but all deal with money of different forms, from counterfeits, to money from the stock market, to the struggling lumpenproletariat; these films concentrate on the contexts within which the characters live as well as their actions to make statements about general human conditions. These films critique the consequences of a capitalistic world by showing the conditions, but do not use the difficult situations to elicit sympathy for the characters.

The most characteristic festival film may still be those personal journeys in which the subject matters are quite devoid of any direct political or social contexts. Films like Bergman's *Persona*, Haneke's *The Piano Teacher*, or Shohei Imamura's *The Eel* (*Unagi*) are fairly apolitical, but deal with basic, essential human emotions. When Abbas Kiarostami presented his 2010 Cannes competition entry, *Certified Copy*, it seemed to depart quite a bit from all his earlier Iranian-based films, but followed in the vein of an European art film about two European individuals' encounter and their relationship and meditation on life.

While mainstream cinema tends to avoid complicated subjects, festivals promote films that tackle volatile issues. Oftentimes, festival films are "political" when there are current affairs that indeed garner the attention of the international press. For France, its complicated relations with its former North African colonies and its present domestic encounters with a multiethnic society as a result of this past colonization are repeated topics in its festival films. The 2008 Cannes Palme d'Or winner, *The Class* (*Entre les murs*), as well as the 2009 entry *A Prophet* (*Un prophète*), arrived at Cannes after the suburban ethnic unrest where television, press, and Internet images were translated into a meditation on ethnic relations in France. Politics has a long history in terms of film festivals, and recent French entries to Cannes includes movies that deal with the new multiethnic France. *The Class* is set in a multicultural Parisian school, a current and pressing concern of contemporary French society. In 2010, Cannes was also haunted by the specter of the Algerian war, with two controversial films on that theme in competition.

Festivals' embrace of more controversial subject matter follows a long tradition of seeing art as free and touting festivals as zones that champion that freedom. The early film societies and film clubs that I discussed in chapter 1 were set up because they wanted to show *Potemkin* from the Soviet Union, or *L'Age d'Or* by Buñuel and Salvador Dalí: the first for political reasons, and the second for moral reasons dealing with sex and the Church. Festivals, then, have been ideologically constructed as free spaces where films of all subject matters are welcome, be they about taboo and politically sensitive subjects or excessive in their portrayal of sex and violence—bulwarks against the censorship real or implicit in Hollywood and national cinemas. The official selection at Cannes in 2009 included several films that have fairly uncomfortable contents, raising controversies about sex and/or violence as domains of pornography. Lars von Trier's *Antichrist*, for example, includes scenes on a variety of genital mutilations, torturous sex, and violence. The Ecumenical jury of the SIGNIS Award gave the film an Anti-Award, protesting its "misogyny." This was met immediately with a protest from the festival director deriding the jury's decision as close to censorship, and the film's primary actress, Charlotte Gainsbourg, won the best actress award.[33] Meanwhile, Brillante Mendoza's Filipino film *The Execution of P* (*Kinatay*), which won him the best director award, also has extremely graphic depictions of sexuality, violence, "torture, beheading, and disembodiment of a prostitute."[34] These are hardly mainstream cinema materials; many considered this film misogynistic as well. But they were validated at festivals by their screenings, by the awards they received, and by the debates they provoked as not belonging to the mainstream, celebrating the unbounded quality of art. This, too, is a tradition. Looking back to the 1960s, Antonioni's *L'avventura* showed a woman undressing while *Blow-Up* was considered extremely daring in its portrayal of sex and drugs.

Sometimes, extreme violence and sexual portrayal have become associated with specific national cinemas and auteurs. While not all Korean entries to top film festivals are R/NC-17-rated films, Park Chan-Wook and Kim Ki-Duk are the two Korean directors who have garnered the most nominations and prizes at the top three European festivals. Park is famous for his Vengeance Trilogy, and Kim's films have also been criticized for having many masochistic female characters. These complaints do not seem to bother the selection committees of major festivals—if the films are artistic, sociocultural elements, especially those based on unequal gender relations, are considered secondary concerns. Kim has made films that include extremely graphic scenes of genital mutilations and "unusual" sexual practices. Park's latest Cannes's nomination, *Thirst*, has a devoted priest turn into a vampire after volunteering for a vaccine experiment. He eventually develops a relationship with the wife of a childhood friend.

Festivals, in the end, whatever their selections, are freer to show movies that would be considered extreme, because art demands this freedom. Programmers claim that the first quality festivals look for in cinema is aesthetics, and because art transcends mundane political and social issues, the resulting universality is what festivals yearn to show to their audiences. Yet themes as well as mise-en-scène constitute critical elements of the festival genre and the definition of a canon of great films against which new entries will be measured. Still, perhaps almost paradoxically, festival programs cannot simply repeat what has been successful before. As they respect and stabilize the old, festivals seek and compete in defining that which is new, albeit within the paradigms that programmers, filmmakers, and audiences have already constructed.

Novelty and Discoveries: The Opposite of Genre

After the long discussion of what constitutes festival films, I have to acknowledge that festivals are also about innovation and discoveries. The newness of the films, auteurs, and film movements is perceived because, first, it is current, and also because it is new in terms of its contribution to cinema, either formally, thematically, or the interaction among the two. Venice had Emerging Cinema and Best First Work awards in the 1980s; it gave Emir Kusturica the Best First Work award for *Do You Remember Dolly Bell?* in 1981. Cannes has had the Camera d'Or since 1978. The Camera d'Or has been given to Jim Jarmusch (who was first "discovered" at Sundance), Mira Nair, Jafar Panahi, and Naomi Kawasé, but also to the likes of Vadim Glowna and Nana Dzhordzhadze, who have continued to work but have not gained more international recognition. The Tribeca festival has a section called Discovery that premieres both documentaries and narratives. Some of these films come from the Tribeca All Access program, which provides initial funding for promising works. Some small festivals also give awards to new directors, such as the Rhode Island International Film Festival and its Directorial Discovery Award. The Kolkata Film Festival in India and many other festivals also have sections called "Discovery."

This chapter so far has relied heavily on the films and auteurs who have shown their films at Cannes, the festival of all festivals. However, Cannes is not known to be the festival that really discovers talents; it affirms past festival auteurs after they have been discovered in other comparatively smaller or regional festivals. Such films and filmmakers might appear initially in Un Certain Regard or the Directors' Fortnight, which is independent of the official festival. Subsequently, works by these auteurs, such as Loach, the Dardenne brothers, and Kiarostami, gained recognition and started competing at the major competitions. But this was scarcely their entrée to a festival world.

If discovery means the first to honor or promote this talent, then smaller festivals have been the place to locate them. Rotterdam's Tiger Award, for example, was specifically founded to promote directors' first or second works, and it has a reputation for discovering Asian cinema. The Pesaro festival is dedicated to new cinema, Locarno has a first film competition, and the Festival of Three Continents has a wider global gaze. These definitely showed more Iranian cinema before Cannes. Cannes, nevertheless, with its power, its ability to attract the most prominent international press, is able to substantively disseminate these "discoveries" to a larger audience even though other festivals discovered the films before they landed at Cannes.

Local and regional festivals also play a key role. Hong Kong and Chinese filmmakers were brought onto the festival stage at the Hong Kong International Film Festival, where programmers from Cannes, Berlin, and Locarno scouted them. Iranian filmmakers use Fajr as their springboard, while Romanian filmmakers make their debut at Transylvania before moving to Sarajevo and Thessaloniki. This is a delicate balance which has recently been challenged by programs to develop young global filmmakers in Europe, echoing the earlier migrations of auteurs like Wong Kar Wai and Jia Zhangke from Hong Kong to Cannes and Venice (or even the European migration of Sundance alumni like Steven Soderbergh and Quentin Tarantino).

Relations to place are complicated since films and directors from certain countries become identified (and even canonized) with specific film styles that reshape further discoveries. That is, discovery makes sense within the festival paradigm, but a film or director may find it difficult to escape festival expectations thereafter. Japanese cinema, for example, was "discovered" by Venice when it screened *Rashômon* in 1951. Textually, the film was "new" because it presented three versions of the same event, yet it was a fairly classical text in every other way. As a result, Cannes and Venice invited Japan to submit films to their competitions throughout the 1950s and early 1960s. Subsequently, Akira Kurosawa and Kenji Mizoguchi became prominent auteurs for these festivals. Japanese films that were exhibited at film festivals and eventually were distributed in art house cinemas and became historical dramas that took Western viewers to a different and exotic world. From 1952 to 1955, all of Venice's Japanese entries were directed by Mizoguchi, who is celebrated as a director sensitive to women's issues.[35] Subsequently, Indian films, represented by the work of Satyajit Ray, became the next "discoveries" of the mid-1950s—although, India's mainstream cinema—Bollywood—has never broken into the festival circuit.

By the 1960s, the new trends were French New Wave, New Italian Cinema, and New German Cinema and other Europeans. Japanese films only regained their festival status since the 1990s in new genres—the noir of Takeshi Kitano and the animated films of Hayao Miyazaki.

Chinese films have also been a site of continual discovery and rediscovery, as fifth- generation mainland filmmakers were linked to the rise and fall of film-making in Hong Kong and Taiwan. Some directors have become canonical—Wong Kar Wai, Jia Zhangke, Hou Hsiao-hsien—others have become more identified with popular films, like John Woo or Zhang Yimou. And festivals have looked farther afield, to find Chinese in Malaysia, Australia, and other areas as discoveries within a tradition. Meanwhile, filmmakers like Wong have left their regional base behind—as Thierry Fremaux proudly proclaimed in 2007: "Film has become global. The best proof is the opening film, *My Blueberry Nights*, directed by a Chinese man from Hong Kong, produced with European money, shot in America and in English."[36]

Discovery still has its limits. In the case of Cannes, two-thirds of all winning directors since 1949 have held European citizenship (and another sixteen have had American citizenship). All but one have been male. And only Mohammad Lakhdar-Hamina of Algeria (*Chronicle of the Burning Years* [*Chronique des années de braise*], Cannes, 1975) and South Africa's Mark Dormford-May (*U-Carmen e-Khayelitsha*, Berlin, 2005) have gained prizes as African directors among all major festivals.

Once discoveries "become established," they become traditions through invitations to film festivals. Using Romanian cinema as a recent case, I will show how "discovery" took place within the film festival world and examine the textual elements of these films to find out what is "new" about this cinema to frame my final reading. I will also show how a school became established as a part of the festival world rather than a fringe.

Discovering Romania

Until Nicolae Ceausescu was executed in 1989, post–World War II Romanian cinema followed a trajectory similar to that of most communist bloc Eastern European countries' cinema: many propaganda films as well as underground films that did not see the light until after the 1989 Romanian Revolution. Romanian films were shown at the Balkan Film Festival, which wandered from Turkey (1979) to Slovenia (1980); they were also shown in China because of the ideological affinity of the second world. Meanwhile, Romania joined other Eastern Bloc countries in withdrawing its films from the Berlin festival in 1979 in protest of its showing of *The Deer Hunter*.

This period has taken on a certain mythic power in the story of Romanian cinema—not unlike the rivalry with Hollywood that shapes American independents. For example, a *Washington Post* article of 1990 spent almost more time on what could not be shown than on the first Romanian films making it to Western screens:

> "Ceausescu didn't really let people make contemporary stories," says AFI programmer Eddie Cockrell, curator of the festival. "They could only make fantasies or stories on historical figures. But the filmmakers coded things into the films—like, they'd make a medieval fantasy about an awful king who is overthrown by the people. You don't have to be a film school student to figure that one out."
>
> Cockrell would visit Bucharest every year after attending the Berlin Film Festival. Each time he would ask officials at the state film office if he could see the highly regarded "Carnival Days," the festival's comedy, and, he says, "they always came up with some excuse. They couldn't find it or whatever. You read between the lines and know that the film has been banned."
>
> This year, when he walked into the office, the film canisters were sitting on the desk. "They all looked so proud," he says, "finally being able to present this film."[37]

By the early 1990s, with the breakdown of the communist bloc in Eastern Europe, many banned Romanian films and other films from Central and Eastern Europe gained wider exposures in different festivals, from the post-communist Karlovy Vary to Berlin. By the mid-1990s, Balkan films were gaining prizes, with Emir Kusturica winning his second Palme d'Or for *Underground* at Cannes in 1995. Lucian Pintille, a Romanian director, also scored festival accolades, including nominations at Cannes and Venice, with *Next Stop Paradise* (*Terminus paradis*, 1998) winning the Grand Jury Prize in Venice. However, regime change also posed a historical problem raised by a transitional official: "Every good film in Eastern Europe was an anti-Communist idea," said Adrian Sarbu, chief of the Bureau of Cinema and Television for Romania's governing National Salvation Front. "We have good filmmakers . . . now we have to find the ideas."[38]

The Romanian cinema that became the talk of the festival circuit responded to this challenge through filmmakers who were very young when the revolution took place in 1989, including Cristi Puiu, Cristian Mungiu, Corneliu Porumboiu, Sinisa Dragin, Radu Muntean, Radu Mihauleanu, Catalin Mitulescu, and the late Cristian Nemescu. Their films screened at the local Romanian festival, Transylvania, before "graduating" to regional festivals in Sarajevo, Thessaloniki, and Karlovy Vary. From there, they were "discovered" by larger Western European festivals like London, Locarno, Copenhagen, Rotterdam, and Cannes. In 2006, for example, Corneliu Porumboiu's *12:08 East of Bucharest* reached the British Film Institute's London festival; it took the Golden Swan in Copenhagen in 2007, following Radu Mihauleanu's *Live and Become* that had taken the same prize in 2005.

Soon, discoveries became established on the festival circuit—becoming new knowledge to be shared with wider local audiences after the films had been recognized by film elites. In North America, Toronto, Telluride, Chicago, and the New York Film Festival programmed new Romanian films. In 2008, the New York Film Festival also organized a special Romanian retrospective program that showcased eighteen features from 1965 to 2006. When a cinema is "discovered," it is not uncommon for festivals to search for old and new movies from this region, reinforcing the history and complexity of this national cinema. By 2007, Romanian film had become a canonical discovery for festivals outside the Euro-American context: that year, they were also showcased in Hong Kong as a discovery for the audiences of the HKIFF.

Films and filmmakers have been caught up in the process of discovery. After Cristian Mungiu received his Palme d'Or at Cannes in 2007, he noted in a press conference in Bucharest, "If I had presented the same film in 2002, the likelihood that I would have received the Palme d'Or would have been almost nil. . . . But I capitalised on the growing sympathy for Romanian cinema."[39] Mingiu articulated the fact that discovery is a process: the wave of successes gained by Romanian films in the previous years and the reception they received made it possible for 4 *Months* to win the Palme d'Or. *California Dreaming* won the Grand Prize in Un Certain Regard that same year, following the tragic death of its director, Cristian Nemescu, before he finished editing his film; Cristi Puiu, whose *Stuff and Dough* (*Marfa şi banii,* 2001) was one of the harbingers of the new wave, was on the jury that year. Subsequently, *Police, Adjective* won a Jury Prize in Cannes in 2009 and Florin Serban's first feature, *If I Want to Whistle, I Whistle,* won the Silver Bear in Berlin in 2010.

Is there any stylistic coherence in this group of New Romanian Cinema besides an historical one? According to A. O. Scott of the *New York Times,* beyond historical circumstances, a social cohesion among many filmmakers evokes the sociability of the French New Wave: "Mungiu, Porumboiu and Nemescu are all U.N.A.T.C. graduates, and Puiu currently teaches courses there in screen acting."[40] Many use the same pool of behind-the-scenes technicians as well as the same actors. In terms of basic style, they favor hand-held cameras (as well as long shots with stationary cameras) in many of their movies, but these qualities are hardly unique to Romanian films. Stylistically, the very fluid hand-held camera in *The Death of Mr. Lazarescu* works very well with the chaotic and depressing environments Mr. Lazarescu inhabits, from his seedy apartment to the different rundown hospital emergency rooms he wanders through. Similarly, the one very long shot on the television show in *12:08 East of Bucharest,* which simulates bad television studio camerawork, is extremely well done and exposes the farce of the whole enterprise. As in many festival films, locations use different rooms in everyday people's apartments, drab offices, and bland cityscapes, but overall ordinary places. These create a sense that the New Romanian Cinema is a neo-realist cinema built on the absurd but actually debilitating lives Romanian people led before the revolution that have somehow continued since.

If discovery did not mean new styles, what about themes? All these films come from—and respond to—the same political, cultural, and social milieu. Many directly deal with Nicolae Ceauşescu and the Romanian Revolution of 1989, like *12:08 East of Bucharest*, or *The Paper Will Be Blue*. The former is a comedy about a festival in a small town, while the latter follows a soldier on the night of the revolution who decides to fight for the cause. Other films tackle the absurdity of Romanian transitional society, including the bureaucratic horrors of socialist medicine in *The Death of Mr. Lazarescu* or *Police, Adjective*, where a small crime story is intertwined with meditations on language and action. The most recent films have a somewhat more global gaze: *If I Want to Whistle, I Whistle*, though set in Romania, centers on prison, family relationships, and European migration. *California Dreaming* deals with American and Polish peacekeepers in 1999 Yugoslavia, confronted by small-town Romanian bureaucracy. Reading the films as a group, they seem to have created a mythic Romania, where pre-1989 meant only a very oppressive communist regime, while since 1989 the country has become lackluster dystopia with a government that seems to have inherited many of the old communist ways of running things. Filmmakers thus echo the position of Cristi, the hero in *Police, Adjective*: "His position is a hyperbolically blunt statement of an impulse that drives much recent Romanian cinema, away from metaphor and toward a concrete, illusion-free reckoning with things as they are."[41]

Further twists come in attitude. Many films insist that one way to deal with the unhappy situation of the country is dark comedy, an absurd humor that permeates *The Death of Mr. Lazarescu*, *12:08 East of Bucharest*, and *California Dreaming*, where corrupt buffoons run different institutions and other everyday people are incompetent, uncaring, or liars. Many of these characters are not particularly malicious; they are portrayed as they are because the society they live in tends to produce unthinking, selfish individuals who have ambiguous moralities. The individuals are not villains, but byproducts of a corrupted system that becomes a dark farce glimpsed through small, almost insignificant moments. In most places, when a sick person needs help from an emergency room, he is admitted, but obviously this is not in the case for Mr. Lazarescu. When there is a television talk show, one expects a knowledgeable host and guest, but in *12:08 East of Bucharest*, a retiree who once played Santa Claus and a drunken teacher are ingredients for great comedy.

Thus, many of the tropes of new Romanian film are familiar characteristics of the film festival genre—serious themes, meditative cinematography and texts, absence of closure and happy endings. Overall, there are more thematic similarities and innovations among these movies than purely formal elements that are considered new. The tastemakers of film festivals seem to be more excited about works coming from a "new" area, an area that has not experienced the kind of cinematic fervor, at least in the context of the festival world, that favored Iran in the 1990s. There was little exposure to communist or post-communist Romanian life on the movie screen until these new films arrived at these Western European, then global festivals. Obviously, by all accepted standards, these are very good movies that brought a freshness both in terms of subject matter and style. Hence, discovery enriches and develops the genre and, ultimately, the canon of films we consider important in cinema as a field.

As these discussions show, there is no simple definition of what a festival film should be. I have identified certain formal, textual, and contextual characteristics in narrative feature films that seem to recur in many works that are either shown or have won prizes in the major festivals. In the following section, I use these different criteria to read a recent Romanian Cannes winner within the parameters of the festival film.

4 Months, 3 Weeks, and 2 Days:
Reading the Festival Film

4 Months, 3 Weeks, and 2 Days won the Palme d'Or at Cannes in 2007 and went on to win twenty-three other prizes all over the world, in the Americas, Europe, and Australia. It was a low-budget film that cost only 600,000 euros to make.[42] It was Cristian Mungiu's second feature; he had trained as a filmmaker in Bucharest and produced shorts before his first feature, *Occident* (2002), which had been included in the Directors' Fortnight at Cannes and had won a few prizes at local and regional festivals, such as Transylvania, Thessaloniki, and Sofia (Bulgaria). *Occident*, considered a bitter comedy, tells different stories about Romanian immigrants seeking the illusory happiness of the West. By contrast, *4 Months, 3 Weeks, and 2 Days* is a dark, hopeless portrayal of an abortion in Bucharest, Romania, during the last days of communist rule. Mungiu's latest work, *Tales from the Golden Age* (2009), an omnibus comedy on life in late communist Romania, also premiered at Cannes.

4 Months focuses on two female university students, Gabita, who is pregnant, and her friend, Otilia, who helps her to make the illegal abortion happen. The film is minimalist even though there is a great deal of "action" and drama. The women have to get enough money, procure the supplies, and check into hotels: the first hotel will not let them in, so they must find another hotel that costs more. Otilia carries the movie because she is the one who runs around the city to help Gabita, all the while negotiating her relationship with her own boyfriend and everyone else in Romania. She also meets the abortionist in some street and must deal with his anger that there is a change of location and that Gabita is four months pregnant, rather than three months as she had told both Otilia and subsequently the "doctor." He is abusive and demands more money and sex with both women. After the abortion, Otilia leaves to attend a dinner party with her boyfriend, where moral issues are raised in conversation against the offstage drama of the hotel room. Otilia returns to the room, drops the fetus in a trash chute, and the girls end up at dinner, where they agree that they will never talk about this subject again.

The camerawork is austere, with very controlled camera movements, long takes, and lighting that projects a depressed, oppressive environment all through the movie. It was shot on location in a university dormitory, hotel lobbies and rooms, family homes, and the streets of Bucharest. The sets all share dreadful lighting and colors. The first two shots of the film last for about five minutes. The first is a hand-held medium shot inside the bland but lived-in university dorm room of the two women. The camera points toward the window, but moves slightly forward and backward to show specific actions, which situates the audience as witnesses of the story to be unfolded. Gabita and Otilia are packing, making small talk on what is needed for some trip away. The second shot follows Otilia out of the dorm room to look for the small things that Gabita needs. The hand-held camera takes the audience through the dark hallway of the university dorm and reveals some aspects of student lives, into the shower and bathroom as well as another dorm room that also serves as a general store for the students. A simple exchange between Otilia and another student in the bathroom reveals the everyday "rules" of this society. Otilia is told by the other student that the lady officer is looking for her because she was not there on Thursday—a form of constant surveillance. In that short exchange, Otilia ends the conversation by asking if the lady officer smokes and what brand—a minor act of bribery is anticipated and expresses the everydayness of corruption. The audience, without much probing, comes to understand certain aspects of Romanian life of the time—from surveillance and the power of people in certain positions, to the need to bribe someone in authority and the underground economy of the students on basic consumer goods. What is presented is the routine of that Romania world; minute details are expressed without specifically asking for the audience's attention.

The film has many long shots that last for three minutes or more. After the abortionist has sex with Otilia, she talks with Gabita and asks why they chose Mr. Bebe. It is a medium-profile shot of Otilia sitting across from Gabita, who is in bed. Another very long shot is filmed with Otilia sitting at the dinner table with her boyfriend's family and friends. Otilia has just been forced to have sex with Mr. Bebe in order to have him perform the abortion; Gabita is in the process of having the abortion. No one surrounding her knows or cares what she is going through. The one long shot simply lets the conversation take place without Otilia; the fear apparent on her unsettling face dominates the scene, yet all the minute gestures and small talk around the table meld together to sums up the oppressive environment of the last days of Romanian communist rule.

The film makes no direct political statements of any kind, but simply shows, with a great deal of care and craft, the quotidian tyranny people lived with under Ceauşescu. There is not a single government official of any kind in the movie; instead, the movie shows how ordinary people act under such a repressive regime. The film is demanding because it presents situations and asks the audience to work with it to find the many meanings. For example, except for the two leads, most characters have an air of dictatorial authority and no empathy, whether hotel clerks, the families and friends of the boyfriend, or the abortionist.

While the narrative is linear and the film follows clear temporal and spatial continuity, it does not start or end with classical equilibrium. It starts with a crisis and ends with the conclusion of a horrific event that demoralizes all involved and which the characters are determined to erase from their memory. At the same time, the form, narrative, and questions of the film have made it difficult for spectators to do precisely that, sparking debates that have spilled out of screenings ever since. This, too, is part of the power of a great festival film.

Conclusion

The old Eastern Europe provided film festivals with a fresh area to explore in the twenty-first century. Even though it had been nearly two decades since the collapse of communism in the area, Western Europeans want to learn more about this area. Festival programmers want to explore the impact of communism in unknown sites, even though the festivals are only several hundred miles away, especially when "truth" is presented with a festival aesthetic and new twists by a strong group of young filmmakers. Communism and totalitarianism are favored topics and areas in film festivals; Chinese and Iranians have both received considerable successes at film festivals, in counterpoint to their regimes. Yet, even as Romanians relish their success, programmers are looking for the next wave, whether from Israel, Argentina, Malaysia, or some other vantage.

Overall, there is not a single formula for festival films or festival success. However, if we study the "successful" festival films, those that have won prizes and garnered a great deal of attention, we see that almost all are "serious" films, films that require work and do not allow the audience to just sit back and be manipulated. Carefully constructed rather than spectacular, austere and evocative rather than pedestrian, novel but referential, festival films may not constitute a genre per se but do constitute a process of genrification, to use Altman's terms. As mentioned at the very beginning of the chapter, it is far easier to define what festival films are not than what they are or will be. Nevertheless, they are anchored by their relationships to production, markets, discussion, and audiences, as we will see in future chapters.

3

Auteurs, Critics, and Canons

EXTRATEXTUAL ELEMENTS
AND THE CONSTRUCTION
OF FESTIVAL FILMS

In the last chapter, I explored festival films as textual objects in order to elucidate features and structures that loosely mark them as a group. Textual examination of film, however, is always incomplete and can only provide partial meaning for the practices of festival films. These texts demand coordinated or competing efforts by different parties and contexts to endow them with meanings and values. This chapter thus complements the last with a focus on the extratextual elements of festival films. In particular, I move beyond films as texts to look at people and institutions of filmmaking and their roles in festivals. Borrowing from Rick Altman's approach to film genre, I begin to situate these films in the contexts of the different agents who are related to the films, including directors/auteurs, the festival apparatus, and the critics and how all these audiences contribute to the meaning of festival films. Altman's use of Ludwig Wittgenstein's game theory proves relevant in explaining how festival films can be identified and used from very different, competing angles and contexts as a "struggle among users." By examining the processes in which some "successful" figures and their films became canonical in film studies, I dissect how different communities—programmers, producers, institutions, viewers, and critics—compete to define festival films and film knowledge. I also show how festivals support this process by reinforcing meanings and strategies of the auteur and training "future masters," as well as reading works in conjunction with other institutions. As in the previous chapter, I will work with concrete examples of auteurs and films, looking first at Michelangelo Antonioni and his L'avventura to illuminate the classic festivals of the 1960s before turning to Abbas Kiarostami and Taste of Cherry (Ta'm-e guilass, 1997) to illuminate contemporary trends. In both cases, I begin with an examination of the director and context and the work. Later, I return to the film and filmmaker as foci of critical discourses. The chapter concludes with reflections from both filmmakers and retrospective festivals on the processes through which film knowledge has been constructed.

This intimate relationship is not, of course, a mystery to those who construct film festivals. In a 2007 interview, Gilles Jacob and Thierry Fremaux of Cannes stressed the interplay of festival, film, and auteur over time:

Jacob says Cannes has been "a sentinel before its time. It has always resisted pressure, it has always fought against all censorship. . . . It saw the arrival of a *cinèma d'auteur* and rode its ascension. Finally, it knew to invite the biggest international stars along with the most unique film-makers."

That mix has made Cannes unique over time. Fremaux, who is charged with putting together the official selection, says: "We mustn't close the door to anyone. The best is when stars are in auteur films such as Nicole Kidman in *Dogville*, Brad Pitt in *Babel* and this year Angelina Jolie in *A Mighty Heart*. It's also good to see Leonardo DiCaprio produce an important documentary like *The 11th Hour*. Stars protect the auteurs but without the auteurs there wouldn't be a festival."[1]

Canonical films emerge from a process of creation that involves both artists and finance, often triangulated through festivals. After a film has found a place in a festival, film critics, festival programmers, and scholars may extend or curtail its reputation, distribution, and the career of its director/auteur beyond the festivals. Reception can be measured by circulation of the film through festivals, which often garner more reviews and more retrospectives and help the work reach a larger audience. Positive reception is crucial to the success of young filmmakers, who need to continue to make films and build their reputations. Reception practices, especially in the form of film criticism and film studies, contribute to legitimation and canonization of certain works, and of mature directors as master artists of significant viewpoints (auteurs) as well.

Yet, most films and directors screened in film festivals do not enter the elusive, ever changing world of competing film canons. Only a handful gain the kind of attention that would lead to inclusion in the pantheon of great cinema that I have loosely labeled the canon. As much as there are complicated, codependent relationships between Hollywood and film festivals, Hollywood and festival films also share many top one hundred film lists generated by different institutions worldwide.[2] Moreover, film festivals do not control the composition of art film canons either; they form parts of larger communities—critics, scholars, museum curators, film archivists, cinephiles, and film business people—who negotiate the status of these films: precisely those voices identified in chapter 1 as Miriam Hansen's discursive horizons. Hence, Peter Wollen describes canon formation as "a complex process of cultural negotiation among a motley set of cultural gate-keepers, ourselves included."[3] In canon formation, the main roles associated with film festivals are to launch new cinemas—individual films, auteurs, traditions, and movements—and to reproduce and add value to these films and their affiliates. The former is managed by selection; the latter process means continued invitation of auteurial films to festivals and competitions, selection of filmmakers as jurors, and hosting critical panels and retrospectives. Finally, film festivals bring different people together to see and talk about these films, allowing them to network with one another and to continue conversations on the films depending on their different capacities.

By scrutinizing the production and reception of these films, I bring the analysis back to the role of film festivals in promoting primary aspects of films beyond the screen. Rick Altman's insistence on genres as processes that undergo constant "genrification" and modifications is especially illuminating. Even though festival films constitute a vague genre, and are oftentimes antigeneric, as discussed in the last chapter, Altman's argument that "genre production is regularly allied with decorum, nature, science, and other standards produced and defended by the sponsoring society"[4] converges with Pierre Bourdieu's idea of habitus to illuminate how certain film festivals' standards are refracted in some of these films and filmmakers and in the processes that support them. Film festivals are indeed one of the "sponsoring societies" of festival films, where critics and theorists "always participate in and further the work of various institutions." Here the institutions for Altman's idea about genre are "production companies, exhibition practices, the critical establishment, and government agencies"[5] that parallel many festival-related institutions.

Genre is tied to audience expectations as well. The festivals' varied audiences include "regular" moviegoers, programmers, critics, scholars, and film professionals. The festivals themselves articulate views in their Web sites, blogs, publications, and above all in their selections of films to be included in the programs and the juries' articulations of why certain films deserve accolades. In film festivals, though, specific audiences may have expectations and readings that overlap or differ with those of the critics and jurors. When discussing reading positions, are there intertextualities intrinsic to festival films? Altman's ideas about genre communities and constellate communities are helpful in studying the festival films' interpretive communities. Business and critical communities of the film festivals often have interpretative lenses that diverge from those of the films' or auteurs' home communities. Local communities diverge in standards and preferences from those of the global (albeit often Western-oriented) film communities. Many festival filmmakers are better known around the film festivals circuit and abroad than at home, whether Abbas Kiarostami, the early Zhang Yimou, or Emir Kusturica. Indeed, when Zhang Yimou became better known in China by the turn of the century, his films became less important in the festival world. His stature within China, for both the government and the general public, has grown a great deal as a result of his shift from austere festival films to dark comedies, large expensive costume epics, and works like the opening ceremony of the 2008 Beijing Olympics. This counter example demarcates the complicated rewards an auteur can win in different contexts, including but transcending the film festival.[6]

Beyond interpretive communities, national and regional politics shape readings, reception, and promotion of films. As we have seen, geopolitics influences the selection and readings of films in festivals, while national funds support art films as well as European festivals, and the MEDIA program of the European Union has played a major role in promoting European films.[7] The place of American cinema in festivals, as discussed in previous chapters, also has a great deal to do with specific interpretations of what Americanness means globally at particular times. American films that won prizes in the Victoria War era, for example, were fairly critical of U.S. politics and culture.

Moving beyond Western Europe and the United States, cinemas from diverse countries have been favorites of film festivals in different times. While films from the "West" have always remained central to film festivals, movies made outside these regions became successful in successive waves, meeting the need for novelty discussed in the last chapter. There is no single clear geopolitical reason why Japanese and Indian films were popular in the 1950s, any more than one might have predicted the rise of Iranian and Chinese cinema in the 1990s or Korean, Romanian, and Israeli cinemas in the twenty-first-century festival world. The very idea that these cinemas were new, different, and exotic to the Western European sensibilities would better explain the kinds of positive festival reception these cinemas have received over the years. This inevitably involves ideas about otherness and difference that Bill Nichols has raised in analyzing the relationship between the Western audience and Iranian cinema in a festival setting. Nichols asserts that encountering these films allows one to experience "going native," to have a "fascination with the strange," and to qualify one to be "citizen[s] of a global but still far from homogeneous culture."[8] However, this othering is not always between equals: the top festivals are the ones holding the power to decide what "others" are to be liked. Hence, Malaysian filmmaker Mansor Bin Puteh replied in a July 1997 letter to Cannes via *Time*:

Why are the same film makers from Asia getting recognition in Cannes? The answer is that they are making the types of films which are liked in Cannes. Basically there only five types of films; those that deal with, 1) poverty or illiteracy, 2) homosexuality or incest, 3) anti-government sentiments, 4) anti-colonialism, and 5) historical or costume epics. Asian filmmakers must make one of those types in order to win recognition at Cannes. Abbas Kiarostami, Zhang Yimou, Chen Kaige, etc., are making only the type of film which deals with homosexual characters or which demeans their religion or society. China and Iran, which are rich in history and tradition, must surely have other interesting stories that could be put on the screen. Cannes has destroyed the very essence of cinema and made the medium one for forcing film makers to scream propaganda for them.[9]

The reception of broad international cinemas sheds light on the intricate interplay of film festival power in shaping global cinematic taste and individual careers.

This chapter begins with European art cinema, recognizing the intimate relation I have underscored for art and festival films in the last chapter. Most of the auteurs of European art cinema had their works shown at film festivals from the 1960s to the 1970s. David Bordwell, Steve Neale, and others have written extensively on this particular film movement and have provided the English-speaking world with an idea of European cinema as art cinema.[10] Andre Kovacs and Mark Betz have examined further the discourse surrounding European art cinema and assert that this movement is a product of overlapping "political, industrial, intellectual, and institutional forces" and the result of certain paradigms adopted by film history and film studies.[11] Using Michelangelo Antonioni's L'avventura (1961), I will explore how Antonioni's film festival successes contribute to the discourse of this particular film and auteur, and to a lesser extent, of European art cinema. While not gaining the Palme d'Or at Cannes, L'avventura won the Grand Prix; meanwhile, the negative audience reception at the premiere was legendary.

Moving away from Europe, this chapter will also examine Abbas Kiarostami and Taste of Cherry (1997), which was initially slated to compete at Venice in 1996. Postrevolutionary Iranian cinema was one of the most successful art film movements of the late twentieth century. The 1979 Islamic Revolution was not friendly to cinema, considering it to be a medium that was tainted by Western influence left over from the deposed shah. However, with an established film production infrastructure and very delicate interplay among filmmakers, audiences, and the Islamic authorities, Iranian cinema has enjoyed both domestic and international successes since the 1980s.[12] Due to technical difficulties, Taste of Cherry did not finish on time for Venice and went to Cannes instead—a mark of the status Kiarostami had already attained as an auteur. Before arriving at Cannes, the film was initially banned from export in late April, but it was eventually cleared by the Iranian authorities in early May.

By scrutinizing these two directors and specific films and their reception, I show how film festivals' critical discourses have guided these films and directors to the status they enjoy today. Both films are recognized as cinematic masterpieces, evident in the amount of critical works devoted to them. While they represent two different periods, in both cases there is a history of reflection and dialogues of interpretation that we can follow over years of change. Other examples of auteurs and films will also be introduced as necessary to highlight relevant aspects of this extratextual cinematic discourse.

Michelangelo Antonioni

The discourse on European art cinema extends beyond the film texts to a movement that galvanized a whole generation of cinephiles on both sides of the

Atlantic from the late 1960s. Its controversies and successes, in fact, made possible the growth of film festivals in the subsequent decades and the extension of discursive horizons around film as art into universities, museums, and multiple journalistic outlets from the press to the Internet.

The New York Film Festival's reputation in its beginning in 1963 was very much tied into the success of European art cinema. The Americans Amos Vogel and Richard Roud looked to Europe and European film festivals to program the New York festival. This included the auteur cinema of the late 1950s to about the late 1970s, a realm of production, discovery, and critique that encompassed the reevaluation of old Hollywood masters, the French Nouvelle Vague, the British New Wave, New German Cinema, and New Italian Cinema, among other movements. The names are those whom we now easily recognize from film textbooks, university courses, and festival retrospectives: Michelangelo Antonioni, Federico Fellini, Roberto Rossellini, Jean-Luc Godard, François Truffaut, Alain Resnais, Rainer Werner Fassbinder, Werner Herzog, Margarethe von Trotta, Wim Wenders, Lina Wertmuller, Ingmar Bergman, Carlos Saura, Andrzej Wajda, and others. Scholarship also "discovered" auteurs in earlier cinema, including Hollywood, to extend and round out this canonical unity.[13]

Postwar Italian cinema had an abundance of prominent directors, from the neorealists—Roberto Rossellini, Vittorio de Sica—to the personal styles of Luchino Visconti, Pier Paolo Pasolini, Federico Fellini, and others. Michelangelo Antonioni was very much a colleague of these filmmakers. While his films are demanding, they also have garnered a great deal of commercial success both inside and outside Italy. He became an absolute international sensation after *L'avventura* was screened for competition with Fellini's *La dolce vita* at Cannes in 1961. *La dolce vita* won the Palme d'Or and *L'avventura* won the Grand Prix. The following years, Antonioni's *La notte* won the Golden Bear at Berlin, *L'eclisse* (1962) gained a Grand Jury Prize at Cannes, and *Il deserto rosso* (1964) received a Golden Lion at Venice. These films also sparked debates that continue into the present.

Antonioni was born in 1913 to a wealthy family in Ferrara, a small city north of Bologna. After graduating from the University of Bologna, he became a film critic for a Ferrara newspaper. He moved to Rome in 1938 and wrote for the film magazine *Cinema* for a few months. In Axis Italy, he collaborated with Rossellini on the 1942 *A Pilot Returns* (*Un pilota ritorna*), a Fascist film that celebrates Italian efforts in the war, based on a novel by Vittorio Mussolini. He was then drafted, but was never sent to the front. He started making a documentary, *People of the Po Valley* (*Gente del Po*); due to the war, the film was not finished until 1947.

After the war, Antonioni worked as a translator, film critic, and scriptwriter for Visconti's "Furore" and "Il processo di Maria Tarnouska," scripts that were never made into films. He also made several short films. While not a neorealist, Antonioni's documentary works exhibit the influence of that period and style.

He worked consistently in the 1950s, making *Story of a Love Affair* (*Cronaca di un amore*) in 1950, and gaining successes in Italian-friendly festivals—*The Girlfriends* (*Le amiche*, 1955) for a Silver Lion at Venice, and *The Cry* (*Il grido*, 1957) taking the grand prize from the Association de la Presse Cinématographique Suisse at Locarno. His rise amid the upswing in Italian cinema in the 1960s propelled his career onto the international stage. Yet *La dolce vita* and *L'avventura* also had strongly national roots. Peter Brunette agreed with Italian critic Gian Piero Brunetta that 1959–1960 constituted the "annus mirabilis of postwar Italian cinema."[14] Italy had recovered from the war, and its subsequent soul searching in understanding the failure of Fascism is expressed in these films. According to Brunette, citing Brunetta, monumental changes in Italian society, including the birth of a center- left government, the rapid process of industrialization, migration, and changes in social norms, allowed cinema to comment on these conditions.[15] As in American cities like New York at the turn of the twentieth century, the discourse of cinema contributed to how one defined the new societies with new experiences in time and space, class, gender, and ethnicities.

Yet these films were not products for a working-class nickelodeon. Italian cinema of the 1960s was serious, artistic, and very middle class, reacting to the demands of the renewed affluent bourgeois society after the trauma of being a defeated and bombed nation. In fact, according to Pierre Sorlin, because of the decline of cinemagoers since the 1950s, film exhibitors and, in turn, producers had devised new strategies to confront this situation. There had been an increasing division between the demands for content of the urban audience and the rural or small-town audience, at least as perceived by the film producers. In the center city, fewer tickets were sold, but they charged more. And other cinemas might sell more tickets, but commanded a smaller market share. Since urban tickets cost more, there was incentive to make "quality" films that attracted the educated and affluent class; the proliferation of Italian art cinema, supported by the Italian industry, can partly be attributed to this trend.[16] These serious films also found a wider audience around the world, making it possible for Antonioni to continue to make fairly large-budget films with major actors. Along this career trajectory, film festivals were one of the driving forces to keep, nurture, and renew his status within the larger discourse of serious cinema.

L'avventura cemented the reputation of Antonioni on the world stage. Like many of Antonioni's films, *L'avventura* focuses on the follies of upper-middle-class Italians. A plot synopsis cannot do justice to the film, but its very sparseness illustrates the irrelevance of plot. A group of well-off haute and petite northern Italian bourgeoisie goes on a yachting trip off Sicily. Anna, who is the girlfriend of Sandro, disappears when the group docks next to a barren rock called Bianca. The group initially tries earnestly to look for Anna; however, after a while, her disappearance becomes irrelevant. Sandro starts a relationship with Anna's best friend, Claudia. They eventually become lovers, yet Sandro once again cheats on

Claudia. Then the movie ends with a long shot of Sandro crying, with Claudia standing beside him lightly touching his hair against the backdrop of Mount Etna and a concrete wall dividing the two halves of the screen.

The film's initial screening at Cannes, however, became a scene of film mythology. Angry audiences jeered and walked out because of its "incoherence." Penelope Houston, the editor of *Sight and Sound,* explained her initial viewing of the film, "At Cannes . . . attention had to be agonizingly divided between the screen and one's neighbor. A long love scene set off a fusillade of angry jeering and one wondered whose moral susceptibilities were being outraged; a reiterated shot of a girl running down a corridor brought bellows of 'cut': and the last scene went through to derisive howls of 'He's crying! Look, he's crying!' It was an ugly and unforgettable reception, compounded in about equal parts of moral indignation and boredom, and it effectively wrecked concentration for the rest of us."[17] An open letter, signed by the likes of Rossellini and members of the jury and the press, was sent to protest the hostilities exhibited the previous day in the film's screening. The subsequent and fervent embrace of the film by critics helped make Antonioni a favorite of the film aficionados.

Antonioni continued to make *La notte, L'eclisse,* and *Il desserto rosso,* which all garnered awards and commercial successes. With the success of the European art

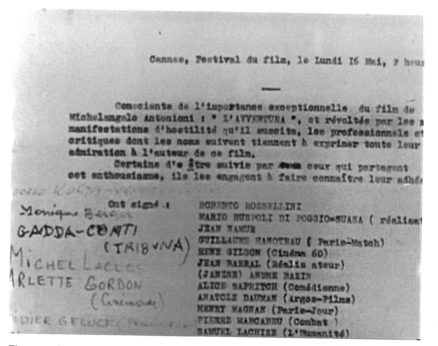

Figure 6. Letter in support of *L'avventura,* signed by Roberto Rossellini and others, May 16, 1961, one day after the screening at Cannes.
Source: Gianfranco Mingozzi, *Antonioni: Documents and Testimonials,* 1966.

film on the world stage, Antonioni was able to secure a major three-film production deal with the backing of major producer Carlo Ponti and the Hollywood studio MGM. The three films were *Blow-Up* (1966), *Zabriskie Point* (1970), and *The Passenger* (1975), all in English—which raised his questions of meaning and alienation across wider North American screens and audiences. However, after *The Passenger*, Antonioni's career never regained the flair that characterized his earlier prominence.

In the early 1970s, the Chinese communist government invited Antonioni to shoot a documentary about China. Chinese authorities were not happy with the final product, and it was banned there along with all the director's films until 2004. Nonetheless, the film, *China* (*Chung kuo–Cina*, 1972), has enjoyed a revival in recent years, including a new reflective documentary, *China Is Far Away— Antonioni and China* (2008) by Liu Haiping that was screened with it at the 2009 Hong Kong International Film Festival.

Antonioni also made a television movie, *The Mystery of Oberwald* (1981), his only period piece, with Monica Vitti. In 1982, his *Identification of a Woman* was nominated for competition at Cannes. The film is about a director looking for a female star and a girlfriend. It is not a remake of *8½*, but a more conventional film than his earlier work, with more psychologically credible characters. Besides making films, Antonioni published *The Architecture of Vision: Writings and Interviews on Cinema* (1996), which explains, in his own words, his theories on cinema.

Antonioni had a stroke in 1985 that left him paralyzed on his right side and took away his ability to speak. With the help of his wife, Enrica, he continued to make a few documentaries. In 1995, he and Wim Wenders made *Beyond the Clouds*, which premiered at the Venice festival. He also contributed to two omnibus films, one to celebrate the World Cup in Rome in 1990, and another one, *Eros* (2004), with Steven Soderbergh and Wong Kar Wai. The latter also premiered at Venice, out of competition. Antonioni died on July 30, 2007.

Two points emerge from this biographical overview. First, Antonioni's career was shaped by filmic opportunities built around the seriousness of his cohort and the festivals of his eras, which not only showcased but promoted his work. He was not averse to "popular" films, nor to work with mainstream producers like Carlo Ponti or stars like Jack Nicholson or Monica Vitti. At the same time, he continued to explore issues across fields, including not only features but also documentaries, which embodied both his first and final productions.

Second, although Antonioni is an undisputed auteur, not all his films are undisputed masterpieces. Because of his stature, his later films—*Identification of a Woman* and *Beyond the Clouds*—continued to be invited by all different kinds of festivals and younger directors sought to collaborate with him. Once a director is recognized, festivals see the acknowledgment as some kind of assurance of quality, and many audiences react this way too. Festivals are more likely to repeatedly invite his or her works, even though the reception to the film could be more lukewarm. This contributes to a narrative that emphasizes Antonioni's most "important" works as those that define him. A more detailed discussion of the process of the construction of this auteur and *L'avventura* will follow after an introduction to Iranian cinema and the dominant figure of Abbas Kiarostami.

Abbas Kiarostami

Iran has undergone great changes during Abbas Kiarostami's lifetime, from rule by a despotic shah, Mohammad Reza Shah Pahlavi—who was "Westernized" through intense U.S. influence—to the forward-looking and hopeful Islamic Revolution in 1979, which evolved into another repressive regime under the Ayatollah Khomeini and subsequent administrations. Kiarostami also experienced the devastating eight-year-long war between Iran and Iraq and the turbulent domestic situation between the conservative and relatively liberal fractions of the Islamic government since 2009 as well as a series of earthquakes that have killed thousands across Iran. Almost all these changes have become the stuff of his filmic vision.

Abbas Kiarostami was born in Tehran in 1940. He attended Tehran University in the Faculty of Fine Arts and started working in advertising, where he made over one hundred film advertisements. He then joined the Centre for the Intellectual Development of Children and Young Adults (Kanun) in 1969.[18] This center had been set up by the shah's photogenic wife, Farah Diba, in 1965 to promote print publications. The center became the major training ground for Kiarostami, and he directed his first ten-minute film, *The Bread and Alley (Nan va koutcheh)* for the center's nascent film section. The film won an award at the Tehran Fifth International Festival of Films for Children and Young Adults. He made quite a few short and feature films at Kanun with relative freedom until he left in 1992.

From the 1960s to the 1980s, meanwhile, amid great changes in Iranian society, the New Iranian Cinema emerged, influenced by masters of French cinema, such as Godard and Bresson. Mohammad Reza Shah Pahlavi supported cinemagoing as a modern mass entertainment, and commercial cinema was thriving. The shah and his wife launched the glitzy Tehran International Film Festival in 1972, "forerunner" of the Fajr festival today. At the same time, Daryush Mehrju's simple *The Cow (Gaav,* 1969) appeared, often described as the dawning work of New Iranian Cinema; this is a visual story about a man's deep bond with his cow, with much social commentary. The film was banned by the shah, but it was smuggled out and received both the Critic's Grand Prize at the Venice festival in 1971 and recognition from the Catholic Cinema Organization (OCIC) in Berlin in 1972. Subsequently, however, Iranian New Wave films of the 1970s were banned by the repressive Pahlavi government because of their progressive nature.

After the revolution, New Iranian Cinema, ironically, was again suppressed by the new regime, since the commercial cinema of Iran was regarded as a propaganda tool of the shah, spurring frequent attacks by the anti-shah groups before and after the revolution. Postrevolutionary cinema started to revive around 1983, with the establishment of the Farabi Cinema Foundation and the Fajr International Film Festival. Iranian cinema also started to gain recognition in Western film festivals. Amir Naderi's *The Runner* (1985) was shown in Venice and London and won the Grand Prize at the Nantes Festival of Three Continents. In 1990, the Pesaro Film Festival, in Italy, held a large-scale retrospective of Iranian cinema and helped launch it to the festival circuit.

Kiarostami's career took shape within these changes. In 1977, he made a relatively conventional narrative about a tax collector and his life, *The Report* (*Gozaresh*), aimed for the commercial market. According to film historian Alberto Elena, the movie was "rigidly censored" after the outbreak of the Islamic Revolution.[19] Amid turmoil, Kiarostami continued to make films with Kanun. These were not overtly political and often dealt with children. *Homework* (*Moshgh-e Shab*, 1989) is a documentary asking children what they think about their homework, while *Where Is the Friend's Home?* (*Khane-ye doust kodjast?*, 1987) chronicles a child's experience of returning a notebook to his classmate, who faces expulsion if he fails to do his homework again. These films show children's relationships with schools and homework, an indirect comment on the state apparatus of education, and also avoided problems that might be raised by Iranian censorship of male-female stories. *Where Is the Friend's Home?*, which had won awards at Fajr, propelled Kiarostami to the international festival scene when it won the Bronze Leopard at Locarno in 1989. Locarno, after Nantes and Pesaro, subsequently became an important festival gateway through which New Iranian Cinema moved onto the world stage.

Since 1990, all of Kiarostami's films have won awards in different festivals, from *Close-Up* (*Nema-ye Nazdik*, 1990) at Montreal and Istanbul to the Palme d'Or for *Taste of Cherry* (1997) at Cannes and a Grand Special Jury Prize at Venice for *The Wind Will Carry Us* (*Bad ma ra khahad bord*, 1999). He also was invited to contribute to the collective film project of *Lumière and Company* (*Lumière et compagnie*, 1995), where forty directors made shorts using Lumière equipment, a recognition that he had entered the cohort of world film auteurs. According to Azadeh Farahmand, the political and financial situations in Iran in the 1990s were also conducive to the positive reaction Iranian cinema received. Iranian film producers actively promoted Iranian cinema to the world, partly because of a more liberal government under Khatami that saw films as cultural tools to cement better global relationships. Financially, the removal of state subsidies in film production prompted more coproduction opportunities between Western European countries and Iranian filmmakers, resulting in coproduction with MK2, a French production and distribution company, and the likes of

Marco Müller, who was both a festival programmer and a film producer for Fabrica Production.²⁰

Kiarostami continued to be productive in the new century. He was also invited to make *Tickets* (2005) with Ken Loach and Ermanno Olmi, which premiered at Berlin in 2005, and another omnibus film celebrating the sixtieth anniversary of Cannes—*Chacun son cinéma*. Kiarostami has continued to make films, but his works have started to become more abstract and "cinematic" rather than merely spare. For example, *Ten* (2002) recounts ten conversations in a woman's car with her son and other women and *Five Dedicated to Ozu* (2003) offers five long shots of a beach area. *Shirin* (2008) literally reflects the theatrical staging of a twelfth-century Persian epic in the faces of its audience; the film premiered at Venice. Kiarostami returned to narrative art film with *Certified Copy* (2010), his first European production with a European cast, including the professional actress Juliette Binoche, and an Italian crew, which was in competition at Cannes. Binoche received the best actress award for her portrayal of a gallery owner living out a fictional history of marriage. Such collaborations, of non-Western auteurs working with European casts and crew, are not uncommon; Juliette Binoche, who had previously worked with Godard, starred in Hou Hsiao-hsien's 2007 *Flight of the Red Balloon* (*Le voyage du ballon rouge*). At the time of this writing, she is working with Jia Zhangke and Zhang Wen. This intricate relationship between these filmmakers and the film festival world, between the non-West and the West, between people who cannot really be defined as East or West, posits interesting questions about transnational negotiation on how and what films should be made. These negotiations are often played out at film festivals. Kiarostami's next project is *Father and Son*, with the actor Hamed Behdad from *No One Knows about Persian Cats*, hardly a newcomer to the festival world.

Like many other Kiarostami's films, *Taste of Cherry* can easily be labeled minimalist. It chronicles a man, Mr. Badii (played by Homayoun Ershadi), who drives his Range Rover on the dirt road outside Tehran. He stops many times to ask if people are interested in making some money. He is initially rejected by one man, who might have thought he was soliciting homosexual sex and returns his solicitation with angry reactions. Subsequently, he manages to invite a Kurdish soldier on holiday to his car and continues the drive and the conversation. When he stops the car, Mr. Badii finally explains his purpose—he is planning to commit suicide that night, and wants someone to go to the hole he has dug the next morning to see if he is still alive or dead. This frightens the young soldier, who runs away. Badii's proposal is then rejected by a religious Afghani seminarian. Eventually he is able to recruit a taxidermist, Mr. Bagheri, who is Turkish and has a sick child, to do the "work." During the drive, Bagheri tells him that he once tried to kill himself, but on his way he smelled mulberries, which he brought back to his wife to share. After the long drive sequences, the film shows Mr. Badii from the outside of his apartment in the evening, seemingly looking for things and turning the lights off. In the dark, he drives to the spot and lies down in the hole he has dug; a shot of the dark sky with moon and cloud follows and the screen fades to black. The last scene of the film, shot in video, has the actor playing Badii, Ershadi, smoking a cigarette, with the film crew and the soldiers who appeared in the film, and Louis Armstrong's "St. James Infirmary Blues" playing in the background.

Kiarostami came from a social, cultural, and political world quite different from that of Antonioni. His films reflect that world, although they have become increasingly abstract (and in ways, closer to the enigmatic seriousness of Antonioni). While he retains ties to Iran, sometimes conflictive, he has also become a fixture on the "A"-level festival circuit and has gained recognition as a modern auteur and, like Antonioni, a representative of an important national tradition of cinema. Having introduced these two auteurs and two major films in this festival context, I now turn to the broader extratextual discourse that surrounded these films, and in turn these filmmakers, to understand how all discursive horizons converged in the creation of the auteurs and their cinema as we know them today.

The Press, the Critics, and the Scholars

The 2009 Cannes festival drew 3,469 journalists from eighty-four countries.[21] They represented the trade press, film magazines, the general press, and television; most publish online versions of their reports. They are the major disseminators of information on film festivals to those who are not in attendance, and a primary link that connects diverse constituents of the festival—the lay audience, the cinephiles, the critics, the programmers, the producers, as well as the filmmakers—who all read these publications.

During the festivals, reviews of films and reports of deals circulate with intensity. The reviews from trade publications like *Screen International, Hollywood Reporter,* and *Daily Variety/Variety* often are the first major reviews festival films receive beyond blurbs in festival catalogs. At Cannes, major publications like the *New York Times,* the *Guardian, Le Monde,* and other global papers publicize these films in their respective countries. Papers from all over the world report on films, filmmakers, or stars, concentrating on participants in Cannes, rather than Cannes itself. These papers also highlight their national stars, filmmakers, and other related events. In addition to the traditional press, in the last two decades many Web sites' on-line publications have been devoted to cinema, including "fan" sites, official sites for specific films, and critical studies of films, like Senses of Cinema, which is based in Australia at RMIT University, and Film Reference (www.filmreference.com). These sites provide further layers of critical voices to many of the films shown in festivals.

Generally speaking, while the press covers the films and auteurs in a timely fashion, and in subsequent books, most scholars differ from film critics and journalists in that they have more time to do long-term research. Film scholars oftentimes are more detached from the direct business of film festivals, and most do not have the kind of access that journalists and film critics have to the film-makers and producers. There are exceptions: the late Peter Brunette, while chairing his film department at Wake Forest University, was a correspondent for *Hollywood Reporter*, and many film scholars have been regular contributors for film journals. When writing on their experiences at film festivals, they mostly report on the films. Nonetheless, their publications are academic, following the conventions of academia—that is, references to other sources, less breaking news, but more history and theory. Students as well as their peers culturally recognize their subject matters as worthy of studies in higher education. Even with the advent of cultural studies that affirm the value of mass popular culture, academic publications on cinema still concentrate on auteurs and "important" films, oftentimes festival films. More importantly, since they are part of the community of higher learning, they help legitimate the value of their studies—in this case, of cinema as a serious pursuit, as art. The rise of cinema studies as an academic field in the 1970s is part of the larger discourse on the changing values of cinema. Through my study of both the press and scholarly reception of Antonioni and Kiarostami and their films, I elucidate how these discourses cement the reputations of these auteurs and their works.

L'avventura was first mentioned in the *New York Times* in long-time critic Bosley Crowther's report on the Cannes Film Festival, "Another special prize was given to Michelangelo Antonioni's Italian film, 'The Adventure,' which had caused wide division in critical reaction at a showing earlier in the week."[22] Crowther concluded in the same piece that 1960 had not been a good festival year for Cannes. Eight days later, agreeing with his colleague, Robert Hawkins wrote under the headline "Focus on an Unimpressive Cannes Film Fete." Hawkins averred that "'L'Avventura' ('The Adventure') won a questionable jury prize. To be sure, its intentions are worthy and director Michelangelo Antonioni used his camera and actors with great skill. Yet the total effect of this diffuse and overlong film is one of continued boredom," hardly an endorsement.[23]

The event at Cannes in 1960 continued to circulate, and some saw the film differently. New York's *Village Voice* later recalled, "A mystery that casually abandons its ostensible premise midway through, *L'avventura* was the scandal of the 1960 Cannes Film Festival. Booing, which began before the movie's midway point, gave way to jeers with infuriated members of the international press hooting, 'Cut! Cut!' during the lengthy silent scenes or odd, yet purposeful, camera maneuvers. Nevertheless, *L'avventura* did receive a jury award and 35 critics signed a petition in its support. Cinema as temporal sculpture, *L'avventura* would be among the most influential of '60s movies."[24] Even World Socialist Web Site referenced the booing at Cannes: "When *L'Avventura* first premiered at the Cannes Film Festival, there were audience walkouts and booing from those offended by its rejection of conventional cinematic techniques. But the next day a group of leading filmmakers issued a statement praising the movie and it was given another screening, a 'special achievement' prize and quickly secured an international release."[25] Overall, there were different opinions on the film, not unlike the initial responses at Cannes.

Later in the year, the *New York Times* reported that the French Cinémathèque had presented a day-long retrospective of the works of little known but highly appreciated Italian director Michelangelo Antonioni: "The exhibition of 'L'Avventura' resulted in ecstatic effusions from every French intellectual worth his salt."[26] The report highlights the different reactions between the United States and France, which go far beyond Hollywood and art films, or aesthetic tastes.[27]

When *L'avventura* was shown in New York in 1961, the *New York Times* reported anew on a "Roman Team on an Intellectual 'Adventure.'"[28] The report included an interview with Antonioni, where Eugene Archer gave Antonioni the opportunity to explain that "my film is a deliberate act of defiance—an attempt to demonstrate that neither plot nor dialogue is as important as the underlying motivation—the personality of the individual artist," asserting his status as an auteur. Bosley Crowther, however, added two less complimentary articles on the film. In the first, he asks if the film has lost several reels.[29] In his article "Way Out Films: 'L'Avventura' Is a Case of Going Too Far," he labels the film too brainy, despite the subheading—"Brain Sells." Quoting Antonioni's statement about the excess of eros, Crowther demands, "Well, if that's what he means, let him show it or state it verbally in such terms as will take us into his isolated and often elusive images and provide the connecting logic that will make his concepts conclusive and clear." Crowther also accuses "Signor Antonioni" of not having "rounded out a full experience of cinematic stimulation."[30] Crowther, using general standards of high-brow mainstream cinema, pillories *L'avventura* for its lack of clarity and "connecting logic."

On the other side of the Atlantic, the more reflective cinema journal *Sight and Sound* had a different take on Antonioni. In the winter issue of 1960/1961, after the London Film Festival had screened most of Antonioni's earlier works as well as *L'avventura*, *Sight and Sound* offered three pieces on Antonioni, an interview with *L'Express* film correspondent Michèle Manceaux,[31] a review of five earlier Antonioni works by Richard Roud,[32] and a review of *L'avventura* by Penelope Houston.[33] The interview was conducted at a golf club in Milan where Antonioni was filming *La notte*. Manceaux primarily asks Antonioni about his earlier filmmaking experiences and allows Antonioni to express his views about filmmaking. When asked if there is a line of progression in his work, Antonioni responds, "I'm tempted to answer; I just make films, and that's that. I don't feel, in any case, that the things a director has to say about his own work really go very far towards illuminating it . . . and in my own case, I just define a particular moment or state of mind, or throw a certain light on the imaginative process . . . films aren't 'understood' simply by spying out their content. You have to ask much more of a film or something different."[34] Here, Antonioni refuses to explain his work, his ideas about cinema, and the understanding of certain films. He is asking his audience to do the work and to find out what certain films mean to them, situating his filmmaking process squarely in the realm of imagination. Throughout his long career, however, Antonioni has given many interviews, and both he and the press benefited from the exposure these interviews provided to define who Antonioni was. Antonioni often was able to control this discourse.

The other two pieces from *Sight and Sound* are fairly straightforward reviews of his works. However, these reviews treated Antonioni as an auteur and in many ways, together with other reviews, affirmed the process of canonization. Roud, who had a connection with Henri Langlois and later on the New York Film Festival, had been the London correspondent for *Cahiers du cinéma* in the 1950s and wrote the annual report on Cannes for *Sight and Sound*. Success at this film festival, in this case the Jury Prize for *L'avventura* at Cannes, brought the possibility of reevaluating Antonioni's earlier works. Older films that would otherwise not be viewed again were given new life. This kind of simple excavation of a filmmaker's oeuvre prepares the ground to examine one director's work in its totality: in this case, all the major narrative works Antonioni had made up to 1961. Structurally, choosing to examine the works of an auteur leads one to find commonalities among these works and to attribute these similarities to the director, his craft, his art, and his vision. In Roud's review, he states that since Antonioni's first feature, *Story of a Love Affair* (*Cronaca di un amore*, 1950), set "in the milieu of the rich Milan industrialists," he has not been an Italian neorealist, distinguishing him from the dominant Italian filmmakers of the day. Roud states, "As Antonioni declared, his own interest would have been in the mind and emotions of a man whose bicycle has been stolen, whilst De Sica and Zavattini had chosen rather to portray the man in terms of the stolen bicycle."[35] He continues to make general statements, like, "Throughout all Antonioni's works, one finds unsentimental illustrations of his belief that the emotions are often conditioned by social factors and tastes."[36] Roud attributes these commonalities to Antonioni's individual genius; he also believes that the absence of "social preoccupations" in many of Antonioni's films make his works stronger. Roud, in discussing *I vinti*, for example, states, "Whenever Antonioni's social preoccupations gain the upper hand, however, his work seems to suffer." Roud continues to conjecture the motivation of Antononi, "One can speculate that Antonioni felt impelled to make *I Vinti* after *Cronaca di un Amore* in an attempt to satisfy that side of him which is genuinely concerned with immediate social issues—and that *Le Amiche* was followed by *Il Grido* for similar reason."[37] The critic is using textual elements from different works and attributing a psychological motivation to the director to create a coherent narrative—that Antonioni is not good at social issues, but that when he does tackle them he is reacting to his genuine heartfelt concern, but not his artistic calling. The narrative of the auteur constructed from disparate pieces of data brings together the different characters in his films that come from different classes.

To argue that a filmmaker is a master of his art, most critics comment on formal elements. Roud comments on Antonioni's lack of close-up and his preference of using "the two-shot combined with long takes . . . action within the shot and a great many tracking and panning movements." This observation is then followed by Antonioni's comment, "I need to follow my characters," he says, "beyond the moments conventionally considered important for the spectator: to show them even when everything appears to have been said."[38] Insightful and nuanced dialogic observations like these cement a particular formal auteurist signature for Antonioni that is then repeatedly observed in his subsequent works.

The last article in that issue reviews *L'avventura*. As quoted earlier in this chapter, Houston opens the piece with her reaction and observation at Cannes, stressing that the audience members who objected were wrong: "It is the public, not the film that got out of hand. . . . *L'avventura* has been criticised here . . . by people who feel that the weighting of the images is some sort of trickster's device. They, at least, are not going to let themselves be taken in by that subtlety and find shading."[39] This establishes a bellicose divide between those who know (us) and those who do not (them). Antonioni is valorized as a new and innovative art cinema scarcely comprehensible to all, denigrating reviews like those of Crowther in the *New York Times*. Houston explains that "oblique comment is Antonioni's method, comment emerging through reactions, details, and off guard moments of self-awareness."[40] As discussed in the previous chapter, meanings are not obvious in festival films; the audience can only grasp the film by paying full attention to indirect comments and details. Houston continues to stress the seriousness and difficulty of Antonioni's work: "There is a wide suspicion at present of the rarefied atmosphere, in which the air is a little thin for easy breathing and the ghost of Charles Morgan's cerebral passions hover at one's shoulder. One ought to remember, though, that a plain statement is not necessarily either more true or more valuable than a subtle and complex one, only a little easier to grasp."[41] Subtlety and complexity are essential to Antonioni's cinema (and to its critique); if the reader cannot grasp the reference of Charles Morgan,[42] she or he would find it hard to appreciate *L'avventura*. These three contemporary pieces at *Sight and Sound* represent the kind of weighty journalistic articles that established Antonioni as an internationally recognized auteur. These articles do not portray him as a discovery per se, since his works had been seen since the 1950s, but consecrate him at another level of cinematic master. Moreover, one might also note that the very controversy over his works underscores their seriousness and affirms their presence in a public sphere of filmic discourse.

As Antonioni continued to win prizes at film festivals, Peter Hawkins of the *New York Times* seemed to change that newspaper's magisterial opinion of Antonioni. Hawkins covered the story that Antonioni was shooting *L'eclisse* at the Rome stock exchange in 1961 and stressed that Antonioni had experienced a "fantastic year" with his successes at Cannes and Berlin. From this point, Antonioni's reputation was enshrined with the films he made in the 1960s.

The immediacy of journalistic debate is easier to trace than the abundance of academic works on Antonioni, most of which discuss *L'avventura*. Even today in 2011, fifty-one years after *L'avventura*, any casual browsing among academic film books in the United States will turn up five or six books on Antonioni at the top of the shelf; many other works have been published in other languages.[43] In these texts, Antonioni often is compared to other great artists, even beyond film, and the analysis of his works is filled with references to artists and great thinkers, reifying film as high culture and Antonioni as its saint.

Peter Brunette's 1998 study of Antonioni, for example, compares him to James MacNeil Whistler in their formalist approach to films and paintings, respectively.[44] William Arrowsmith, a classicist and expert of Euripides, also writes extensively on Antonioni. In Arrowsmith's analysis of *L'avventura*, he quotes an interview Antonioni gave in 1961 where Antonioni cited Lucretius, saying that "Nothing appears as it should be in a world where nothing is certain. The only thing certain is the existence of a secret violence that makes everything uncertain."[45] Thus he connects classic poetry and its Greco-Roman heritage to modern art cinema. Seymour Chatman, in his introduction, refers to Roland Barthes's "encomium, in the form of the letter Cher Antonioni," a letter presented to Antonioni in 1980 in Bologna when Antonioni received the Archiginnasrio d'oro from the city.[46] Barthes, himself canonized as a great thinker of the twentieth century, names "vigilance, wisdom, and . . . fragility" as Antonioni's three virtues. Barthes continues to stress that Antonioni makes "subtle the meaning of what man says, tells, sees, or feels and this subtlety of meaning, this conviction that meaning does not crudely end at the thing said, but keeps on going, fascinated by what is not meaning."[47] Chatman also compares this aspect of Antonioni with Georges Braque and Henri Matisse.

Few auteurs receive this kind of treatment by the intellectual classes, thus firmly situating Antonioni within an elite group of established global artists, writers, and philosophers. Antonioni's films may have gone in and out of fashion over the years since 1960, yet he is firmly ensconced within the cinematic canon. Interpretation and exaltation of Kiarostami, in fact, shares similar discursive characteristics.

The *Times* in London considered Kiarostami's *Where Is the Friend's Home* as "Locarno's real discovery" where the film "had appeared nowhere."[48] *Le Monde* chimed in that, "A new Iranian cinema exists. We know it because La Sept is giving it a cycle now. . . . It is a discovery. Abbas Kiarostami's *Where Is the Friend's*

Home? (1987), first recognized with prizes last year at Locarno and Cannes, is a tale of childhood friendship which, in certain ways, makes us think of the universe of Luigi Comencini. It is difficult to speak of influences, since beyond the theme of childhood, the reality of the Iranian countryside—poor, isolated, emergent—admirable integrated into the action, so grabs you by the throat."[49] The myth of origins/discovery is again asserted, as is the unique vision combining formality and themes. Reference to Comencini links him to neorealismo rosa (pink or lighter neorealism). Many subsequent journalistic reviews followed Kiarostami's growing consolidated reputation as he won more awards at film festivals and gained theatrical distributions all over the world.

Recognition came with voice for the filmmaker. Farah Nayeri, for example, published an interview with Kiarostami in 1993 highlighting Kiatostami's invitation to be a juror at Cannes, the very first Iranian director to be selected. Kiarostami was also able to articulate and share many of his thoughts through interviews. When speaking to Nayeri, for example, Kiarostami stressed that "Life is a film." He pointed out that he had not seen many films, so his greatest influence was "reality." Good films come from real life, but this does not mean that his films tell stories. He also established links across his own career. Kiarostami talked about how *Life and Nothing More* does not tell a story about looking for the two boys who acted in his earlier film *Where Is the Friend's Home?* in the aftermath of the 1990 earthquake. Instead, in the press book for *Life and Nothing More,* Kiarostami stated that after he arrived at the village, the two boys were among many other boys of that region and he felt that it was more "important to help the survivors who bore no recognizable faces, but were making every effort to start a new life. . . . Such is life, it seemed to tell them, go on, seize the day."[50]

Before *Taste of Cherry* was shown at Cannes in May 1997, the press started covering the film, prejudging what would become another masterpiece for the auteur while inscribing it with geopolitical drama. First, news arrived that "Tehran authorities have banned Iranian director Abbas Kiarostami from presenting his latest film, 'The Delicious Taste of Cherries,' at the Cannes festival next month, he said late Wednesday."[51] Then *Variety* reported that there might be hope that the ban would be revoked.[52] And in another week, "Iran relents, clears 'Cherry.'"[53] By the time the Palme d'Or was announced, like most films in competition, it had been reviewed by different news organizations, generally positively. The *International Herald Tribune,* for instance, nonetheless noted that "the jury, headed by Isabelle Adjani, made a bold move, rewarding Kiarostami's 'Taste of Cherry,' a small film from a poor country, over gunplay and gore titles and warning labels like 'Assassin(s)' and 'Nil by Mouth.'"[54] The *Australian* heralded the award as Cannes's "show of support for their battles against censorship."[55] The distinguishing point here is that it is a small film, it is a film different from the others, and one that is not violent. Unlike reviews of *L'avventura,* here, the social context is dramatically invoked: the idea that Iran is repressive and that it is poor is prominent. *Le Monde* emphasized how "extraordinary it is that . . . THIS IS an exemplary history of contemporary cinema. That of a man, living in a country excluded from cinematographic circuits who has conquered the place he is due, that of being one of the greatest living directors."[56]

Shortly thereafter, Steve Erickson's reflective review of *Taste of Cherry* in *Film Quarterly* situated the film as a continuation of Kiarostami's previous works, comparing the endings of his last three films—*And Life Goes On, Where Is the Friend's Home?* and *Through the Olive Trees* to *Taste of Cherry*. Erickson wrote, "These films' abrupt endings open up questions about the real-life events behind the films; they suggest that people are more important than characters and experiences more important than narratives," thus asserting the film's otherness to classical narrative.[57] Erickson also compared Kiarostami's landscape to that of other great auteurs, including Antonioni: "The land itself looks ready to give up. It's an emblematic use of landscape, worthy of Antonioni or Rossellini (or J. G. Ballard, for that matter)—simultaneously a real landscape and a projection of Badii's mental state."[58] Erickson set Kiarostami apart from other "Western" auteurs like Truffaut and Godard because he is not a cinephile, since Kiarostami "boasted" of having only seen a few dozen films in his life; at the same time he recognized that Kiarostami had indeed become a "critics' darling." In fact, critics make claims about the uniqueness of Kiarostami by asserting that "his explorations never run the risk of getting trapped in a hall of pop-culture-reference mirrors," because he is not a cinephile.[59] (Who then would be the cinephiles who are trapped in the hall of pop-culture-reference mirrors—Fellini? Welles? Truffaut? Tarantino?)

In this review, then, the critic helps establish a specific style for Kiarostami as an internationally recognized auteur. Yet, Erickson emphasizes Kiarostami as non-Western and makes a leap in declaring that Kiarostmi's inattention to the idea of cinephiles allows him to have "a suspicion of the image and an awareness of the tremendous power of filmmakers over ordinary people with a belief in the healing power of cinema."[60] The review ends with, "It's a shame that there's no one making films like his in the United States, where the class differences between image-makers and image-consumers dwarf the ones in Iran."[61] While all these statements applaud the achievements of Kiarostami, they separate him from the West and allow that global category to become more universal by his inclusion. Still, this very "non-Westernness" orientalizes some romantic non-West that escapes the ills of the West.

Joan Dupont of the *International Herald Tribune* also read *Taste of Cherry* within other non-Western films, "Getting 'Taste of Cherry,' banned by the authorities, out of Iran, was the kind of drama the festival had not known since 1982, when Yimaz Guney's 'Yol,' a film on prison life, was banned in Turkey and came to Cannes to win the Golden Palm."[62] Her article contains excerpts of the reporter's interview with Kiarostami, where he explains that the subject of suicide disturbed the authorities, but adds that once they "had time to see the film and analyze it, there was no problem." Dupont also compares Kiarostami to Egyptian director Youssef Chahine, who had won the special fiftieth anniversary prize. Kiarostami, however, did not denounce his country's regime: "I don't feel it's necessary. In our country too, there are radical religious movements and sometimes they cause problems. You have to talk with people to resolve the problems. I think that Iran's internal problems are better resolved from inside the country, rather than from the outside. As I say in this film, life is not fate; it's a matter of choice. I choose to live in Iran; I could leave, but I don't; despite the problems, I feel at home. In our neighborhood, we don't see any violence." Whether read as a general Middle Easterner amid Turks or Arabs, or positioned in relation to his own Persian traditions, Kiarostami is often asked these questions about the problems in Iran. Often, he seems to take the opportunity to explain to Western journalists that the West should leave the problems of Iran to the Iranians. However, this would change as the Iranian regime became more repressive in 2010 with the arrest of Jafar Panahi.

Censorship, especially censorship in totalitarian regimes, has always interested festival programmers as well as the press in their coverage of international film festivals. Jonathan Rosenbaum asserts that Gilles Jacob "orchestrated" the arrival of Taste of Cherry like a "cliffhanger." He goes on to critique the press for its "self-righteousness . . . in denouncing state censorship" when the press never addresses the other form of market censorship that the United States experiences.[63] In the same year, Zhang Yimou's Keep Cool was withdrawn by the Chinese authorities from competition at Cannes because the festival had selected the forbidden Zhang Yuan's East Palace, West Palace, with its treatment of homosexuality, for Un Certain Regard. While Dupont does not mention these Chinese interventions, many other newspaper and trade papers covered the story at the times of the festival. Similarly, in a review in Film International on Weerasethaklul's Syndromes and a Century, the reviewer John Berra started by describing the "six contentious scenes" that the Thai authorities had either cut or "scratched": "The offending scenes included a doctor passionately kissing his girlfriend, a Buddhist monk playing a guitar, and a doctor drinking whiskey from a bottle concealed in a prosthetic leg."[64] This cross-cultural interpretation of an equally transnational, globally produced film (Thailand/France/Austria) made by a Western-educated Thai filmmaker exemplifies an unsuccessful intercultural communication where each seems to have held on to certain expectations of the other. From the West, censorship is wrong or a bit ridiculous, but for Thailand's authorities, censorship is necessary to protect Thai images, especially to the West.

The well-known feminist film critic Laura Mulvey, writing in Sight and Sound, compared Kiarostami's success at Cannes with that of Kurosawa at Venice in 1951.[65] She put Kiarostami's international success in the context of film festivals' ability to bring "Asian art cinema to the international circuit" and identified Rashômon as the point where "major festivals have launched art cinema from the First, Second and Third Worlds into limited, generally élite distribution."[66] While acknowledging the complicated relationship between Western festivals and world cinema, Mulvey recognizes that festivals have "moulded cinema in their own image, imposing a universalising festival taste on emerging cinemas worldwide."[67] Nevertheless, she admits that without film festivals "the appearance of *A Taste of Cherry* in London would not have been possible."[68]

Like many scholars on auteurs, Mulvey looked at Kiatostami's corpus of works for some kind of repeated motives. She concluded that "Kiarostami's narratives tend to take their protagonists on journeys. Both actually and metaphorically, the journey becomes a space of personal transformation—not, as in traditional folktales, a transition to a new status in the world or to the successful accomplishment of a quest, but to a new level of understanding. . . . *A Taste of Cherry* continues the themes of quest and transcendence explored in the less self-reflexive films. On the other hand, *A Taste of Cherry* does refer, in the last resort, to cinema, using its metaphoric potential to end the film outside the storyline." Mulvey continues to comment on the director's use of driving, the car, and the road. But ultimately, it is the "principle of uncertainty" that becomes the signature of Kiarostami.[69]

Kiarotami galvanized a fascination about the Orient and censorship within the press of the West. In film festivals today, in the case of most films that come from a "repressive regime," the director is asked about issues of censorship. In 2005, when I was attending the question-and-answer section following the screening of *Oxhide* (*Niu pi*, 2005) by Liu Jiayin at Berlin Forum, the first question asked was if there had been interference during production in China. Liu simply replied no, and explained that students at the Beijing Film Academy were allowed quite a bit of freedom in doing their work. Shot entirely in Liu's own home with herself and her parents playing the family, the film won the FIPRESCI prize. It is formally challenging, with only twenty-three static shots; however, there were few questions on the art of the film. The audience seemed to be more interested in the working conditions and censorship for cinema in China. It is very hard to say whether it is a manifestation of orientalism, a hidden sense of hierarchy between the free world and the Orient, or simply an institutional ingrained practice of the press which shared this unbalanced historical subjectivity within global representation. In many ways, film festivals often find films from non-Western countries sociologically more interesting because they are perceived to be made under difficult situations, while the enlightened festivals provide a free space for these creative ideas to thrive. However, reception at home for some of these film festival auteurs can be quite different. Mahrnaz Saeed-Vafa states that local responses to Kiarostami "have been divided. Some Iranians call Kiarostami's work uncinematic, journalistic, and unworthy of all the international attention it has received . . . a favorite of Western festivals who makes films for foreign audiences. . . . Others have suggested that the French and

Iranian governments conspired to give Kiarostami so much attention. . . . Kiarostami has sold himself to the Islamic government to gain fame."[70]

Is Kiarostami universal? In the epilogue of Alberto Elena's work on Kiarostami, he stresses that many have compared him to "Rossellini, De Sica, Olmi, Bresson, Godard, Murnau, Tati, and even Eastern maestros such as Ray and Kurosawa, already victims of a similar exercise."[71] Yet many have "obscured the deep-rooted Persian influence" and "neglect[ed] the Iranian context or underestimate[d] its importance."[72] Here, in evaluating the art of Kiarostami films, other critics seem to have ignored Kiarostami's Persian roots.

Today, with Kiarostami making a thoroughly European coproduction, *Certified Copy*, the press has reacted to him as "ventur[ing] into European arthouse cinema."[73] Rob Nelson at *Daily Variety* calls Kiarostami a "deep-thinking writer-director," and adds that "Kiarostami appears condescending to the bourgeois melodrama, and commercial prospects could suffer for it."[74] Nelson goes on to compare Kiarostami with auteurs like Wong Kar Wai and others, while *Certified Copy*'s characters are "channeling Ingrid Bergman and George Sanders in Roberto Rossellini's 'Voyage to Italy.'"[75] During the press conference for *Certified Copy* at Cannes on May 18, 2010, journalists asked Kiarostami why he chose to film in Italy, how this film differed from his other films, and how this fit the political and social context of his films. His general answer was that this is a film that takes place in Tuscany, so the location is dictated by the text.

In the case of Kiarostami, like Antonioni, we find the convergence of discursive horizons around his festival-recognized films situate him in a pantheon alongside other auteurs. Yet, in his case, his non-Westernness is not only an emblem but a paradoxical affirmation of the universalism of the Western world that includes him. Aesthetic judgments, moreover, are linked to political and economic position—especially as the film is read not only on its own terms but also as a work that has grappled with censorship that is anathema to art. Yet, while Antonioni is linked to Lucretius or Whistler, Kiarostami is linked to Antonioni—neither to a longer Western cultural heritage nor to his own Iranian literary and artistic world. Here, the discourses are clearly written for and by Western receivers of his work. Once again, the film festival provides a point of convergence and control, even in their own discourse on auteurs and films.

The Film Festivals Present Themselves

While the roles of directors, the press, or scholars evoke independence, the festivals themselves also offer their own interpretation of their own activities. Every festival publishes its own catalog (although there is considerable flow and borrowing among these texts, acknowledged or not). Some, as I have noted, publish longer studies on specific films, national or regional cinema, genres, and works of auteurs. In addition to print, all film festivals have their Web sites, which provide elaborate and rich information on the films, the directors and actors, and even reactions to the films shown. Thus, the myth of films and filmmakers are reformed into the myths of festivals as well.

Robert Chazal recalls in *Cannes Memories* that facing "Curses, catcalls, and insults for '*L'avventura*,' Antonioni, extremely upset, leaves the screening room arm-in-arm with Monica Vitta who has tears streaming down her face. They turn to tears of joy, however, when the film receives an award from the forward-thinking Jury presided by George Simenon."[76] The now famous reception of *L'avventura* was reprinted forty years later to show how the "forward-thinking" Cannes jury was able to spot a talent even under a cloud of insults. Alberto Elena's work on Kiatostami, similarly, stems from a retrospective on him at the Gijón Film Festival. Film festivals have the ability to reproduce themselves as institutions by showing that they are the arbiters of good cinema, having chosen the "right" film in competition and by hosting special programs and retrospectives for the established auteurs.

After the initial "discoveries" and continued validations of the works of an auteur by both the press and scholars, some auteurs are ultimately canonized by retrospectives launched by film festivals and other film centers and museums or even by tributes in their names. Once these auteurs have been established, many festivals invite them to be on juries and to host or comment on retrospectives of their works. Locarno, Venice, San Francisco, Hong Kong, and Melbourne have all hosted retrospectives on Antonioni. In 1995, the American Film Institute festival (AFI FEST) premiered Antonioni's just completed *Beyond the Clouds*, which was shown earlier as a work in progress in Venice. In 2004, Cannes introduced a new sidebar, Cannes Classics. Included in its first program was the premiere of Antonioni's short, *Michelangelo's Eye*, as well as a restored print of *Blow-Up* to be released by Warner on DVD. In 2009, *L'avventura* was again selected by Martin Scorsese to be included in Cannes Classics. Kiarostami, somewhat more recently, has been on the jury for Cannes, Venice, San Sebastián, Marrakesh, and many other festivals. Among his many festival retrospectives, the latest was at the Munich Film Festival of 2010.

Outside film festivals, the stature of the auteur is reproduced and nurtured in other more accessible art house venues. For example, in 2007, the Gene Siskel Film Center in Chicago did a retrospective on Antonioni. The retrospective states that "A giant of the European Art Cinema movement, Michelangelo Antonioni has combined themes of contemporary alienation, a breathtaking precision of composition, and a resonant use of modern environments to create one of the most significant bodies of work in cinema history."[77] In 1999, the Castro Theater in San Francisco held a two-week retrospective, labeling him as the "Italian master of angst."[78]

Retrospectives are also held in museums. The University of California, Berkeley, Pacific Film Archive also held a retrospective that saw Antonioni as the "most elegant proponent of modernism" who "made absence a presence on the screen."[79] After Antonioni passed away in 2007, the National Museum of Singapore held a retrospective, where he was lionized: "One of the world's most celebrated and innovative filmmakers, Antonioni created a body of startlingly beautiful, original and still amazingly resonant works of film art spanning six decades that examined the anomie of modern life."[80] In the same vein, Kiarostami has been the subject of retrospectives at the Berkeley Museum of Art/Pacific Film Archive, the Museum of Modern Art in New York, the British Film Institute, and other high-culture venues.

Furthermore, film festivals are publishers themselves of their own histories as well as of special volumes on auteurs, stars, film technologies, national cinemas, and film movements. For example, in Berlin, the Deutsche Kinemathek is responsible for conceiving and publishing works to accompany the retrospectives or special programs the Berlinale hosts.[81] Locarno also helps publish quite a few volumes on their special programs, including *Out of the Shadows: Asians in American Cinema*, which was edited by Roger Garcia, one of the earliest directors for the HKIFF. (He returned as director of the festival in 2010.) These publications not only reinforce the festivals' roles in history, they put the festivals on par with other respected academic publications. The processes involved in some of these publications also create stronger networks among different film professionals, from programmers to critics to scholars.

The Voice of the Auteur

The present moral standards we live by, these myths, these conventions are old and obsolete. And we all know they are, yet we honor them. Why? The conclusion reached by the protagonists in my film is not one of sentimentality. If anything, what they finally arrive at is a sense of pity for each other. . . . Why do you think eroticism is so prevalent today in our literature, our theatrical shows, and elsewhere? It is a symptom of the emotional sickness of our time. . . . The tragedy in *L'Avventura* stems directly from an erotic impulse of this type: unhappy, miserable, futile. To be critically aware of the vulgarity and the futility of such an overwhelming erotic impulse, as is the case with the protagonist in *L'Avventura*, is not enough or serves no purpose. And here we witness the crumbling of a myth, which proclaims it is enough for us to know, to be critically conscious of ourselves, to analyze ourselves, in all our complexities and in every facet of our personality.[82]

Antonioni delivered this famous prepared speech at Cannes in 1960. In many ways, such a public statement from the director is rare. While almost all directors are willing to talk to the press and attend press conferences, few have prepared statements for their films. Antonioni was asking the audience/press to read *L'avventura* in a particular way, neither didactic nor straightforward, but with a general sense of how one should approach the film and its characters. Film festivals are fora that allow filmmakers to express their views, and structures like press conferences create dialogue between the filmmakers and the press. Most films, especially those in important sections, have well-crafted press packages that document the thoughts and ideas of the filmmakers. Yet unlike the programmers, the press, and the scholars, the director may offer another voice and image, and these, in turn, may guide his audience and reader to see him in a particular light.

Indeed, at festivals, the director becomes an event; often the director is the primary focus of the press conference, accompanied by actors, producers, cinematographers, writers, and others who have participated in the making of the movie. This forum allows the filmmakers to talk directly with the audience, primarily the press. Some directors preface this speech with the idea that they cannot tell you much about the films they have made—like Antonioni, who famously asserted, "I am convinced that whatever a director says about himself or his work is of no help in understanding the work itself."[83] Yet, Antonioni freely contradicted himself by making strong statements concerning his films.

The *New York Times*, for example, interviewed Antonioni with Monica Vitti when *L'avventura* was released in New York in 1961. Thus Eugene Archer conveyed to a wider viewing public Antonioni's assertion that "I want the audience to work. . . . I ask them to see the film from the beginning and devote their full attention to it, treating it with the same respect they would give a painting, a symphony, a novel, or any other work of art. I treat them with the same respect by inviting them to search for their own meanings, instead of insulting their intelligence with obvious explanations. When the viewer participates directly in the search, the film becomes an intellectual adventure, a mystery on many levels—for the personages, for myself, and for the audience as well."[84] Antonioni was never shy in explaining his films, as seen in his original statement at Cannes when *L'avventura* was premiered.

Directors like Antonioni and Kiarostami have given hundreds of interviews over the years many of them published. Therefore, they have quite a bit of control over their presentation in the media as well as in the academic world. Besides the filmmaker himself, his voice might also resonate with his own production company or publicity created to help promote the film. In 1995, for example, the Farabi Cinema Foundation published a pamphlet that listed all of Kiarostami's film exhibitions at film festivals all over the world.[85] The document was probably distributed to anyone who was interested in Kiarostami's work, because it is a factual public relations piece. The document makes it abundantly clear that Kiarostami has been receiving prizes since the early 1970s, mostly in Iran, but that his Western recognition began later, in 1989, with Locarno.

Kiarostami has used interviews to control specific readings of his film. Jonathan Rosenbaum wrote about Kiarostami's response to a question about the ending of *Taste of Cherry*, where he said, "I believe in a cinema which gives more

possibilities and more time to its viewer . . . a half fabricated cinema, an unfinished cinema that is completed by the creative spirit of the viewer, [so that] all of
a sudden, we have a hundred films."[86] Kiarostami thereby sums up the many
features I discussed in the previous chapter, that the film does not provide all the
answers and that the audience's job is to complete the film. This shared expectation about festival films can in turn be interpreted as a form of intertextuality
that is embedded not only in the film texts, but also reproduced, articulated, and
disseminated by the filmmakers as well as the critics.

Directors may also take us in other, more personal directions. At the premiere of *Taste of Cherry* at Cannes, Kiarostami told the press, "Without the possibility of suicide, I would have killed myself long ago."[87] In 2010, at the press
conference at Cannes for *Certified Copy*, when asked about his experiences at
the festival, Kiarostami described his first visit, where he received the Rossellini
prize for *Life, and Nothing More . . .* :

> I did not know what I have done, I was almost in despair, . . . I did not know
> whether my film could be considered as a film at all, and the fact that it was
> received as such, the fact that people liked it, enabled me to realize that
> I existed as a filmmaker, far from the agitation at Cannes, far from all the
> special effects, far from the narrative model which one regularly see here,
> I have been able to create something which was recognizable as a film, I was
> visible, my film was visible and it is that recognition that I still feel today.[88]

Kiarostami articulates what his films are not and expresses his gratitude to
Cannes as a festival that has recognized his kind of cinema, thus affirming, in a
circular fashion, the power of that discourse.

With the advent of DVD technology, distributors increasingly use words of
the directors, actors, cinematographers, and critics to add layers of meaning and
economic value to the film in its wider distribution. The Criterion Collection was
established by Janus Film, a major film distributor in the United States. It has
been responsible for distributing European art cinema since it arrived in the
United States more than half a century ago; it remains a prestige distributor for
quality works on DVD. *L'avventura*'s DVD set from Criterion includes "audio
commentary by film historian Gene Youngblood," "*Antonioni: Documents and
Testimonials,* a 58-minute documentary by Gianfranco Mingozzi," and "Writings
by Antonioni, read by Jack Nicholson—plus Nicholson's personal recollections of
the director." The DVD for *Taste of Cherry* includes an interview with Kiarostami
by "Iranian film scholar Dr. Jamsheed Akrami." Other directors oftentimes also
get their say in a DVD presentation. Jean Renoir was able to speak to the audience directly about *The Rules of the Game* and explain the initial reception of the
film and his intention of presenting a classical story to the audience. Lucrecia
Martel explains to the audience of *The Swamp* (*La ciénaga*) that her film does not
follow narrative convention. Sometimes, more interesting exchanges occur

between critic and director. In the commentary on the *Tropical Malady* DVD, for example, a film critic tells the director, Apichatpong Weerasethakul, that "this is my second favorite sex scene in Thai cinema." The director responds, "No, this is not a sex scene." When I first watched the film, I also did not read this scene as a sex scene. Instead, I saw a naked native-looking man who might be more appropriately interpreted as the spirit of a tiger roaming in the jungle being chased by the Thai soldier whose job it is to catch this tiger, which has supposedly destroyed livestock in the forest. It is a long shot of the soldier in fatigues chasing the naked tattooed man and the ensuing struggle that follows. Yet, how many people will hear the director and how many the critic, framed by preconceptions of Thailand and sexuality, especially in a festival filmic discourse.

Antonioni and Kiarostami, as auteurs, have been able to create and respond to the discourse surrounding and creating them. Yet, an auteur cannot completely control this discourse so much as engage in it as a dialogue. Moreover, insofar as each auteur and film is categorized and placed as part of a larger paradigm—of great directors, master films, techniques, or images—it is harder to provide an independent or contrary reading that claims to be original, much less correct. The auteurs, like the films, become creations. And yet, readings also evolve over time, as the festivals themselves remind us in their meta-role as extratextual discourse.

Conclusion

Films as texts meet textualized directors and events in the worlds of festivals. Yet, besides all these printed words or videos, for a film to be "successful," people and institutions dealing with the business side of film and film festivals are extremely important. The markets, coproduction fora, and filmmaker seminars for emerging directors are all crucial in that they make possible the continued circulation and reproduction of festival films; chapter 4 will go in depth to examine these institutions. However, it is important to understand that many of these different agents have multiple roles—as producers, sales and acquisition agents, and distributors—and increasingly these people help move many films to first get into film festivals, and then beyond.

Nonetheless, with film festivals offering all these institutional structures—different sections, publications, retrospectives, markets—the most important aspect I continue to affirm about them is the relation between the global and abstract system and the festival as lived experience, a world of personal connections, interactions and interpretations. Film festivals, in the end, offer a place for people who share similar interests, be they artistic, business, or something hybrid. The filmmakers meet other filmmakers to discuss their craft; depending on which stage their projects are at, they (or their people) meet investors to finance the next project, or to finish the present project. The publicists, distributors, producers, sales agents, and investors all work hard to make sure that they do their job well, which in the end all comes down to how well one notices or discovers a "good" film, or the potential for future development. The festival organizers' job is to bring the right kinds of people and the right kinds of films and build structures that enable a fruitful exchange among all these people with different interests. Once the festival is over, festival participants go home, or go to another festival, and continue the work they do, from writing the newspaper articles, film criticisms, or scholarly pieces to organizing other festival programs. This brings us back to the beginning of this chapter, where we discussed Altman's constellated communities, where each group has a slightly different agenda. Nevertheless, they work together, albeit with different levels of self-interest, toward making the films the kinds of works they want, as art, as commodities, and both, as the next chapter shows.

4 Film Festivals and Film Industries

While film festivals play pivotal roles both in defining a shared canon of "great" cinema and in adding cultural value to films, they also are significant because they create nodes of global business in which films circulate as commodities. For some, this marketing function denotes antagonistic goals within the festival world,[1] while others respond that however strong cinephilia may be, films mean little if they are not seen. Circulation, even if films move through a festival circuit, remains rarefied and economically problematic. Since their origins, however, film festivals actually have been associated intensely with national film industries, visibility, and distribution. Festivals mean premieres, screenings, and prizes, but many now offer film markets, coproduction fora, funding competitions, producer platforms, and master classes. These opportunities attract filmmakers, stars, producers, distributors, investors, exporters, publicists, lawyers, journalists, and film commissions from different countries: even auteurs need to pay their staff. These agents, in turn, form networks in which film production, finance, and distribution are negotiated beyond the festival world.

Festivals were active components of the film industry rather than mere backdrops in Mussolini's promotion of Italian films in Venice and the French response at Cannes. Film festival organizers and sponsors subsequently have continued to reevaluate their status in the cinematic world and change their roles when useful. Since the foundation of the Marché (market) at Cannes in 1959, festivals have become increasingly involved with film sales and distribution. As selection committees have taken over from national nominations since 1972 (when Cannes changed its policy), festivals have become conduits for active distributors in their own right. And since the 1990s, festivals have learned to play the role of promoters and, increasingly, of coproducers for international independent cinema, from Sundance to Rotterdam.

Festivals and their participants may include Hollywood brokers who bask in festival publicity and glamour with films out of competition. Many festivals are nonetheless instrumental in providing film with an alternative business structure that promotes a global and artisanal process of filmmaking, giving special albeit limited opportunities to women, minorities, and agents from "underrepresented" regions. Film festivals thus have become multilayered global industrial events that link different players and entities in getting films made and shown by assembling necessary financing, nurturing talents, facilitating coproduction, and finding global distributors.

In this chapter, I explore both institutional structures and more "casual" networking conditions that make film festivals central components of the global cinema business. While present since the beginning of film festivals, in recent decades these functions have shaped the evolution of individual and competing festivals in significant ways. As markets become central to truly global film festivals, organizations and people like producers, sales agents, investors, and distributors become increasingly important players. These are not the auteurs or the stars that festivals generally highlight, but players behind the scenes. Yet these people provide the apparatus that make the production and distribution of alternative cinemas viable.

These functions rely on webs of communication as well as face-to-face contact. While the mainstream press, with its general readership, concentrates on the glamour and art of film festivals, with minor detours into business coverage, for the trade press—*Variety, Hollywood Reporter, Screen International, IndieWIRE*—festival business coverage is essential. During festival weeks, many of them publish special daily issues and updates. Festival-goers, glued to their reviews, follow deals and evaluate negotiations in these as well as festival media. In the 1980s, Cannes alone had three newspapers "which run lists of prominent industry figures with the names of the hotels where they are staying and then one of two words: *Buying* or *Selling*."[2] Tear sheets are posted on bulletin boards around the press office, and festival Web sites make press conferences and other coverage available worldwide. Through the year, the industry trade press follows competition for support and changes in the leadership as well as the scouting that leads to programs for their festivals. Festivals themselves circulate their own publicity to filmmakers, producers, audiences, and learned colleagues. Meanwhile, filmmakers and festival organizers distribute and comment on this information through more personal connections, seeking, fostering, and even competing for new talents who will provide the future of the film industry and festivals themselves. And then, for a few brief days, film, people, and opportunities converge beside the Mediterranean, or Lake Ontario, or Hong Kong Harbor.

While one cannot discuss business without reference to other cultural and political issues, this chapter concentrates on the concrete foundations of film festival businesses. It first addresses relations that represent the nexus of business linking film festivals and film industries, with a keen awareness of the presence of Hollywood at Cannes in relation to issues of filmic form and authorship that I have already discussed. Again, I bridge constructs that are often taken to be a major cultural divide in cinema, as prizes and visibility, which already have been analyzed as features in the creation of film knowledge, become public relations and commercial tools as well. The chapter then examines issues of exhibition and distribution. Finally, it turns in more details to the recent rise of training and production of cinema within the film festival contexts.

Through these lenses, I elucidate the roles different stake holders play in these exchanges. Besides filmmakers, stars, and producers who act as private agents, for example, national film commissions are involved in the promotion of their respective industries, whether making and selling film or making their countries and cities available for location shooting and production support. Regional issues, individual aspirations, and competing festivals are all players in this business world. Business, of course, cannot be divorced from the nurturing of filmmakers. Film festivals in fact have increasingly arranged to support the film workers who will meet these needs of films festivals, as I show through the career of Chinese filmmaker Jia Zhangke.

The chapter concludes with a review of the interconnectedness of the various film festivals and their business features. Shared business structures and networks entail uneven power relations in this global network that remind us of systemic struggles in defining what film is and who has access to it.

The Early Days: Exhibition and Hollywood

In the first decades of film festivals (1930s to 1960s), they showcased serious, respectable cinema underpinned by values of national industry and representation. As exhibition venues, they did not generate significant direct revenue for the screened films, which companies were expected to provide for free. Mussolini cared more about Fascist propaganda and national pride than making money out of Mussolini Cup winners *Lo squadrone bianco* (1936) or *Scipio Africanus* (1937), even if the festival might bolster a weakened Italian film industry. Geopolitical concerns were paramount in the establishment of these festivals, with aesthetic dimensions following behind.

Participating nations understood these rules of cultural political economics. The early film festivals received films from either studios or national film commissions; to have their films shown only once or twice at the festival provided enough prestige to make the economic bottom line negligible. Still, many films were high-quality mainstream studio productions. For example, in 1952, *Two Cents' Worth of Hope* (*Due soldi di speranza*), a comic love story set in the slums of Naples and rural southern Italy with neorealist influence, produced by Universalcine, shared the Grand Prize at Cannes with Orson Welles's *Othello*.

Karlovy Vary, shaped by the rise of communism in Czechoslovakia, tells a different story. During its first decades, it served largely as a "propaganda tool."[3] Business in the capitalist sense did not play a large role in the festival, although, "generally speaking, politically correct output was traditionally sent to Moscow, while artistically significant films would compete at Karlovy Vary."[4] Since the Velvet Revolution of 1989, it has reasserted itself as a center for Eastern European filmmaking.

This engagement of festival and national industry continues to be an element in contemporary global festivals. Governments are major players still. Locarno, for example, showcases the small array of Swiss films produced each year; the Swiss film office holds a party for official participants. Hong Kong gained fame as a showcase for Hong Kong and Greater Chinese cinema and meshes with other campaigns to sell Hong Kong artistic products, including FILMART, the Hong Kong film market. Its program also includes short films from students at local public university film schools who may be entering the business in the future. In San Sebastián, the state film industry is flanked by delegations from Spain's other autonomous regions, such as Cantabria, Catalonia, and Madrid, touting locations, resources, and productions. Local Basque films program an entire day. While these collaborations of the national industry and festival are less heavy-handed than those of Mussolini's Venice, the connections of art, politics, and national industry are clear. These nationalist foundations frame the presence of Hollywood as a major national film industrial complex—and apparent competitor—within the festival world.

Despite the ties I have shown in terms of film style, direction, and the experience of festivals, Hollywood seems to be the mythic antithesis of the festival world for many. Hollywood, after all, produces predictable, profitable mainstream fare with bankable stars and formulaic plots rather than those perceived as serious, edgy, inventive, or confrontational. The Lido and the Croisette seem worlds away from Rodeo Drive and Beverly Hills. Yet, the deepest relationships between film festivals and Hollywood have always been about business: the creation of global good will, public relations, and the constant exposure of stars. The seals of approval that film festivals provide are all parts of the profit-making enterprise of Hollywood.

Hollywood actually found a place for its films to shine in the early Venice project, where *Anna Karenina* won the best foreign film in 1935. However, as the Axis powers started to collaborate beyond the political and military fields, every prize in Venice for Best International Film from 1936 to 1942 went to Italy's Axis ally, Germany. Hence, Hollywood joined the French to find another venue to screen films as global art . . . and more. In the summer of 1939, for the inauguration of Cannes, "the Americans quickly sent over a few of their biggest stars in September: Paul Muni, Gary Cooper, Douglas Fairbanks, Tyrone Power, Norma Shearer, and Mae West."[5] These stars were ready to cross the Atlantic despite threats of war; some, like Mae West, actually had arrived in France before Hitler invaded Poland on September 1 and aborted the first Cannes festival. Eight Hollywood films, including *The Wizard of Oz*, were also scheduled for screening in that first festival.

Vanessa Schwartz's research on the Cannes festivals of the 1950s deftly illustrates the extent of cooperation between the postwar festival and Hollywood in the constructing of cosmopolitan film culture.[6] The films shown were international, but confined to the Western world. Among the films Cannes screened in the 1940s and 1950s, Hollywood followed only France itself. Hollywood not only sent *many* films, but its studios sent big films—*Gilda, Gaslight,* and *Notorious* in 1946, *Dumbo* and *Ziegfeld Follies* in 1947, and *House of Strangers* in 1949, for which Edward G. Robinson won the Best Actor award.

In the 1950s, important films from Hollywood continued to capture Cannes awards. *All About Eve* won the Grand Jury Prize in 1951, Lee Grant (*Detective Story*) and Marlon Brando (*Viva Zapata*) garnered Best Actress and Best Actor in 1952. Walt Disney received the Legion of Honor at Cannes in 1953, and in 1954 *From Here to Eternity* was honored. In 1955 and 1956, the Palme d'Or was awarded to *Marty* and *Friendly Persuasion*, respectively. In thinking about the confluence of business and art at this stage, it is worth noting that both *From Here to Eternity* and *Marty* won Oscars in the same year, while *Friendly Persuasion* was nominated for the Academy's Best Picture, losing, ironically, to *Gigi* and America's image of France. U.S. cinema may no longer win both the Palme d'Or and the Oscar, but there are crossovers even today, like *No Country for Old Men* (2007), which was nominated at Cannes and won the Oscar (though it was rather different from most Oscars wins), in 2008, or *Inglourious Basterds* (2009), which was nominated for both.

Hollywood studios continued to send films for competition at Cannes in respectable numbers until the 1960s, when they began to place their films in a different category. Starting in 1955, Hollywood films generally screened *hors compétition* (out of competition), including *Carmen Jones* in 1955, Oscar-winner *Around the World in Eighty Days* in 1956,[7] and *The Diary of Anne Frank* in 1959. Over the next decade, Hollywood films clearly preferred the *hors compétition* status, including epics like *Ben-Hur, Exodus, The Fall of the Roman Empire,* and *Doctor Zhivago* as well as popular films like Hitchcock's *The Birds, Mary Poppins,* and *In Harm's Way.* All were high-quality products from the studios, as opposed to the "B" movies then being discovered by the critics of *Cahiers.* Many were Oscar contenders and winners. This change of placement, moving major films out of competition, suggests that Hollywood started seeing Cannes more for its potential for exposure than for the awards, which carried the risk of failure and negative press.

This pragmatic division has become even more prevalent today. Studios regularly use Cannes (out of competition) as a launching pad for big summer blockbusters, from *Star Wars* to *Indiana Jones.* Meanwhile, newly minted American competition and sidebar entries tend to be independent, auteur, or more unusual films. Still, Hollywood remains a presence. As noted in a report on Cannes 2010, which saw only one American director, Douglas Liman, in competition, "The jury is chaired by a [relatively] mainstream American filmmaker, Tim Burton, and it contains a pair of actors who've made their share of major studio hits, Benicio del Toro and Kate Beckinsale—but that doesn't mean the Cannes Film

Figure 7. Promotion of *Up* at the Sixty-sixth Venice Film Festival, September 6, 2009. Source: 66ème Festival de Venise (Mostra), by Nicolas Genin, http://www.flickr.com/photos/nicogenin/3893646803/in/faves-52138611 No 2, CC By 2.0.

Festival looks to Hollywood to stock its competitive lineup. On the other hand, Cannes does love those Hollywood stars on the red carpet."[8]

Beyond any films that Cannes wanted and Hollywood sold, the Hollywood package comes with stars, glamour, and global publicity. What is better to infuse the myth of Hollywood into the fiber of the festival than the story of Grace Kelly and Prince Rainier, who supposedly met during her publicity visit to Cannes? Publications on Cannes shimmer with images of stars, both American and European—Grace Kelly, Kim Novak, Gina Lollabrigida, Brigitte Bardot, Kirk Douglas, Alain Delon, Sophia Loren, and Marcello Mastroianni. The stars also have advanced the business plans of the producers, the agents, the studios, and their own careers. Stars generate press, enticing journalists to show up. The press, in turn, receives great material for adding glamour to their pages and gives exposure to stars, their films, and the festivals. Festivals participate in a cycle of other publicity vehicles, from Hollywood press to modern talk shows, although they add a cosmopolitan cultural cachet to the image of a star that Oprah and Jay Leno do not.

By the 1950s, Hollywood stars and other figures took on institutional roles within the festivals that assumed this cultural/intellectual status as artist, especially in terms of award juries. While France initially loaded Cannes juries with icons of French high culture, such as André Malraux, Jean Cocteau, and André Maurois, by 1953 prizewinner Edward G. Robinson was on the jury. Director

George Stevens followed in 1957 and Gene Kelly in 1959. In 1965, with actress Olivia de Havilland, Hollywood took the presidency of the jury for the first time. As in out-of-competition screening, jury duty provides a planned showcase with few risks and interesting exchanges, with the president being a powerful figure in constructing networks around her selection of jurors.

The agency that stars have in these festivals becomes complex in conjunction with discussions with the dominant figure of the auteur and the less visible roles of producers and agents. In contemporary festivals, Hollywood and global stars have become more calculating about the value of their ability to attract festival sponsors and publicity; some even charge festivals for their appearance. It was rumored that the inaugural Rome festival paid "an outrageous amount" to have Nicole Kidman show up but thought this worthwhile in terms of press and support. Glitz has always been a publicity tool for all those who are involved in the festivals and for the success of the festival venture.

Other people are less visible in the global public eye, but have always managed intense local visibility, especially in the more freewheeling world of distribution that followed the demise of the studio system and the rise of new independents in production and distribution.[9] This was epitomized by Roger Ebert's 1987 description of distributors Menahem Golan and Yorum Globus with Cannon Films at Cannes:

> A decade ago, they were peddling soft-core sex comedies like *Lemon Popsicle* in the market. . . . At the festival, they have built themselves into the most important single entity at Cannes, a company that this year had two films (*Shy People* and *Barfly*) in the official competition, another film (Norman Mailer's *Tough Guys Don't Dance*) as an out-of-competition film selection, and dozens of other films in the marketplace, ranging from *Death Wish 4* to a 'family film festival.' Cannon is the biggest advertiser in all of the daily festival papers, Cannon's *Superman IV* billboard dominates the front lawn of the Carlton Hotel, and in the days to come more people will see more Cannon films, attend more Cannon parties and drink more Cannon booze than will be involved in all the activities of the next three distributors together.[10]

In fact, like many business endeavors, "the Golan-Globus Empire" did not last much beyond Ebert's reporting its extravagance at Cannes in 1987. These two players may be gone, but others continue to fill the roles of distributors and sales agents who wield a great deal of power in controlling film festival business.

Hollywood involvement with festivals through public relations and promotion, finally, not only intersects with public relations and negotiations but also with the business of the press. In modern day Cannes, the number of journalists participating has grown from 700 in 1966 to 3,767 in 2010, operating through global networks of print journalism, radio, television, and multiple Internet channels.[11] In the early, "pre-Marché" Cannes, although connections were made, there were fewer business connections: Hollywood primarily used the festivals as a public relations arena for great parties. Deals had been made before the gathering of beautiful people to party. After the market was added, this business component of the festival became more salient even for Hollywood films. The original deal for *Star Wars* was struck at Cannes in 1971.[12] Sheer publicity remains an important reason to see and be seen. In 2007, for example the Coen brothers said, "The Cannes film festival is actually one of the platforms that we can use . . . to get over the fact that in other respects, the movie [*No Country for Old Men*] is not simple to market. . . . It helps publicize the movie to, no small thing, for the European audience, the French audience. . . . It's a great platform just to raise the awareness of the movie."[13] Not surprisingly, auteurs know the value of marketing and publicity.

Hollywood products and festival films are often taken as aesthetic and cultural opposites, although I have challenged this simplification in earlier chapters. Yet, insofar as Hollywood is about film as business, whether studios, stars, or public relations, Hollywood figures and films have been present in and around major film festivals since their beginning and have shared the industrial basis of these festivals. To understand this evolving symbiosis, however, we must also look at the transformations of the festivals that began with their own local and global markets in the late 1950s.

The Markets

Despite their obvious connections to national film industries, in the early decades of these festivals no institutional structure was devoted "solely" to business. The first major accompanying market, the Marché du Film at Cannes, was created in 1959: "Two members of the Chambre Syndicale des Produceurs de Film Français, Emile Natan and Bertrand Bagge, had the idea of taking advantage of this annual meeting of professionals from all round [*sic*] the world to arrange screening of French films, not a part of the official competition, with a view to possible business for international buyers."[14] Three themes stand out even from this initial plan—"taking advantage of this annual meeting," "international," and "business." The market promotes business by using film professionals from the world already gathered in one place. Festival organizers and programmers can attract people in the business to attend the market, while markets can build on the people who are there "for art." While festivals may showcase national industries, this is not the essential raison d'être for many films and audiences, because festivals cross borders in content, distributions, and impact.

Unlike the highly selective Cannes festival, as I have noted, the Marché welcomes anyone who can pay the registration fee; in 2008 there were nearly 600 exhibitors, spilling out of the Palais de Festival into nearby hotels. More than 10,000 people attended. Registration for a day pass can be as cheap as 20 euros a day, giving limited access. Showcasing a film becomes more expensive; screening rates ranged from 620 euros to over 1,000 euros. Renting a booth can cost 4,000 to 6,000 euros in addition to staffing and materials.

As Marijke de Valck notes, the range of the Marché has been much more diverse than that of the festival: "Because movies shown to potential buyers in the market were not subjected to the French censorship board, the porn niche market grabbed its opportunity and grew exponentially at the Côte d'Azur. In 1973, people would fight over a certain little red book on the film market, which listed an impressive number of porn films, including everything produced in the U.S., Germany, and Sweden."[15] Festival officials have responded to official pressure with a prior reading of synopses for films in the market; this gentle censorship led to a new shadow Marché for films and even the production of porn films like *Emmanuelle Goes to Cannes*. Still, Roger Ebert added in the 1980s that "the marketplace is often the scene of some of the festival's greatest vitality. Here the movies have no pretensions of artistic greatness; they only promise to sell tickets."[16]

Hence the Marché at Cannes represents a "democratic" forum alongside elite screenings, an arena open to all who can pay the fee to attend and rent spaces, even if differentiated, for film screenings. Even the tradition of pornographic and extreme films continues despite festival controls: "Titles available at the market can be so wild and crazy it's tempting to arrange them in potential double bills. How about 'Betty Blowtorch' and 'Lady Godiva, Back in the Saddle'? Or 'Oh, My Zombie Mermaid' and 'Shira: The Vampire Samurai'? Or even 'Death to the Supermodels' and 'Bachelor Party Massacre'? One of the most intriguing titles is for a Korean film, 'No Mercy for the Rude,' apparently about a gentleman who is intent on killing those with bad manners. Clearly made with Cannes in mind."[17]

The Marché screens films at different stages of development, looking for business opportunities and selling participation as well as products. Hence, it also connects festivals to production and film as process. Production funds can be raised through pre-sales for distribution rights. Distribution rights are territorial, format-related, and temporal (e.g., rights for Dutch television broadcast for two years). Finished films, if they win prizes, have a better chance of wider distributions. The Marché is democratic, diverse, crass, and rampantly commercial, mixing high and low culture, big and small budgets.

Some who are associated with Cannes have worried that the market challenges the nature of the festival. Gilles Jacob has stated that "we are fully aware of the emergence of a new style of international film festival." Pushed a bit further, he concluded: "This is the opposite of what André Malraux once said. We have shown that the industry of cinema is also an art."[18]

Few other markets existed beside the Marché until the 1970s. In 1973, Film Messe was the market for the Berlinale. It then became the European Film Market (EFM) in 1978, aiming to cement better relationships with the German film industries. It takes place in Berlin in conjunction with the film festival, which now has assumed control over it. The EFM, however, did not become a major player until early 2000, when the American Film Market moved to early November and EFM gained a valuable February slot after Sundance. Its move to the glorious Martin-Gropius-Bau exhibition hall in 2006 signaled the increased importance of the EFM.

In the last decade, many film festivals have advanced the symbiosis of market and festival as a way of ensuring programming, participation, and publicity. Hong Kong Filmart was established in 1997, although it was only brought into direct connection with the HKIFF a decade later; the Pusan Asian Film Market followed in 2006. Other festivals do not directly run a market themselves, but related markets are often held at the same time and make use of the "gathering" of interested parties to make the event a success. San Sebastián 2008, without a market, still boasts that 1,171 industry professionals from fifty-eight countries used the services of the sales office. Describing distribution deals made there, the festival said, for example, that the winner of the "New Directors award, *Li mi de cai xiang (The Equation of Love and Death)*, was purchased by Barton Films." And its claims for hegemony in a Spanish-language market raise important postcolonial questions.[19]

This symbiosis is especially true in North America, where films have faced new questions of distribution since the collapse of the Hollywood studios. Toronto, for example, does not officially have a market, but has gained a reputation for mega-deals made with the likes of Sony that identifies it as the primary market for North American independents. Again, sales and industry delegates can purchase all kinds of passes, from C$260 to $870. Toronto also has an Industry and Sales Office, and specific industry or press screenings; it has been seen as the launching pad for the Oscars as well. Sundance, meanwhile, has for many become dominated by the hunger of studios and distributors for the "next *Little Miss Sunshine*." Even in its early stages, as John Anderson reports, this was part of the discourse of the event:

> Every year at Sundance, in the weeks and months before, everybody identifies the 'buzz' films. They're convinced these are the buzz titles, and how they become buzz titles is a combination of agents hyping them; a genuine—perhaps—creative quality; and a bunch of people on the networks of information trying to angle and pop different things—it's a completely corrupt process. Not necessarily a malicious process, but a corrupt process.
>
> And inevitably, the rule of thumb is, no matter what the buzz titles are, something's going to come out of left field. . . .
>
> The classic examples, overall, are *Strictly Ballroom* and *Shine*.[20]

The size and celebrity of North American markets may be the envy of smaller markets in film festivals; however, these festivals have edged closer to a platform for commercially oriented cinema than the kind of festival films I have described.

Manohla Dargis of the *New York Times* thus dismisses Sundance as a "frenzied meat market."[21] And James Shamus of Good Machine, Inc., notes acidly, "Sundance is the most commercial festival on earth. There is no discourse about film, even independent film, in a public fashion, in the halls of the festivals, on panels, that is not about the following, 'You really made it for this little and you sold it for that much?'"[22]

With the importance of global markets today, no major festival wants to do without one, but each must grapple with those that already exist. While the older Italian festival of Venice has worked to strengthen its position in many ways, its new rival Rome had more ambitious plans for its role in this network of festival markets. Teresa Cavina, Rome's artistic director, asserted, "We think it is possible to concentrate on three key markets: Toronto, which is the door to North America; Rome, which we want to be the European rendezvous; and Pusan, which is a great fall appointment for Asian buyers and sellers."[23] Rome wanted to position itself as the center for the European market, nestled between North America (Toronto) and East Asia (Pusan), pushing aside Cannes and Berlin. As mentioned, this proved overly ambitious, especially given the career of its primary backer, Mayor Veltroni.

Just as festivals existed before and without markets, a few independent film markets have emerged without connections to film festivals. The American Film Market (AFM) was founded in Santa Monica in 1981; its eight thousand participants and three hundred screenings revolve around Hollywood.[24] MIPCOM (Marché International des Programmes), another Cannes trade show for all kinds of media content, has been attended by the likes of Michael Eisner and Elisabeth Murdoch, daughter of media tycoon Rupert Murdoch. The nonfestival markets are all business, yet some want to "steal" glamour from festivals as well. Since 2004, for example, the AFM has collaborated with the AFI FEST in an FIAPF-accredited festival that tends to showcase Hollywood or English-language films.[25] In 2009, for example, the festival's gala offerings were *Fantastic Mr. Fox* and *The Imaginarium of Dr. Parnassus*.

As Roman ambitions suggest, markets also have an annual calendar, discussed below from the vantage of distributors. Within this international network of film festivals and markets, regional markets intersect with annual cycles. These markets provide different contexts for regional cinema to be incorporated into a world market while keeping their local contexts both in cinematic forms and in diverse business practices. Specific markets also promote local talents, settings, and film professionals seeking international coproductions. As cinema has become increasing global, it has become possible for many more Asian films to be distributed in different formats (theater, DVD, Internet, etc.) in the West. Doing business with Asia thus has become more important, attracting filmmakers and distributors to that region. These markets reinforce the simultaneous connections and inequalities of global film festivals that have already appeared in my discussion of texts and organization.

In East and Southeast Asia, for example, Korea, Japan, China, Hong Kong, Thailand, the Philippines, and Singapore now all host markets. Hong Kong and Pusan see themselves as primary but competitive Asian markets.[26] The late Wouter Barendrecht, chairman of Fortissimo Films, was credited with creating the Filmart in 1997, and Asian Film Financing Forum (HAF) in 2002. HAF believes that "For buyers, it is important to meet in an Asian context because that's how Asians do business. . . . It is a different mindset than just meeting in some cold convention center in Milan."[27] Over time, the HKIFF pioneered an integrative trend in Asia with Filmart, originally an independent marketing venture before converging with the festival, awards, and a production forum to make each part of a series of events that cater to different, yet related interests.

While the Pusan market was not established until 2006, the Pusan Production Plan (PPP) had been in existence since 1998. The Pusan market has a $2.8 million budget, with the city of Pusan contributing $1.5 million. As in the initial establishment of the festival, the Korean national and municipal governments and the national film industry have invested heavily. Its September festival has taken a prime annual spot between Toronto and the AFM, and it trumps Hong Kong with its huge budget. However, as the Korean film industries started to wane in late 2000, the Pusan Asian Film Market began to encounter some difficulties.[28]

Regional rivals Pusan and Hong Kong face competition from the revitalized Tokyo Tiffcom and the new Shanghai market. Both bring powerful national economies into cultural marketing. The Shanghai International Film Festival launched its film market in 2007, positioning itself more as a market for studio products, stressing its participants as "local studio reps" and the likes of Harvey Weinstein and Luc Besson.[29] Shanghai market planners wanted to help integrate the Chinese market into the world's film market through coproduction with foreign producers as well as trying to launch China as a location for shoots, replicating the motivations of the PRC on a global stage. Hence, they are most interested in mainstream international commercial filmmaking rather than regional or smaller scale films.

Meanwhile, in the Middle East, as oil-rich kingdoms have started their own film festivals to gain global cultural status, Dubai and Abu Dhabi have been interested in film markets. Dubai launched its market in 2007; its star program, the Dubai Film Connection, works with the Cannes Producers Network to promote projects with Arab themes. Abu Dhabi, meanwhile, planned "brand[ing] itself as a film financing conference."[30] Both of these new markets are more interested in promoting production, rather than distribution, partly because there are now too many markets and newcomers can scarcely compete with the established venues. Yet these newcomers, with their oil money, can always promote projects.

In Africa, the PanAfrican Film and Television Festival of Ouagadougou (FESPACO), one of the oldest and most prominent festivals, actually has no market. Since 1995, Cape Town has held the Sithengi Film and Television Market, which partners with the Cape Town World Cinema Festival. It partnered with Berlin to hold its own Talent Campus in 2006, with funding from the Goethe Institute. However, it has faced serious turmoil, with a total change over of board members in 2007, so it is hard to assess its future. In 2006, FIAPF visited the Cairo International Film Festival and, acting as a producers' organization, stressed to the festival that it "must establish a market for cinema production."[31] The Web site for the 2008 festival lists a film market at the festival, but offers scant information. The lack of a stable film festival/film market pair in Africa reflects the limited power Africa has in this alternative film business world, forcing filmmakers to seek support through other festivals or even African festivals outside the continent.[32]

Latin America also lacks major film festival markets. Mar del Plata has the Intercine—International Business Hub; however, it emphasizes Argentine films. In 2006, it had around two hundred industry representatives, with only 35 percent being from outside Argentina. The Festival Internacional de Cine in Guadalajara has created an Ibero-American Film Market, which reached its fourth edition in 2006. Still, neither São Paulo nor Bogotá has a film market. Many Latin American filmmakers simply go to the European film festival markets, like EFM or San Sebastián, to sell their films. Among the twenty-three members of the FIAPF, only Argentina is in Latin America.

The markets at these global film festivals are said to "ADD VALUE"[33] to the festivals, allowing them not only to be showcases, but also to be channels through which films are made, distributed, and exhibited. They bring together the world of film, create a forum for competition, and, as in the case of film knowledge and selection, stratify it globally. In many ways, the markets are about the bottom line of the film business, and the traditional cultural aspects of film screenings and competitions are the more public faces of the festivals. Yet, film festivals today cannot survive by only showing films to film lovers—or perhaps even business people. Organizers see the market as a means to guarantee wider press, more movers and shakers of the industries, stars, and ultimately sponsors and revenues, while remaining a public event of some sort. Let me now explore these sales from the vantage of the distribution end of the cinema business, so as to understand how audiences in the end get the opportunity to see many of these films promoted by film festivals.

Distribution: Buyers and Sellers

Unsuccessful independent producers say that looking for a distributor is when you finally pay the price for your independence. And it's true that an indie film that no one wants to distribute is not even an orphan in the storm, since storms pay enough attention to smack you around. Orphan indies waste away in a desert of neglect. On the other hand, if the fruit of your independence is a film that a distributor covets, you can write your own ticket and use it to ride into festivals, general release—and even a deal for your next movie.[34]

Markets share spaces at festivals, but they themselves do not sell films or even tickets for films. Instead, they offer independent contemporaneous venues in which people negotiate rights to sell tickets for films in different markets. In the trade of films as commodities, the sellers are (primarily) producers and the buyers are distributors. There are also sales agents, who can be at times producers and distributors; sales agents buy the rights to distribute the film from the producers, then find distributors for different regions and formats. When the media report that deals are made at Sundance or Cannes, generally they are talking about distribution companies such as then Artisan Entertainment that acquired *The Blair Witch Project* (1999) or earlier distribution rights negotiated during production phrases. Other major distribution companies include Sony and IFC in the United States, and Cinéart for Europe, and many more for other parts of the world. These deals have replaced the vertical integration of Hollywood and its own theater chains, for example, with more fluid and competitive intermediaries whose negotiations, themselves, become news at festivals.

In 2007, for example, Wild Bunch, one of the most important European sales agents and distributors, was selling Cristian Mungiu's Romanian competition entry *4 Months, 3 Weeks, and 2 Days* in Cannes before it even won the Palme d'Or.[35] According to its exporter, Vincent Maraval, Wild Bunch does one-third to half of its annual business at Cannes.[36] At Cannes 2008, its competitor, Fortissimo, picked up John Woo's next project, *1949*, which was dropped in 2009; IFC Films took U.S. rights to South Korean potential smash *The Chaser*. Meanwhile, Fox bought Steven Soderbergh's *Che* for Spain as two separate films while Celluloid Dreams purchased Bruce Beresford's *Mao's Last Dancer* for international sales. Then, in Toronto, Maximum Film Distribution bought the rights for *Disgrace*, which had won the international critics' prize from Fortissimo. La Fabrique de Films bought *Gigantic*, also from Fortissimo. Fox Searchlight paid $4 million for U.S. rights to *The Wrestler*, winner of the just-concluded Venice festival's Golden Lion.

Many deals were concluded without exact knowledge of markets to follow. *Gigantic* gained minimal revenues and *Mao's Last Dancer* found diverse audiences, while *The Wrestler* built its critical acclaim into a slow and steady revenue even before its Oscar win for Best Actor. As public relations specialist Laura Kim observed a decade ago at Sundance, "A lot of distributors are out to prove they have more money and make splashy buys. If they had any sense or talked to their marketing people or went back to L.A. and thought about it, they wouldn't buy a lot of these movies. These movies need more support when they open."[37] Even so, when John Anderson surveyed all feature films screened at Sundance in 1999 a year later, only half had U.S. distribution in place.[38]

Festival markets also encompass the ambience of sales, the "buzz" and "frenzy." Every day during a festival, the trade press writes about many, many deals that attest to the centrality of the festival event itself. That means these distribution deals are read as integral to the market and the festival as a whole. The "successes" in distribution deals, in turn, validate the programs of the festival. Hence festivals and markets become dual film emporia. The Marché at Cannes had over sixteen hundred screenings in 2008; the European Film Market at Berlin had eleven hundred; Venice, on the other hand, only had around forty-five.[39] In Toronto, while the organizers "still pretended they were not operating a market, simply a fest with some very well-managed industry screenings,"[40] providing opportunities for visibility and deals remains extremely important.

Since the market is all about business, good management is essential for success. More importantly, good management leads to the market's ability to attract important people to the screenings, thus allowing good products to be sold to good buyers. Festival organizers never stop talking about whether a festival is well run or not. It is indeed all business, the business of selling art and culture, where bad management has tangible negative impacts on the festival, whatever the films' artistic values.

The success of a market can be measured quantitatively and qualitatively. The number of screenings as well as the qualities of the films screened and the qualities of the buyers determine importance for distributors. Some distributors have also started to use the concept of "market premiere." For example, Kim Ki-Duk's *Dream* had its market premiere at Cannes's Marché in May 2007, then its official world premiere at San Sebastián in September 2008. Yet, sellers and buyers use the festival circuit as a game board with their own strategic interests. Sal Ladestro, vice president of Sony Pictures Marketing, brought their film *Across the Universe* to Rome in 2007. Meanwhile, Albert Lee of Hong Kong's Emperor Motion Pictures went to AFM, Cannes, and Hong Kong Filmart to sell his films.[41]

Distributors also make use of the festival calendar. Planners for Hong Kong Filmart, held in March, see this event as nicely sandwiched between Berlin and Cannes. The fall is then left to Venice, Toronto, AFM, and Pusan, before film businessmen start the year all over again in freezing Utah at Sundance in January. This calendar, while never officialized by any governing body, is very important to make sure that films move from one festival/market to another and find the right distributors. Besides the spatial and temporal dimensions of these markets, there is also hierarchy among film festival markets (just as there is with the film festivals). The bigger festivals, such as Cannes, Berlin, Toronto, Sundance, and Pusan, have more important markets, meaning that top sales agents, distributors, and acquisitions people are gathered to make deals with the festival films that circulate within and beyond the festival circuit. Cannes has the widest global reach, Toronto is more about distribution in North America, and Pusan is more about Asian films and Asian distributions.

When the AFM moved from February to early November in 2004, people at Berlin were quite excited. Promoters visiting the EFM told me how it would grow with this move, which it indeed did. In 2008, it had "6,000 participants [with] 700 films from 430 companies."[42] The EFM has made itself more relevant to other festivals as well: in Berlin, films shown at Sundance that have not picked up distributors are screened in a section called "Straight from Sundance."[43] This establishes a codistribution structure across two festivals: those who cannot attend Sundance have the opportunity to purchase some of these films at Berlin. As Patrick Frater at *Variety* has pointed out, "The fall season now offers so many permutations of festivals and markets to attend that bizzers nowadays make difficult choices about allocation of their time and resources—and then spend three months looking over their shoulder to see if they have picked the right events."[44] The many choices offered in markets, festivals, and film screenings create headaches for distributors; however, this underscores the importance and attraction of these combined festival/market events—they *are* the places to buy and sell films.

Distribution also becomes a form of aesthetic gate-keeping situated in the festival. If films are not distributed, are they somehow intrinsically worse than those that gain such exposure? In some ways, this is an impossible question to answer, since the films that lack distribution will not be seen or even reviewed, precluding judgment. Hence, festivals, in conjunction with their markets, become conduits for the exposure and survival of films, auteurs, and even national industries. This adds an economic twist to taste and canon in the form of a prior filter on what much of a global audience will see. To find a comfortable zone where the business and artistic sides can coexist is never an easy task; nevertheless, the two have never truly been set apart.

The roles of sales agents and distributors themselves has changed in the new world of film festivals. Companies like Fortisimmo, Wild Bunch, and Celluloid Dreams not only distribute to more traditional outlets like cinema, DVD, or television broadcast, but also distribute to film festivals.[45] Non-"A" festivals may need to pay distributors $500 to $2,000 in rental fees for festival films. Only two to three decades ago, distributors would send their films for free (charging only shipping, handling, and insurance), because they wanted exposure from festivals; here, they were also dealing with expensive prints rather than the disposable videos and DVDs of contemporary film festival circulation.

With the ever increasing number of festivals, the festivals themselves have become a market for the distributors. A festival film that has not won big prizes can still have a festival run of about two years. Revenue generated through the festival circuit becomes important for many of these low-budget, limited-audience films. In the end, this growth of the distributor as agent in the festivals, however "behind-the-scenes," inevitably has changed the world of the festivals. As one European festival programmer told me, "In the past, you went to festivals and you talked to filmmakers, directors, and their films; today, you go to festivals, and you deal with distributors."[46] But even more, festivals have begun to work directly with producers and sellers to create the products in which they as well as commercial enterprises ultimately trade: the films themselves.

Film Festivals as Producers

While the creation of the Marché at Cannes in 1959 changed the business climate of festivals, the introduction of Rotterdam's CineMart in 1984, followed by the Hubert Bals Funds in 1988, Pusan PPP in 1997, and other coproduction fora and funds from Locarno and Berlin to Buenos Aires and Hong Kong has meant that film festivals have started to control, at least indirectly, the business of film production.[47] While festivals are not studios, through their markets and production and coproduction forums, they are becoming places where connections, negotiations, and financing of films take place. They are increasingly a necessary destination for young filmmakers who work outside the commercial studio system, be it in Hollywood, Hong Kong, Algiers, or Rio de Janeiro. Furthermore, festivals, through their historic public connections, can funnel government funds from the EU, the oil rich UAE, or emergent Asian funds into targeted production. Even the numerous prizes that are given at film festivals and the prominence of international distributors, like Wild Bunch or Fortissimo, in their organizations have meant that film festivals have established institutions that in some way parallel the production, distribution, and exhibition processes for mainstream cinema, including their own share of failures and unproduced works.[48]

Festivals are more flexible, diverse, and selective (at least in "artistic" value) than mainstream studios. And they aim for different markets. While they are obviously not vertically integrated like Classic Hollywood Studios were, collectively they form a complicated, competitive global network, spatially as well as temporally, that also constitutes an annual pilgrimage calendar and provides benchmarks for success that shape the lives of alternative, independent cinemamakers around the world. Yet, critics have also raised the question of how these funds, especially from the North, may channel filmmaking and tastes in global coproductions and undercut the role of local circuits as alternatives.[49]

These creative business roles also have changed festivals. Through these institutions and processes, film festivals consolidate their roles as legitimate arbiters of prestige for films, filmmakers, and ethnic and national cinemas. Being involved in the production processes of these movies provides the festivals with films for their own lineup (in competition with other global festivals). These films give the festivals a steady supply of movies, not unlike the old Hollywood studios. This supply, of course, is more fragmented, based on much smaller budgets and incomplete projects, and oftentimes anti-Hollywood in form and content. Over time, production support, from money to classes like Berlin's Talent Campus and San Sebastián's Film School Meeting, foster themes, forms, and even stars (directors/auteurs) within the system as well; many directors gain their first experiences with film festivals this way.

I was able to participate in one of these school events because one student film from my school, *Woman as Property* by Norie Taniguci, was selected to be part of the International Film School Meeting at San Sebastián in 2008. Seventeen film schools from all over the world, from Africa, Europe, and North and South America, were invited. Each school sent the filmmaker, another student as juror, a teacher, and an administrator. The students were able to work with Amos Gitai, who, together with the student jurors, chose the winner. During the four days of the program, the students watched and critiqued each other's works, attended workshops ranging from the latest 3D technologies to seminars offered by professionals (sales agents, the press, and officials from MEDIA), and soaked in the film festival air. We had a great time, going to many parties, mingling with other student filmmakers, and cemented some good relationships.

The festivals are using these "schools" as training grounds for future festival filmmakers. Some learn how to get matching funds to complete their productions, how to package their films, and how to get the maximum exposure. If finished, many of these small projects enter the festivals' sidebar or second tier sections; as the directors become more important, the "successful" ones eventually move up to the major competitions. If some of these directors become "big," the sponsoring festival will take credit and may put the director into a new position in the jury or offer some prominent recognition, further consolidating the festival's position as donors of film prestige.

These changes have taken place within wider political histories as well. After the restless political climate of the 1960s, new sections like Directors' Fortnights at Cannes and the incorporation of the Forum of Young Cinema into the Berlin program opened spaces for new directors and cinema from the so-called third-world countries or the "South." Meanwhile, Hubert Bals's International Film Festival of Rotterdam in 1972 focused the festival on alternative cinema from the Far East and developing countries. Festival dialogues also became more globally diverse. FESPACO, the Panafrican Film and Television Festival of Ouagadougou, was founded in 1972, while in 1978 the Hong Kong International Film Festival became one of the first Asian festivals. Global voices also found new European homes: Nantes's Festival des Trois Continents was established in 1979, specializing in cinema of Africa, Asia, and Latin and Black America followed by the Fribourg International Film Festival (1980), specializing in third-world cinema and Pesaro. Film festivals gained new identities, moving away, in some ways, from the safe prestige and box office that the contemporary Oscar or César promotes to positions that are more inclusive and alternative.

Evolving technology, including the introduction of VCRs, DVDs, and digital technology, also has changed film production. While big movie budgets continue to grow, it is also possible to make cheap feature-length digital products for as little as $50,000 (like Jia Zhanghe's *Pickpocket* (*Xiao Wu*), changing the landscape for independent production. This has altered the possibility of festivals as sponsors as well as exhibitors for independent films, yet it has also reinforced their role in shaping a visible canon.

This support, though, ensures that festivals will have products and even stars for the future in an increasingly competitive world. While film festivals take place in real urban and national space, all major festivals are international, creating interesting issues that test the relationships between host countries, the festivals, and diverse international communities. Marco Müller, Locarno's director from 1992 to 2000 (and the director of the Venice festival since 2005), conceives of the festival as "a way of thinking about the world."[50] Meanwhile, in 2007, the focus of "Berlinale Talent Campus . . . [was] on a current and burning theme addressed by world cinema: the search for cultural identity in a global—and globalized—film business."[51]

Since most prominent film festivals are located in Western Europe, the coproduction system also reproduces inequalities, raising important questions about the power dynamics of global cinema. Film festivals have sought to discover and nurture new talents, especially in what Europeans call the "South" (developing/third world) and may also target minorities recognized in Western terms, as in larger trends in film production, form, distribution, and viewership. Randall Halle, for example, has explored the influence of European Union funding and coproductions on film through programs like MEDIA and Eurimages. Eurimages works closely with various film festivals' coproduction markets, like CineLink at Sarajevo, New Cinema Network at Rome, and CineMart at Rotterdam, and provides production funds, to the tune of around 30,000 euros annually for different individual projects. Oftentimes, some of these films are typical festival films that are premiered at festivals and circulated through the festival circuit. Halle finds various forms of imagined European community at play in continental coproductions of "works that reflect the multiple facets of a European society whose common roots are evidence of a single culture."[52] More troubling is when these European funds are used outside Europe. Halle uses the examples of Eurimages-funded works by Yesim Ustaoglu, *Journey to the Sun* (1999) and *Waiting for the Clouds* (2003), to assert that the themes these films tackle— "suppression of Kurdish population" and the "destruction of Greek Ottoman population" in Turkey—are "in line with European political agendas."[53] The press kit of *Waiting for the Clouds* lists the festival-related lineage of this film, which had support from the Sundance/NHK International Filmakers Award and the Hubert Bals Fund of Rotterdam as well as various production funds from the European Union.[54] Halle is careful not to "contest the value of opening up for discussion the atrocities committed by military and dictatorial regimes," but he warns about a new form of Orientalism, where these funds and support from the West produce "a set of cultural texts that speak the truth of the other on behalf of that other,"[55] where the filmmakers are structurally dependent on European funding. Film festivals, specifically European film festivals, are operators that facilitate this kind of complicated cooperation and exchange. Festivals help provide funds, either from the festivals, or other agencies that use the festival to distribute these funds, then festivals screen these films and help distribute them to the rest of the world.

Within this general panorama, it is important to explore both coproduction fora and festival-controlled production funds. I also address the addition of more competitions to festival programs insofar as filmmakers can use these prizes to secure either distribution or capital for production. These selection and funding structures epitomize the crucial emergent role of festivals in creating films even before arbitrating and extending film knowledge. After I describe and analyze some major coproduction and project markets and the funds associated with them, I complement my analysis of funders with filmmaker Jia Zhangke, who has gained a major international platform through world cinematic festivals. These production and funding issues frame broader questions of capital, knowledge, and power that these changing film festivals and their funding/production now embody.

Coproduction Fora/Project Markets

"'The future of cinematography is not to be expected from Europe or the United States, but all the more from lesser known film cultures.'"[56] Hubert Bals, the founder of International Film Festival of Rotterdam (IFFR), sought to remold the film festival from a showcase of the stale establishment to inclusive film events that celebrated innovation, risk, and diversity. IFFR now is renowned for discoveries without a red carpet. Besides screening films, Rotterdam now hosts the CineMart, the Hubert Bals Fund, and the Tiger Award, all EU institutions that foster the making and circulation of international independent cinema. Among its better known protégés are Chen Kaige, Cristian Mungiu, Zhang Yuan, Christopher Nolan, Hong Sang-soo, Kelly Reichardt, and Todd Haynes.

CineMart, founded in 1984, was initially a film market. Since 1991 it also has pioneered international coproduction. Each year, forty-five projects are selected out of hundreds of submissions. The producers of these projects "present their film projects to co-producers, bankers, funds, sales agents, distributors, TV stations and other potential financiers."[57] CineMart serves as a filter to ensure that the qualities of both the projects and the financiers are reliable, making itself a seal of confidence. CineMart, however, only accepts projects that have never been pitched anywhere else, although it also encourages projects to have secured some financial backing at the outset. This is not unlike what "A"-level festivals do in terms of the selection of movies for their competitions, where only premieres are allowed. Situated at the beginning of the year, CineMart is the oldest project market and by now has an impressive track record. Clearly, such claims to exclusivity not only promote film in general but serve to maintain CineMart's position as the major coproduction forum.

Following the success of CineMart, the "A"-level festivals have added competing coproduction fora for established filmmakers and younger students. Cannes's Marché du Film has the Producers Network (2004) and Cinéfondation Atelier (2005); Berlin has a coproduction market within their European Film Market (2004); and Locarno has Open Doors (2003). Even a new festival like Rome began with New Cinema Network (2006). In Africa, Cape Town has Sithengi Film and Television Market; in Asia, Tokyo has Tokyo Project Gathering (2005), Pusan has the Asian Film Market (2006), and Hong Kong has Filmart (1997). In Latin America, the Buenos Aires Film Festival has Buenos Aires Lab (BAL), and the Sarajevo Film Festival has CineLink. Project markets are scattered all over, with each having its own regional specialization, again forming a global system.

These coproduction or project markets bring international directors and producers together with international film financiers. Unlike the Classic Hollywood Studios, which were very centralized, or contemporary Hollywood, which can demand large sums of capital in the boardroom, money for independent cinema must be assembled from multiple sources. Festival producers have know-how and connections to other producers and sources of money, be they government funds, or equipment investments/donations from studios/labs or manufacturers, or distributors. Many companies are small and can only contribute a fraction of the total budget for a film. Although digital festival films can cost as little as $50,000 for beginners or independents from poor countries, even small sums need to be raised through diverse channels, so coproduction markets are perfect for these small films. More importantly, these markets, as well as film festivals in general, are excellent places for networking with people who can tell you who is interested in what project.

Thus, production networks like CineMart or the Hong Kong and Pusan project competitions use the fund-raising, production, and distribution models from mainstream films, but apply them to small global movies. Using these structures, international independent film production has become more institutionalized. Again, scale is important. Hollywood may pay millions for one star; those millions are enough for many low-budget independent films. Some films can recoup their production costs simply going around the festival circuit. Sometimes governmental investors care more about cultural rather than monetary returns. Some films will never recover even modest investment, making it difficult for their directors to find funding for the next project.

Funding Films

For the filmmaker, production demands management—arranging, balancing, and allocating funds. Some coproduction markets also have their own funds to distribute to worthwhile projects. Any single fund is rarely sufficient to cover the complete budget, forcing these projects to be coproductions. The HBF, for example, has five categories of funding: (1) Script and project development (maximum 10,000 euros); (2) Digital production (funding up to 20,000 euros for digital production of a film with a maximum budget of 100,000 euros; (3) Post-production funding or final financing (maximum 30,000 euros); (4) Distribution (maximum 15,000 euros); and (5) Hubert Bals Fund Plus (additional funding up to 50,000 euros for a Hubert Bals Fund project that already received script and project development support, coproduced by a Dutch producer).[58] The money is modest and the projects themselves are also modest, at least in monetary terms. The funds also can only be applied to one aspect of film production or distribution, again forcing the director and producers to find other resources to complete the project. Funds for digital production were introduced in 2007, making Rotterdam one of the first festivals to recognize the importance of digital filmmaking, continuing its status as a vanguard.

Another important qualification influences distribution and the form of festival films, while recalling Halle's concerns with Orientalism. While CineMart is open to all international participants, HBF only supports projects that originate from developing countries. This carries on the strength of the IFFR, which has always been the promotion of innovative cinemas from developing countries.

HBF is not the only European fund to target its support. Cooperating with the German Cultural Foundation, the Berlin World Cinema Fund (WCF) was launched in 2004 to fund projects for production and distribution. As its organizers noted, "It is the World Cinema Fund's intention to finance film projects from countries whose film industries are endangered by political and economic crises. Up through 2007, the Fund will focus on promoting the production and distribution of films from Latin America, the Middle East, Central Asia and Africa."[59] They also stressed that "the fund is to help the realization of films which otherwise could not be produced. . . . Another goal is to strength the profile of these films in German cinemas."[60] The WCF also seeks films "with strong cultural identities, outstanding aesthetics and compelling stories that give an authentic picture of their countries of origin."[61] In 2007, the WCF awarded a total of 230,000 euros to five projects from Argentina, Angola, Columbia, Israel, and Iran. The WCF expresses a desire to bring Germany closer to parts of the world of which it knows little; it is striking, however, that some of these nations also figure prominently in cinematic politics and other critical international affairs.[62]

Vincenzo Bugno, the project director of the WCF, ran Locarno's Open Doors. This fund, launched in 2003 with the support of the Swiss Federal Department of Foreign Affairs' Agency for Development and Cooperation (SDC), focuses on "developing" countries, with a different regional focus each year. It commenced with Cuba and Argentina in 2003, and over the years it has covered such varied regions as the Mekong delta, the Maghreb, Southeast Asia, Greater China, and most recently Central Asia in 2010. In 2007, when Open Doors selected Mashrek (the eastern Mediterranean from Turkey to Israel), thirteen projects were chosen out of 121. The directors and producers of these projects first went to a workshop on pitching. After the workshop, two days of one-on-one meetings followed with potential coproduction partners from Europe, North America, Japan, and South Korea. In addition to providing a forum for directors to meet other producers and financiers, Locarno, through the Swiss Agency for Development and Cooperation, provided two grants, amounting to 100,000 Swiss francs. France also contributed 10,000 euros for development.[63]

The Swiss Federal Council sees the festival as a "political forum," indicating a Swiss interest in interacting with the rest of the world. According to Bugno, Open Doors "always tries to get in touch with cinematographic cultures outside Europe. The idea behind Locarno's Open Doors initiative is to connect the many talented producers from different regions with European producers, sales agents, television agents, and anyone who can help improve or finance a project."[64] He also stresses that visiting and constant contacts with these countries are keys to developing a workable strategy for these funds. Still, the overlap of nations with Berlin and with global politics is striking.

Both a coproduction forum and a fund, the New Cinema Network of the embattled Rome International Film Festival also represents a mixed coproduction forum, and is run by Teresa Cavina, who had five years of experience at Locarno's Open Doors. In 2007, it received twenty-six projects, fourteen from Europe and twelve from the rest of the world. Rome's New Cinema Network, however, sought to coordinate with other coproduction events around the globe and the calendar, affirming festivals as production systems:

> The international projects being showcased by New Cinema Network have a different mission: to link the Rome event with similar initiatives throughout the year. They include the Sundance's year-round directing and screen-writing labs, Rotterdam's CineMart in January, the Berlinale Co-Production Market in February, the Hong Kong Asia Film Financing Forum (HAF) in March, and the Cinefondation's Atelier du Festival at the Cannes film festival in May. HAF and Cinefondation's Atelier formally cooperate with Rome's New Cinema Network by sending three top projects from their own events, enabling the film-makers to obtain fresh exposure at Rome.[65]

In March 2007, HAF in Hong Kong, for example, awarded 10,000 euros to Kim Jee-woon from money from Rome. The coordination of coproduction fora and festival funding sources echoes the competitive but cooperative global festival calendar.

European-based competitions, even when they invite outside submissions, face an interesting contrast in developments in Asia, whose film festivals have generally occupied a second tier in global prestige despite the growth of their cinematic industries and global critical evaluation of their films and personnel. In Asia, the Pusan International Film Festival (PIFF) was launched in 1996, and the Pusan Production Plan (PPP) followed in 1998 to promote Asian cinema as well as Korean cinema. In its initial run, the PPP only accepted projects originating from Asia. Some projects were exclusively limited to emerging Korean directing talents with "New Directors in Focus." In 2002, more established names in Asian cinema, like Hou Hsiao-hsien, and Mohsen Makhmalbaf—directors whose films have won major prizes at the "A" festivals—became producers at PPP.[66] In a way, these masters were nurturing the next generations of filmmakers in their regions.

Unlike some other festivals, which launched their film market before their project market and funds, Pusan only began its Asian Film Market in 2006.[67] In this year, the PPP also started to accept project submissions from outside Asia, making it more international. Since this time, the PPP has also worked closely with other coproduction markets and funds, from HBF to the HAF, consolidating the tight network these institutions form to create some kind of an international coproduction apparatus.

Production and connections also constitute elements of competition among festivals. In Hong Kong, as Hong Kong cinema was enjoying international success in the 1990s, Filmart began with colonial government support to make Hong Kong an attractive place to do film business, modeled after other film markets in Europe and the United States. The HAF, Hong Kong's coproduction market, is an outgrowth of Filmart that was launched in 2000, concentrating on Asian production. However, it had a rocky career in years of crisis, economic and epidemiological: there was not enough money in 2001 and 2002, and the SARS epidemic greatly curtailed the 2003 HAF, allowing Pusan to move ahead. After 2005, HAF was run by the Hong Kong Trade and Development Council; only in 2007 was HAF taken over by the administration of the HKIFF.

In 2007, HAF selected twenty-five out of 155 Asian projects to be presented to investors in carefully prepared bilingual Chinese and English texts. Even the process of preparation and translation, as participants have told me, can raise issues about cogency or presentation for new filmmakers; there is a real give and take as editors raise questions that may have an impact on eventual production and sales. HAF aims at picking up projects after Rotterdam and Berlin (February) but not competing with Cannes (May), while some of its projects go to Rome and Pusan (September). It partners with CineMart, HBF, PPP, Rome, Paris Cinema, and J-Pitch from Japan. It also has a relatively high rate of eventual completion of funded projects—roughly 25 percent.[68]

Project markets, like festivals and distribution, have increasingly developed into an integrated global network both in time and space: some are literally run by the same people or overlap in selection and support. Given the risks of European hegemony, the Asian markets and funds, with their counterpart Pan-Asian orientation, or new initiatives from the Middle East can create spaces for different voices and visions.

Besides creating funding opportunities for projects from different countries, these coproduction fora and funds also assist smaller film festivals to replicate their models. CineMart has several partners, including the Independent Features Project (IFP) in the United States, the Hong Kong Asia Film Financing Forum, the Sithengi Film and Television Market in South Africa, the Marché du Film (Producer's Network) at Cannes, and Cinelink in Sarajevo.[69] This network also indicates that CineMart recognizes that film festivals, with this structure of coproduction, are essential in its quest to promote independent film production, and also to consolidate its position in this production circuit. In 2006, the African Co-Production Forum initiative was introduced in the Sithengi Film and Television Market in Cape Town with funding from HBF and the Göteborg Film Fund from Sweden. The initiative wants to source African projects and have them pitched at the Feature Film Co-Production Forum at Sithengi, and then at CineMart. Travel grants were awarded to two directors—Jide Bello for *My Brother's Sin* and Musekiwa Samuriwo for *Cup of Glory*,[70] upcoming filmmakers who still had to struggle to finish their work and put their names out. Sites of new funds and coproduction markets are sprouting at an incredible rate; however, their scale remains relatively small, both in production and reach.

The products of these project markets and funds rely on festivals for eventual exhibition beyond their own sites. All of these support mechanisms, in turn, measure their success by what projects are completed and are shown in major festivals. CineMart, HBF, WCF, PPP, and HAF all issue press releases that highlight the success of their funded project. Has this mixture of funds made the idea of national cinema less relevant? Berlin's 2006 Golden Bear winner was Jasmila Zbanich, who had participated in Thessaloniki's 2003 Balkan Fund meetings. There she secured script development funding for *Grbavica*, about a Bosnian woman raped in a detention camp during the war. The film has been touted as a success story for coproduction, with diverse subsequent sources of funding from HBF and various western European government funds, as well as private production companies from the Vienna-based Coop99 to television distributor ZDF/arte.[71] Yet one must also recall Halle's warning about other coproductions, that "Under the guise of authentic images, the films establish a textual screen that prevents apprehension of complexly lived reality of people in not-too-distant parts of the world."[72] Thus, the career of Jia Zhangke allows us to examine more closely how film festivals, project markets, and coproduction funds have helped to catapult a career and reshape Chinese and global cinema.

Funding and the Auteur: Jia Zhangke

Like many of his contemporaries in the sixth or urban generation of Chinese filmmakers, Jia was a graduate of the Beijing Film Academy. His first short (fifty-seven minutes), *Xiao Shan Goes Home* (*Xiao Shan hui jia*), won the top prize at the second Hong Kong Independent Short Film and Video Awards in 1997. With this first accolade from a small competition, in 1998 Jia went on to win awards at Berlin, Vancouver, Pusan, Nantes, and San Francisco with *Pickpocket (Xiao Wu)* (1997). Here, he also asserted his voice and his vision of a China that is modern and alienated, and whose citizens are trapped in rapidly changing local, national, and global environments that socialism has not prepared them for.

While the first two films were primarily self-financed, recognition from various festivals and the accompanying reviews attracted investors for Jia's next project. *Platform (Zhantai)* (2000), the story of a petty thief in a small Chinese city, received investment from Kitano Film,[73] coproduction funds from Pusan, Hubert Bals, Fonds Sud, and Fondation Montecinemaverita (Swiss), including both cultural funds and funds from the clothing company Benetton. *Platform* also made waves at global festivals: it was in official competition at Venice, won the Netpac Award there, and gained other awards at Nantes, Fribourg, Buenos Aires, and Singapore.

Jia's next picture, *Unknown Pleasures (Ren xiao yao)* (2002), did not use any government or festival funds. Still, this small film about young friends received international private financing from Japan, France, Korea, and Hong Kong. This film continued to climb the festival hierarchy; it was selected for competition at Cannes. In 2003, Jia and Hong Kong's Chow Keung and Nelson Lik Wai Yu (his cinematographer for many films since *Pickpocket*) formed their own independent film production company, XStream Picture, which subsequently coproduced many of Jia's films, including *Still Life (Sanxia heoren)* and *24 City (Ershi si cheng ji)*. The company is based in Beijing and Hong Kong, thus capitalizing on the increased production opportunities bridging the two places. Being his own producer has given Jia a great deal of control over his movies, yet he has had to continue to raise more funds.

With these successes internationally, Jia finally received official funding from his own country. The Shanghai Film Group, together with French, Japanese, and Hong Kong companies as well as Fonds Sud, supported his next project, *The World (Shijie)* (2004), set in and around a Chinese amusement simulacrum of the world, complete with costumed characters and pavilions. Chinese support made his movie above ground, officially approved in China. He continued to compete successfully in Venice.

In 2006, *Still Life* won the Golden Lion at Venice, with primary financing from the Shanghai Film Group; it was also a Rotterdam CineMart project of 2005. Jia had managed to balance above-ground support with a project that has inflected criticism of the Three Gorges Dam (never made directly in the film but raised in every discussion).

In 2007, nonetheless, Jia pitched HAF with a spy story set in Hong Kong of the 1950s, *Shuang xiong hui*.[74] The project received the Hong Kong Cyberport Award ($13,000) for the most imaginative narrative and technical excellence. As such, Jia also became part of the global film festival establishment: in casual conversation at San Sebastián, fellow filmmaker Amos Gitai had talked highly of Jia's work. Now, Jia himself selects/guides future filmmakers—Jia headed the jury for Cannes's Cinéfondation and Short Film section in May 2007. Jia's documentary *Useless (Wuyong)*, was shown in Venice in September 2007 and won the documentary award. *24 City* (2008), which transmutes documentary, memoirs, and reenactments in Chengdu at the moment of transition from factory 154 to bourgeois housing in a grim portrait of the new China, premiered at Cannes and went on to other festivals in Mar del Plata, São Paulo, Toronto, New York, and Hong Kong.

Having built an international reputation, Jia now uses this fame to negotiate for more domestic projects, such as *I Wish I Knew (Hai shang chuan qi)*. The Shanghai Expo of 2010 actually commissioned Jia to make this documentary of the city, made up of interviews of different people. In preparation for the film, a press event took place in June 2009 at the site of the Expo. After the film's premiere at Un Certain Regard at Cannes, it was supposed to open in Shanghai on June 14, but the showing was canceled. Some have reported that because one of the interviewees, Han Han, makes controversial remarks in the movie, the authorities had to reconsider.[75] *I Wish I Knew* opened in Beijing on July 1, and on July 2, 2010, nationally, with a slightly edited version that is ten minutes shorter than the one shown at Cannes. At the opening in Beijing, when a reporter asked Jia if the film was a propaganda film because it was the Image Movie of the Shanghai Expo, meaning a movie just for show, Jia replied that "it is a movie that respects human memories and it boldly addresses many issues that could not be articulated in the past."[76] When asked about the business side of the movie, Jia told the reporter that the movie had recovered two-thirds of its cost and there should be more distribution deals made in Toronto the following September. Jia also expressed his desire to work on more commercial films, saying that he was first attracted by John Woo and Ringo Lam's action movies, and that he can make commercial films as well as art films.[77]

As of the time of writing, he is still working on *The Age of Tattoo*, adapted from a novel of the same name set after the Cultural Revolution. Juliette Binoche has said that she will be working with Jia. Jia's next project, *In the Qing Dynasty*, is considered a big-budget costume period piece. In some ways, he seems to be drifting away a bit from the festival world. On the other hand, he seems to be negotiating the many demands from different communities—global film festival, Chinese authorities, Chinese film industries, Chinese popular audiences. The Museum of Modern Art in New York held a retrospective on him, and at Locarno he was awarded the Leopard of Honour in 2010.

Jia's development as an auteur has worked through layers of funding, screening, and audience. His stories continue to explore a changing and uncertain China in a way that avoids the historicism of many past directors (Chinese and foreign) and the ideological claims of more mainstream Chinese filmmakers.

He has shepherded this vision into official support and "critical" portraits of contemporary China and a big-budget costume drama. Yet, as he becomes a global player and agent, this may influence his trajectory and evaluation, as it did with Zhang Yimou in the fifth generation. Festivals may seek discoveries, but their funding and coproduction cannot guarantee continued independence, even if that were an unalloyed aim.

Conclusion: Rethinking Production and Power

The evolution of film festivals as sponsors of production in addition to exhibition and distribution is tied into multiple roles through which institutions, agencies, and people of film festivals produce global film knowledge. Yet, this support also embeds elements of national and international power into this creation and circulation of knowledge, as Bill Nichols has noted: "Like the tourist, we depart with the satisfaction of a partial knowledge, pleased that it is of our own making. . . . Hovering like a spectre, at the boundaries of the festival experience, and those deep structures and thick descriptions that might restore a sense of the particular and local to what we have now recruited to the realm of the global."[78]

Most of these coproduction markets and funds, for example, evoke investment as much as tourism and neocolonialism. They are sponsored by (national/international) government funds. The prizes for these funds are not large, ranging from 50,000 euros in Berlin, to around HK$100,000 (US$13,000) at the HAF. Western European governments perceive these sums as small and as providing good public relations for the countries involved, but for an independent filmmaker from Sri Lanka, Bolivia, or Angola, 20,000 euros is a large sum. This partly explains, in fact, why there are fewer markets in the United States, where government money to support the arts has been limited and disconnected from foreign policy.[79]

Still, some of these funds stipulate that the funded projects must have a coproducer from the funding countries. For the World Cinema Fund, for example, a funded project must have a German producer. Fonds Sud from France also requires a French producer to be on board, while the HBF Plus Fund, the higher and more advanced funding opportunity from Rotterdam, requires projects to have a Dutch producer. Eurimages requires participation of two member countries as producers. This can be seen as a new form of colonialism, yet it also speaks to issues of global voices and independent positions within distinctive local and global settings as well as distribution.

On the one hand, it is indisputable that government money makes these funds possible, whether from the Netherlands, Germany, France, Switzerland, Japan, South Korea, or Hong Kong. In terms of dollar (euro) amounts, the Europeans contribute more than their Asian counterparts, and European festivals are older and more established, perpetuating longstanding divisions of economic and political power as well as competition with emerging Asian partners.

When some of these European establishments became the producers of films from developing countries, they also have exerted control over these movies. This resonates with discussions earlier in the book on how the most established film festivals in Europe control film knowledge, defining what constitutes art in cinema. Exerting any kind of control in production would inevitably contribute to further debate on this issue, since production conditions cannot be separated from content.

On the other hand, if left with the unregulated global capitalist market and even national support, many of these films would not even be made. While having rich countries fund projects from poorer countries smacks of neocolonialism, in practice, there are other nuances. Sonja Heinen, project manager of the WCF, is careful to stress that "One of our main aims is, not to act in a Eurocentric or even German-centric way. 'The smell of money' is an often-discussed topic in this field."[80] The WCF wants to make sure that local production companies are involved in the project, so projects will not be seen through "German eyes."

Hence, Bugno stresses that "the funding of film productions in developing countries should not be misinterpreted as a kind of philanthropic foreign aid. It's all about co-operation. . . . Most of these films then will be made for the international festival circuit and audiences in the 'first' world. This situation often influences the choice of subject matter and style, unconsciously or deliberately, when film projects are being conceived. The WCF's goal, however, is to support projects that preserve their distinctly original cultural identity and so we should always be asking ourselves what cultural identity means."[81]

The choices made by both filmmakers and funders further complicate issues. Artistic integrity may be the criteria for selection, but what is it? With all these funding structures established, as Bugno suggests, filmmakers learn to adapt their projects so that they can be funded. A Hong Kong filmmaker told me in Berlin, "You know what they [the festivals] want, and you can't help but be reminded about it." There is still a perception in the West that the People's Republic of China is repressive (which is, in many ways, not inaccurate). *Beijing Bastards* (1993)—on China's urban underground rock scene—is the kind of film that festivals like, gritty realism of the PRC. Recent Malaysian films, made primarily by ethnic Chinese, can also be looked upon as festival favorites because of their anti-mainstream Malay and anti-Muslim cultural stances.

Festival organizers, especially those from the West, remain aware of unequal power relationship and the threat of neocolonial tendency in their actions. If filmmakers and festival organizers are to work productively within the entrenched global inequalities, dogmatically sticking to positions like "not working with colonial powers" would not provide any satisfactory answers, nor would they open up discussions of any of these issues in silenced regimes. In an image that invokes the specter of anticolonial theorist Frantz Fanon, in fact,

Halle quotes critic Ferid Boughedir, "It is almost as though an African who looks at himself in the mirror sees a European looking back at him."[82]

In the end, projects also are very diverse, like films and festivals themselves. The 2006 HBF included Chilean director Sebastian Campos's *La sagrada familia*, about middle-class angst in Chile, and *Opera Jawa*, by Garin Nugroho, an Austrian/Indonesian coproduction celebrating Mozart with new visions of the Ramayana and traditional Javanese drama. *Walking on the Wild Side*, directed by Han Jie, became a French-Chinese coproduction about three youths in a mining town in Shanxi province, and their experience in a newly transformed China in the 1990s: not an Orientalist view of China, but one that definitely stresses the alienated lives in a new China. Most of these films I just described do not have strong narratives. They are all quite challenging and formally, if not innovative, at least, unconventional. And their future impact on film knowledge and visions remain to be seen.

There is no clear-cut answer to evaluate this funding structure as either purely neocolonial, capitalistic, or altruistic—any more than we might once have imposed simple dichotomies of business and art, or popularity and message on the films and filmmakers of the festival world. Film festivals belong to a rarified world where they show movies that few may see, but in the lively encounters, competitions, and debates of this world, they distill the creativity and promise of film. Hence, both their engagement with global film business and their contemporary evolution in production and sponsorship demand our close attention as they inflect further our vision of global film.

5   Festivals as Public Spheres

While my previous chapters primarily have engaged festivals through the art and business of film, they have paid attention at the same time to the human elements of the film festival. This includes those people involved in making films, those who evaluate them, and those who sell them, as well as those who organize events, socialize, and watch films. Together, these people constitute the crowds and the buzz of festivals, the local and wider imagined global community of cinephilia. And the buzz itself—praise, critique, scandal, and inspiration—constitutes the stuff of an important public sphere, or of a set of overlapping public spheres, where engaged people debate film and its issues.

It is important from the beginning to understand that no single community or sphere delineates the commingled actions of intense festival programs of films, panels, press conferences, and socializing. The birth of film festivals was national in nature, for example, and the inclusion of a national film section or showcases even in Cannes, Berlin, Locarno, and Venice continues to engage the complicated imagination of nation building.[1] Cities, regional governments, and other political agencies also engage the festivals as funders, neoliberal collaborators, and occasional censors guiding participants toward local identities through media.

At the same time, the international and diverse nature of festival offerings forces participants to confront more difficult issues of global interaction and power and even to challenge local constraints. Even under the most dictatorial conditions, film festivals and their organizers have not simply replicated the established structure of political power in cities, nations, or the world. The people and places of the festival, in fact, may be envisioned by organizers and participants as members of civil society embedded in national culture yet talking in counterpoint to it as well.

Hence, in exploring wider social and cultural meanings of festivals, this chapter looks at film festivals as public spheres, following the generative theories of Jürgen Habermas's bourgeoisie public sphere.[2] This theoretical framework, of course, has been complicated by subsequent interpretations of the nature, limits, and meaning of public sphere, with special reference to extensions and counterpublics as envisioned by Nancy Fraser, Oscar Negt and Alexander Kluge, Miriam Hansen, and Michael Warner.[3] Building on these analysts, I read film festivals through the prism of ideas about proletarian public spheres, alternative counterpublics, and public spheres that articulate critically with the mass industrial cultural productions that fascinated and worried so many thinkers of the Frankfurt School tradition.

This discussion, nonetheless, must continue to recognize the variety of film festivals, their texts, their contexts, and their participants. All festivals have the advancement of cinema as a primary goal, promoting works that break new grounds and reclaiming old works that shore up the legacy of cinema, while they facilitate production and distribution of films. All introduce their varied audiences to an enriched selection of films as they conduct the business of film and film knowledge. Certain festivals and networks of festivals, however, have additional, even dominant goals that entail furthering other agendas beyond cinematic arts. Many of these make claims to better the world through programming around very concrete goals, whether promoting transnational linkages, seeking intergroup understanding, advancing human rights, demanding equalities for people of all sexual orientations, or promoting environmental agendas. Such specific goals give these festivals well-defined identities because they have narrower foci in films and interpretation and serve particular constituents. While similar issues may be raised by individual films or by sections within larger festivals, focused festivals distill important questions about the discourse and social impact of film.

These festivals or themes may not gain the same attention of the world press as Cannes or Berlin, yet they embody in special ways the diversity of voices created by the festival world that push the boundaries of cinema. They promote cinemas that articulate different experiences and expressions, and in doing so, they constitute alternative public spheres/counterpublics where ideas, oftentimes repressed or ignored in larger contexts, are exchanged and explored. These festivals do not see art as the ultimate goal of cinema in the same way as Cannes, Venice, Toronto, Pordenone, or New York, or at least they do not do so without incorporating specific social and political articulations. Nonetheless, in nearly all major film festivals, even when the art of cinema is the publicly expressed goal of the festivals, non-filmic values—human rights, freedom of speech, equality, and recognition for different groups—are also celebrated for pedagogy as well as art. Cinema, of course, can never be divorced from the worlds in which films are produced, nor be "art for art's sake," or else it would become irrelevant to the world around it. Still, the relationship between specific agendas and larger, multidimensional showcases raises important questions to be considered below.

At the same time, I believe that even the more traditional film festivals themselves constitute public spheres, in the sense of "a public arena of citizen discourse and association"[4] that expresses a different vision than that of Hollywood, Bollywood, and other mainstream cinemas. Film festivals evoke a place and position that is very close to the traditional bourgeois public sphere, given the middle-class status and locales in which they foster informed debates and discussions—"an institutionalized arena of discursive interaction."[5] Like coffeehouses and the halls of parliament, given the economic and business aspects of film festivals, they are never pure public spheres as described by Habermas. Yet, their themes of national identity and international relations can certainly echo the most Habermasian of global domains.

Theme-specific festivals, then, can shape alternative public spheres, closer to Nancy Fraser's and Michael Warner's visions of counterpublics, differentiating themselves from the big, businesslike festivals, or in some instances, competing with them for films and interpretation. For example, gay and lesbian festivals have been called counterpublics by critics—and have faced issues raised by the incorporation of their films and discourse into wider networks of "A"-level festivals.[6]

It is also important to note that film festivals (especially issue-oriented events) are, by and large, sites of leftist or liberal practices. Here, I am reminded of the observation of Roland Barthes in his study of myth that those on the Right tend to not question the myths and actually reproduce them to constantly reinforce their constructed meanings.[7] On the other hand, film festivals celebrate innovations, breaking new grounds, question the status quo—the myth. This partly explains why film festivals, by and large, remain on the fringe of mainstream society and the political Right does not see a need to voice their ideas through film festivals. The mainstream film industry very much expresses the myths that sustain the established ethos; therefore, despite protests, those on the Right see few gains in promoting their point of view in film festivals. We might find this orientation in the American Film Renaissance Institute Film Festival, which celebrates "America's timeless, traditional, and foundational values such as free speech, free enterprise, religious freedom, and rugged individualism," but this is a very small festival without any established network.[8] Instead, both major festivals and smaller, specific ones favor the critical discussion and deconstruction that Barthes associates with the Left. Despite the permeation of cinematic capitalism, organizers, critics, and even "stars" often share a liberal, left-of-center orientation.

Nonetheless, film festivals clearly construct their own myths of film knowledge, modernity, and diversity, as I have shown. In fact, the constructed hierarchy of the current film festival circuit also means that the top festivals, with their ability to endow distinctions in their specific film world, can be seen as analogous to the idealized liberal bourgeoisie public sphere that limits voices of women and the lower classes or less powerful regions. Yet, these fora also act as training grounds for the (film) elite that dominate that world.[9]

Issue-oriented festivals also extend extremely complex questions about global relationships, especially the dialectic between the so-called West and non-West, or North and South, as these are often framed in filmic geography we have seen mapped onto business and aesthetics. The subjects of human rights issues films, for example, are heavily concentrated in poorer countries around the globe, whatever the origins of filmmakers or capital behind them. Amy Gutmann, in discussing the ramifications of human rights, generally supporting universal pluralistic human rights, observes that "if human rights are based exclusively in Eurocentric ideas, as many critics have (quite persistently) claimed, and these Eurocentric ideas are biased against non-Western countries and culture, then the political legitimacy of human rights talk, human rights covenants, and human rights enforcement is called in question."[10] Hence, festivals—often in the West—that concentrate on human rights raise questions about who speaks, with what foundations and to whom, within a larger concern about how to protect "human rights" without simply destroying the local cultures (or ignoring the global ones) within which the human rights abuses take place.[11]

Another related issue that these festivals bring out in terms of public sphere evokes Fraser's idea of a multiplicity of competing public spheres.[12] While small events cooperate and even overlap with the more established festivals, like Sundance or Berlin, festivals devoted to human rights and LGBTQ (Lesbian Gay Bisexual Transgender Queer) issues offer different publics a specific discursive space to articulate their public and political concerns to each other. Fraser refers to these publics as subaltern counterpublics, and constituents of these alternative festivals are indeed mostly people whose voices do not speak loudly to hegemonic discourse. We must also distinguish between those who appear as representatives of the oppressed (the Dalai Lama, Rigoberta Menchu) or "are spoken for" in Western human rights festivals and participants in other loci and arenas in which producers, presenters, and audiences share experiences and agendas, an experience that I will explore through the issue of LGBTQ events.

The chapter begins with a more general discussion of the relationships between film festivals and various formations of public spheres. After looking at how film festivals succeed or fail to engage in different forms of public spheres, the section concludes with an analysis of how Iranian filmmakers have used film festivals to voice their causes over the years and how the process continues and refracts today in a time of high political turmoil in Iran. This section also intersects with questions about transnational/imagined communities discussed through a wide selection of articles recently assembled by Dina Iordanova and Ruby Cheung.[13]

The second part of the chapter addresses two specific circuits of theme festivals—human rights festivals and festivals with LGBTQ issues as their major organizing foci. It first examines the Human Rights Watch Film Festival, one of the largest and oldest film festivals of its kind. In terms of queer festivals, I consider San Francisco, the oldest festival of this large network, and MIX New York, an alternative to the more mainstream queer festivals. As in the discussion of other film festivals, I treat not only the films being shown, but also the kinds of spaces, discussions, and experiences these festivals generate during the events as well as the way these festivals themselves form networks of connections.

These issue-oriented festivals have grown to create their own global networks that echo the hierarchies and interactions I have outlined with regard to larger festivals as well. The Human Rights Film Network, for example, was founded in 2004 in Prague as an organization that provides support to human rights festivals. The international network of lesbian and gay film festivals also constitutes an extremely well-established circuit of film festival screening and distribution. All these events participate in wider networks of people, knowledge, distribution, and, in recent innovational strategies, even production.

Film Festivals and the Public Sphere

To speak of film festivals as a discursive horizon that promotes cinema, the first electric mass media of the turn of the twentieth century, suggests analogies to the nineteenth-century bourgeois public sphere and the salons, coffeehouses, and book clubs that constituted the discursive arenas for open and informed debates. Film festivals provide / transform public spaces, again echoing the experience of more literary public spheres. In festivals, people can discuss political, social, and cultural ideas through the medium of cinema as well as engage in conversation about the nature of the medium itself. Indeed, the physicality of many festivals as they take over public venues and spill over into lobbies, streets, and coffeehouses evokes the vivid spatialities of Habermas's first examples of the bourgeois public sphere itself.[14]

Habermas saw the public sphere as a space for the emergence of an inclusive civil society, even though a great deal of subsequent debate has focused on the exclusionary character of the bourgeoisie public sphere in terms of gender and class. However, a closer analysis of film festivals yields similarly contradictory impulses in them as well. Just as the engagement of early coffeehouses demanded a literate public, film festivals, especially the most powerful ones, allocate major discursive roles to a selected few. In theory, for example, film festivals are open to all genders, but in practice, men (straight and gay) outnumber women in all aspects of film festivals (save audience), except for those festivals that are organized specifically around women's roles or issues. In terms of class, many festivals consciously build on an elite sense of distinction, in Bourdieu's sense, that means that whatever their attractions for those outside this field, working classes are rarely targeted as audiences or listened to except as "witnesses." Moreover, film festivals are generally international; hence, as we have seen, class issues are manifested even more powerfully in the relations between rich and poor countries, and to a lesser extent, between better-resourced cosmopolitan film producers / directors and those who are forced to work with shoestring budgets or scholarships from the first world. However, since film festivals vary in their scales, goals, constituents, and content, their relationships to the public spheres also change depending on events and contexts.

Yet, if this fairly bourgeois public sphere created, when audiences attend screenings or even read about Cannes, Venice, Berlin, or Locarno, is exclusionary, film festivals at the same time create spaces where different kinds of ideas can be represented and where discussions may ripple beyond immediate events or settings in terms of publicity, publications, blogs, or classroom dynamics. Key ideas may articulate bourgeois/high-brow or so-called universal concerns, as in other forms of high art and literature—middle-class ennui is a recurrent theme in festival offerings, from *L'avventura* (1960) to detached meditations on life and death exemplified by Bergman's *Wild Strawberries* (1957), in Kiarostami's 1997 *Taste of Cherry*, or in Moretti's *The Son's Room* (2001). This does not preclude more marginal issues or alternative perspectives even within "Northern" visions, however, whether intercultural interactions, as in *The Class* (*Entre les murs*) (2008), the portrayal of the dead-end lives of the Belgian working class in *Rosetta* (1999), or the postcolonial issues that have haunted Cannes from *Battle of Algiers* (1966) to *Days of Glory* (*Indigènes*, 2006), *Des hommes et des dieux* (2010) and *Outside the Law* (*Hors-la-loi*, 2010). At the same time, even oppositional cinema can be infused with elite discourse and agendas when transformed into aesthetics rather than protest.

Thus, film festivals incorporate very contradictory impulses in their texts, audiences, and discussions. On the one hand, most festivals are fairly high-brow and exclusionary. On the other, precisely because of the exclusivity that distances film festivals from the industrial mass cinema, they have the freedom to represent and even debate marginal, sensitive, and difficult subject matters. In fact, as shown in chapter 2, film festivals welcome films that transcend and challenge the boundaries of everyday sensitivities and norms. Therefore, Lars von Trier's vividly cruel *Antichrist* (2009) competed for the Palme d'Or with the disturbing violence of the Filipino *The Execution of P* (*Kinatay*, 2009) before being replaced by the oneiric lyricism and animistic roots of the 2010 award winner, *Uncle Boonmee Who Can Recall His Past Lives*. An African interpretation of the classically Western tale of Carmen, *U-Carmen e-Khayelitsha* (2005), won Berlin's Golden Bear, while other festivals have explored the reinterpretation of American noir in France and Hong Kong. Venice, meanwhile, has screened films that address Chinese problems like *Durian Durian* (2000), which grapples with a much neglected issue of migrant children from Mainland China in Hong Kong, or Jia Zhangke's prize-winning *Still Life* (2006), which focused world attention on the social and ecological problems of China's Three Gorges Dam.

Audience participation is a vital component of the public sphere. Most film festivals are theoretically open to all, although Cannes is an important exception. Many align closely with segments of their local populations, especially in their regular audience base. The ticket prices are not prohibitive, and may include special arrangements for cinephiles or specifically interested/targeted, educated populations such as students. Audience awards also provide a public arena for audience voices that may erupt in boos, applause, or Q&A's after presentations. Still, this audience voice can be influenced by discourses presented in catalog copy and criticism and, oftentimes, lacks any true power in the general selection process unless special arrangements have been made about program consultants (and/or support). Film festivals are once again open and closed, allowing access to different groups of people, valuing certain voices over others, and juxtaposing different texts and agendas of interpretation.

An even more central question may be that of whose ideas are articulated in film festivals and by whom? Who uses film festivals as an arena to promote specific viewpoints? The closing down of the Cannes festival in 1968 marked a unique protest from a counterpublic who saw the official festival as opposing the voices of the cinematic publics with the earlier firing of Henri Langlois as the head of the Cinémathèque. Furthermore, the closing of Cannes was a show of solidarity with the students and workers of Paris in May 1968 against a more shadowy bourgeois establishment. Often, struggles for festival control entail more exclusionary conflicts among competing elites. For example, in West Germany, the Oberhausen Manifesto of 1962 of the Oberhausen Short Film Festival asserted that "short film has become in Germany a school and experimental basis for the feature film." The manifesto further demanded new freedoms: "Freedom from the conventions of the established industry. Freedom from the outside influence of commercial partners. Freedom from control of special interest groups."[15] This manifesto used the forum provided by film festivals to articulate new cinematic practices that eventually gave rise to the New German Cinema of the 1970s. While these practices coincided with social and political developments in West Germany, they were also distinguished from them by their aesthetic ideology.

While perhaps not so dramatic, internal and external debates at Cannes in 2010, stimulated by a documentary from Italy and a feature film from France, exemplify everyday contests over who controls the public sphere. *Draquila: Italy Trembles*, directed by Italian satirist Sabina Guzzanti, chronicles the 2009 earthquake in L'Aquila that killed over three hundred people. Prime Minister Silvio Berlusconi became concerned by media coverage of Italian government corruption in granting reconstruction contracts. The Italian culture minister, Sandro Bondi, who is also national coordinator of Berlusconi's People of Freedom party, even refused to attend Cannes because "the film is propaganda, he charged, and 'insults the truth and the entire Italian population.'"[16]

Meanwhile, following up on his prize-winning *Days of Glory* (*Indigènes*, 2006), which recuperated the history of North African soldiers fighting with the French in Europe during World War II, Algerian-French director Rachid Bouchareb was again in the official competition, with his film *Outside the Law* (*Hors-la-loi*). The film is a fairly conventional narrative in the mode of *The Godfather* exploring French atrocities against Algeria, seen through three Algerian brothers in the struggles leading up to Algerian independence in 1962. Outsiders, many of whom had not seen the film, led public protest demonstrations in Cannes against it. *The Guardian*, for example, reported that "police were out in force as about a thousand people protested in Cannes, some of them members of the far-right National Front. Cinema-goers were frisked as they entered the Palais des Festivals and water bottles confiscated." Protesters carried signs demanding "respect de l'histoire de France."[17] Unlike 1966, when *Battle of Algiers* was banned in France but won prizes at Venice, the festival this time invited *Outside the Law* even though it had been criticized by Lionnel Luca—a member of Nicolas Sarkozy's Union pour un Movement Populaire, who had not seen the film. As historian Benjamin Stora commented, "The Algerian war is still not over in our minds and hearts, because it hasn't been sufficiently named, shown, come to terms with in and by collective memory."[18]

Government protests or street demonstrations may be less successful than censorship by corporate sponsors or municipal governments that grapple with the actual presence of films. Government agencies, including film boards and other government officials of many countries, have forbidden certain films at film festivals under their jurisdictions. Furthermore, historical political issues have also affected festivals' potential to either assert their independence or to cave in to the political winds, sometimes taking debates far away from the festival screenings, as we will see in the case of the colonial Hong Kong International Film Festival and organizers' negotiations of Hong Kong's fragile position between Great Britain and China. Yet, many global examples point to the continual negotiation of "what we talk about" in these constructed public spheres.

In 1995, for example, in Tasmania (Australia), the state attorney general banned twelve films scheduled for the first Tasmanian Queer Film and Video Festival, even though the films had received the go-ahead from the Australian federal attorney general. One, the documentary *Coming Out Under Fire* (1994), about gays and lesbians in the American military, had received funding from the American Corporation for Public Broadcasting and won a Peabody award as well as recognition at Berlin. While they were screened elsewhere in Australia, local pressure triumphed. Through censorship, audiences were denied collective encounters with the films themselves.[19]

Similar issues arose in the Mumbai International Film Festival (MIFF) in 2003. MIFF was run by the Ministry of Information and Broadcasting, which threatened that all Indian entries to the festival would need to obtain official censor certificates. The authority was sensitive to Indian films that were critical of Indian affairs, ranging from Hindu militarism to homosexuality. The requirement for the certificates was only lifted when Indian filmmakers protested, but the air of censorship has persisted.[20]

The public sphere also involves negotiations and control of the subject matters of films that are affected by transnational imaginations and sensitivities. *Final*

Solution (2003), an Indian documentary that chronicles the 2002 Hindu-Muslim conflict in Gujarat, won awards in both the Berlin and Hong Kong festivals. However, it could not be shown in the Singapore festival because the Singapore censor board considered it "potentially inflammatory."[21] In 2004, when the ruling Hindu-nationalist Bharatiya Janata party lost the election, further complicating the situation, *Final Solution* was banned in India and was never shown in the Mumbai film festival.[22] Local politics influence festivals' selections, but the considerations are intricate: Germany and Hong Kong, without substantial South Asian populations, did not have to worry about local Hindu-Muslim conflicts and could bring a distanced (neutral?) gaze to the documentary. On the other hand, Singapore is a multiethnic city-state that negotiates a balance of South Asian Hindus as well as Muslims with Malay Muslims. *Final Solution*, from the point of view of the conservative local government, was deemed problematic. When the film went back to its original country, where the events themselves had taken place (and certainly had been debated), the Indian government banned it, while the major film festivals simply refused to include the film in their lineups, avoiding all controversies. This does not mean that Berlin and Hong Kong were more open or that they have embraced all topics. If in many ways, the programmers appreciated the value of the film and were free to show *Final Solution*, but these festivals were also far from the conflict portrayed in the film, a free zone where screening of the film would not likely generate new disputes or engender any political changes.

This case underscores more complicated issues in the theory of public sphere. Nancy Fraser's discussion on the feasibility of a transnational public sphere, where it does not follow a Westphalian framework, points out the difficulties of evaluating the transnational public sphere film festivals try to occupy.[23] What kind of efficacy can be assessed if the publicity is transnational but displaces the agents of nation states who might demand change in any meaningful political structure? The problem of Muslim/Hindu conflict is not a German or Hong Kong issue, and citizens of these places cannot effect much change on the matter. On the other hand, citizens of India and Singapore are affected by the issue, yet the film festivals of these places refused to show this piece publicly that would address the conflict in a way not sanctioned by the authorities.

In fact, as mentioned in chapter 1, the Berlin festival is a product of the cold war, and its relationship with the GDR and the Eastern Bloc meant that this film festival was for decades the showcase and agency of the government and the NATO West. Only in 1974, twenty-three years after the festival was launched, did a film from the Soviet Union participate, followed by a film from the Germany Democratic Republic the following year.[24] The Berlin festival might have be open to other concerns, but in the early years it kept to its objective of being a representative for the West.

Hence, while controversial films like *Battle of Algiers, Antichrist, Final Solution,* and *Outside the Law* have found multiple places within the film festival circuit and canons, their individual trajectories and diverse readings remind us that film festivals cannot create a single global public sphere, a monolithic world civil society. On the one hand, they embody a generalized mandate to be an open forum for all kinds of cinematic exchanges that might stimulate debate. On the other hand, they also represent their respective governments, industries, and communities. Still, just as elites use festivals to make their statements, individuals also use festivals to present their points of view. These individuals, because of the global aspects of film festivals, come from all over the world, and diversify points of view by their works, while evoking multiple interpretations from varied audiences. To understand this negotiation more coherently, I return to the relationships among Iranian cinema, governments, and international film festivals to shed light on how film festivals and their participants constitute and delimit public and counterpublic spheres.

Iranian Cinema, Cinematographers, and Debates in Global Public Spheres

As we have seen in earlier chapters, modern Iranian cinema is one of the most feted and successful non-Western cinemas in the festival world, represented by masterful works and consistent auteurs, such as Abbas Kiarostami, Jafar Panahi, Mohsen and Samira Makhmalbaf, and Rakhshan Bani-Etemad. Since the dawn of contemporary Iranian cinema in the 1960s, Iranian filmmakers have balanced local audiences and mores with Western festivals as a platform to showcase films that sometimes have been banned in Iran. At the same time, despite decades of attention to both the art and complex political and cultural issues involved in making films under the regimes of the shah and the subsequent Islamic Revolution, it is not uncommon that directors and films from Iran and other "troublesome" countries face barriers in participating in global film festivals. In 2002, both Kiarostami and Bahman Ghobadi were denied visas to the United States to attend the New York Film Festival and the Chicago Film Festival, respectively. The State Department officials in charge obviously saw these agents and contexts as threatening and used political power to prevent voices of Iranian directors from being heard. The festivals, though prevented from being the arenas for these voices, were recognized as a potentially dangerous public sphere that celebrates these diverse voices.

In 1990, the Pesaro Film Festival in Italy held a retrospective of Iranian cinema, celebrated as "a different cinema which is neither narrative or documentary."[25] The Iranian film journal *International Film—A Cross Cultural Review* also lauded the achievement of Iranian film aboard. However, in the same issue, the editor in chief, Behzad Rahimian, lamented that transnational success foreclosed careers and truncated discussions as well:

> There are more than a few filmmakers who were discovered in one edition of a festival and forgotten in another. The directors of international film festivals and editors of smash movie magazines seldom remember their

names. This does not merely lead to going astray by the filmmakers who could at least have a future in their national film industries. What else this caused was a major recession in the cinema of one country or a whole region. Also more than a few are filmmakers secured attention for themselves outside thin national borders and forgot about the audience in their own country, and when their days were numbered to the last as a foreigner, they never found an opportunity to work at home.[26]

The film journal strikes an ambivalent note as it showcases the accomplishment of Iranian cinema in Western festivals while also chastising film festivals and film magazine editors for not truly valuing Iranian cinema. The attack becomes more pointed when the editor identifies filmmakers who appeal to international film festivals as having abandoned their home audience, suggesting that international film festivals create brain drain from Iran. If film festivals are global public spheres that allow some Iranian filmmakers a space to speak their voice, like that of Behzad Rahimian, film festivals outside of Iran are also colonial devices that take people from their native countries and appropriate their craft to the Western/world stage. These kinds of evaluations undercut any other alternative public sphere that might be fostered within Islamic Iran itself, a stand that echoes the internal criticism of Abbas Kiarostami.

Indeed, it is important to realize that from some Iranian perspectives, that which "the West" values as a public sphere is corrupt or tainted. In 2006, for example, when Danish cartoons depicted the Prophet Muhammad and sparked a firestorm of protest from Muslims around the world, Iranian director Majid Majidi withdrew *The Willow Tree* from the Denmark International Film Festival. In 2009, Majidi complained to the Supreme Leader that there "is no respect for human rights, and the government is so ideologically motivated, our hands are tied."[27]

Political unrest in Iran since 2009 has once again pushed Iranian directors beyond their roles as artists. *No One Knows about Persian Cats* by Bahman Ghobadi, a film that documents the rebellious counterpoint of youth, indie music, and the Iranian theocratic regime, won the Jury's Special Prize from Cannes's Un Certain Regard in 2009. Since its premiere at Cannes, it has followed the regular festival route and was shown in over ten other festivals just in 2009; the film also can easily be downloaded from the Web. For Western critics, this film itself seems to embody the promise of a universal youthful alternative public sphere.[28] Ghobadi himself explained it in counterpoint to controls he had lived with as a Kurdish filmmaker exploring the lives of that minority in Iran, while completion of *Persian Cats* also coincided with the arrest and imprisonment of his fiancée, Iranian American journalist Roxana Saberi. Neither returned to Iran after Cannes, choosing to live in exile. Nonetheless, Ghobadi sought to reinsert his film into alternative public spheres in Iran:

> I sent my [most recent] film to Iran. The first country where it was screened was Iran. I gave it out for free; I told them that I didn't need money and that

they could copy it. This was only for the Iranians in the country, not for those outside of Iran, because they'll bring some 20 foreigners with them to see the movie.

Since I gave the film out freely, everyone is watching it. And I told them, look around you and if there is any money, give it to these young people who are trying to create art. Now I'm getting emails from the young people in Iran telling me, "The people are looking at us differently; we're getting much more positive reception."[29]

Iran's own approved film festival, the Fajr International Film Festival, creates a different kind of filmic discussion within the country. Run by the Ministry of Culture, it takes place on the anniversary of the Islamic Revolution in February. During more liberal years under the reformist administration of Iranian president Mohammad Khatami after 1997, the festival was "a place of discovery and surprise." However, as the hardliners took control in Iran, they imposed strict censorship and oversight on the festival. With the political upheaval with the Iran election of 2009, where many believed that Mir Hussein Musavi should have been the legitimate winner, Iranian artists who had supported him boycotted the festivals. Moreover, according to Mehdi Abdollahzadeh, it has been badly run by people outside the cinematic world who were simply government bureaucrats.[30] Unlike previous years, in fact, jury members were not even announced after the opening of the festival. Similarly, according to Western reports, a group of directors "boycotted a recent documentary festival in Tehran because they could not show the truth."[31]

Debates over Fajr and film have recrossed national boundaries. Diasporic media outlets, like Radio Zamaneh, a Dutch-funded Persian-language radio station, and cyber space, were active in promoting opposition to the government. One *Los Angeles Times* blog asserted that some Iranian artists called for a boycott of the Fajr International Film Festival in 2010; others called for foreign artists to boycott the festival because of the Iranian "government's violent treatment of the people." Meanwhile, like Ghobadi, Narges Kalhor, a young director who is the daughter of President Mahmoud Ahmadinejad's cultural advisor, sought political asylum after showing her film at the Nuremberg Human Rights Film Festival. In this case, Iranian filmmakers as well as the Iranian expatriates sympathetic to the oppositional candidates used multiple film festivals as a platform for their protest.

Established directors have sustained opposition voices inside and outside Iran. Exilee Mohsen Makhmalbal denounced the Iranian government when he accepted the Freedom to Create Prize in London and dedicated the award to the recently deceased Ayatollah Hossein Ali Montazeri, the opposition's spiritual leader. In the Montreal Film Festival in the summer of 2009, Jafar Panahi asked all the judges to wear green scarves—the symbol of the opposition movement in

Iran. In a YouTube video titled "Jafar Panahi President of Montreal World Film Festival Jury," other supporters of the Mir Hossein Mousavi, the opposition candidate, wore green t-shirts with the phrase "Where is my vote?" Panahi, stopped on his way at the red carpet, posed for a picture with the demonstrators to show his support for their cause. The video then shows green balloons released into the air and the demonstrators shouting "Democracy for Iran."[32]

After this event, the Iranian government barred Panahi from going to an Indian film festival and the 2010 Berlinale. He was arrested by the government in March 2010,[33] after which he was invited to be a jury member for Cannes that year. In May, at Cannes, France's Culture Minister Frederic Mitterrand read a letter from Panahi from jail in which he stated, "I am innocent. I have not made any film against the Iranian regime." The festival also arranged to show a clip of Panahi describing a police interrogation. Tim Burton, the head of the jury, joined others, including Steven Spielberg and Francis Ford Coppola, in calling for Panahi's release.[34]

During the press conference for *Certified Copy* at Cannes on May 18, Abbas Kiarostami asked the moderator to let him address the issue of Panahi's imprisonment before talking about his own film. Kiarostami asserted that the fact that "a filmmaker is in prison is intolerable. . . . That art as a whole is being attacked. . . . Iranian independent filmmakers live under constant pressure and cannot do their job." He then asked to distribute a letter he had written in March after Panahi's arrest. According to Kiarostami, the letter written in March did not get much circulation, except for one paper in Iran and the *New York Times*. Kiarostami used the festival, a major media event with thousands of journalists, to disseminate his message. He also even asked if there were any Iranian journalists on the floor who wanted to add anything. A journalist announced that Panahi had just started a hunger strike, which elicited strong emotion from the platform. Juliette Binoche, who had worked with Kiarostami on his first European movie, was visibly shocked and broke into tears, a Western gaze that was subsequently reported by many news sources. Later, at the final awards ceremony, when Binoche won the prize for the best actress, she held up a sign, "Jafar Panahi," and added, "I hope Jafar Panahi will be here next year."[35] One day after the conclusion of Cannes, news came from Iran that Panahi would be released on bail. No one can say with certainty that the festival and its community forced Panahi's release, but it points to some of the power of festival. If the impact of festivals as transnational public spheres on politics is tangible, Cannes, with its well-known participants (from cultural ministers to famed auteurs to award-winning actresses) and its massive press coverage, is effecting some form of transnational efficacy. However, this power can be elusive. In late 2010, the Iranian Ministry of Justice sentenced Jafar Panahi and Mohammad Rasoulof to six years in prison and barred them from travel abroad and writing scripts for twenty years. In reaction to this drastic action by the Iranian judiciary, many film festivals and filmmakers

Figure 8. When receiving the Best Actress Award, Juliette Binoche holds a sign reading "Jafar Panahi" during the closing award ceremony of the Sixty-third Cannes Film
Festival, May 23, 2010. Iranian director Jafar Panahi could not be part of the jury as he
was imprisoned in Iran.
Source: © IAN LANGSDON/epa/Corbis.

responded with strong, albeit symbolic, gestures. Cannes, Berlin, and San Sebastián
protested the arrest, as did Hollywood directors, including Martin Scorsese,
Francis Ford Coppola, and Steven Spielberg. Berlin, besides asking Panahi to join
its jury, honored him with screening of his works and a panel discussion on film
censorship. At the time of writing, both directors were out on bail.

With this example in mind, we can now turn to more tightly focused alternative thematic festivals. Here, I explore festivals tackling fundamental issues of power (human rights) and of social-cultural order embodied literally in sex, gender, and sexuality (LGBTQ festivals), while raising questions of aesthetics, place, and connection.

The Politics of Human Rights

Almost echoing Habermas's formulation of the public sphere, the Web site of the Human Rights Watch Film Festival (HRWFF) stresses "the power of film to educate and galvanize a broad constituency of concerned citizens."[36] Many human rights film festivals have emerged worldwide since the 1990s; in an interview I conducted with John Biaggi, director of the HRWFF, on January 27, 2010, he said that he believes that the proliferation of human rights festivals reflects a greater concern about human rights on the global scale. These particular theme festivals recall early debate on the function and effects of cinema when it was first introduced one hundred years ago. For these festivals, content becomes their primary focus, with the hope, not necessarily the reality, that these films will indeed effect change or promote more dialogue, which leads these festivals to constitute themselves as civic spaces for the public sphere and opportunities for networking to advance human rights issues. However, human rights film festivals are still film festivals and follow much of the same logic and practices of other festivals, even as they constitute a special subset of that world.

In terms of format, most human rights film festivals rely heavily on documentaries. While they screen feature fictions as well, documentaries offer flexibility, immediacy, and personal connections in describing current events. The preponderance of documentaries reveals an epistemological predisposition to the documentary form, which has a different relationship to truth from fiction films. There is a hierarchy of truth between fiction and nonfiction, and images captured in "real life" have a power that fiction is less adept in delivering.[37] Documentaries also demand fewer resources than fiction films; with a lessened financial burden, filmmakers are freer to choose their subject matters with less concern for audience or box office.

Sensitive issues that more mainstream cinema tends to overlook because of perceived controversies are stock topics for human rights festivals, ranging from the question of Tibet to the Palestinian/Israeli situation. Marginal films that have few economic prospects for distribution are also screened at human rights festivals, whether films addressing the situation of Liberian women's political participation, Peru's Shining Path, or human rights issues in states of the former Soviet Union. In many ways, topics that have received little attention due to political or economic pressures are welcome in these festivals, representing a public sphere where voices from private global citizens are addressed. And the films, in turn, become not only texts but also springboards, creators of discussion in panels or question-and-answer times that follow, as well as further reporting in local and wider press or online fora.

Many organizers and spectators share the idea that documentaries are more educational. Most human rights film festivals see their mission as educating and empowering the audience about human rights abuses in the world; educators form their audience as well as advocates. The opening night film for the 2005 Seoul International Human Rights Festival, for example, was *China Blue* (2005), by Micha Peled, which chronicles the lives of Chinese sweatshop laborers. The reviews provided for this film, through its distributors, come primarily from academics from Columbia University and the University of California, Berkeley. Voices of educators become valuable endorsements of the actions described in the film as well as the subjects, facilitators for the public sphere. The reviewers provide nuanced assessments of the complicated issue of cheap Chinese sweatshop labor while also making suggestions for the film's classroom potential. Thomas Gold, director of the UC Berkeley China Initiative, for example, states that "the film makes an excellent tool for stimulating classroom discussion on a broad range of topics impacting not only China, but the rest of the world as well."[38]

Many global human rights festivals have close affiliations with human rights groups. These human rights organizations then use cinema as a tool for achieving the goals of their respective bodies and may support the festivals as well. The Movies that Matter Film Festival, for example, is the successor of the Amnesty International Film Festival, established 1995 and held in Amsterdam under the aegis of the Dutch branch of Amnesty International. The One World International Human Rights Documentary Film Festival, founded in 1999 in Prague, is affiliated with People In Need (PIN), a postcommunist Czech human rights organization and a grantee of George Soros's Open Society Institute. These film festivals form parts of a rich network of global human rights organizations as well as parts of the festival world. Other human rights film festivals have taken root in Cairo, Seoul, South Africa, and Russia; however, there are no human rights film festivals in countries like China or Saudi Arabia.[39]

The Human Rights Watch Film Festival is one of the oldest and largest of this genre of festivals. HRWFF, established in 1988, is organized by Human Rights Watch (HRW), a recipient of the Nobel Peace Prize in 1997.[40] HRW, a nonprofit group that was established in 1978, strives to expose human oppression worldwide and to promote human rights. HRWFF has two locations, New York and London, and traveling festivals from which other festivals or institutions (Cornell, University of Virginia, Peabody Essex Museum) in the United States and Canada can rent films and have their own HRWFF. The New York event is cosponsored by the Film Society of Lincoln Center, which also hosts the New York Film Festival.

The statement on the HRWFF 2009 brochure encapsulates many ideas shared by other human rights festivals:

What power is there in watching? Why is investigating abuses such an important weapon? Because experience tells us that abusive leaders will go to great lengths to avoid being publicly exposed. Why do films that illuminate injustice matter? When we witness the impact of oppression, threats to freedom and dignity are made real. Borders and politics become less important, and individual names replace collective numbers. The story of a single, courageous activist reminds us of our own power. Together we can uncover the truth, make justice possible, and bring greater protections to people everywhere. Your power to watch is your power to protect.

HRWFF believes that cinema first exposes the wrongdoers, who always want to hide their misdeeds. Because of cinema's mimetic power, concrete individuals replace statistics and make actions and situations real. More importantly, HRW is invested in using cinema to "uncover the truth and make justice possible." Film itself, then, is an agent of dialogue and change and has the power to do good in society.

Although specific to HRW, which is an organization that fights for human rights through the court system, the HRWFF remains committed to exposing the abuses to a wider discussion. For HRWFF, film's primary function is to communicate a message: "The idea was that a film festival would allow HRW to get their message out in a different medium than printed matter," Biaggi says. "Films bring an immediacy and an emotional level that reports do not. The visual medium is the arena where human rights can really be detailed and brought to an audience who can understand it on a personal level."[41] Films situate otherwise dry data on human rights to an intimate, personal plane and thus demand a human response from the audience.

When the HRWFF began, there was little coordination between the festival and the larger HRW organization. According to Biaggi, the festival was conceived as another means to reach people. However, around 2007, the film festival started to begin the process of integrating the festival closely with the larger HRW organization, having the festival dovetail with the foci of the larger organization. The festival organizer would try to identify films that would resonate with HRW projects. For example, when women's rights became a major focus of HRW in 2010, the 2010 festival showed *Mrs. Goundo's Daughter* (2009), by Attie and Goldwater Productions, which followed a Malian mother in her fight for asylum in the United States for her two-year-old daughter so as to escape female circumcision.

The integration of HRW and HRWFF not only has brought the two organizations closer in terms of message, but it also has enhanced outreach efforts. For example, when a film on women's rights is shown, the festival can organize a reception and invite potential donors interested in the subject (one should not neglect the sociability of the public sphere). Coordinated organizational effort, in turn, helps all the branches of HRW in their work, from getting the message out to private fundraising.[42] The festival has even come up with a new "messaging tool kit." Before 2010, the catalog was organized alphabetically. Since 2010, it has been organized by themes; regions and countries are color-coded. The three themes of the 2010 festival were Closed Societies: Iran and North Korea, Accountability and Justice, and Development and Migration. The catalog explains why the festival programmed certain films and shapes the readings of them. With its decades of experience, the festival is now refining its message and striving to better communicate with its different constituents through film.

Since outreach is a major goal of human rights film festivals, many festivals create social fora in and around screenings in which filmmakers and activists gather to exchange ideas and discuss possibilities of cooperation. The Movies that Matter Film Festival hosts A Matter of ACT, where the festival invites both the directors and human rights defenders to their gatherings so that subjects of the films have a chance to meet with people involved with organizations that might further their causes. After most screenings, most festivals (including major and nonthematic events) invite the filmmaker to attend question-and-answer sessions. Q&A's develop the themes of specific works and add value to the experience of being in the room. Biaggi informed me that contentious issues like Tibet or the Israeli/Palestine issues always stimulate heated discussions.

In 2008, HRWIFF initiated Youth Producing Changes—Adobe Youth Voices. The program seeks to empower youths from underserved communities worldwide to make works that concern them and their communities. Adobe, the corporate sponsor, wants to nurture young people who are adept at new media technologies, while serving nonprofit educational institutions.[43] To enhance such programs, festivals have sought support from the philanthropic arms of large corporations.

While content and outreach are major goals of the festivals, human rights film festivals retain a cinematic agenda as well. They show works by major auteurs: in 2009, for example, Costa-Gavras's *Eden Is West* opened London's festival. The film, which was the closing film of Berlin's official selection, offers a "lighthearted take" on internal European illegal immigration from poorer to rich European countries.[44] Costa-Gavras had already established political credentials—and mainstream pull—with movies such as *Z*, *State of Siege*, and *Missing*. Amos Gitai's reflection on Holocaust memory, *One Day You'll Understand* (*Plus tard tu comprendras*) opened the 2008 Toronto Human Rights Festival after screenings in Berlin and Locarno. In 2006, Michael Winterbottom and Mat Whitecross's famous docudrama, *The Road to Guantanamo*, was screened at the New York HRWFF after it won a Silver Bear in Berlin. Due to its timely subject, this film garnered theatrical distribution in many parts of the world.

Unlike the comprehensive "A" festivals, human rights festivals rely less on premieres than on audience and show many movies that have been around the festival circuit. Biaggi stated that he primarily went to the Toronto International Film Festival and then the International Documentary Film Festival (IDFA) at Amsterdam to scout for films. Because of human rights festivals' reliance on documentaries, large documentary festivals like IDFA are more important to them than Cannes or Berlin. Since subject matter is the driving concern, fiction films in these festivals are often conventional narratives on appropriate subjects, like *Triage* (2009) by Danis Tanovic, whose *No Man's Land* won the best foreign film Oscar in 2001 after being nominated at Cannes for a Palme d'Or. HRWFF also shows historical documentaries, like *The Battle of Chile* (1976). However, few if any films shown at human rights film festivals receive wide theatrical distribution in the United States. In some ways, these festivals are removed from both mainstream cinema and art cinema, but serve a very specialized and highly committed audience.

The sense of a public sphere as a place of discussion is reinforced by John Biaggi's explanation that for a film to be included in the festival, it needs to have balance. Balance does not mean that the film has to show both sides of an argument, but that it has to acknowledge that there are other sides and that as much as possible it needs to be factually accurate rather than sheer polemic. He added that it was important for a film to be artistic. While issues and content are more important, a film can only be successful if it communicates with the audience. The festival's primary goal is not the pursuit of art for art's sake, yet if the film fails to be persuasive, it fails in communicating its message.

With the proliferation of human rights film festivals worldwide, the Human Rights Film Network was established in 2004 in Prague, partly initiated by directors from different human rights film festivals, including John Biaggi of HRWFF, Taco Ruighaver of the Movies That Matter Film Festival, and Igor Blaževič of the One World festival. This is an informal network through which members can exchange ideas and share the resources of the different human rights film festivals. It has grown from its initial seven members to twenty-nine.[45] The network now bestows the International Human Rights Film Award; rather than giving the award to a film or filmmaker, however, the award goes to "a human rights defending organisation or activist portrayed in a recent feature or documentary film." In 2008, the network awarded 5,000 euros to Afghan politician and activist Malalai Joya for "her efforts for peace, women's rights, and democracy in Afghanistan."[46] Joya is the subject of *Enemies of Happiness* (2006), directed by Eva Mulvad, which follows her campaign for the 2005 Afghan election. By giving the award to the subject rather than the filmmaker, the festival reinforces the extracinematic meaning of the text.

The growth of human rights film festivals as a system also has entailed concerted efforts to support established festivals, like Movies That Matter. Since

2009, the organization has provided up to 5,000 euros as well to organizations in Africa, Asia, Latin America, and Eastern Europe "to organize various types of human rights film events." In the two years since this program started, sixteen projects have been selected. These events are not limited to film festivals, but also include "mobile cinema programmes, film and debate programmes, small-scale screenings for specific target groups, rotation within a network of film houses, school and university screenings, and distribution through multimedia platforms."[47] These diversified film events can be seen as a harbinger of the future of generalized film distribution and a more comprehensive approach to reach potential audiences. This project also highlights the difference between the major film festivals and specialized festivals, like human rights festivals, that embody very different relationships with movie audiences.

HRWFF also wants to distinguish itself from festivals like the Margaret Mead Festival that are more anthropological than argumentative. Therefore, a film about a community that does not directly address broad human rights issues would not be selected even though, according to Biaggi, there is often a great deal of overlap in terms of the issues these films address. Like most other festivals, HRWFF scouts films from other festivals as well as through individual submissions. Its festival year starts in September with Toronto, then IDFF; finally, the festival may pick up a few titles from Sundance. The festival also accepts open submissions. However, more than a thousand titles have arrived each year in the past few years, affirming the democratic qualities of video but straining the staff, who had to review all the submissions.

This public sphere, while speaking to potentially universal issues, nonetheless has limits. HRWFF shows films that touch on familiar human rights issues, such as war, international justice, journalistic rights and abuses, women's issues, transgender issues, and many others. However, in terms of geographical distribution, there is a clear concentration on films about "poorer" countries. The 2009 HRWFF, for example, showed twenty-one films. Only five of these films were set in the West, with two of them treating immigrants who have migrated to France and the United States.[48] In the 2009 Movies That Matter Film Festival, twenty-one films/programs were shown, with only two films set in the West, with one on Muslim American standup comics and another a Barcelona protest about Western treatment of Darfur. Other festivals share similar patterns in terms of the political economic geography of the films screened. This returns us to the disparity discussed earlier about human rights film festivals and human rights in general by Amy Gutmann. With a great deal of influence coming from the West, are human rights film festivals dominated by a Western gaze? If so, what are the implications of that power relationship?

The reality remains that there are many films on human rights issues made and financed in the West, yet most deal with subjects outside these wealthy industrial societies and their middle classes. John Biaggi suggests that this is a matter of resources, economic as well as technological, and more permissive space for filmmaking of this kind. Increasingly, many diaspora filmmakers are making films about their home countries. For example, Rithy Panh is a Cambodian filmmaker who fled the Khmer Rouge in 1975 and was educated in France. He primarily makes films about Cambodia, including *The Land of the Wondering Souls* (2000), which screened at the Amnesty International Film Festival and One World. He is now based in both Cambodia and France. Such transnational global citizens increasingly lead the charge to speak on global issues that afflict their home countries.[49] Many of these filmmakers have been educated in the West, yet remain fluent in their native culture. Once again, Randall Halle's analysis of Western financing of non-Western films echoes this extremely complicated situation concerning unequal relations among nations and regions and the neo-Orientalism of who is creating the image of whom. As human rights become a wider global issue, an issue that garners international attention and sometimes international solutions, from the International Court at The Hague to responses from the United Nations, the trajectory for human rights film festivals will be intimately intertwined with the larger global discourse on human rights. Here, Nancy Fraser's thesis on the possibility of a new kind of transnational public sphere may indeed be conceptualized through a more concrete transnational public power.[50] Yet, as in other festivals, the presence of the local and national are also parts of the constitution of public place and public sphere.

Lesbian and Gay (Queer) Film Festivals

The Kids Are All Right, a light lesbian family comedy directed by Lisa Cholodenko and starring Julianne Moore and Annette Benning, became the subject of a high-stakes acquisitions drama at Sundance and won the Teddy Award at Berlin in 2010; Benning was touted as an Oscar contender. Its very success, though, makes it instructive to examine what role gay and lesbian, LGBTQ (Lesbian, Gay, Bisexual, Trans, Queer), or queer film festivals have played in bringing us to the gay cinema of today,[51] including mainstream media presence as well as argumentative or revolutionary media. *The Kids Are All Right* represents just one kind of LGBTQ cinema, with national distribution and major stars. The diversity of this cinema is very much refracted by the many different queer film festivals, audiences, and issues that have constituted a lively and growing public sphere.

These events represent one of the oldest thematic clusters among festivals since the first major festival in San Francisco in 1977. San Francisco was soon followed by Chicago in 1981, Outfest (the Los Angeles Lesbian and Gay Film Festival) in 1982, the London Lesbian and Gay Film Festival, and MIX (New York Lesbian and Gay Experimental Film Festival) in 1987. Networks became global with the Festival du Films Lesbiens de Paris, Lesben Film Festival Berlin, and the Asian Gay Film/Video Festival in Hong Kong in 1989.

Figure 9. U.S. director Lisa Cholodenko with her Teddy Award for the film *The Kids Are All Right*, Berlin, Germany, February 19, 2010.
Source: © JENS KALAENE / epa / Corbis.

One can also see these events in terms of an historical engagement of festivals with issues of gender and sexuality that challenged the borders of censorship and mainstream social and cultural orders of many films, exemplified by the Production Code that constrained Hollywood. Gay and lesbian actors, directors, and other agents in filmmaking were present from the origins of film; by the

1960s and 1970s, a gay sensibility became present in film festivals through well-known auteurs, including Pier Paolo Pasolini, Luchino Visconti, and Rainer Werner Fassbinder. As Harry Benshoff and Sean Griffin note in *Queer Images:* "Many of these films (and others not lucky enough to earn distribution deals) were first screened in America at newly formed lesbian and gay film festivals. . . . The growth of festivals allowed people in urban areas to see internationally produced queer films, as well as documentaries and experimental films made by domestic queers."[52]

The films LGBTQ festivals screen range from very mainstream to the very fringe. For example, the closing night film for the San Francisco festival in 2009 was *Hannah Free*. This is a conventional narrative, starring Sharon Glass, about "an adventurous, butch lesbian with gruff charm—and Rachel, a pristine, married homemaker."[53] It has traveled the queer film festival circuit, winning numerous awards at gay and lesbian film festivals. It gained limited theatrical distribution (one week at New York Quad cinema) and has garnered press coverage in the *New York Times*, Huffington Post, and *Veja São Paulo*. Also on the program was *Thundercrack*, a 1975 film that is "the world's only underground kinky art porno horror film, complete with four men, three women and a gorilla. . . . This film will arouse, challenge and question you through every torrid moment of solo, gay, bisexual, and straight couplings, voyeurism and more."[54] Similarly, the 2010 Philadelphia QFEST complemented its international survey with a live and in-person encounter with Michael Lucas: "From his award-winning takes on *Dangerous Liaisons* and *La dolce vita* to his ground-breaking 2009 epic *Men of Israel*, Lucas Entertainment is one of the world's most recognized and prominent porn studios. But if you've only seen those famed lips in action yet have never heard the voice behind them, you're in for an eyebrow-raising and pulse-pounding earful."[55] These festivals showcase narrative features, shorts and documentaries join discussions and parties—not unlike diverse events in other festivals, even if advertised with a more overt sexual element.

These events have not been defined simply by content but in fact have taken on many characteristics of counterpublics and counterpublic spheres.[56] Many of these festivals promote broader LGBTQ agendas: to fight for the rights of LGBTQ people, to foster expression by and for LGBTQ people, to build alliances with LGBTQ community groups, and to educate the larger community about queer issues. Moreover, they have embodied a visible public presence of queer audiences and issues—a place for socialization and entertainment, for business, and for activism. Just as queer is an alternative to the dominant heterosexuality, these festivals very much established queer film festivals as alternatives, and at times oppositional spheres, vis-à-vis more mainstream film festivals and their discussions.

This is not to say that such festivals denigrate film or even the business of film, so much as they reframe it around different extratextual and spectator issues. The umbrella organization for the San Francisco International Lesbian and Gay Film Festival is Frameline. Besides running the film festival, Frameline also works in community liaison. It started its distribution arm in 1981, renting films to other festivals as well as educational institutions. Since 1991 it also has provided completion grants to filmmakers, echoing the practices of Rotterdam and Hong Kong. Other festivals participate in archival work. Outfest in Los Angeles, for example, in collaboration with the UCLA Film and Television Archive, is running the Outfest Legacy Project, which aims to preserve LGBTQ moving images.

Even so, queer festivals differ from human rights festivals, which fight for human rights for all (and abstract) people, in that queer festivals are first and foremost of, by, and for queer people: a place of presence. These festivals are heavily tied in with complicated identity politics. They were also born after the Stonewall riots (1969) and grew up with the AIDS crisis that transformed and galvanized gay communities. Since queer identities are not stable and are contested, queer festivals manifest themselves in different guises around spatial and social formations of the public sphere.

Hence, not surprisingly, such festivals have a strong history in place, even neighborhood. The iconic Castro Theater, on a street identified with gay history, is Frameline's major venue where most of the features are shown. The Anthology Film Archive in Manhattan's East Village was the home of MIX and many experimental art films, even though in the last two years MIX has moved to the trendier Chelsea section of Manhattan. Festivals also create place and sphere. According to Ruby Rich, the San Francisco festival conducted a survey in the mid-1990s that found that "80 percent of the audience never went to movie theaters the rest of the year" and "80–90 percent of the works shown at gay and lesbian film festivals never play elsewhere."[57] Given that these festivals are deliberately self-contained or bounded, tensions and interactions emerge within the festivals themselves as well as within their relationship with the larger film festival circuit and cinematic institutions. Rich poses the question, "Is a gay, lesbian, bi, or trans film festival comparable to a bar? a gym? a club? a community center? a softball game? a queer conference? a magazine? a daytime talk show?"[58] What make queer festivals stand out is that they started out as oppositional and alternative and paid less attention to the world outside. Richard Fung adds that "when one programs a festival, one also programs the audience and the community."[59] Here, identity becomes primary, displacing at least partially mainstream festival concerns with both aesthetics and business.

Place has been important in the globalization of film festivals, especially as activism, film, and identity have combined in areas where gay activities have been hidden or criminalized. GAZE, the Dublin Gay and Lesbian Film Festival, which began in 1992, proudly notes on its Web site that "From its humble beginnings in 1992 (when homosexuality was still a criminal act in Ireland!), GAZE has grown from strength to become the largest LGBT film event in Ireland, and one of the most respected in the world."[60] The first Beijing Gay and Lesbian Film Festival premiered with Chinese films for some three thousand spectators in a one-day event in 2001. A second internationalized edition did not follow until 2005. Both were shut down by police.[61] A more successful rebirth followed in 2009, when "the auditorium for the film festival's opening movie, a story of a Chinese man who searches for the soul of his dead Swiss lover, was packed with a lively crowd of about 100 people, mostly young and proudly gay. Others who came were simply curious to know more about gay issues, a segment sought out by organizers who wanted to encourage dialogue between the gay community and the wider public."[62]

Such festivals now complement each other as parts of the global queer film festival circuit, marked by an awareness of global issues. In its 2009 lineup, MIX showed the documentary *Queer Sarajevo Festival 2008*. It captures one of the few queer festivals in the Muslim world, how it was put together and how it was forced to close after violent assaults on the first day of the festival. MIX thus becomes a vehicle that transmits images and sounds from one queer festival to another, reinforcing a global community of queerness, sharing its struggle as well as its pain, while educating others to understand the many hardships queers in other parts of the world still face. The film was included in the section "Do It to It," which treats community building as part of the mission of the festival.

At the same time, globalization can also turn queerness into a destination brand that reproduces differences of metropolis and smaller city, or North and South. Out Film CT in Hartford, Connecticut, received the Outstanding Project Award by the Connecticut Commission on Culture and Tourism in 2007.[63] On the Web page of Damron, a travel agency specializing in gay and lesbian travel, there is a page on LGBTQ film festivals, obviously noting the festivals as potential niche travel destinations,[64] affirming the commodification of some gay and lesbian film festivals.

Globalization, finally, underscores queer festivals' multiple intersections with the presence of queer filmmakers and films in larger festival circulation worldwide. While a queer film might not win the Palme d'Or or Golden Bear, the Teddy Award was established in 1987 in Berlin, as a sidebar to Berlinale. It is now one of the most important queer awards. The Berlinale, especially the Forum, has worked closely with queer communities, sharing curators or programs. Other major festivals, like Sundance and Toronto, have also been important to queer cinema, and Cannes has recently seen an unofficial Queer Palm to meet the Queer Lion of Venice.[65] This coexistence became especially notable for gay cinema since the emergence of the phenomenon that Rich termed New Queer Cinema in 1992, where she credits film festivals as a whole, not just gay and lesbian film festivals, for helping the development of this cinema (which many suggest is too male oriented).[66] For example, Gus Van Sant's first feature

Mala noche (1985) was screened in Berlin as well as at Frameline in 1986 and at the Los Angeles Lesbian and Gay Film Festival in 1987. Even with no theatrical release at the time, the film "won the L.A. Film Critics Association's best independent feature award in 1987."[67] While not mainstream, films shown at gay and lesbian film festivals drew the attention of film critics in the 1980s. *Mala noche* finally gained theatrical release at Film Forum in New York in 1988. Two decades later, with Gus Van Sant an established filmmaker in more mainstream circles and "A" festivals, *Mala noche* has come to form part of queer film history, and has been screened retrospectively in numerous film events in Cannes and Thessaloniki, in 2006, and the London Lesbian and Gay Film Festival in 2008. Rich has also placed more emphasis on features than alternative formats, like experimental and avant-garde works. Nonetheless, besides identifying Sundance and Toronto as nurturers of New Queer Cinema, works done previously by gay and lesbian film festivals like Frameline and MIX are of equal, if not greater, importance. MIX, while starting as an oppositional film festival, has launched the career of filmmakers and programmers, including Todd Haynes, who screened his Brown University thesis project, *Assassins: A Film Concerning Rimbaud,* there.[68]

Over time, queer festivals have faced social divisions within gay life and have created sections or festivals for specific ethnicities (Black, Latino, South Asian), agents and sexual orientations (lesbians and transgender film festivals), and more mainstream versus less mainstream. While fiction features center most festivals, documentaries have also played an important part in the recuperation of history and the statement of problems for public discussion. At the same time, unlike human rights festivals, queer festivals cover a wider terrain of subject matters and forms since they not only show films with queer content, oppositional or otherwise, but also show works by queers, thus opening the festivals to virtually boundless opportunities. While debate continues as to what "queer" means, issues relating to gender and sexuality are at the forefront of queer festivals. Since queer encompasses so many people belonging to different genders, classes, races, and ethnicities, queer festivals always have to struggle to define their own inclusiveness.

Nonetheless, queer festivals have been accused of being unable to extricate themselves from the entrenched power relations in the mainstream society, where white males control and own more resources. Patricia White asserts that the most stubborn divide is a split between male and female works at these festivals.[69] Rich also underscores the difference between the male-oriented queer cinema at Toronto and Sundance and the smaller, less "important" (because it has received less publicity) Amsterdam Gay and Lesbian Festival, which was more friendly to lesbians and was a more female-oriented festival.[70]

Queer festivals, moreover, are more vibrant in the West than in other parts of the world. While most embrace differences, they share the dilemma that refracts the global imbalance on issues of gay rights. Just as the human rights festivals face the questions of who is speaking for whom, queer festivals also have to reckon with the fact that the West speaks more than the non-West. In discussing globalization, Suzy Capo at MIX Brazil, São Paulo, asks, "Globalization means 'Americanization' of queer culture, right?"[71] Nanna Heidenreich, who has curated queer festivals in Germany and MIX Brazil, also commented on the intersection of identity politics, demanding that queer festivals tackle assumptions such as "gay means German means white and that Turkish means Muslim means straight means homophobic."[72] Some queer festivals, in fact, have started to confront this issue of diverse global concerns and representations with more diversified programming.

To deal with such divisions of community, even more than genres of film, many larger queer festivals now see themselves as entities that encompass different components. Roya Rastegar, for example, has investigated the Fusion Festival—Los Angeles LGBT People of Color Film Festival, a festival within Outfest.[73] To have a festival devoted to LGBT people of color both affirms queer people of color and raises the old question of whether Outfest ghettoized people of color. Like Rich and Fung, Rastegar asserts that "film festivals matter. They play a significant role in not only bringing together films but also defining and shaping a community." Yet, she asserts that Outfest had "a reputation of alienating audience of people of color."[74] Hence, Fusion was born in collaboration with Asian Pacific Islanders for Human Rights in 2004, a logical connection, since gay and minority rights are indeed human rights.

However, the competing and at times contradictory demands from very diverse constituents of these festivals also prevent the formation of a coherent community goal and a collective queer identity. This itself is not a hindrance; however, it crystallizes the challenge that LGBTQ festivals face when they have to negotiate the diverging goals of a complex web of expectations. In Rastegar's research, she interviews different participants—"artists, activists, industry professionals, and scholars"—for a Fusion conference called "Ignite the Fuse" and finds that the major divide seems to be between people who are more interested in the industry and those who see Fusion more as an activist community-based event.[75] The two orientations lead to very different kinds of programming decisions as well as the overall cultures of diverse festivals.

Such differentiation is apparent in New York City, for example, with a large and diverse queer population and two major longstanding queer festivals: MIX, originally known as the New York Gay and Lesbian Experimental Film Festival, since 1987; and the NewFest, established in 1988. Since there is no unified queer identity, people constantly explore appropriate strategies to approach issues concerning LGBTQ lives. Joshua Gamson's article adroitly described how these two New York festivals negotiate their organizational collective identities. MIX was devoted to experimental cinema while constantly questioning the boundaries of what constitutes gay or queer. On the other hand, the NewFest started as a

Figure 10. Poster for the Third Gay and Lesbian Experimental Film Festival, New York, 1989. .
Source: Jim Hubbard.

pluralistic festival, one which strives for gay visibilities, without questioning much what constitutes gay or queer. Yet with the change experienced by larger queer communities, the two festivals also share new relationships with commercialism while retaining their varied goals.[76]

Jim Hubbard and Sarah Schulman created MIX in 1987, the same year ACT UP (an activist organization to combat the AIDS crisis) was established. Many who were involved with the festival were also involved with ACT UP and felt an urgency to rely on one another across the Lower East Side of New York. According to Schulman,[77] the festival organizers felt that many other film festivals, including the few gay and lesbian festivals of the time, reinforced the status quo that made it difficult for people at the margin to become artists. Hubbard and Schulman believed that experimental forms could present more authentic gay experiences and representations. MIX was from its origins extremely concerned with race, class, and gender as well, even though the first festival was very "white." Reaching out to populations with less means was always a primary goal. The fourth festival, in 1990, focused on gay black men and screened works by Marlon Riggs and Issac Julien.

Even after two decades of festivals, "MIX's work challenges mainstream notions of gender and sexuality while also upending traditional categories of form and content."[78] The name of MIX with the word experimental already suggests that MIX is not a "mainstream" festival. The festival has always sought to understand what queer identities mean. It seldom shows feature-length films, but instead programs short films, defined by content or subject matter. Through this dedication to experimental films, the early festival had close relationships with high art institutions, like the Whitney Bienniale and a mainstream European "A" festival, Berlin. Over the years, MIX also has expanded globally, helping to launch MIX Brazil and MIX Mexico in the 1990s.

Yet, MIX remains rooted in its local communities. For example, in 2009, MIX's opening program was "Making All Local Stops," which covered work from New York's five boroughs. Another program was "Bulldozed," which consisted of eight short films, dealing generally with gentrification. In its more recent editions, MIX (New York) sometimes has also foregone strictly queer themes for broader themes of social justice, although oftentimes these works are produced by queer filmmakers. MIX also runs a program called "A Different Take" that offers a video workshop for LGBTQ youths and young adults, where the youths spend ten weeks together to learn the craft of filmmaking. Finally, MIX also has a section devoted to installation, again questioning the boundaries of film form and content. These installations, in turn, create spaces for the communities to mix.

Another project that MIX has been involved with is the ACT UP Oral History Project, organized by Hubbard and Schulman. The project secured grant money from different foundations to collect testimonies of over one hundred people who had been involved with ACT UP in New York. The unedited interviews are archived at the New York Public Library; most can be downloaded for free from its Web site. Again, MIX pushes its mission beyond showing films, including preserving the history of LGBT struggles.

Even though MIX has undergone many changes, it still adheres to the principle of "supporting completely original, completely queer, and completely uncompromised experimental art."[79] When the Bank of New York Mellon withdrew its support of the festival because the bank considered the festival too controversial, MIX sent an open letter to its supporters explaining its continued mission and asking for financial support to continue its operations.

The New Festival (NewFest), the other major LGBTQ film festival in New York, was established a year after MIX, in 1988. According to Gamson, NewFest's base is "the more market oriented independent film world."[80] Conversations with audiences who have attended the festivals show that they feel that NewFest is very much like any other film festival in the city, except that it has a gay theme. Audiences attend the festival to see movies, rather than seeing the festival events as gatherings. The festival also holds a Filmmakers Forum, which brings "audiences together with filmmakers and industries,"[81] validating Gamson's point that the festival strives to work closely with the more business-oriented independent film world.

Queer film festivals as specialized film festivals are grounded within the very diverse histories of queer struggle as well as the very uneven journey in defining queer in society. As LGBTQ issues became relatively more conventional and mainstream in the last two decades, many have asked questions about the purposes and nature of queer festivals. As Sarah Schulman pointed out to Joshua Gamson in 1995, the wider acceptance of mainstream gay cinema like *Philadelphia* (1993) and *Go Fish* (1994) should be read as part of a larger shift for the organized lesbian and gay population "from an ignored community struggle to represent itself to a consumer group that is being niche marketed by the most powerful corporate influence." This is indeed a result of the "successful organizing for visibility and self-representation."[82] In 2000, Ruby Rich once again asked if queer cinema had become "just another niche market?"[83]

In the earlier decades, queer festivals, not yet diverse, tended to speak mainly to nascent and urbane queer communities, but with gay themes becoming more mainstream since the 1990s, many queer festivals are now more integrated into the larger society and art independent film and film festival circuits. Hence, different queer festivals struggle to define how they see themselves in wider communities by their actions as well as their texts and gatherings. The question for the future is how a group of alternative, oppositional festivals contend with increased mainstreaming. And in so doing, how do values of film (aesthetic and commercial) and the constitution of audience and filmmakers as public sphere coexist?

Conclusion

When investigating film festivals through their focus on ideas, audiences, and discussion, with or without political underpinning, this chapter has moved away slightly from dominant themes of art, form, and business. Yet as anyone who has experienced a festival knows, talking and meeting is a central feature of these events, unlike regular screenings at a local cinema, viewing a DVD, or watching on-demand programs at home. As Walter Benjamin and Siegfried Krakauer observed long ago, film creates new collective publics. Recognition that film festivals provide audiences and sites for debate, in turn, has opened up intentional organization for the promulgation of liberal human issues like human rights, ecological consciousness, immigration, globalization, and gay identities.

Within mainstream and dominant festivals, the practice of the public sphere echoes both the strengths and weaknesses of Habermas's formulation. Interested (often bourgeois) people raise issues around filmic events and in the streets and cafes of London and San Francisco and mingle with starstruck gawkers and dealmakers in an exuberant and ephemeral heterotopia. Controversy may arrive from the street or diffuse in newspaper coverage of key films and speeches. Yet, at the same time, controversy makes reputations and even sells films: aesthetics and business never completely disappear.

By examining two smaller networks of festivals dealing with human rights and queer issues in some detail, while not neglecting these issues as themes within larger festivals, I have tried to bring into clearer relief this vital component of people and place that sets apart film festivals once again from other viewing experiences. These events distill rather than contravert themes we have already seen in festival organization and impact: the development of networks of knowledge, agents, and distribution, the formation of canons and auteurs, and even the problems of hegemony that have undercut the position of voices from women, minorities, and filmmakers from the third world.

The human contacts and debates characterizing the public sphere also insist that festivals, thematic and omnibus, are not inflexible but are sites of change and exchange. This vision, in fact, becomes clearer through the elucidation of history, content, and meanings of a particular regional and global festival between the small-scale ones and the "A"-levels, the long-running Hong Kong International Film Festival, to which we now turn.

6   The Hong Kong International Film Festival as Cultural Event

Throughout this work, I have dissected festivals into varied components—history and function, film and aesthetics, auteurs and critical knowledge, production and business, audiences, debates, and impacts. While all of these perspectives map festivals as a living, multilayered system with complex and changing individual units, festivals also embody intense convergent experiences of people, places, and film. Hence, to bring the system into final focus, I turn to a systematic discussion of a single film festival—the Hong Kong International Film Festival. I begin with a synthesis from my field notes in 2007 that conveys how this event transpired for viewers and participants.

> Just after Chinese New Year and the 2007 Hong Kong International Film Festival program catalogs are out! Cinephiles, students, and the curious pick up the thick, glossy red-and-gray pamphlets in movie houses, performance halls, and libraries. They scrutinize them on line, calculating how many movies they can catch. "Can I make it across the harbor from the Science Museum in Tsim Sha Tsui [Kowloon] to catch the next screening in City Hall in Central [Hong Kong Island]?" "There's a section on new Romanian cinema: is that the next hot thing?" "We need to order quickly for the European and Japanese films—they sell out every year." "Are you going to see these documentaries from Africa?—I should, I know, but the one on the U.S. rating system might actually be fun." "The Korean pop star Rain is going to be in town for this cyborg movie and also is going to compete in the first Asian Film Awards—is it an Asian Oscar? Is this selling out?"
>
> While audiences constitute themselves, festival banners fly everywhere in the city. Despite its specialized draw, they seem to outnumber even the propaganda promoting Hong Kong as Asia's World City. Or do they reaffirm this claim for the postcolonial city? Soon, mass media, English and Chinese, start to cover the festival. Opening night is still a month away.
>
> Of course, since December, the festival staff has been busy putting this catalog together. While some selections came to mind when they visited festivals at Pusan, Delhi, Berlin, Cannes, and Locarno, others were still being lined up in February, especially those that would be making world or regional premieres. Jacob Wong and Li Cheuk To, the programmers, have guided these selections. Staff grapple with the logistics of accommodating

filmmakers and other important visitors and making sure that the prints arrive on time while circulating ubiquitous DVDs to catalog writers. Being the director of the HAF, the Asian Film Financing Forum, Wong also needs to make sure that all these incipient film projects are ready to be presented to potential investors. Chinese and English editors have been scrambling to see clips and write 100-word catalog blurbs—completely independently of each other—but must cooperate to polish the dozens of project descriptions and translations for the HAF. In the office downtown, other staffers juggle schedules and venues—with gala events in the elegant central theater of Cultural Centre, while other, more specialized films are tucked into smaller halls in the film archives or the Broadway Cinematheque in Mong Kok.

The catalog designer's office is just minutes away from our apartment at the staff quarters of City University. Almost every night in early February, my husband, who worked as English-language editor, joined full-time staff like Li Cheuk To and my brother, Jacob Wong, to work late into the night to fit the pages together, adding and or subtracting words, double-checking the spelling of names and places on draft after draft. And after that went to the printer, it was back to work to assemble criticism and comments for the massive festival reference catalog available on opening day. The city—and the festival—shut down momentarily for New Year's . . . and then the rush began.

By mid-March, red carpets are out at the Convention Center in Wanchai, built for the 1997 Handover and the Cultural Centre across the harbor in Tsim Sha Tsui. Actor Tony Leung is the ambassador for the Film Expo, which kicks off the festival. Critics, filmmakers, financiers, and stars arrive for the film financing forum and the deals to be made at the Filmart (which used to be a separate event). Many stay for the glamour of the first Asian Film Awards. And all these events are wrapped into a cultural calendar that will host weeks of markets and expositions dealing with Hong Kong design, music, and other arts, claiming a place for Hong Kong as a design/marketing center for Asia to complement its finance and services roles.

We take my teenage daughter and her friend to the opening ceremony for the Expo and the AFA ceremony. They find it dull, with too many bureaucrats talking and two few glamorous stars, despite the special award for longtime Hong Kong star Josephine Hsiao. When Rain shows up, his fans scream wildly and flash homemade signs, but they leave when he fails to win an award. The AFA even includes an award for film criticism, given in this inaugural year to David Bordwell, who has studied Japanese cinema as well as Hong Kong production. Many people in the HKIFF adore him, and rumor has it that director Johnnie To would only show up if Bordwell were honored. The award is preceded by an elegantly edited clip on his work; still, it is hard to imagine the Oscars engaging academic film studies in the same way.

By the end of the evening, it seems almost every Asian film industry wins some award, with best picture going to the popular Korean horror film *The Host*. And Hong Kong has pulled off the awards before this honor can be claimed by Korea or Australia, who have similar programs in the works.

With the film festival now officially under way, minor problems and discoveries crop up constantly. Some spectators are still not getting the tickets they ordered through the new online booking system, distracting busy staffers. Some of the prints are not as solid or finished as they should be. One day the festival office calls my husband to act as a Spanish interpreter as well: the young Chilean director of *Anger* [*La rabia*], Oscar Cardenas Navarro, is not comfortable speaking English for interviews with media or Q&A sessions. When we meet him, he has already made his pilgrimage to Chungking Mansion, immortalized in Wong Kar Wai's *Chungking Express*, but we also explore the city with him during the short stay the Chilean government has supported to expand its own industry abroad.

Crowds fill the many theaters used as venues. Youth-oriented programs like *I See It My Way* are packed; French and Japanese movies still get their dependable audience; smaller, challenging, esoteric films from smaller places still get their diehard seekers in half-empty halls. Herman Yau, known for shocking films like *Human Pork Chop*, reveals many other dimensions in his retrospective and the world premiere of his character-driven examination of Hong Kong prostitution, *Whispers and Moans*, a gala event in the Cultural Centre main theater whose catalog was the last publication to be finished. Some old-timers, who have observed the festival for a long time, lament that it is not what it used to be—too commercialized, too many red carpets. . . . Yet, audiences stay after the film for Q&A with filmmakers from around the world and coffeeshops at the Cultural Centre and the universities are always packed with people talking about discoveries and disappointments.

And the festival finds new audiences. My five-year-old, Graciela, enjoyed *Komaneko—the Curious Cat*—a film in stop-motion animation whose dialogue is done through "meows" and she has a front row seat for Luc Besson's *Arthur and the Invisibles*, although she is afraid to ask him a question in the exchange that follows. Some of my students at City U complain in class that they just could not stand the film *Betelnut*; "The director said that he just used long shots because he did not want to use many different shots; how could it have won the prize at Pusan?" It goes on to win a FIPRESCI prize in Hong Kong as well. Venice Golden Lion winner Jia Zhangke was the focus of a special symposium, and some thought that was the best thing about the festival. Bill Guttentag, one of the directors of *Nanking*, came to City U to talk to students at the School of Creative Media about the film as well as his other works on TV and the ethics involved in them.

Figure 11. Chinese filmmaker Jia Zhang ke kisses the Leopard of Honour after receiving the award at the Sixty-third Locarno International Film Festival, in Locarno, Switzerland, August 5, 2010.
Source: © JEAN-CHRISTOPHE BOTT / epa / Corbis.

Festivals also mean parties in many places, where participants meet outside the public eye. I missed the Jia party because I got the wrong day. But in another party, I talked with organizers and visiting critics while my husband talked to the political candidate who was the subject of the delightful Japanese documentary *Campaign*. He is wearing his campaign banner, even though we really could not understand one another too well. There is a reception before the Yao gala and time to meet other people for dinner or drinks around the city. . . .

After twenty-three long days and 300 films, the festival finally ends. A Luchino Visconti retrospective still spins on for those who have not had enough classic festival films. The Hong Kong Film Archive also stretches its retrospectives, having taken over production of the reference work long associated with the festival itself. All the staff breathe a sign of relief, even if the online ticketing still demands refunds. Many, hired part-time for the event, move on to other jobs. There is little time to think about strengths and weaknesses before the Board of Trustees invites everyone to a celebratory dinner at a fancy restaurant in Hong Kong Park. After a little rest, some are then off to Cannes, some off to Locarno as the festival year starts all over again. (From author's fieldwork notes on the 2007 HKIFF)

As a native citizen of Hong Kong, I have been going to the Hong Kong International Film Festival (HKIFF) since I was a teenager there in the late 1970s. This was an era of an increasingly wealthy, cosmopolitan but colonial Hong Kong, before the signing of the Joint Declaration of 1984 between Deng Xiaoping and Margaret Thatcher that guided the return of Hong Kong to the People's Republic of China (PRC) in 1997. After being a spectator, over the years, the festival offerings became part of my academic studies of media and the city and provided a natural platform as I expanded into ethnographic and archival work, interviewing programmers, rethinking audiences and spaces, and attending a wider range of events with new interests in 1997, 2004, and 2007 while I worked on other aspects of Hong Kong media and society.[1] I saw the festival through new processes and places, ranging from screenings to parties to editorial work. My brother had been involved in the festival since the 1980s as the Asian film programmer and then curator, giving me new access to this world, while he recruited my husband as an English-language writer and editor in 2006, 2007, and 2008. When I taught cinema at the City University in Hong Kong as a Fulbright Fellow in 2006–2007, I saw the festival through the eyes of my students and my children as eager participants in its heady whirl of screenings and events.

Yet, beyond my personal connections, the HKIFF represents an important film festival to balance materials more commonly drawn from the major European and North American events. The HKIFF, founded in 1977, is the oldest continuous film festival in East Asia. As the premier Asian festival, it has helped place Asian films, including those of Hong Kong and new Chinese cinemas, into the international film festival circuit and art house cinemas. With the Hong Kong New Wave in the late 1970s and the debut of the Chinese fifth-generation masterpiece *Yellow Earth* in 1985 at the Koshan Theatre in Kowloon, the HKIFF became a showcase for diverse Chinese cinemas and a window for those (including critics and festivals) seeking new dimensions of global cinema.

In the last decade, the festival has weathered the decline of the Hong Kong film industry, competition from neighboring countries and cities, including Pusan, Shanghai, Bangkok, and Tokyo, and the changing regional-global position of Hong Kong itself. Moreover, the HKIFF evolved from a government-run operation into a privatized neoliberal corporation dependent on sponsors as well as government aid.[2] Additions like the Asian Film Financing Forum (HAF) and the Asian Film Awards (AFA), which link the festival to production of mainstream as well as independent cinema, are strategies we have already explored that allow festivals to compete in the film festival world of the twenty-first century. To understand the HKIFF, one has to understand colonial and postcolonial governance, Hong Kong's relationship with China and Taiwan and their global positions, the people of Hong Kong who negotiate these shoals as programmers, filmmakers, audiences, and citizens, and how all these articulate with the dynamic global film festival culture. Hence, situating three decades of the festival in its evolving contexts shows how the global demands of film festivals interact with local and regional film industries as well as the political, cultural, and social demands of a colonial and postcolonial hybrid Chinese city.

In this chapter, I begin with a brief historical sketch of Hong Kong and its film culture, especially since the mid-twentieth century, to provide a context for the film festival as a cultural institution within changing Hong Kong society. I then explore the HKIFF through four interlocking perspectives that develop roughly chronologically. First, I show how the festival began in interaction with the colonial city, culturally and politically, in the 1960s and 1970s. Second, I show how the definition and preservation of Hong Kong film culture in the 1970s and 1980s, linked to a growing local identity, came to distinguish the HKIFF and gain it critical recognition from *Cahiers du cinéma,* other global critics, and festival planners. Third, I show how promotion of Hong Kong cinema became enmeshed in the 1980s and 1990s with bridges among Chinese peoples and cinemas, locating a diversity of Chinese voices within international cinema, whether in the "A"-festival circuit or the canonization of Chinese cinema in critical and academic worlds. Finally, I situate today's HKIFF within the larger contemporary but cutthroat network of international film festivals to investigate how individual festivals, while unique, must negotiate their roles within regional and global networks. This complete sequence of events and contexts allows me to reflect on the present and future of HKIFF and, through it, on festivals as a wider world.

Hong Kong, Colonial Culture, and Early Film

After the British claimed the "Barren Rock" of Hong Kong at the mouth of South China's Pearl River in 1841 as a spoil of the First Opium War,[3] the territory evolved for 158 years as a crown colony, separated from China by law but not by people. During this time, China itself changed from a decaying imperial bureaucracy to a divided republic to a communist state that has passed through convulsive and destructive decades to reach its present position of a dynamic one-party state modifying capitalist techniques to achieve global power. From 1841 to 1997, Hong Kong never ceased to be a Chinese society with a majority Chinese population, although it was ruled by a transient expatriate colonial government appointed by and loyal to the British. Nonetheless, the legal separation of the colony made Hong Kong an important staging ground for change in China and connections with overseas Chinese as well as Western modernities, from Sun Yat-Sen to Falun Gong.[4]

Hong Kong Island is a small place (thirty square miles). The early port and warehouses in Victoria (Central) controlled only one side of a deep-water harbor until China was forced to concede the tip of the Kowloon peninsula to Great Britain in 1860 as spoils of the Second Opium War. As the dense clusters of warehouses, commercial establishments, and Chinese tenements along both waterfronts continued to grow into a polyglot trading entrepôt, the British leased the rural New Territories—broad paddy fields and villages on the peninsula and hundreds of islands—for ninety-nine years, beginning in 1898. These were to act as a buffer with China, but this lease brought significant clan villages with centuries of history into the diverse Chinese populations of the colony. The combined territories cover 423 square miles (1,100 square kilometers) and now have a population of 7 million, still concentrated around Victoria Harbor. This includes the soaring skyscrapers of the Central, Wanchai, and Causeway Bay districts on the Hong Kong side and the neon-washed, bustling Kowloon-side neighborhoods of Tsim Sha Tsui, Prince Edward, Yau Ma Tei, and Mong Kok.

By the mid-nineteenth century, Hong Kong replaced nearby Portuguese Macau and upriver Guangzhou as the major port for transferring opium from India and other sources into China. It also became a gateway that allowed people and goods to move into China and out of it to different parts of the overseas Chinese world. Still, most Westerners saw it as a colonial backwater compared to the splendors of the Raj in British India. They established their businesses, churches, sporting clubs, and other institutions while retreating from the workaday city to residences on the segregated Peak that overlooks the harbor (with Chinese servants, of course).

For the Chinese, meanwhile, including some Eurasians who took on important intercultural positions, Hong Kong was a place of opportunity and even a center for resistance to the late Qing or foreign incursions. But for China, Hong Kong was also a reminder of weakness. Chinese exiles who fled Shanghai for Hong Kong in World War II found it a place without culture: "while everyone is Chinese . . . it has no Chinese flavor, it lacks a Chinese soul."[5] Nor did these exiles find refuge from the Japanese, who invaded in 1941 and occupied the territory for four years, challenging European superiority.

The end of the war in 1945 was followed by civil war on the mainland and communist success in establishing the People's Republic of China (PRC) in 1949. Hong Kong became an important entrepôt for an embargoed regime and a place of escape. Many capitalists, including filmmakers, fled mainland China, bringing their money to Hong Kong. They jumpstarted the colony's incipient industrialization, including the film industry. Thousands of other refugees fled to Hong Kong as well. The population, depressed to less than a million by Japanese occupation, mushroomed from 1,600,000 in 1946 to 2,360,000 in 1950 and reached 3,526,000 in 1962, 98 percent of whom were Chinese. A poor working class from nearby Guangdong and Fukien provinces mixed with affluent industrialists and cinema people from Shanghai, as refugees provided cheap labor for burgeoning industries, fomenting Hong Kong's economic takeoff in the next generation.

The colonial government was forced to deal with these changes, despite its general hands-off ideology. A dramatic conflagration at Shek Kip Mei on Christmas day 1953, for example, destroyed the homes of 50,000 squatters.[6] Such fires, which had swept through hardscrabble settlements cobbled together on dangerous slopes and unoccupied lands, haunt Allen Fong's *Father and Son* (1981) and the television project *Under the Lion Rock*.[7] In order to deal with the increased squatter population, the government embarked on massive public housing projects over the next decades, developing new towns across the Kowloon peninsula and New Territories: Sha Tin grew from a small farming and market town to an urban settlement of more than 1 million. The British also provided education to children of immigrants who would enter industry, sales, and finally the growing service economy of the postwar Hong Kong economic miracle. By the 1960s, Hong Kong, under the watchful eye of Britain and the United States, was becoming a modern city with a growing middle class, a strong working class, and a core of institutions and buildings that underpinned the skyscrapers and wealth of today.

Nonetheless, in the globally turbulent 1960s, Hong Kong experienced riots and civil unrest as Chinese protested over local issues and the Cultural Revolution in China spilled across the border in 1967. While the colonial government put down all the protests, it was forced to become more responsive and inclusive to Chinese colonial subjects seeking their own voices and hybrid identities.

While Hong Kong film culture is often associated with this postwar expansion, it actually had begun earlier as part of the global colony in relation to Chinese markets and industry. While film palaces were built for expatriate audiences and Hong Kong elites, Hong Kong Chinese produced their first film in 1913: Li Minwei's *Zhangzhi Tests His Wife,* which relied on Chinese American capital and the possibilities of audiences in Chinatowns worldwide. Run Run Shaw established a studio in Hong Kong in 1934, and by the end of the 1930s Hong Kong produced one hundred films per year in Cantonese, the dominant language of South China. These dramas, translated into Chiu Chao and Amoy dialects, found little favor with the Mandarin-speaking Chinese Republican government but did play to audiences in the Chinese diaspora worldwide. After Japan took Shanghai, Hong Kong became a new center for Chinese filmmaking, at least until 1941.

After the war, Hong Kong's peace and prosperity fostered an even more vibrant film industry in the 1950s and 1960s, with Shaw Brothers and Cathay making glossy Mandarin films from their studios, Cantonese films coming from other smaller production companies, and even leftist films made by those sympathetic to the PRC.

In addition to local movies, Hong Kong people also have watched Hollywood cinema as well as British films sustained by a protected market (colonial laws required that British films show seven days out of seventy in first-run theaters). The 1955 *Hong Kong Report,* for example, noted 227 locally made films (one-quarter in Mandarin), apart from which "a preponderance of American films is shown. British films are third, averaging about fifty, in comparison with four hundred American. Japanese, French, Indian, and Italian films are shown occasionally."[8] All these films were censored by a Board of Review concerned with politics and sexual mores.

At this time, the report noted, Hong Kong had sixty-five cinemas, with twenty-three in the downtown Victoria district and twenty-six in urbane Kowloon across the harbor. Here were the first-run palaces for foreign films. Other smaller cinemas served working-class and rural Chinese with vernacular films in continuous screenings. Due to its relatively small local audience, Hong Kong film studios continued to have strong ties with overseas markets, from Southeast Asia, East Asia, and Taiwan to diasporic Chinese communities. Television, which arrived in the colony in 1957, became a competitor with films, although it often recycled older Hong Kong films, reintroducing Cantonese films to younger audiences.[9]

It was under such a political, economic, and cultural climate that Hong Kong established a film festival in the late 1970s. By this time, industry, tourism (fomented by American cold war interest in East Asia), and finance were making Hong Kong a global Chinese city, a position its citizens would continue to enhance through decades of spectacular growth. This is also a period scholars associate with the emergence of a concrete "Hong Konger" identity despite the paradox of the absence of decolonization.[10]

Indeed, the future of the territory soon became a different question. While Hong Kong and Kowloon were held in perpetuity as British spoils of war, the New Territories, which had become the seat of growing populations and industry, were due to return to China in 1997. Unlike decolonization in British colonies worldwide, independence was almost never seen as an option for Hong Kong, leading one author to describe it by the phrase "Borrowed Place, Borrowed Time."[11] Its residents shared language, family, and cultural ties with Guangdong and by the 1960s depended on China for rice and food. In 1979, when Deng Xiaoping identified South China as an area for new, capitalistic development, this further resituated Hong Kong into its historical context as an economic motor for the Pearl River Delta. In 1984, British-Chinese negotiations made reunification with China inevitable, although guaranteeing the Hong Kong way of life for fifty years after the handover.

Shortly thereafter, the events of Tiananmen in 1989 sent shock waves through the colony, although its citizens worked, protested (occasionally), and survived. By the 1990s, Hong Kong's glassy skyscrapers, flashy films, and fervent consumer culture became emblems of postmodern urbanism worldwide even as its citizens wondered what would happen on July 1, 1997. Yet, even this transition became a stage in defining Hong Kong, rather than a beginning or an end. Hong Kong became ever more embroiled in a growing economic powerhouse region (the Pearl River Delta) as well as a changing nation and region, positions its leaders and citizens continue to grapple with today.[12]

Film cultures reflected evolving urban success, global connections, and popular fears. Hong Kong commercial cinema of the late 1980s and early 1990s became both extremely exciting and extremely successful worldwide, with John Woo and Ringo Lam leading the pack in reinventing the gangster genre;

Tsui Hark imagining alternative worlds; and Wong Kar Wai, Ann Hui, and others creating artistic visions. Filmmakers and stars—Jackie Chan, Brigitte Lin, Andy Lau, Michelle Yeoh, Maggie Cheung—showed themselves at home in Hollywood, European, and global Asian cinema. Films spoke of Chinese martial arts, urban romance, postmodern alienation, and scenarios that occasionally—as in the sci-fi drama *Wicked City* (1992)—included fears for the future.

Through all this development, Hong Kong has enjoyed a peculiar space in relation to China, Taiwan, and the West, including both the United Kingdom and the United States, the latter of which has acted as an interfering uncle in colonial and postcolonial affairs. Being neither Communist China nor Nationalist Taiwan, it has had relatively freer cultural attitudes and fora than the other two Chinas, even with heavy-handed colonial as well as postcolonial censors. It also has been an important entrepôt that linked China to the world, whether overseas Chinese worldwide, Western worlds, Japan, or Southeast Asia. Yet, while across the border from burgeoning Guangdong, with which it shares language, history, and culture, Hong Kong has never been fully a part of China. Even today, after the 1997 handover, Hong Kong remains a Special Administrative Region (SAR) that has its own currency, its own elections, and its own government, albeit with China overseeing military and diplomatic affairs. Hong Kong, therefore, has played crucial roles as a mediator among China (and after 1949, Taiwan) and the rest of the world in politics, economics, and culture. A decade after the handover, it remains a freer space for debate, while negotiating a delicate balance between China and the West, tested by epidemics, protests, pollutions, and experiments with democratization. All of these features of political, economic, and cultural history have shaped the film festival since its inception.

The Festival and Hong Kong Film Culture, 1952–1980

Hong Kong film culture in the postwar period meant dual worlds—with English-language subtitled Hollywood films playing in air-conditioned palaces like the King's or Queen's Cinema in Central and elegant Mandarin musicals as well as "chiyitshi" ("made in seven days") Cantonese comedies amusing audiences in Shaukeiwan, Mong Kok, and Tai Po. To expand this Hollywood-Hong Kong palette, the Sino-British Club, an organization under the aegis of the British Council that catered to the social and cultural life of the British expatriates in Hong Kong, started a film group in 1952. Somewhat different from other cineclubs discussed in chapter 2, the club sought to show quality British films to expatriates, nevertheless emphasizing Western colonial culture that defined film as art within an elite milieu. Yet, it was also an unofficial colonial establishment for those in power who might not be interested in cinema. However, these screenings had low attendance and difficulty finding venues. Censorship was also an issue; *High Treason* (1951), an espionage thriller written and directed by Ray Boulting that showed enemy agents planning to bomb London factories, was actually banned. This reflected sensitive relationships between the colonial government, Britain, and Communist China. The club sponsored a Festival of French Film in 1953 but became inactive after 1954, although it incorporated some documentary films into its role as a sponsor of the Hong Kong Festival of the Arts.[13] The division of reporting categories in Hong Kong Report 1955 portrays a divided world: British Council activities were discussed as art and culture, while more popular films were lumped into a section on media and communication, dividing film as art and entertainment along cultural/linguistic lines.

Despite these problems, some audiences still demanded movies beyond those shown in commercial theaters. In 1961, veteran members of the film club started Studio One, which was incorporated the next year as the Film Society of Hong Kong, Limited. One of its objectives was to "promote better appreciation of film as a contribution to the artistic and cultural life of the community." Studio One, the Alliance Française, and the Goethe Institute ran film series that made European production visible in a more cosmopolitan city. The governmental Urban Council also funded the Phoenix Film Club in 1974; both civic and private entities saw films as cultural activities. Many of these organizations rented venues at the City Hall, a government building next to the harbor that houses performance spaces, libraries, and some services. Built in 1962 in the International style, City Hall remains an inclusive governmental cultural institution that, despite its name, serves no central civic electoral or administrative function; it is a performance space for high cultural events, coupled with libraries and offices.

During the 1960s, however, as Hong Kong's Chinese citizens explored wider identities through economic success and political action, it is hardly surprising that such top down British/expatriate cultivations of film as art faced challenges from a generation of post–World War II Hong Kong university graduates who had been exposed to European art cinema, who read Sight and Sound and Cahiers du cinéma, and who had fallen in love with Italian neorealism and the French New Wave. These Hong Kongers found an outlet in Chinese Student Weekly (Zhongguo Xuesheng Choubao) (1952–1974), their own film periodical aimed at readers in high school and university. In my conversations with him, veteran film critic Law Kar described the Chinese Student Weekly as a reaction to the communist takeover of China, started by young anticommunist college students who had moved from China to Hong Kong. The Weekly was not overtly political but aimed to promote cultural activities outside the more rigid and practical curriculum of the schools in Hong Kong. Here, a group of students from the University of Hong Kong, including Law Kar, Lin Nien Tong, Shu Kei, Ada Loke, and Ng Ho,[14] started publishing a column on cinema in 1961. They tried to understand local cinema through what they had learned from European art cinema.[15] These young writers differed from the earlier generation of film critics who had evaluated cinema from a Confucian standpoint—wenyizaidao—that art is the conduit for morality.[16] Instead, these young people looked at auteurs, form, and cinematic languages, using Western (global) cinematic theories to read Hong Kong cinema. These students also ran the College Cine Club from 1967 to 1971, where they screened Cantonese and Western films and held seminars on the cinematic art. Their special morning shows might include Bergman's *Wild Strawberries* in a Wanchai cinema or discussions with Chinese directors like Chu Yuan and Long Kong. John Woo was a member of the club when he was a high school student. In many ways, this club shaped the next generation of filmmakers, critics, and audiences for serious film.

In the 1970s, other cultural institutions also emerged in Hong Kong for discussing film and even changing its production. The Art Centre in Wanchai was built in 1977. This building houses many performance spaces and has hosted sponsored film series ever since it started; Studio One and the Goethe Institute both have used this venue. A magazine, *Dianying shuang zhoukan* (*Film Biweekly*), began publication in 1978. The Film Cultural Centre, a grassroots film center run by those who were involved with the magazines, was established in Portland Street in Kowloon in a Chinese working-class district.[17] At this center, which lasted from 1978 to 1988, productions as well as critical studies classes were taught. Baptist College (Hong Kong Baptist University since 1996), meanwhile, established its Department of Communication in 1968; in the early 1970s, it started cinema and television programs.[18] The Chinese University of Hong Kong also offered extracurricular classes, expanding discursive horizons around film as art. All these developments mirror the same kind of infrastructure for the development of cinematic art in the West from the 1920s on.

These film enthusiasts did not have very close ties with the commercial Hong Kong film industries; however, many worked quite closely with government-run television. TVB-Television Broadcasting Limited, the first broadcast television in Hong Kong, had replaced initial cable offerings in 1967. Over the next decades, TVB became the training ground for many future filmmakers and critics. While much of its programming was popular (music, films, sports), long-running series like *Under the Lion Rock*, where Allen Fong, Ann Hui, and Patrick Tam all worked, shaped new views of the city and filmic realism. These filmmakers had been educated abroad and were also drawn to global art cinema of the 1960s and 1970s, as sustained by European film festivals.

Hong Kong cinema underwent a rebirth in the 1970s, especially with regard to Cantonese cinema, which had been eclipsed by Shanghainese money and stars in Hong Kong's Mandarin cinema. With the global success of Bruce Lee and the then new studio Golden Harvest, and the comedies of the Hui brothers, local audiences returned to theaters to patronize Cantonese cinema, while global audiences began to discover Hong Kong. By 1966, Hong Kong had over one hundred cinemas, with an annual attendance of more than 90 million. Hong Kong filmmakers produced three hundred movies. While attendance dropped in the 1970s, the number of venues and productions, as well as distribution overseas, steadily increased, which eventually created the Golden Age of Hong Kong cinema of the 1980s, as David Bordwell notes:

> By the early 1980s, virtually all Hong Kong films were in Cantonese, and a new generation of directors came to the fore. Often trained in the West and in television, less tied to Mainland traditions than older hands, these young filmmakers turned away from the martial arts and toward gangster films, sword-and-sorcery fantasy and dramas of contemporary life. Many of the films garnered acclaim in festivals and foreign exhibition, the most notable success being Ann Hui's *Boat People* (1982). Although this 'new wave' did not overturn the mass production ethos of the industry (most of the young directors wound up in the mainstream), its energy reshaped Hong Kong cinema into a modern and distinctive part of the territory's mass culture.[19]

The following decades were dominated by powerful filmmakers, including John Woo, Ringo Lam, Tsui Hark, Ann Hui, and Jackie Chan (who reinvented the kung fu film), and successes abroad, both artistic and commercial, for Hong Kong cinema. Still, one also notes early problems in declining spectatorship (which fell to 27 million in 1996) and complaints about repetitive themes and effects. These contributed to a full-grown crisis for Hong Kong cinema in the twenty-first century, as stars and directors left for Hollywood. Despite new generations of filmmakers, including Wong Kar Wai, Fruit Chan, and Johnnie To, local and global crises have been part of Hong Kong cinema for the last decade.

While there had been sporadic film festivals in Asia beforehand, including a pan-Asiatic festival with mobile venues, the HKIFF emerged in 1977 from this intersection of cinephiles, colonial culture, and diverse film production. Its first outing was organized by the Urban Council of the British colonial government with the help of people from the City Hall, *Film Biweekly,* and Studio One. Many of the critics who write for *Film Biweekly* and the *Chinese Student Weekly* served on the advisory board of the early festivals. The Urban Council played a central role as the major cultural branch of the colonial government.[20] Not only did it channel money to urban services, but also from the 1960s to the 1980s it was the only branch of government that allowed a limited amount of citizen participation, with elected officials serving as representatives for their constituencies.

Their support, though, was galvanized by Paul Yeung, the manager of the City Hall. In 1975, he had gone to England to pursue an advanced degree in arts administration and had visited the London International Film Festival. When he came back to Hong Kong, he immediately proposed a Hong Kong festival. He was aware that he had to work with other film institutions in Hong Kong to make the festival a success and brought in local film aficionados to assemble a program in three months. Though initially a government-funded initiative, HKIFF became a joint collaborative project dominated by Chinese (but Westernized)

Figure 12. The sixth Hong Kong International Film Festival, 1983.
Source: From the sixth HKIFF, Leisure and Cultural Services Department, Hong Kong.

university-educated Hong Kongers open to creative negotiations and creative arrangements to expand the range of available cinema.

Still, the colonial Urban Council had a fairly narrow definition of culture as elite, modern, global, and Western. Therefore, they supported the HKIFF as a "cultural" event, and had little interest in working closely with the local film industries. Popular movies were mass entertainment; there was a clear line between culture and commerce, which remains evident in formal government reports. Moreover, the government felt that it did not want to inadvertently support one company over another. Yeung asserted, in fact, that the festival would show "films of cultural value in a territory long dominated by commercial products."[21] Thus the film festival fell under the category Recreational Activities (minyuhuodong), colonial strategies offered after the 1967 riot to give the people something to do, rather than to form local identity or to turn the population into active citizens. As one central figure of the festival noted in an interview: "the government was not interested in informing people or making them thinking subjects."[22] Besides the film festival, the Urban Council was responsible for the Hong Kong Arts Festival (started in 1972) as well as the Asian Art Festival (1976–1996). Local film studios and distributors, from their vantage, viewed the festival as elitist.

As one major contributing figure, Ada Loke, noted in an interview with the influential local newspaper, *Ming Pao*, this first festival "was not in the position to solicit either new works of well-known directors or first features of new talents. It could only enlist the support of various embassies to secure films that had appeared on the international film festival circuit in the past few years."[23] The first festival in 1977 showed thirty-seven films in forty-seven screenings that attracted 16,515 people; tickets sold out in four days despite a catalog released only two weeks beforehand (with no film blurbs). Many films were older European and art films. The opening film, for example, was Roberto Rossellini's *Italy Year One* (1974), a historical biography of postwar statesman Alcide de Gaspari. But half of the films were Asian, including the Philippine classic *Human Imperfections* (*Tinimbang ka ngunit kulang*, 1974) by Lino Brocka, who would make his debut at Cannes the next year, evoking the later association of HKIFF and discoveries for Asian cinema. The festival also included short films by Hong Kong independent filmmakers, like Allen Fong. The final film was King Hu's *A Touch of Zen* (1969); this, too, already had been screened at Cannes, in 1975. All this was done on a budget of HK$100,000—roughly US$13,000.

By the next year, films were more contemporary: Spain's 1975 Carlos Saura masterpiece, *Cría cuervos*, and Marco Bellocchio's 1977 *Il gabbiano*. Attendance soared to 55,000 and the budget reached $150,000 for 113 screenings, with high audience demands for the Cantonese cinema retrospective. According to Li Cheuk To, in fact, the colonial administrative officer just wanted the festival workers to get things done; there was no incentive for the festival to excel or to strive for an international presence. The programmers were not civil servants, but contract workers who were paid for ten months. Therefore, there was little consistency of staff in the first ten years; the government provided few incentives to transform the festival into a truly international showcase. No funds were set aside for programmers to attend other festivals; Freddie Wong had to use his own money to go to the London International Film Festival.[24] Only after the sixth festival, in 1982, were limited funds provided by the festival for its programmers to attend Cannes and Toronto to scout for films and to network.

Even by the tenth festival, the budget had risen to only $200,000, which allowed 139 features and 284 screenings for an audience of 119,236. As late as 1992, staffers like Li Cheuk To, Shu Kei, Wong Ain Ling, and Leung Mo-Ling[25] all contributed their own money to screen a new African production, Idrissa Ouedraogo's *Tilai,* and retrospective views of Mikio Naruse's *Sudden Rain* (1956) and *Daughters, Wives, and a Mother* (1960) at the fifteenth festival.[26] This level of support contrasts with later competitors, like Pusan, which the city and national government supported from its inception in 1996.

Through the years, the festival has played the role of cinema educator by showing world cinema to Hong Kong audiences, doing retrospectives, hosting seminars with auteurs, and, of course, screening the most current international films. In its third edition, in 1979, the festival hosted a seminar with Satyajit Ray; in 1980, with Paul Schrader. Numerous auteurs have visited the festivals, including Martin Scorsese (*The King of Comedy*) and Nagisa Oshima (*Merry Christmas Mr. Lawrence*) in 1984, Agnès Varda with Jacques Demy (*Kung-fu Master!* [*Le petit amour*]) in 1989, and Krzysztof Kieslowski (*Three Colors*) in 1994.

The HKIFF reminds us that many festivals, however important to the industry, to a nation, or to a region, only have survived because they have been run by people who are passionate about the festival and about cinema, basically cinephiles. This has permitted a gathering like the Hong Kong International Film Festival to grow into many cultural, intellectual, and commercial roles despite changing pressures from industry and politics. Just as political and economic events shaped the HKIFF, so did film production and film culture. In the 1960s and the 1970s, diverse segments of the Hong Kong population, from expatriates to university students, took an interest in cinema beyond what the popular theaters could provide. Film clubs, classes, film schools, and magazines prepared Hong Kong to demand a more vigorous film culture to expand the cinematic horizon of Hong Kong audiences. The Hong Kong audiences were becoming more cosmopolitan every day and thus shared in trends we have noted for European and North American audiences. Hong Kong as a whole was becoming more prosperous, despite large gaps in income distribution. The festival would bring together many of these themes. But it would also change the course of film culture for the Golden Age of Hong Kong cinema itself. Here we turn to the festival's emerging role not only as a window for Hong Kongers and resident expatriates but also as a window on Hong Kong for locals and the world.

Showcasing and Creating Hong Kong Cinema in the 1980s

Without the initial funds or interest in creation of a global film venue, organizers worked in new ways with local films as well as wider regional visions. Roger Garcia, for example, was working at the Cultural Service Department of City Hall. He became involved in the second film festival, where they inaugurated the HK retrospective section, and became festival director in 1979. (Garcia is once again the festival director in 2010.) The retrospectives were a local hit from their first program, "Cantonese Cinema in the 50s" (1950–1959), which curated and showed nineteen movies in forty-one packed screenings. By the third festival, a Hong Kong film (with some Taiwanese financing) opened the event: the world premiere of King Hu's *Raining in the Mountain* (*Kong shan ling yu*). An Asian section also was added that year, as the festival assumed the structure it would generally follow thereafter. Hu, Satyajit Ray, and Filipino filmmaker Kidlat Tahimik were all in attendance. Although the budget shrank, attendance topped 80,000.

Meanwhile, the festival began to produce not only sales catalogs but also volumes on specific topics about Hong Kong cinema. These bilingual collections cover topics ranging from *Cantonese Cinema Retrospective (1960–1969)* (1982) and *Cantonese Melodrama* (1986) to *Phantoms of the Hong Kong Cinema* (1989) and *Early Images of Hong Kong and China* (1995).[27] These anthologies were generally written by local film critics and scholars. They include important data such as biographies of different film personnel—actors, directors, producers, cinematographers, editors, and screenwriters. The program notes of these issues provide comprehensive information as well as individual descriptions of the films shown in that year's festival. *Cantonese Cinema Retrospective (1960–1969)*, for example, published for the 1982 festival, consisted of a forward, a postscript, eleven bilingual pieces, and an additional three Chinese articles and one English article by various film critics who all belonged to the group that had been responsible for the blossoming of 1970s Hong Kong film culture. The authors included Shu Kei, Yip Fu-Keng, Lai Kit, Lin Nien Tong, Yu Mo-Wan, Li Cheuk To, Lau Shing-hon, Law Kar, Law Wai-Ming, Deng Shiu-Yue, Tian Yan, Roger Garcia, and Leung Mo-ling. The first three articles looked at the relationships between these films and changes in Hong Kong society, some observations on this decade of movies, and how these films were viewed in the 1980s. Institutional studies on the Zhong Lian Film Company and the apprentice system of the studio followed. Auteur studies centered on directors like Zuo Ji, Qin Jian, Chu Yuan, and Long Kong. Two addition pieces dealt with two famous actresses of the time, Chan Po-Chu and Fung Bao-Bao. The pieces are quite diverse—some are interviews, some are observations rather than essays, and some are more traditional cinema articles dealing with aesthetics, narratives, genre, montage, verisimilitude, realism, and how these relate to Hong Kong society of the time. Through such volumes, the film festival assumed an important role in shaping knowledge about films and the city.

While highlighting Hong Kong cinema, other tomes moved beyond local confines. The 1988 volume *Changes in Hong Kong Society Through Cinema*, for example, analyzed outside visions such as *The World of Suzie Wong* (1960). The 1994 volume compared the cinemas of Hong Kong and Shanghai, while the 1995 issue, *Early Images of Hong Kong and China*, discussed how cinema came to Hong Kong and China and explored outside images of Hong Kong and China. The HKIFF's interest in and promotion of Hong Kong film culture remained salient as it explored wider definitions of Chinese cinema on screen and in writing.

Through these publications, the film festivals and related institutions were busy compiling a complete filmography of Hong Kong cinema. This creation of a coherent body of knowledge established a canon for Hong Kong films and a platform to incorporate this knowledge—and Hong Kong film—into global film knowledge and academic studies.

HKIFF involvement in archives constituted another part of this canonical task, arising from the sheer difficulty of finding prints of Hong Kong films. According to Law Kar, during the third festival, in 1979, Roger Garcia consulted with film experts from the West about the possibility of establishing a film archive. A veteran Hong Kong film expert and writer, Yu Mo-Wan, scoured production companies. The Hong Kong film critics and festival programmers knew that it would be impossible to study Hong Kong cinema at the level demanded by global film studies without such an archive, inspired by the Cinémathèque Française. Initially, there was little enthusiasm from the colonial government. Eventually, in 1993, the government gave some money to start the archive that was housed in a temporary hut in eastern Tsim Sha Tsui.[28]

Since there had not been any systematic cataloging or storage of Hong Kong cinema until the beginning of the festival in the late 1970s, it was extremely difficult to build a collection of Hong Kong cinema. However, due to the export orientation of Hong Kong cinema, where foreign audiences and distribution had enlarged the market for Hong Kong films, prints were left all over the world. According to Frank Bren, Hong Kong had no technology for developing color films in the 1950s and 1960s; color negatives needed to be processed abroad, either in Tokyo or London. Some negatives had never returned to Hong Kong. The archive itself embarked on the work of finding prints across the globe. Cynthia Liu, director of the Hong Kong Film Archive, found prints in London's Rank Laboratories, the World Theatre in San Francisco, Japanese laboratories, a private American home, and throughout Southeast Asia.[29]

Besides preserving old films, the archive collected old film posters, leaflets, and popular film magazines to provide scholars materials to understand cinema beyond the texts themselves. As the film archive became a reality, newer films were archived and the production companies that made them became willing to donate prints and related materials. The archive finally moved to its permanent home at Sai Wan Ho in east Hong Kong Island in 2001. At this point, the

Hong Kong Film Archive took over the responsibility of the Hong Kong cinema retrospective section from the HKIFF, and it has since been running a longer festival that starts within the two-to-three-week time frame of the HKIFF and continues thereafter for another four weeks at the archive itself.

Finally, besides publications and archives, the HKIFF, from its very inauguration, has offered lectures, seminars, and exhibitions during the festival to make the gathering an educational/discursive event. With the introduction of the Hong Kong retrospective catalogs, most of these auxiliary programs were related to the publication of that year. Yet other seminars covered international film movements, film workers, and auteurs, including James Wong Howe, Theodoros Angelopoulos, Buster Keaton, the French New Wave, Satyajit Ray, Ozu Yasujiro, and filmmaking in the Philippines. In 1997, a three-day international conference on Hong Kong cinema invited international authors to discuss Hong Kong film at the moment of transition, compiled in the volume *Fifty Years of Electric Shadows* (1997). The festival has continued to celebrate Chinese auteurs, with the hosting of the Chinese master forum with Hou Hsiao-hsien, Jia Zhengke, Zhang Yuan, and Ann Hui in 2006. In 2007, the Chinese Urban Generation was the topic of discussion. The festival also became a catalyst for other film events. In 2004, for example, a Fulbright Conference on Chinese cinema was held at the University of Hong Kong. While not organized by HKIFF, many participants came to the conference because they could also go to the film festival. In all these ways, the festival anchors and promotes the discussion of film in discursive horizons across the SAR and wider connections.

Despite its colonial baggage, the festival as a site of local and regional film also came to attract a great deal of attention from abroad. Ulrich Gregor from the Forum at the Berlinale began to bring Hong Kong cinema to Berlin. While David Bordwell saw his first Hong Kong films in the 1970s, he notes that his later scholarship also was based on the fact that "my old friend Tony Rayns saw to it that I was sent the annual catalogues of the Hong Kong International Film Festival, and so I came to learn something of this cinema's history."[30] Rayns passed on Hong Kong information through his role at the British journal *Sight and Sound*, especially after it was taken over by the British Film Institute in 1990. BFI would later publish Stephen Teo's 1997 *Hong Kong Cinema*.

Meanwhile, French critics from *Cahiers du cinéma* were coming to the festival as well. After scattered Hong Kong articles appeared in *Cahiers* in the early 1980s, the journal devoted a whole issue in 1984 to Hong Kong cinema. French director Olivier Assayas, who was introduced to Hong Kong cinema when he was working with *Cahiers*'s editor, Serge Daney, in 1981, recalls:

> In 1984 we went to Hong King and made the special issue on Hong Kong cinema. It was the first issue dealing with this cinema—not only its present, but also its roots. It's still in print, people do buy it once in a while. It was the

first serious Western work on popular Cantonese cinema and it was like discovering a new continent. We had no notion of who were the directors, what
were the films, what were the classics . . . it was like discovering something
completely new, which is very rare in cinema.[31]

This issue complemented the local vision of the festival I have given so far.
It began with a gushing introduction to Hong Kong itself:

> There are (still) in the world some strong cinematographic poles: Hong Kong
> is a unique one. Its industry, founded on a studio system like Hollywood,
> produced genre cinema for a vast public spread across East Asia (Taiwan,
> Singapore, Malaysia, Burma, and more and more Japan). And for the entire
> world, thanks to the complex network of Chinatowns, true counters, for the
> world, of Chinese culture. In the West, we know martial arts films, generally
> through secondary works. Yes, their place is crucial whether we are talking
> about kung fu films, cape and sword or the fights of Bruce Lee and Jacky
> Chan. But melodrama and comedy have their place. As does the cinema of a
> new generation of young filmmakers born in Hong Kong, coming out of
> television and forming a "New Wave."[32]

The team from *Cahiers* made contact through Tony Rayns and Marco Müller,
who had programmed Asian films for Pesaro before he moved to Locarno and
Venice. They talk about the HKIFF, whose eighteenth edition closed just before
television carried images of the joint declaration that shaped Hong Kong's
future. They photographed the cinemas and sights of the city, with Assayas
emphasizing Hong Kong as "a city of contrasts, more violent than any other
Asian metropoles" and one of constant motion—"one passes from one place to
another at great speed."[33]

Their report showed the perspectives on Hong Kong film culture that had
already emerged through the festival. The retrospective articles included an
interview with King Hu, a report on comedian Michael Hui, and a lengthy
analysis of martial arts films. Other pieces explored the studios: Shaw Brothers,
Golden Harvest, and leftist films. Finally, Assayas introduced the new wave—
"the Generation of 1997," highlighting Allen Fong, Ann Hui, and Tsui Hark.
And, like the film festival catalogs and retrospectives, *Cahiers* included pages of
photos and data—terms, bios, and history—that situated Hong Kong films
within global/festival canons of film knowledge. Finally, *Cahiers* brought the festival home in another way in its own two-week celebration of these films, "Made
in Hong Kong," screened at the Studio des Ursulines in mid-September 1984.
The issue also included notes on access to Hong Kong films in France through
cineclubs and art houses.[34]

By the mid-1980s, then, the HKIFF and new generations of Hong Kong film
and filmmakers had become global. Indeed, it is interesting that *Cahiers* did not

use its time in Hong Kong to look across the border at all, nor to explore the screenings of other Asian films at the festival. This would change as Hong Kong and the festival renegotiated their place in China and Chinese cinemas in the decades ahead.

Negotiating Chineseness: 1980s Onward

Since all film festivals other than on-line festivals take place in real space with specific geopolitical situations, film festivals always have to negotiate with different political forces to assert their place within specific locales. In the three decades since the HKIFF began, the festival, like the territory and its citizens, has proven very nimble in its ability to change and create a space for its existence. Other film communities in Hong Kong also have participated in this negotiation with the government. Hence, HKIFF again illuminates how evolving local political conditions affect local and global film culture.

As I noted, the HKIFF was born in the late stages of the British colonial government. Throughout its existence, the British colonial government had to negotiate with very different Chinese political entities—the decaying empire, an unstable state, warlords in South China, and then the People's Republic in its various transformations—but showed little concern for its own Chinese subjects. After 1949, the colonial government needed to maintain a sort of neutrality between the PRC and Taiwan, not taking sides with either Chinese governments (although it recognized the latter until 1972, when it began to negotiate recognition of the PRC as the sole legitimate government for Hong Kong). By 1977, when the HKIFF was inaugurated, the colonial government was aware that the final negotiation with the PRC regarding the future on the colony was imminent. When the Joint Declaration was signed in 1984, the future of Hong Kong was decided by the present and future rulers, without much participation of the Hong Kong people.

Nonetheless, the last fourteen years of colonial rule witnessed an unprecedented clash of cultures as the two governments sought to define the future of Hong Kong. The British, after nearly one and a half centuries of rule, finally introduced some forms of participatory democratic practice to its colonial subjects and encouraged new exploration and expressions of identity.[35] China, on the other hand, just emerging from a decade of turmoil (the Cultural Revolution, 1967–1977), started to experiment with a state-controlled market economy, while remaining firmly a totalitarian country with one-party rule. Its laboratory was the South, using Hong Kong as a filter for investment and expertise as factories migrated across the border into special economic zones of the Pearl River Delta. Shenzhen, a village of 30,000 near the Hong Kong border in 1978, has become a metropolis of 10 million today, larger than the contiguous SAR. This economic development has introduced new public access and lifestyles while China continues to control political expression and media, whether film, television, or the Internet—control that its filmmakers, in turn, have tested and challenged.

In the first four years of the Hong Kong festival, no Chinese films from either the PRC or Taiwan were shown (although King Hu had close ties to Taiwan). The colonial government simply did not want to engage in anything that had the slightest hint of controversy. According to Law Kar, when asked why there was no Taiwanese cinema shown at the festival, government officials answered that since the local people were already showing these Taiwan films, the film festival saw no reason to duplicate the effort.

Censorship among different imaginations of the two Chinas extended even further, in fact. Allen Fong, one of the most prominent Hong Kong New Wave directors, made two films with so-called leftist money linked to communist China. Hence, neither *Father and Son* (1981) nor *Ah Ying* (1983) was chosen to be the opening film of the respective festivals of those years despite their importance in Hong Kong cinema. Still, the festival had latitude to show most films, and films of local award-winning directors would be shown, just not accompanied by fanfare like the festival openings. Nonetheless, Fong turned down any invitation for *Father and Son*, which would only appear years later in retrospectives.

During this time, the Nationalist Party (followers of Chiang Kai-Shek, who had fled defeat on the mainland) still claimed to be the legitimate ruler of China from Taiwan, the Republic of China. Chiang himself only died in 1975, and his son ruled until 1988. Given regional tensions that sometimes threatened to boil over into war, no Taiwan films appeared in the HKIFF for nearly a decade, even though New Taiwan Cinema had started to make waves in Taiwan. The Film Cultural Centre was even stymied when it attempted to organize a screening of Taiwan New Cinema in 1983. Organizers sought to rent the Space Museum screening room for the show. The films had passed the Hong Kong censors, but two weeks before the screening, the Space Museum (which was under the administration of the Urban Council) refused to rent out the space. Not renting the museum's lecture hall reproduced a practice of seeming neutrality, confirming the apolitical stance of the Urban Council. The government used this passive censorship to avoid perceptions of controversy.

The first Taiwan film was not shown at HKIFF until 1987, when Edward Yang's *The Terrorizer* opened the eleventh edition of the festival. Programmers at the festivals, however, saw themselves as ambassadors of Chinese cinema. They arranged meetings between directors from both sides of the Strait, between Zhang Yimou and Hou Hsiao-hsien, for example. They saw the Hong Kong festival's role as creating a network for Chinese cinema and providing Chinese cinema a conduit to the international scene.

Since the 1980s, Taiwanese films and filmmakers have been prominent contributors; 2008 featured a highly personal and emotional tribute to Edward Yang, who had died in 2007 at the age of fifty-nine. Hong Kong has also provided venues for global Chinese filmmakers, especially those from Southeast Asia: Malaysian Chinese films, for example, came to prominence in 2007 and 2008.

The PRC, however, has been more complicated in film and other Hong Kong relations.

After the broad censorship of the Cultural Revolution, Chinese directors of the fifth generation, such as Chen Kaige and Zhang Yimou, started to make interesting works in the 1980s. In 1985, HKIFF organized the premiere of *Yellow Earth*, directed by Chen Kaige, with Zhang Yimou as the cinematographer. This phenomenal success galvanized these two filmmakers' careers and vaulted their names onto the international cinema circuit. Tony Rayns writes, "It's tempting to put an exact date to the birth of the 'New Chinese Cinema': 12 April 1985. That was the evening when *Yellow Earth* played to a packed house in the Hong Kong Film festival. . . . The screening was received with something like collective rapture, and the post-film discussion stretched long past its time limit."[36] According to Li Cheuk To and Law Kar, most mainstream PRC film critics did not like the film: "The film was denounced by the cultural bureaucrats of Beijing, who complained that it glorified ignorance and poverty, that it demeaned the 'revolutionary ardor' of the era, that it was, in the final analysis, too hard to understand."[37] Ironically, the local Urban Council also did not pay much attention to this event. The international film community, however, recognized it as a major turning point for Chinese cinema, Chinese fifth-generation filmmakers, and HKIFF's role in promoting Chinese cinema worldwide. Hong Kong became a place of discovery for films, a gateway onto a global circuit that critics and programmers would travel in order to establish connections and break new ground.

This attention, however, forced other global issues as well. In memoirs of the eleventh and twelfth festivals (1987 and 1988), threats of Chinese censorship met other interests: "Edward Yang's *The Terrorizer*, if not for the timely intervention and good will of the concerned parties, would have given up the HKIFF and bounded westward for a small town called Cannes."[38] The next year, the planned opening film from the mainland, Chen Kaige's *King of Children*, was lost to Cannes, although screening Zhang Yimou's *Red Sorghum* still became a major event. Global competition remains an area of concern for Hong Kong, as films by Jia Zhangke and Wong Kar Wai have veered toward Cannes and Venice after the filmmakers built their careers in the HKIFF.

Hong Kong and Chinese relations remained sensitive despite increasing connections of business and population in the 1980s. During the early 1990s, especially after the 1989 Tiananmen massacre, many people in Hong Kong became apprehensive of Chinese interference in Hong Kong affairs. The festival continued to show Chinese films; however, Chinese authorities posed new obstacles.[39] According to an article in *The Economist*, in 1992, the festival asked for a documentary on the aftermath of Tiananmen Square, but it was told that because the documentary was a television production, the film bureau had no authority over it. The festival also asked China for two films that had been denied the previous year, *Bloody Morning* and a documentary on the handicapped. The Chinese said no. The festival tried to get *The True-Hearted*, but the Chinese wanted to send the film to other festivals. In 1993, *Compassion in Exile*, a documentary on the Dalai Lama, screened in Hong Kong, but was met with some protest from the left-wing (pro-Beijing) press.[40]

In 1994, the festival was working on a retrospective investigating the cinematic relationship between Hong Kong and Shanghai. The festival chose to show He Jianjun's *Red Beads* (1993) and Wang Xiaoshuai's *The Days* (1993), critical films made outside the studio system that explored uncomfortable sexual and social issues. China also objected to the highly sensual coproduction *Temptation of a Monk* (1993). According to interviews and *The Economist*,[41] the PRC simply did not want the festival to have the autonomy to show "unofficial" films. *Temptation of a Monk* contains sex scenes and apparently the producers had broken the production contract with Guangzhou Studio.[42] As a counter-tactic, the Chinese Film Bureau threatened and then withdrew nine films that would have contributed to that year's retrospective. *Beijing Bastards*, which later became quite famous in the Chinese cinema critical dialogue, was one of those films pulled.

Withdrawing films has been a Chinese state practice for decades, an exercise of power that extends beyond Hong Kong. In 1987, for example, Chen Kaige's *The Big Parade* was withdrawn from competition at Cannes because of ambiguities in its text.[43] Being a totalitarian country that has sought to control information tightly, from the Confucian hierarchies of the Empire to today's Great Firewall of China that monitors the Internet, these state practices have reinforced its international stand, even if a changing China has already allowed alternative voices that film festivals have seized upon. Certainly, a city like Hong Kong, with a complicated relation to Chinese unity, obviously engages these films of resistance or reinterpretation in different ways. This reading, in context, differs from the Orientalization of the same films as heroic voices of dissent in more distant contexts. These discourses with Chinese cinema in Hong Kong are well within the Westphalian traditions of the traditional public sphere.

The press in Hong Kong has become involved in this dialogue between the HKIFF and the Chinese Film Bureau. *Hsin Pao*, another reputable local newspaper, publicly interrogated the Chinese Film Industry Administration about the reason why the nine movies were pulled in 1994.[44] The editorial asked why Beijing withdrew these films and if the HKIFF had breached any agreement. Beijing's reply was basically bureaucratic, stating that the producers of both *The Days* and *Red Beads* had failed to follow the requisite procedure for export. They also named Wong Ain Ling, the HKIFF's Asian film programmer at the time, as someone who had given "her consent to our views right away."[45] Their wishes were that the HKIFF "would not select films without our administration's screening and authorization or programmes unfriendly to our country or even willfully vilifying our social system and policies and that only with mutual respect and equal treatment can both sides continue to cooperate with each other on a long-term basis."[46]

In the end, the festival ignored the threats and showed the "unofficial" films, while China refused to send films for the retrospective. In the following years, this complicated relationship with China continued to create disturbances for the festival as new Chinese filmmakers sought to be seen and heard. In 1995, China basically boycotted the festival and sent no official films.[47] The festival showed three "independent" films, Zhang Yuan's *The Square*, He Jianjun's *Postman*, and Guan Hu's *Dirt*. Members of the Urban Council who were Democrats were very protective of the autonomy of the film festival in its ability to select films based on "artistic" merit; one Democrat asserted, "If all the films in the festival are screened by their government of origin, the prestige of the festival will be adversely affected."[48] Beijing continued to demand that films made in China needed the Chinese Film Bureau's permission before they could be shown, but the Hong Kong Urban Council effectively concluded that the HKIFF did not have to send Beijing a list for approval, asserting the independence of HKIFF programmers.

In 1996, the festival's Asian programmer, Wong Ain-ling, resigned after China once again pulled films in protest; "the three films withdrawn include Hong Kong-Chinese joint ventures *Warrior Lanling* and *The King of Masks*, and the Beijing-made video *The Story of Wang Laobai*."[49] None was "sensitive."[50] In 1997, Zhang Ming and Duan Jinchuan submitted their films, Zhang's *In Expectation* and Duan's *No. 16, Barkhor South Street*, set in Lhasa.[51] However, China withdrew *In Expectation*, a drama on the controversial Three Gorges Dam, and replaced it with Huang Jianxin and Yazhou Yang's social satire *Signal Left, Turn Right*. The latter film actually makes fun of local bureaucrats, but the film does not directly critique the overall idea of bureaucracy, only its human agents. Sometimes, Beijing has objected to the content of a film; often, however, withdrawing films was more a power struggle between the Chinese Film Bureau and outside film festivals rather than a debate about substance.

In response to all the controversies, the 1997 festival created a special session, "I Have a Date with the Censors."[52] The program included such films as *Battle of Algiers* (1966), *Dersu Uzala* (1975), and *China Behind* (1975), which had been banned by the colonial Hong Kong censors for being anticolonial, anti-Chinese, and too sensitive as it discussed the Cultural Revolution, respectively. This was obviously a protest against China's meddling with censorship over the years, but done in a way that put the spotlight on the British colonial government instead. In all these interactions, the organizers of the film festival shaped the HKIFF as a space of debate and contestation, a rich cinematic and political public sphere incorporating international Chinese voices as well as a concerned local citizenship. Where HKIFF offscreen discussions in the past might have focused on consumption, cosmopolitanness, or modernity, this interjection of politics marked a new maturity in Hong Kong citizenship, with citizens demanding the right to speak.[53]

The 1997 HKIFF retrospective, *Fifty Years of Electric Shadows,* obviously marked a momentous change in Hong Kong with its prospective return to China on July 1, about three months after the festival ended. This collection is a sweeping survey on the history of post–World War II Hong Kong cinema, offering a broad stroke on aesthetics of action, urbanism, colonialism, Hong Kong cinema's relations to mainland China and Taiwan, diasporic Hong Kong cinema, distribution, and more. This volume shows the development of these publications, with scholars working outside of Hong Kong and China, including American scholars David Bordwell, Poshek Fu, and Steven Fore, contributing to the issue. After 1997, the new HKSAR government embarked on a new experiment of "One Country, Two Systems," treading carefully (at times, timidly) with the authorities of Beijing. The HKIFF's relationship with China—and more specifically, with Chinese films—illustrates how local protest and limits shape film festivals as a space of meaning beyond film itself, yet also tie to global appreciation of media.

Tensions continued even after the handover. In 2001, not a single Chinese-produced film was shown. The Chinese films shown were all coproductions of one kind or another, including Jia Zhangke's *Platform* and Chin-Hua Lien's *The So-Called Friend* (*Ge er men*). At the same time, this recognizes that Hong Kong filmmakers themselves have become increasingly linked to the mainland in terms of coproduction. As Tony Rayns said later in a 2007 interview in *Offscreen*: "What's happened in Hong Kong has been a 360-degree turn toward China. China is now seen as the salvation of the Hong Kong film business. So most Hong Kong filmmakers, at all levels from the most ambitious to the least ambitious, are working in China and are aiming at Chinese distribution, because that's where they think the audience is. Hong Kong audiences basically stopped going to the movies; it's like Taiwan."[54] Hence, relations of culture and business have evolved on both sides of the border, as the HKIFF reflects and comments on.

In 2002, Chinese officials withdrew films again, because one dissident film was selected in the festival. But the festival has also developed its own strategies. For example, the HKIFF no longer denotes the country of origin of films originated from either China or Taiwan. If it is from China, the language is Putonghua, if it is from Taiwan, it is designated Mandarin.[55] Hong Kong films are still listed with place of production, and the language is generally Cantonese. All these complicated negotiations with China are very much part of the late colonial and postcolonial history of Hong Kong, where the HKIFF, following traditions of the enlightenment and ideas about free expression, maintains that it has the right to choose its own films, while China wants to retain its authority over matters that it deems its own.

Still, as noted, the Chinese Film Bureau did not simply single out the HKIFF in terms of its desire to control China's image abroad, nor has that process ended. In 2007, for example, with Li Yu's *Lost in Beijing,* the Chinese Film Bureau (a.k.a., SARFT, the State Administration of Radio, Film, and Television) did not want the uncut version screened in Berlin.[56] Only after lengthy negotiation was the film screened in competition. The uncut version also was shown widely in the European Film Market at the festival. With its controversies in Berlin, the saga continued in Hong Kong, where the producer of the film, Fang On, told reporters that *Lost in Beijing* would be the opening film of that year's HKIFF. This then prompted Peter Tsi, the director of HKIFF at the time, to respond by saying that many films were being considered for the festival opening and that the HKIFF had not made a decision. Tsi, however, added, "It has been the tradition of HKIFF to program films from mainland China without regard for issues apart from their artistic values."[57] The film was never shown at the HKIFF. Eventually SARFT banned the film in 2008, claiming that it was pornographic.[58]

This complicated relationship has evolved, but it has not ended. In 2008, China pressured producers of three films to withdraw their movies, saying that they had not passed the Chinese censors.[59] The three films were Zhang Yibai's *Lost Indulgence,* Tom Lin's *Winds of September,* and Bryan Chang and Wing-Chiu Chan's *A Decade of Love.* They are all coproductions with Chinese producers. Other than the issue about the censor, no other reason was given.[60] The news wire actually was wrong in saying that "China's growing influence over Hong Kong cinema has promoted producers to pull three films."[61] China had been engaged in controlling movie exhibition in film festivals for a very long time. Yet these are not the only challenges facing the city, its citizens, and the festival today.

HKIFF in the Twenty-first Century

The Hong Kong festival itself faces a looming identity crisis. Run by the Urban Council and its civil servants for 23 years, it passes next year to the government's Home Affairs Bureau and all the present programmers' contracts will cease. Will they be re-engaged by the new dispensation or will control pass to cine-illiterates? It is an open question but some are pressing for the festival to be hived off as an independent body with, for the first time, its own director, like other film festivals.[62]

When 1997 arrived, the Urban Council changed into the Provisional Urban Council and it continued to run the film festival. However, members of the Urban Council were heavily Democratic. Therefore, the then-chief executive and Beijing loyalist Tung Chi Wah wanted to change the structure of the Urban Council and replace it with the Leisure and Cultural Service Department (LCSD). This meant that the HKIFF overseers would no longer report to elected officials, but would be strictly a branch of the SAR government separated from but beholden to China. Facing such governmental meddling, two senior long-time programmers of the HKIFF, Li Cheuk To and Jacob Wong, quit the festival in 2000. They perceived that with the dissolution of the Urban Council and the elected officials who supported the autonomy of the festival, their ability to program the HKIFF as an independent event would be greatly compromised. The 2001 festival was held without the two programmers, and some have claimed that it simply was not the same.[63] It was run by the Film Program Office of the LCSD.

In 2002, however, the festival was taken over by the Art Development Council (ADC). While not directly a government department like the LCSD, its CEO was a retired civil servant and all its funding is from the government, with a twenty-seven-member board (twenty appointed and seven elected). They wanted to set up a "Programme Committee" to select and approve the films for the festival. This would be very different from most international film festivals, which tend to maintain their independence from direct or indirect interference. Peter Tsi, director of the HKIFF, was able to convince the ADC that the program committee would make the HKSAR government look bad. Therefore the committee was never established and the programmers maintained their autonomy.

At the same time, the ADC was exploring the possibility of the "corporatisation" of the HKIFF. Other art organizations, like the Hong Kong Chinese Orchestra, the Hong Kong Dance Company, and the Hong Kong Repertory Theatre, had recently been privatized. Corporatization meant that the HKIFF would no longer be run by the government, or branches of the HKSAR government; however, their major funding would still be provided by the government through the ADC (HK$7 million, less than US$1 million in 2007).[64] The HKIFF would have more opportunities to raise funding through corporate sponsors and other private foundations, or one could say more responsibilities or burdens in terms of fund-raising. The ADC hired Roger Garcia to submit a report about the prospect of corporatization, after consultation with people from the film industries. The report recommended corporatization as a nonprofit company, stating that it would give the HKIFF "greater flexibility in organisation and management, but also allow it to develop its programmes further, and maximize its potential, and build on its unique characteristics, identity and reputation, and turning Hong Kong into a hub of Asian films."[65] The ADC ran the festival for two years, in 2002 and 2003. It then finally became an independent nonprofit entity in 2004—the Hong Kong International Film Festival Society. Meanwhile, both the government and the staff of the HKIFF have explored new ways to fund and run the festival.

Besides internal/local changes, HKIFF has been forced to respond to the wider film festival world, especially as defined by regional integration and competition in East Asia. The festival had started as an audience-oriented local festival, where the major goal was to provide Hong Kongers with opportunities to see more serious movies that regular movie houses would not show. It came about with other festivals organized by the Urban Council to provide cultural activities for the population of Hong Kong, who were demanding different forms of leisure activities and art programs that were more cosmopolitan and challenging. Slowly, with good organizational skills and excellent selections from the programmers, HKIFF built a reputation as a premiere festival for Asian cinema. However, with the slow demise of the local film industries, and the rise of the well-funded and dynamic Pusan International Film Festival (PIFF) in 1996, HKIFF started to face its first strong regional competitor. Around the same time, the Shanghai International Film Festival was launched and the Tokyo festival also started to reorganize. Singapore, Bangkok, and other cities would also try for specialized or general and glamorous film events, linked to both production and tourism.

As we have seen, film festivals in the 1990s were booming all over the world but were also evolving. As mentioned elsewhere in the book, film markets became more important, coproduction fora abounded, festivals started offering competitions, and distributors started charging high fees for screenings. HKIFF could not remain what it had been and survive in the world of international film festivals of the twenty-first century.

In the process of becoming an independent entity, the HKIFF needed to hire a new executive director. Peter Tsi was hired in November 2001; he had extensive experiences with the Hong Kong film and media industries and had negotiated on behalf of the HK industries with China in 1997. With the return of the Li Cheuk To and Jacob Wong (and Freddie Wong), who had resigned in protest the year before, the festival was assembled in three months in 2002. Tsi was the first director who was not a civil servant. He also differed from earlier cinephilia-type organizers who had little experience with the film and media industries in Hong Kong.

The festival had to change in order to survive as an independent entity, where funds would need to be sought from private sources. It needed to add competitive programs and to rethink its programming. The local airline, Cathay Pacific, became the first major sponsor for the festival in 2001 and 2002, but it pulled out after only two years. Cathay Pacific was not interested in sponsoring a festival that was too "niche."[66] In other words, the festival needed to reach a wider audience; Cathay Pacific thought that the festival did not engage the whole city and lacked visibility. According to Tsi, the withdrawal of Cathay Pacific's support was a wake-up call for the festival that it also needed to change its programming to attract a wider audience and make itself relevant to a more diverse population in Hong Kong: "Peter Tsi, the Director, and Li Cheuk To, the General Manager of the Hong Kong International Film Festival, are given the task of re-creating the image of the Festival and they are very enthusiastic about it. Their goal is to establish an event that has to be culturally entertaining."[67] Innovations included competitions, association with market activities in Filmart, new funding fora, and eventually the Asian Film Awards.

Competitions long have been part of the "A"-level festivals of Europe as well as of smaller specialized events. HKIFF started out as an audience festival; therefore, it did not have any competitive section for the filmmakers. However, according to Li and Wong, as more and more directors asked for competitions because the prizes would benefit their careers, the festival started to incorporate some competitive sections. In 1999 it added the global FIPRESCI Critics Award for Asian films, actually using the foreign press as a mouthpiece to bolster the argument of quality. In 2003 came the Asian Digital Award, a humanitarian award for documentaries, Firebird Awards for Young Cinema (Cathay made this money possible), the SIGNIS Award presented by the World Catholic Association, and the Fresh Wave Short Film Competition. The awards are the manifestations of "added values" that many filmmakers demand and the festival can provide.

At the same time as the festival explored links to corporate sponsors, it looked at the business of film. Hong Kong Filmart actually had started in 1997. Strictly speaking, Filmart is not run by the HKIFF; it is run by the Hong Kong Trade and Development Council (TDC), which oversees all trade activities. However, the two events have been linked in different ways. In 2005, Filmart finally moved its date from June to March and further synchronized with the HK Entertainment Expo (started in 2004), where the festival is one of the events. The March date also fits well with the annual film festival market calendar, with the European Film Market at Berlin in February and Cannes Marché in May, and Pusan in the fall, although it is smaller than either and regionally distinctive.

In addition to distribution, many festivals began to explore production guidance. HAF emerged in 2000 under the late Wouter Barendrecht, as a coproduction market like the one in Rotterdam. But a series of problems forced it to only have irregularly scheduled conferences in the first few years. In 2003, the HAF was scheduled to be held two days before the festival, but it was cancelled due to the SARS outbreak.[68] It was taken over by the HKIFF in 2006. Both CineMart and the Hubert Bal Funds of Rotterdam are its partners, as is the PPP in Pusan. It is important that we see in this network of global coproduction an analogy to the development of Hong Kong itself as a center for finances and services rather than production. It has met competition with global festivals and the strong local emergence of Pusan and Korean films with the tools and skills of the city itself.

Still, in 2007, faced with such Asian competition, the HKIFF was worried that it would lose its prominence in the world of Asian film festivals. The festival hired public relations firms to strategize how to better position the HKIFF and to make sure that it continued to be relevant. Consultants told the festival that it needed to put up some "acrobatics," and that it should get film studios and film stars to be involved. An Asian film award made sense to the organizers. HKIFF was also aware that Australia was organizing a pan-Asian film award. The AFA was launched in March 2007; the festival and other relevant organizations had only started organizing the award in November 2006. The March date was considered a win over the Queensland event, which was announced in April 2007 and held its first award—the Asian Pacific Screen Award—in November 2007.[69]

This popular competition risks overshadowing the artistic goals of the festival. Still, it is hard to think of another award ceremony that includes global film criticism as a category.

At the same time, events like AFA sought to attract new local audiences (hence, Rain as well as Josephine Hsiao and Tony Leung). New audiences also influenced packaging and programming, since "mainstream cinema" is included in the festival's new section, "Midnight Heat," a program that screens films at midnight:

> Eerie, absurd, gory and violent, it is everything you will expect from midnight cult screenings. Leading the way is Miike Takashi's *Ichi the Killer*, touted as the most gory film in Japanese history, starring Gohatto's Asano Tadanobu and Hong Kong's Alien Sun. Then there is Wes Craven's early classic *The Last House on the Left*, Ishibashi Yoshimasa's deranged *The Color of Life* and Hong Kong's own Leslie Cheung in Law Chi Leung's psychological thriller *Inner Senses*.[70]

Bringing together all these elements, in 2007 HKIFF produced the longest and most varied festival in its history—as the notes that inaugurate this chapter have described. The festival began on March 20 with the inaugural Asian Film Awards, Filmart, and Asian Film Financing Forum (HAF), and a few films for the festival. It was the first year where the HKIFF, which had always relied on the Easter holidays for local attendance, wanted to start with the Filmmart, AFA, and HAF events in March because of venue as well as the festival market calendar. With a combined opening, launching of all the events together, HKIFF tried to become a bigger and more glamorous event. Jacob Wong, in "Our Cinema, Our Times: 23 Days of Torture and Rebirth,"[71] lightheartedly used Easter metaphors to talk about the hardship and rewards of the festival. He mentioned the frenzies and mistakes, from showing the wrong film, to having reels out of order, to the fiascos with Internet booking. However, at the end, Wong asserted that it was the festival's commitment to screening a Filipino film—*Autohystoria*[72] by Raya Martin—that validated the goals of the film festival. There were six people in the audience in the space museum screening room, and Wong felt gratified, "gratified that there are people who put so much effort and time to make a movie, to openly expose one's body and soul, having to accept the possibility of rejection. I was also gratified that there are people who were willing to enter an unknown space, to lose oneself and to be reborn."[73] Yet, these comments underscore the difficulties many festivals face in showing difficult or inaccessible films or films that have little commercial possibility.

The week before, in the same column, "Our Cinema, Our Times: An Open and Diversified Film Festival," Li Cheuk To responded to critics who claimed that the HKIFF had lost its soul. He discussed the difference between diversification and commercialization, whether the festival has to take the initiative to change, or just "sit still and wait to die" (zuoyidaibi).[74]

> In the past, there was no external competition, films all came from cultural organizations. Locally, there were audiences with high levels of education and English ability; the festival was then primarily a showcase of alternative cinema, depending on the government for all its funding. Things have changed, today, any small and medium size film festivals that cannot provide commercial opportunities or broad press coverage are suffering. The quality of the audience has gone down, film box office results are not good, distribution systems are unhealthy, many mainstream films do not have exhibition opportunities. . . . How can the festival not move forward? . . .
>
> A festival that embodies both the elite and popular could be interpreted as schizophrenia, on the other hand, it simply shows one idea of cinema as narrow, to have absolute definition on what constitutes "Good Cinema."[75]

Thus, even the definition of film itself becomes an issue facing this festival as it moves into its fourth decade and the world of contemporary global cinema. Yet, the festival also functions as a space to see, to experience, and to talk about these questions, within a longer history and a larger system that reconstitutes film each year.

Conclusion

All film festivals are shaped by and comment upon their local environment, cultural, political, financial, and bureaucratic. HKIFF started as a pedagogical event organized by the Urban Council of the British colonial government, drawing on a European culture of cinephilia promoted by Cannes, Berlin, and London. Within a changing context, it has been transformed into a local event of real importance through its dedicated staff and local film communities of production, criticism, teaching, and spectatorship. As HKIFF gained an international reputation and became integrated into an international festival circuit, it also gained more power to attract films and even take a stance with regard to thematic screenings, including Chinese nonofficial films. Yet, in this spotlight, the festival and its selections took on new political meanings as well as civic ones, shaped by changes in China as well as Hong Kong. Meanwhile, the very success of this event made the festival an event to be imitated in other cities across the region, a competition that forces new dimensions and associations onto the older and larger structure of the festival.

Without much push from the government, cinephiles who were running the festival expanded the agenda to produce an institutional structure to promote Hong Kong cinema, both its scholarship and the growth of an archive. Given that there were few Asian festivals at the time, Europeans came to the festival and not only brought Hong Kong cinema into the international arena, but also started seeing the festival as a fertile ground to discover Asian cinema, especially Chinese cinema. At the same time, in the late 1980s and early 1990s, Hong Kong cinema was enjoying its highest achievement in terms of output and local box office.

This reminds us that while the HKIFF is unique in its status as the first East Asian film festival, its roles in bringing Chinese and Hong Kong cinema to the rest of the world, and in its colonial and post-colonial status, it also represents a fairly typical film festival as well as a cultural event that participates in the definition of the place it is situated, in this case Hong Kong. The changes that it has gone through in the last thirty years, from an audience-centered festival to one that promotes its local cinema and negotiates more global concerns, diverge from the early history of Cannes or Berlin but converge with contemporary issues. In this development, HKIFF became recognized as a treasure trove for the excavation of Asian cinema and then a more inclusive event for a broader audience. Today it is a more spectacular event, with red carpet, markets, a coproduction market, and the Asian Film Awards. Some cinephiles lament its popular fare, but they can still find the avant-garde, the challenging, and the forgotten among its many sections. Hence, the HKIFF is unique but at the same time embodies experiences, pressures, and solutions facing film festivals worldwide in the past and the future.

Conclusion

As I finish this manuscript in 2011, echoes from Cannes have filtered through artistic and commercial worlds. Apichatpong Weerasethakul's *Uncle Boonmee Who Can Recall His Past Lives* (*Loong Boonmee raleuk chat*) (2010), despite the tongue-twisting quality of the director's name for many non-Thai audiences, has been screened at the Sydney Film Festival and has been scheduled for other major regional festivals, including São Paulo, Munich, New York, and Tokyo. Meanwhile, it has secured distribution deals with Germany (Movienet), "France (Pyramide Distribution), Spain (Karma Films), Italy (BIM Distribuzione), and the U.K. (New Wave Films), and many others."[1] In New York City itself, Tribeca and the Human Rights Watch festival have ended, and the Asian Film Festival has moved uptown to Lincoln Center, where it juxtaposed the popular *Kung Fu Chefs* with "the arthouse exercises its organizers claim to abhor," including Tetsuya Nakashima's *Confessions* (copresented with the Japan Society), *Echoes of the Rainbow* from Hong Kong filmmaker Alex Law, and Lee Hae-Jun's *Castaway on the Moon*.[2] Sofia Coppola's *Somewhere* took the Lion at Venice, and Berlin is finalizing its program, while the HKIFF prepares a special section on Vietnamese films of the war years. Stars, prizes, retrospectives, and discoveries are in flux from Pordenone (interested in the cache of American silent films recently discovered in New Zealand) to Hong Kong. The cycle—multiple cycles in fact—go on, reproducing the rich, complex, jumbled worlds of film festivals.

Festivals come with delights and problems, captured by critic Nick Roddick:

> Film festivals are like freebies: the people who would really benefit from them don't often get the chance to go, while those of us who go do seem to become increasingly jaded about the whole experience. I know this because, whenever I write a piece about some glitch in the system, some inexplicable failure on the part of festival organizers to pick the right films, serve the right wine or keep the rain from falling, people stop me and say, 'How true!' If, on the other hand, I write a piece about how great the films are and how smoothly the event went, the silence is deafening. . . . Since festivals are now an essential part of the world's film distribution system, they increasingly raise the question of why this system functions so badly.[3]

Throughout this text, I have sought to capture the good and the bad as I have taken apart this world of film festivals from various perspectives—arts and artists, business, place, and public sphere—to explore these multiple values and limitations.

At the same time, I have insisted on holism, the way that disparate pieces come together in a concrete event, whether the HKIFF or Cannes or a local festivity for LGBTQ screenings, as well as the way these pieces make sense with a global circulation of films and knowledge. Festivals in this regard presume each other and depend on each other despite constant competition and complaints of jostling schedules and organizational chaos. Yet they remain unique events and experiences. If films are works of art in an age of mechanical reproduction, festivals remain performances that cannot simply be mechanized or reproduced, despite the claims of online events.

At the same time, no festival is an isolate. A non–Hong Kong film might not premiere in Hong Kong and Venice, Hollywood high-brow fall releases favor the calendar of Venice over Cannes, and New Yorkers will have their eyes on which Cannes films need to be added to their cinematic calendar and whether they will go to Lincoln Center or Tribeca or even a local cinema. A film screened in one festival may find a distributor in another. A star or director may try to change or revitalize her career with a new project or an altered perspective on past products in a festival far from home. A student or young filmmaker with support from Hong Kong or Rotterdam may go on to another festival to complete her work, or to seek an audience, or to find inspiration and colleagues with whom to move on. Business may be the mortar, as critics note (and lament), but films escape these constraints in screenings and discussions, and bridge individual and local expressions in a global enterprise that festivals presume and change.[4]

This intimacy of system and event, reproduction, and performance brings to mind a model underpinning some of the theoreticians who have influenced me most in my analysis, including Pierre Bourdieu and Roland Barthes—the structural paradigm for language constructed by Ferdinand de Saussure. Rather than introducing a model so late in the text, I think of Saussure's work as providing a generative metaphor by which to bring together and reflect on the questions I have raised.

Saussure grappled with the social fact of language (at the same time Freud, Marx, and Durkheim explored the unconsciousness of other social facts) by dividing language (langue) from speaking (parole).[5] The first denoted a system in which "difference is everything" but where the very systematization remained implicit, unconscious, and shared. Here, one can compare distinctions among festivals by the systemic constraints that allow us to compare and distinguish them. Locations and times, for example, form a system that is relatively arbitrary albeit contested—Why Cannes rather than Biarritz? Venice rather than Rome? Hong Kong but not Tokyo or Shanghai? Spring rather than fall? "A"-festival or regional? Despite challenges and complaints, the festival world depends on such implicit systems, with only the loosest vision of FIAPF or other participants.

This model might be extended to films and auteurs as well, as they, too, are distinguished by multiple patterns of both similarities and difference. Antonioni, according to one critic, is like Whistler (an artist), while to film historians he was a colleague and contemporary to Fellini, Rossellini, and Pasolini in a larger New Italian Cinema movement. To a beginning student, he is a demiurgic discovery in a vague world of art films (or history of film exams); to a young filmmaker, a model. Kiarostami, in turn, is compared to Antonioni and yet, at the same time, is situated through the complicated political and cultural world outside the West that is Iran, one that is read as a challenge to the West. And he can also be compared to a filmmaker and even festival competitor within Iran as well as a citizen who might or might not be able to voice concerns or support. Such paradigms of contrast and connection allow us to make sense of new works and new filmmakers by contrasting them with others, fitting them in rather than challenging the whole paradigm, which evolves more slowly.

Contrasts create and stabilize different meanings. Again, Saussure's images of paradigms that entail different kinds of contrasts is illuminating—Wong Kar Wai in Hong Kong has meanings in opposition to Fruit Chan or King Hu, but this is not the same as Wong Kar Wai juxtaposed to Antonioni and Soderbergh in *Eros*—or Wong Kar Wai refracted by Ang Lee and Zhang Yimou among multiple Chinas. At the same time, festivals differ in contents and meanings but offer the shared myth of a larger system of canonical films and global audience. Thus, notions of hierarchy—"A"-festivals versus more local or specialized ones—represent a paradigm of differences that stabilizes a larger system, even if that full system is never made explicit or called upon to act or regulate.

And yet the vitality of film festivals lies not only in this system that stabilizes and frames a world around loosely coordinated tools and institutions—FIAPF, festival programmers, filmmakers, business people, critics, and audiences—but around the experience, the performance of each festival. While Saussure died before elaborating a model for speaking, we can nonetheless play with the analogy to understand a syntax of performative events (openings, sections, fora) that produce unique pronouncements: screenings, readings, contexts. Cannes returns every year, but there was only one May '68 when Truffaut, Saura, Godard, and Geraldine Chaplin clung to the curtains in the Palais to bring it to a halt. Tribeca is institutionalized but can never recapture that first moment of affirmation for the city in response to 9/11. New discoveries come and go—but critics and audience members remember the first moment they saw a work by Antonioni, or Lina Wertmuller, or Zhang Yimou, or Cristian Mungiu, or Apichatpong Weerasethakul, and realized its language and power. And audiences will return in 2011, 2012, 2013 for the possibility of something comprehensible, building on knowledge, taste, and commerce. Among other participants in the experience, they encounter something new.

It is important that as a model for something so basic as language, Saussure's work has been a generative springboard that others have adapted to realms of society, myth, literature, and economics. In analyzing film festivals, while I have insisted on the concreteness of their histories, actors, places, and functions, I have also shown that they *are* places of knowledge, where film knowledge is produced, shared, debated, and canonized. In this, festivals participate in wider paradigms as well—the discursive horizons of film discussion Miriam Hansen elucidates, the structures and processes of art and genre of Rick Altman, the public spheres of Jürgen Habermas and Nancy Fraser—that have guided other parts of my analysis. At the same time, they embody a haunting geopolitics of inequality that separates Cannes from Fajr, Disney, and Cinecitta from third-world videographers, university critics from those starved for images and ideas.

Festivals hold together these functions and possibilities, interlayered with red carpet glamour and backroom negotiations, paparazzi, fans, and accountants. This vitality helps us to understand their futures as well. When Gilles Jacob, whose powerful vision of the film festival appeared at the beginning of this book, and Cannes artistic director Thierry Fremaux were asked about the future of festivals, Fremaux answered that "festivals will continue to be essential in the digital age. Why would all these people come from the ends of the world to see films, to buy them, to critique them, to get them seen, to talk about them, to love them. Festivals are like the World Cup: it's a common passion united."[6]

This does not mean there may not be problems and changes ahead. Filmmakers, organizers and critics with whom I have spoken raise many issues that festivals must face, apart from sheer jumbled proliferation and intense competition, a recurrent theme. Changing technologies are important, for example, as Roddick notes:

> Festivals are kidding themselves if they think they will remain the key to this process. The current arthouse pantheon—Almodóvar, Wong Kar Wai, Haneke—was certainly consecrated by the festival circuit. But the next generation's pantheon could well bypass festivals altogether, using social-networking sites for awareness-creation and relying on broadband technology for distribution. When that happens, all the free flights and hotel rooms in Rome are not going to persuade any serious executive to spend one week in another town. They will be too busy trying to monetize the product flow.[7]

Roddick's words ask us to rethink technological determinism as a theme in the evolution of festivals as places of art, business, and public. While the rise of the DVD and the Internet changed festivals (especially in opening up selections and communication), these were not the first changes to have shaped an old technology becoming new, to borrow a suggestive image from Carolyn Marvin's rereading of the telephone.[8] Festivals, after all, emerged from experiments with the meaning of technology and its limits. As we celebrate the conviviality and convergence of films in Venice or Cannes, for example, we should remember that Hollywood stars failed to arrive at Cannes in 1939 because they were traveling by boat. The golden age of festivals was already an age of airplanes as well as sound and color in film.

Television, meanwhile, was seen as a widespread threat to film in the 1950s and 1960s. Yet, even if television lessened crowds at urban cinema palaces, other spectators found their way to film history by its broadcasts. Hollywood auteurs like Welles and Hawkes played on afternoon television movies across America while Hong Kong broadcasting introduced new generations to Hong Kong film in the 1960s.[9] Government-sponsored stations identified with art—from PBS to Telefrance—converged with the definition of cinema as art and heritage and opened the eyes of new audiences. Sundance, at least, seems to have learned this lesson by launching its own channel to disseminate pieces of the festival.

This is not to say that DVDs, video-on-demand, and the Internet (and piracy) have not and will not have impacts on festivals. But change is not the same as disappearance. Nor is watching via Internet the same experience as discussion in an auditorium among other interested spectators and professionals. Sharing films remains the foundation, while business and communication are intrinsic corollaries. And despite new technologies of dissemination, the success of existing festivals encourages cities and social groups to create even more festivals around genres, problems, and cinephilia itself. Festivals, after all, are scarcely festive without traditional human interaction, and film festivals are most important in their ability to bring people together.

Reassessing my notes on individual festivals and the festival world, I would suggest that the immediacies of these technologies, in fact, may intersect with another longer-term issue facing festivals—inequality among festivals and filmmakers. Certainly, the system as built now, with myriad events, relies on inequality to survive. There can only be so many great films each year to premiere, limiting the prime events even if other, smaller festivals will be able to introduce these films later into local or regional markets. Western/Northern sites and a Western gaze, even in many coproductions, have dominated "A"-level events. Other cinematic cultures have emerged worldwide—the distant cinemas of Japan,[10] the commercial, visual, and aural worlds of Bollywood, the many voices of the Chinese, and the effusive videos of Nollywood. Moreover, we know that watching is global—Bruce Lee films have been popular in Africa as well as Europe; Nollywood DVDs are available in New York immigrant stores even if not screened in film festivals. Yet, if these film cultures have been incorporated into the festival world, this has been done via hybridization, sharing vocabularies and even imposed ideas of film as art. Festivals in Hong Kong, Pusan, Ouagadougou, Mumbai, and other sites contribute to a dialogue but are not prime interlocutors, nor do they present films totally foreign to the canon or the European eye.

Meanwhile, many of these festivals risk losing their best filmmakers and productions to the critics and capital of Europe, as Halle warns. This is no longer a competition around established auteurs, like Wong Kar Wai, Jia Zhangke, or Apichatpong Weerasethakul. As festivals seek out young filmmakers abroad for cultivation in the Atelier of Cannes, they are changing patterns of access and formation for local markets. Still, it is disturbing to see how few women filter through this system. How such inequalities are addressed, by whom, and what emerges may reshape the nature of film knowledge as well as the world of festivals.

Yet if changes occur, they also will be possible through the unique combination of film, people, knowledge, and discussion that festivals embody, individually and collectively, and their creative roles in rethinking film. In this regard, it is worth closing with a return to Gilles Jacob's words from the introduction to reflect on experiences of film by computer screening, individual studies, or even books, classes, and museums:

> To take the pulse of world cinema once a year. To gather the movers and shakers of the profession in one place so they can exchange ideas, show each other their movies and do business. To discover new talents. . . . To spotlight new trends in filmmaking. . . . To promote a type of cinema that's both artistic and of wide appeal. To showcase striking and difficult works that wouldn't otherwise get the attention they deserve. To salute great filmmakers who will add to the festival's prestige. To give the people behind a film the chance to meet the world's press. To generate miles of free publicity for the films taking part, enough to stretch from Paris to Los Angeles . . . And finally, to recharge filmmakers' and producers' batteries once a year so they have the courage to carry on—by showing them movies they'd have been proud to work on and produce.[II]

In this citation, Jacob talks about not only films and festivals but also about people. Festivals involve connections, sharing, debate, and discussion that entail face-to-face connections. Elite festivals like Cannes, Berlin, and Venice may focus this discussion on film professionals, yet these films ripple across audiences, distant programmers, and readers of newspapers and magazines. Smaller festivals, meanwhile, provide glimpses of current Asian films, queer features, or animated inventions—personal experiences that replicate and reinforce other spheres of exhibition and thought and may even alter, slowly, the larger film circuit. And major festivals continue to be the personal sites of deals, critical discussions, and glamour (sometimes operational) that suggest that festivals will not soon fade away.

This book cannot substitute for the experience of festivals, which I recommend to readers even on a local level. By reading this book in conjunction with the films themselves (generally available without a festival online or via DVD) and these experiences, readers can understand the wider world of festival history, experiences, and cultural production. You should now be armed with a roadmap and a sense of history and function to attend festivals and to understand them from afar. And thus you, too, enter into the processes and places that shape the future pulse of world cinema, year to year.

Notes

INTRODUCTION

1. In this book, I will make a distinction between film awards and film festivals. The Oscars, Golden Globes, Bafta, and the Golden Horse in Taiwan are not film festivals; film festivals have to be events where screening of films is a major component, and most of them are not primarily industry events.

2. Derek Elley, "Director Envisions Next Millennium of Fest," *Variety Special Supplement, Cannes at 50*, March 24–30, 1997, 6.

3. Pierre Bourdieu, *Distinction* (Cambridge: Harvard Univ. Press, 1984). Bourdieu's sense of the cultural construction of distinctive aesthetic knowledge and the multiple meanings of social and cultural capital he teases out of French society remain a primary influence on this book even when not directly cited. The brand reference refers to Anna Klingmann's fundamental *Brandscapes: Architecture in the Experience Economy* (Cambridge: MIT Press, 2007); urban motivations are also part of Richard Florida's popular *Cities and the Creative Class* (New York: Routledge, 2004) and Julian Stringer's "Global Cities and the International Film Festival Economy," in *Cinema and the City: Film and Urban Societies in a Global Context*, ed. Mark Shiel and Tony Fitzmaurice (Oxford: Blackwell, 2001).

4. See John Anderson, *Sundancing: Hanging Out and Listening In at America's Most Important Film Festival* (New York: Avon, 2000); Peter Biskind, *Down and Dirty Pictures: Miramax, Sundance, and the Rise of Independent Film* (New York: Simon and Schuster, 2004). Some early Sundance winners, including Steven Soderbergh, the Coen brothers, and Quentin Tarantino, also went on to auteurist careers bridging Cannes and Hollywood. Soderbergh's breakthrough film, *Sex Lies and Videotape*, won at Cannes and Sundance in 1989. More recently, films like *The Good German* screened in Berlin while *Che* (2008) won Benecio del Toro an acting award at Cannes. I will return to this theme in chapter 3.

5. Anthony Kaufman, "Sundance vs. Rotterdam; Differing Styles Bring Forth New International Cinema," *IndieWIRE*, January 14, 2004.

6. Sandy Mandelberger, "Cinemart: US Indies Come to Rotterdam," www .filmfestivals.com, February 2, 2001. American independents who had attended Rotterdam include John Sayles, Jim Jarmusch, and Wayne Wang.

7. E.g., Roger Ebert, *Two Weeks in the Midday Sun: A Cannes Notebook* (Kansas City: Andrews and McMeel, 1989); Cari Beauchamp and Henry Béhar, *Hollywood on the Riviera* (New York: William Morrow, 1992); Steven Gaydos, ed., *The Variety Guide to*

Film Festivals: The Ultimate Insider's Guide to Film Festivals around the World (New York: Berkley, 1998); Lory Smith, *Party in a Box: The Story of the Sundance Film Festival* (Salt Lake City: Gibbs Smith, 1999); Anderson, *Sundancing;* Kenneth Turan, *From Sundance to Sarajevo: Film Festivals and the World They Made* (Berkeley: Univ. of California Press, 2003); Biskind, *Down and Dirty;* Kieron Corless and Chris Darke, *Cannes: Inside the World's Premier Film Festival* (London: Faber and Faber, 2007).

8. For example, *Fifty Years of Electric Shadows* (Hong Kong: Hong Kong International Film Festival, 1997); Gian Carlo Bertelli et al., eds., *Festival internazionale del film Locarno 40 ans: chronique et filmographie* (Lacarno: Festival Internazionale del Film dé Locarno, 1988); *Chronique et filmographie* (Locarno: Festival Internazionale del Film dé Locarno, 1988–1997); Jean-Claude Romer and Jeanne Moreau, *Cannes Memories 1939–2002: La grande histoire du Festival* (Montreuil: Media Business and Partners, 2002); Dalmazio Ambrosioni, *Locarno: città del cinema i cinquant'anni del festival internazionale del film* (Locarno: Armando Dadò, 1998); Wolfgang Jacobsen, *50 Years Berlinale* (Berlin: Filmmuseum, 2000).

9. Skadi Loist and Marijke de Valck, "Film Festival/Film Festival Research: Thematic, Annotated Bibliography," 2nd ed. (Film Festival Research Network, 2010).

10. Stringer, "Global Cities and the International Film Festival Economy," 134–146; Corless and Darke, *Cannes;* Thomas Elsaesser, *European Cinema: Face to Face with Hollywood* (Amsterdam: Amsterdam Univ. Press, 2005); Emmanuel Ethis, ed., *Au Marches du Palais: Le festival de Cannes sous le regard des sciences sociales* (Paris: Documentation Française, 2004); Vanessa Schwartz, "The Cannes Film Festival and the Marketing of Cosmopolitanism," in *It's So French! Hollywood, Paris, and the Making of Cosmopolitan Film Culture* (Chicago: Univ. of Chicago Press, 2007), 56–101.

11. Bill Nichols, "Discovering Form, Inferring Meaning: New Cinemas and the Film Festival Circuit," *Film Quarterly* 47, no. 3 (spring 1994): 16–30; Liz Czach, "Film Festivals, Programming, and the Building of a National Cinema," *Moving Image* 4, no. 1 (2004): 76–88; Schwartz, "The Cannes Film Festival and the Marketing of Cosmopolitanism," 56–101; Dina Iordanova, "Showdown of the Festivals: Clashing Entrepreneurship and Post-Communist Management of Culture," *Film International* 4, no. 23 (October 2006): 25–38.

12. Peter Wollen, "An Alphabet of Cinema: 26 Responses to a Self-Interview," *Point of Contact* 5, no. 1 (1997): 5–17.

13. I will elaborate on this distinction in chapter 2.

14. Rick Altman, *Film/Genre* (London: British Film Institute, 1999).

15. See also Marijke de Valck, "Venice and the Value Adding Process," in *Film Festivals: From European Geopolitics to Global Cinephilia* (Amsterdam: Amsterdam Univ. Press, 2007).

16. André Bazin, *What Is Cinema? Essays Selected and Transcribed by Hugh Gray.* (Berkeley: Univ. of California Press, 2005); David Gerstner and Janet Staiger, *Authorship*

and Film (New York: Routledge, 2003); Virginia Wright Wexman, ed., *Film and Authorship* (New Brunswick: Rutgers Univ. Press, 2003); Barry Keith Grant, *Auteurs and Authorship: A Film Reader* (Malden, Mass.; Oxford: Blackwell, 2008).

17. I am grateful to the work of my graduate students Chan Chui Hing and Yang Tzu Yi at the City University of Hong Kong for their research on these two awards in 2007.

18. This point is emphasized in de Valck, *Film Festival 2007*, as well.

19. Richard Roud, *A Passion for Films: Henri Langlois and the Cinémathèque Française* (1983; reprint, Baltimore: Johns Hopkins Univ. Press, 1999), 81.

20. Iordanova, "Showdown of the Festivals," 25–38.

21. Fédération Internationale des Associations de Producteurs de Films (International Federation of Film Producers Associations), "FIAPF Accredited Festivals Directory, 2008," http://www.fiapf.org/pdf/2008FIAPFDirectory.pdf. Thirty-one other festivals are recognized as specialized events and five as noncompetitive festivals.

22. Thirty-one additional festivals are designated as competitive specialized festivals, ranging from Pusan (South Korea) as a competitive festival for new directors from Asian countries; Sitges (Spain) as a competitive festival specialized for fantasy films; Sarajevo (Bosnia and Herzegovina) as a competitive festival specialized for features and documentary films from Eastern, Central, and Southeastern Europe; Bogotá (Colombia) as a competitive festival specialized for new directors; Toronto as a noncompetitive feature film festival; and Oberhausen (Germany) as a FIAPF-accredited documentary and short film festival. However, many important festivals are not FIAPF accredited, especially in North America. Sundance is competitive but never really sought FIAPF endorsement. This again shed light on how FIAPF remains very much a non-U.S. organization, furthering the perceived division between the two coasts of the Atlantic.

23. In Europe, the South means developing nations that are poorer than those in Western Europe.

24. Smith, *Party in a Box;* James Mottram, *The Sundance Kids: How the Mavericks Took Back Hollywood* (New York: Faber and Faber, 2006).

25. See also Elsaesser, *European Cinema*, 86–88.

26. "What Is the Berlinale Talent Campus?" http://www.berlinale.de/en/das_festival/berlinale_talent_campus/index.html (accessed March 30, 2007).

27. See the Sundance Institute Web site at http://www.sundance.org/.

28. David Gitten, "Venice Film Festival Reviews," *Sunday Telegraph*, September 3, 2007 http://www.telegraph.co.uk/culture/film/starsandstories/3667676/Venice-Film-Festival-reviews-Michael-Clayton-In-the-Valley-of-Elah-Its-a-Free-World . . . -and-Cassandras-Dream.html.

29. David Germain, "Ken Loach Goes to War with Route Irish," Associated Press, May 21, 2010, www.azcentral.com/thingstodo/movies/articles/2010/05/21/20100521ken-loach-goes-war-cannes-drama-route-irish.html.

30. Dai Qing, "Raise Eyebrows for *Raise the Red Lantern*," *Public Culture* 5 (1993): 333–336.

31. His 2009 film, *A Woman, a Gun, and a Noodle Shop*, was nominated for a Golden Bear in Berlin, but it hardly followed the festival circuit and was distributed through mainstream cinemas in Asia and the United States.

32. Ethis, ed., *Au Marches du Palais*. See Ebert, *Two Weeks in the Midday Sun*; William Goldman, *Hype and Glory* (New York: Villard Books, 1990); Beauchamp and Béhar, *Hollywood on the Riviera*; Corless and Darke, *Cannes*; Schwartz, "The Cannes Film Festival and the Marketing of Cosmopolitanism," 56–101.

33. SooJeong Ahn, "The Pusan International Film Festival 1996–2005: South Korean Cinema in Local, Regional, and Global Context" (Ph.D. diss., University of Nottingham, 2008), http://etheses.nottingham.ac.uk/archive/00000513/ (accessed October 15, 2008).

34. Marla Stone, "The Last Film Festival: The Venice Biennale Goes to War," in *Re-viewing Fascism*, ed. Jacqueline Reich and Piero Garofalo, 293–314 (Bloomington: Indiana Univ. Press, 2002); Heide Fehrenbach, *Cinema in Democratizing Germany: Reconstructing National Identity After Hitler* (Chapel Hill: Univ. of North Carolina Press, 1995); Czach, "Film Festivals, Programming, and the Building of a National Cinema"; Iordanova, "Showdown of the Festivals"; Soyoung Kim, "'Cine Mania' or Cinephilia: Film Festivals and the Identity Question," in *New Korean Cinema*, ed. Chi-Yun Shin and Julian Stringer, 79–91 (Edinburgh: Edinburgh Univ. Press, 2005).

35. Thomas Elsaesser, *The BFI Companion to German Cinema* (London: British Film Institute, 1999); Mette Hjort and Duncan Petrie, eds., *The Cinema of Small Nations* (Bloomington: Indiana Univ. Press, 2007); Roud, *A Passion for Films*; Schwartz, "The Cannes Film Festival and the Marketing of Cosmopolitanism"; Hamid Naficy, *An Accented Cinema* (Princeton: Princeton Univ. Press, 2001); Azadeh Farahmand, "At the Crossroads: International Film Festivals and the Constitution of the New Iranian Cinema" (Ph.D. diss., University of California, Los Angeles, 2006), http://proquest.umi.com/pqdweb?did=1317311961&sid=1&Fmt=2&clientId=79356&RQT=309&VName=PQD (accessed January 8, 2009). See Schwartz, "The Cannes Film Festival and the Marketing of Cosmopolitanism," and Roud, *A Passion for Films*.

36. Ebert, *Two Weeks in the Midday Sun*; Goldman, *Hype and Glory*; Gaydos, ed., *The Variety Guide to Film Festivals*; Smith, *Party in a Box*; John Anderson, *Sundancing*; Turan, *From Sundance to Sarajevo*.

37. Senses of Cinema, http://archive.sensesofcinema.com; Hors Champ, http://www.horschamp.qc.ca; Internet Movie Database, www.imbd.com.

38. Romer and Moreau, *Cannes Memories*; Ambrosioni, *Locarno*; Bertelli et al., eds., *Festival internazionale del film Locarno 40 ans*; Jacobsen, *50 Years Berlinale*; Jon Elizondo et al., eds., *56 Festival Catalog de San Sebastián/Donostia Zinemaldia* (San Sebastián: Donostia-San Sebastián Festival Internationale de Cine de Donostia-San Sebastián, 2008).

39. Bourdieu, *Distinction;* Ferdinand de Saussure, *Course in General Linguistics,* ed. Charles Bally and Albert Sechehaye, trans. Roy Harris (Lasalle, Ill.: Open Court, 1983).

40. Michele Aaron, *New Queer Cinema: A Critical Reader* (New Brunswick: Rutgers Univ. Press, 2004).

41. E.g., Graeme Tuner, *Film as Social Practice,* 4th ed. (London: Routledge, 2006).

42. Jürgen Habermas, *The Structural Transformation of the Public Sphere: An Inquiry into a Category of Bourgeois Society,* trans. Thomas Burger, with the assistance of Frederick Lawrence (Cambridge: MIT Press, 1989); Nancy Fraser, "Politics, Culture, and the Public Sphere: Toward a Postmodern Conception," in *Social Postmodernism: Beyond Identity Politics,* ed. Linda Nicholson and Steven Seidman, 287–231 (New York: Cambridge Univ. Press, 1995); Benedict Anderson, *Imagined Communities: Reflections on the Origin and Spread of Nationalism* (London: Verso, 1991).

43. Janet Staiger, *Perverse Spectators* (New York: New York Univ., 2000); Will Brooker, ed., *The Audience Studies Reader* (New York: Routledge, 2002). Michael Warner, *Publics and Counterpublics* (New York: Zone Books, 2002); Turner, *Film as Social Practice.*

44. Jon Frosch, "Eclectic Cannes Line Up Mixes Frosh and New Blood," http://www.france24.com/en/20100415-eclectic-globe-spanning-cannes-festival-line-up-mixes-veterans-new-blood-cinema (accessed April 29, 2010).

45. Ron Holloway, "Cannes Report 2004," *Kinema* (2008) http://www.kinema.uwaterloo.ca/article.php?id=428&feature.

46. An inside look at "jury duty" at Cannes can be found in Goldman, *Hype and Glory.*

47. Monical Bartyzel, "Girls on Film: The Estrogen-Free Cannes Competition," *Cinematical,* April 19, 2010, http://www.cinematical.com/2010/04/19/girls-on-film-the-estrogen-free-cannes-competition.

48. "Festival de Cannes," http://www.cannesinteractive.com/files/Cinefondation/english.pdf.

49. "Cinéfoundation," http://www.festival-cannes.com/en/cinefoundation.html.

50. "Semaine de la Critique," http://www.semainedelacritique.com/.

51. "Quinzaine des Réalisateurs," http://www.quinzaine-realisateurs.com. See Pierre-Henri Deleau, *La Quinzaine des réalisateurs à Cannes: Cinéma en liberté: 1969–1993* (Paris: Editions de La Martinière, 1993).

52. SIGNIS, "Awards," http://www.signis.net/rubrique.php3?id_rubrique=33.

53. For an interesting one-sided look at the Cannes Market, Chris Jones's video at http://vimeo.com/4661897 shows the basic business that was conducted at Cannes for small filmmakers.

54. "Marché du Film," https://www.marchedufilm.com/.

55. See Christine Vachon, with David Edelstein, *Shooting to Kill: How an Independent Producer Blasts through Barriers to Make Movies That Matter* (New York: Quill, 1998).

56. Ibid., 287.

CHAPTER 1 — HISTORY, STRUCTURE, AND
PRACTICE IN THE FESTIVAL WORLD

1. Miriam Hansen, "America, Paris, the Alps: Kracauer (and Benjamin) on Cinema and Modernity," in *Cinema and the Invention of Modern Life*, ed. Leo Charney and Vanessa R. Schwartz, 365 (Berkeley: Univ. of California Press, 1995).

2. Pierre Bourdieu, *Distinction* (Cambridge: Harvard Univ. Press, 1984). See Tatiana Heise and Andrew Tudor, "Constructing (Film) Art: Bourdieu's Field Model in a Comparative Context," *Cultural Sociology* 1 (2007): 165–187.

3. While working on parallel projects and from different sources, my historical overview has benefited from the thought and scholarship of de Valck as she modeled the origins of the film festival circuit.

4. FIAPF stands for Fédération Internationale des Associations de Producteurs de Films (International Federation of Film Producers Associations), www.fiapf.org.

5. Miriam Hansen, *Babel and Babylon: Spectatorship in American Silent Film* (Cambridge: Harvard Univ. Press, 1991); Roberta Pearson, *Eloquent Gestures: The Transformation of Performance Style in the Griffith Biograph Films* (Berkeley: Univ. of California Press, 1992); Leo Charney and Vanessa R. Schwartz., eds., *Cinema and the Invention of Modern Life* (Berkeley: Univ. of California Press, 1995), 362–402; Richard Abel, ed., *Silent Film* (New Brunswick: Rutgers Univ. Press, 1996); Steven Ross, *Working-Class Hollywood: Silent Film and the Shaping of Class in America* (Princeton: Princeton Univ. Press, 1998); Gregg Bachman and Thomas J. Slater, eds., *American Silent Film: Discovering Marginalized Voices* (Carbondale: Southern Illinois Univ. Press, 2002); Frank Kessler and Nanna Verhoeff, eds., *Networks of Entertainment: Early Film Distribution, 1895–1915* (Eastleigh: John Libbey, 2007).

6. Richard Abel, *The Ciné Goes to Town: French Cinema, 1896–1914* (Berkeley: Univ. of California Press, 1994); Richard Abel, *French Cinema: The First Wave, 1915–1929* (Princeton: Princeton Univ. Press, 1984).

7. See David Cook, "'We're in the Money!' A Brief History of Market Power Concentration and Risk Aversion in the American Film Industry from the Edison Trust to the Rise of the Transnational Media Conglomerates," in *Theorising National Cinema*, ed. Valentina Vitali and Paul Willemen, 158–171 (London: British Film Institute, 2006).

8. Noël Burch, *The Silent Revolution Volume 2—She! Denmark (1902–1914)*, 2000.

9. Ana M. Lopez, "Early Cinema and Modernity in Latin America," in *Theorising National Cinema*, ed. Valentina Vitali and Paul Willemen, 209–225 (London: British Film Institute, 2006); Aaron Gerow, *Visions of Japanese Modernity: Articulations of Cinema, Nation, and Spectatorship, 1895–1925* (Berkeley: Univ. of California Press, 2010).

10. See Bachman and Slater, *American Silent Film*.

11. For an introduction to this lengthy process and copious analysis, see David Bordwell, *The Way Hollywood Tells It: Story and Style in Modern Movies* (Berkeley: Univ. of California Press, 2006).

12. Dudley Andrew, "The 'Three Ages' of Cinema Studies and the Age to Come," *PMLA* 115, no. 3 (May 2000): 341–351.

13. Christian Keathley, *Cinephilia and History, or the Wind in the Trees* (Bloomington: Indiana Univ. Press, 2005), 8.

14. Bourdieu, *Distinction*, 87.

15. Ibid., 101.

16. See Pearson, *Eloquent Gestures*; Ross, *Working-Class Hollywood*.

17. Michael Richardson, *Surrealism and Film* (New York: Berg, 2006).

18. David Gillespie, *Russian Film* (New York: Longman, 2003).

19. Klaus Kreimeier, *The UFA Story: A History of Germany's Greatest Film Company, 1918–1945*, trans. Robert Kimber and Rita Kimber (Berkeley: Univ. of California Press, 1999); Thomas Elsaesser, *Weimar Cinema and After: Germany's Historical Imaginary* (London: Routledge, 2000); Frances Guerin, *A Culture of Light: Cinema and Technology in 1920s Germany* (Minneapolis: Univ. of Minnesota Press, 2005).

20. Pearl Bowser, Jane Gaines, and Charles Musser, eds. and curators, *Oscar Micheaux and His Circle: African-American Filmmaking and Race Cinema of the Silent Era* (Bloomington: Indiana Univ. Press, 2001); Patrick McGilligan, *Oscar Micheaux, the Great and Only: The Life of America's First Black Filmmaker* (New York: HarperCollins, 2007).

21. Abel, *French Cinema*, 41

22. Donald Spoto, *The Dark Side of Genius: The Life of Alfred Hitchcock* (London: Da Capo Press, 1999), 71.

23. Heise and Tudor, "Constructing (Film) Art," 185.

24. David Andrews, "Toward an Inclusive, Exclusive Approach to Art Cinema," in *Global Art Cinema: New Theories and Histories*, ed. Rosalind Galt and Karl Schoonover, 63–74 (New York: Oxford Univ. Press, 2010).

25. Spoto, *The Dark Side of Genius*, 72, also see Heise and Tudor, "Constructing (Film) Art," 165.

26. Richard Roud, *A Passion for Films: Henri Langlois and the Cinémathèque Française* (1983; reprint, Baltimore: Johns Hopkins Univ. Press, 1999), 17.

27. Ibid., 37; "Fondazione Cineteca Italiana (FCI)," http://www.filmarchives-online .eu/partners/fondazione-cineteca-italiana.

28. Haidee Wasson, *Museum Movies: The Museum of Modern Art and the Birth of Art Cinema* (Berkeley: Univ. of California Press, 2005), 37.

29. Hisashi Nada, "The Little Cinema Movement in the 1920s and the Introduction of Avant-garde Cinema in Japan," *ICONICS* 3 (1994): 43, http://nels.nii.ac.jp/els/110006677141.pdf?id=ART0008702405&type=pdf&lang=en&host=cinii&order_no=&ppv_type=0&lang_sw=&no=1267475300&cp=(accessed March 1, 2010).

30. Gertrud Koch, "On Pornographic Cinema: The Body's Shadow Realm," *Jump Cut* 35 (April 1990): 17–29.

31. Wasson, *Museum Movies.*

32. See Laura Marcus, *The Tenth Muse: Writing About Cinema in the Modernist Period* (New York: Oxford Univ. Press, 2007).

33. Ibid., 240.

34. See Roud, *A Passion for Films,* 20.

35. Marcus, *The Tenth Muse,* 248.

36. Dana Polan, "The Beginnings of American Film Study," in *Looking Past the Screen: Case Studies in American Film History and Method,* ed. Jon Lewis and Eric Smoodin, 37–60 (Durham: Duke Univ. Press, 2007); see also Wasson, *Museum Movies.*

37. Anthony Slide, *Nitrate Won't Wait: A History of Film Preservation in the United States* (Jefferson, N.C.: McFarland, 1992), 11, 16.

38. Roud, *A Passion for Films.*

39. Fédération Internationale des Associations de Producteurs de Films (International Federation of Film Producers Associations), www.fiapf.org/default.asp (accessed March 9, 2010).

40. Fédération Internationale des Associations de Producteurs de Films (International Federation of Film Producers Associations), "50 International Film Festivals Signed FIAPF's Mutual Trust Contract and Received Accreditation in 2010," www.fiapf.org/intfilmfestivals.asp (accessed March 9, 2010).

41. Ibid. These standards include:

- Good year-round organizational resources.
- Genuinely international selections of films and competition juries.
- Good facilities for servicing international press correspondents.
- Stringent measures to prevent theft or illegal copying of films.
- Evidence of support from the local film industry.
- Insurance of all film copies against loss, theft, or damage.
- High standards for official publications and information management (catalogue, programmes, fliers).

42. Mark Shiel, *Italian Neorealism Rebuilding the Cinematic City* (London: Wallflower Press, 2006), 21.

43. Ibid., 20

44. Information on Italian Fascist cinema is from Mark Shiel, *Italian Neorealism;* Pierre Sorlin, *Italian National Cinema 1896–1996* (London: Routledge, 1996); and Carlo Celli and Marca Cottino-Jones, *A New Guide to Italian Cinema* (New York: Palgrave Macmillan, 2007).

45. Sorlin, *Italian National Cinema 1896–1996*, 70.

46. *Luciano Serra, pilota* is set in the Italian invasion of Ethiopia.

47. Kieron Corless and Chris Darke, *Cannes: Inside the World's Premier Film Festival* (London: Faber and Faber, 2007), 13–14.

48. These points concur with de Valck's historical analysis of the early history of film festivals, along with other specific references cited in the text.

49. Corless and Darke, *Cannes*, 15.

50. Tina Mai Chen, "International Film Circuits and Global Imaginaries in the People's Republic of China, 1949–57," *Journal of Chinese Cinemas* 3, no. 2 (June 2009): 149–161.

51. "A Brief Festival History," http://www.kviff.com/en/about-festival/festival-history/ (accessed March 8, 2010).

52. Heide Fehrenbach, *Cinema in Democratizing Germany: Reconstructing National Identity After Hitler* (Chapel Hill: Univ. of North Carolina Press, 1995).

53. Ibid., 238.

54. Wolfgang Jacobsen, *50 Years Berlinale* (Berlin: Filmmuseum, 2000), 12.

55. Ibid., 23.

56. Ibid., 27.

57. "Festival du Film Maudit. Biarritz 1949," http://www.filmmuseum.at/jart/prj3/filmmuseum/main.jart?rel=en&content-id=1219068743272&schienen_id=1238713588226&reserve-modeactive (accessed April 6, 2010).

58. Antonie de Baecque and Serge Toubiana, *Truffaut: A Biography* (Berkeley: Univ. of California Press, 2000). Originally published in France as *François Truffaut* by Editions Gallimard, 1996.

59. "Oral History: How the San Francisco Film Festival Started," http://history.sffs .org/our_history/how_sfiff_started.php (accessed April 11, 2010).

60. Roud, *A Passion for Films*, 128.

61. A. O. Scott, "A Film Festival with a Penchant for Making Taste, Not Deals," *New York Times*, September 24, 2010, C4.

62. Andrew, "The 'Three Ages' of Cinema Studies and the Age to Come."

63. "The 70s: A New Start after the 1968 Demonstrations," http://www.cannes .com/index.php?Itemid=2457645&id=505&option=com_content&task=view&lang =en_EN.

64. Ibid.

65. Ibid.

66. Steven Gaydos, ed., *The Variety Guide to Film Festivals: The Ultimate Insider's Guide to Film Festivals around the World* (New York: Berkley, 1998), 56.

67. "The Toronto International Film Festival," http://worldfilm.about.com/od/filmfestivals/a/toronto.htm.

68. Liz Czach, "Film Festivals, Programming, and the Building of a National Cinema," *Moving Image* 4, no. 1 (2004): 81.

69. "The Organization," www.tiff.net/abouttiff/organization.

70. Chris McGreal, "U.S. Actor Jane Fonda Backs Away from Israel Row at Toronto Film Festival," *Guardian*, September 16, 2009, http://www.guardian.co.uk/film/2009/sep/16/toronto-festival-israel-tel-aviv.

71. John Anderson, *Sundancing: Hanging Out and Listening In at America's Most Important Film Festival* (New York: Avon, 2000); Peter Biskind, *Down and Dirty Pictures: Miramax, Sundance, and the Rise of Independent Film* (New York: Simon and Schuster, 2004).

72. Robert Koehler, "Cinephilia and Film Festivals," in *Dekalog 3: On Film Festivals*, ed. Richard Porton, 84 (London: Wallflower, 2009).

73. Brian Stelter, "Cablevision Unit Buys Sundance Channel," *New York Times*, May 8, 2008.

74. Peter Cowie, "Memories of Late-but-Not-Always-Lamented Fests," in *The Variety Guide to Film Festivals: The Ultimate Insider's Guide to Film Festivals around the World*, ed. Steven Gaydos, 7–9, 7 (New York: Berkley, 1998).

75. Medhi Abdollahzadeh, "Fajr Film Festival's 30-Year Span since the Islamic Revolution: A Look at the Roots of the Festival Boycott," *Gozaar*, February 16, 2010.

76. More detailed exploration of the 2010 festival is found in chapter 5.

77. Fajr International Film Festival Organization, "Shamagadari: We Want Cinema for 70 Million Iranians," http://www.fajrfestival.ir/28th/en/index.php?option=com_content&view=article&id=179:shamaghdari&catid=1:latest-news&Itemid=50 (accessed March 13, 2010).

78. "FESPACO Through The Years," http://www.fespaco.bf/Mouvement_Fespaco_angl.htm.

79. "India Gets First Mainstream Gay Film Festival," http://www.independent.co.uk/arts-entertainment/films/india-gets-first-mainstream-gay-film-festival-1953047.html.

80. Frameline, www.frameline.org.

81. Jay Weissberg, "Report on the 22nd Pordenone Silent Film Festival," *Senses of Cinema*, http://archive.sensesofcinema.com/contents/festivals/03/29/22nd_pordenone.html (accessed April 22, 2010).

82. "Pordenone Silent Film Festival Highlights," www.fest21.com/en/blog/editor/pordenone_silent_film_festival_highlights.

83. Anna Klingmann, *Brandscapes: Architecture in the Experience Economy* (Cambridge: MIT Press, 2007).

84. Marijke de Valck, and Malte Hagener, *Cinephilia: Movies, Love and Memory* (Film Culture in Transition) (Amsterdam: Amsterdam Univ. Press, 2005).

85. Shay Zeller, "Telluride by the Sea, Bill Pence," *Front Porch*, NHPR—New Hampshire Public Radio, September 15, 2005, http://www.nhpr.org/node/9641 (accessed April 11, 2010).

86. Daniel Shea, "Small and Mighty: Telluride Has Become the Place for Little Films to Build Big Reputations," *W*, November 2008, 214–215.

87. Stefan Berger, "Alternative Barcelona 2000," http://www.filmklubb.no/IFFS.php?id=914&t=iffs_reports (accessed April 22, 2010).

88. Julian Stringer, "Global Cities and the International Film Festival Economy," in *Cinema and the City: Film and Urban Societies in a Global Context*, ed. Mark Shiel and Tony Fitzmaurice (Oxford: Blackwell, 2001), 134–146.

89. Nick Vivarelli, "Rome Film Festival Budget Slashed: Funds Cut from $24 Million to $15 Million," *Variety*, December 18, 2008, http://www.variety.com/article/VR1117997592.html?categoryid=1061&cs=1.

90. Steven Teo, "Asian Film Festivals and Their Diminishing Glitter Domes: An Appraisal of PIFF, SIFF and HKIFF," in *Dekalog 3: On Film Festivals*, ed. Richard Porton, 109–121 (London: Wallflower Press, 2009); also see Kong Rithdee, "The Sad Case of the Bangkok Film Festival," in *Dekalog 3: On Film Festivals*, ed. Richard Porton, 131–142 (London: Wallflower, 2009).

91. "Tribeca Enterprises," www.tribecafilm.com/about/.

92. Please refer to Eric Kohn, "Tribeca's Image Problem: Wrapping Up the 2010 Fest," *IndieWIRE*, May 3, 2010; and Stephen Holden, "12 Days, 132 Films, 38 Countries," *New York Times*, April 15, 2010.

93. Jacobsen, *50 Years Berlinale*, 253

94. Andrew, "The 'Three Ages' of Cinema Studies and the Age to Come."

95. "Terrior of Cinema," Wine Country Film Festival, http://www.winecountryfilmfest.com/Terroir.asp (accessed April 22, 2010).

96. Wine Country Film Festival, http://www.winecountryfilmfest.com/index.asp (accessed April 22, 2010).

97. For Babelgum, visit http://www.babelgum.com/online-film-festival/; for Con-Can, visit http://en.con-can.com/.

CHAPTER 2 — THE FILMS OF THE FESTIVALS

1. Peter Wollen, *Paris Hollywood: Writings on Film* (London: Verso, 2002), 9.

2. Ibid., 161; Dudley Andrew, "Foreword," in *Global Art Cinema: New Theories and Histories*, ed. Rosalind Galt and Karl Schoonover (New York: Oxford Univ. Press, 2010), v–xi.

3. Patrick Keating, for example, raises the question of multiple settings and meanings in his examination of Gabriel Figueroa versus Buñuel in "The Volcano and the Barren Hill: Gabriel Figueroa and the Space of Art Cinema," in *Global Art Cinema: New Theories and Histories*, ed. Rosalind Galt and Karl Schoonover (New York: Oxford Univ. Press, 2010), 201–217.

4. Richard Corliss and Mary Corliss, "Haneke's *The White Ribbon* Wins Cannes Palme d'Or," *Time*, May 24, 2009, http://www.time.com/time/arts/article/0,8599,1900754,00 .html (accessed July 15, 2009).

5. The glasses were recalled, ironically, for their high cadmium content.

6. Louis Althusser, "Ideology and Ideological State Apparatuses (Notes towards an Investigation)," in *Mapping Ideology*, ed. Slavoj _i_ek, 100–140 (London: Verso, 1994); Roland Barthes, *Mythologies* (Paris: Editions du Seuil, 1957).

7. This was a declaration for a New German Cinema signed by twenty-six West German filmmakers at the 1962 Oberhausen Short Film Festival, demanding that "New film needs new freedom," and that "the old film is dead."

8. Steve Neale, *Genre* (London: British Film Institute, 1980), 119.

9. Only one film, *Marty* (1955), won both the Best Picture Oscar and the Golden Palm from Cannes.

10. Roger Ebert, "The Leopard," *This Great Movie Review*, September 14, 2003, http://rogerebert.suntimes.com/apps/pbcs.dll/article?AID=%2F20030914%2 FREVIEWS08%2F309140302%2F1023&AID1=&AID2=%2F20030914%2FREVIEWS08% 2F309140302%2F102 3 (accessed May 15, 2010).

11. Derek Elley, "Auteurs Today: To Do Is to Be," *Variety*, May 6–12, 1996.

12. David Bordwell, "The Art Cinema as a Mode of Film Practice," *Film Criticism* 4, no. 1 (fall 1979): 1–8.

13. Neale, *Genre*, 119; see also Rosalind Galt and Karl Schoonover, eds., *Global Art Cinema: New Theories and Histories* (New York: Oxford Univ. Press, 2010).

14. Apichatchong Weerasethakul, in fact, has also created installations that provide different perspectives on his cinema. See Jihoon Kim, "Between Auditorium and Gallery: Perception in Apichatpong Weerasethakul's Films and Installations," in *Global Art Cinema: New Theories and Histories*, ed. Rosalind Galt and Karl Schoonover, 124–139 (New York: Oxford Univ. Press, 2010).

15. Wollen, *Paris Hollywood*, 18.

16. Andrew Pulver, "Review: Shirin," *Guardian*, August 29, 2008, http://www .guardian.co.uk/film/2008/aug/29/shirin.venicefilmfestival.

17. Altman, *Genre*. See further discussion in chapter 3. This is a theme that has also been picked up by Azadeh Farahmand in his "Disentangling the International Festival Circuit: Genre and Iranian Cinema," in *Global Art Cinema: New Theories and Histories*, ed. Rosalind Galt and Karl Schoonover, 263–284 (New York: Oxford Univ. Press, 2010).

18. Visconti's *Leopard* obviously has an elaborate set.

19. Richard Maltby, *Hollywood Cinema* (Malden, Mass.: Blackwell, 2003), 454–455.

20. Michael Budd, ed., *The Cabinet of Dr. Caligari: Texts, Contexts, Histories* (New Brunswick: Rutgers Univ. Press, 1990).

21. Wollen, *Paris Hollywood*, 74–75.

22. Andras Balint Kovacs, *Screening Modernism: European Art Cinema, 1950–1980* (Chicago: Univ. of Chicago Press, 2007), 61.

23. Keith Reader, *Robert Bresson* (Manchester, UK: Manchester Univ. Press, 2000), 31.

24. *Uncle Boonmee Who Can Recall His Past Lives*, press release, http://www.festival-cannes.com/assets/Image/Direct/033783.pdf (accessed May 22, 2010).

25. Oftentimes, in movies from small cinema-producing countries like Thailand, the international audience would not know that certain actors are local stars or nonprofessional actors. The requirement of having a blank slate in the audience mind can be achieved simply by the ignorance of the audience/critics.

26. Jeff Andrew, "Abbas Kiarostami: Interview," *Time Out London*, http://www.timeout.com/film/features/show-feature/7995/abbas-kiarostami-interview.html (accessed May 22, 2010).

27. Ibid.

28. Altman, *Genre*.

29. There have been a few comedy film festivals, but most are very small. A festival called the International Comedy Film Festival, referring to itself as the "Cannes of Comedy Film," seems to have only a 2008 edition. Please refer to www.icff.co.uk.

30. Elley, "Auteurs Today."

31. Refer to Sean Homer, "Retrieving Emir Kusturica's Underground as a Critique of Ethnic Nationalism," *Jump Cut*, no. 51 (spring 2009): http://www.ejumpcut.org/archive/jc51.2009/Kusterica/index.html.

32. Chris Berry, "East Palace, West Palace: Staging Gay Life in China," *Jump Cut*, no. 42 (December 1998): 84–89.

33. Michael Dwyer, "Cannes Jury Gives Its Heart to Works of Graphic Darkness," *Irish Times*, May 25, 2009, http://www.irishtimes.com/newspaper/world/2009/0525/1224247325203.html?digest=1 (accessed September 26, 2009).

34. Corliss and Corliss, "Haneke's *The White Ribbon* Wins Cannes Palme d'Or."

35. For a discussion of the interaction between Japanese and Western articulations of Japanese film history, see Scott Nygren, *Time Frames: Japanese Cinema and the Unfolding of History* (Minneapolis: Univ. of Minnesota Press, 2007).

36. Nancy Tartaglione-Viloatte, "Without the Auteurs There Wouldn't Be a Festival," *Screen International*, May 18, 2007, http://www.screendaily.com/without-the-auteurs-there-wouldnt-be-a-festival/4032535.article.

37. Dana Thomas, "Romanian Films: From Ban to Boom," *Washington Post*, September 16, 1990, Sunday Show, G3.

38. Carol Pugh, "East Block Filmmakers Lack Ideas and Money since Communism Fell," Associated Press, February 9, 1990.

39. Agence France Presse, "'Growing Sympathy' for Romania Secured Cannes Prize: Director," May 31, 2007, http://www.lexisnexis.com (accessed May 18, 2010).

40. A. O. Scott, "New Wave on the Black Sea," *New York Times*, January 20, 2008.

41. A. O. Scott, "Jiggers: Take Out the Dictionary," *New York Times*, June 22, 2010.

42. Ibid.

CHAPTER 3 — AUTEURS, CRITICS, AND CANONS

1. Nancy Tartaglione-Violatte, "Without the Auteurs There Wouldn't Be a Festival," *Screen International*, May 18, 2007, http://www.screendaily.com/without-the-auteurs-there-wouldnt-be-a-festival/4032535.article.

2. Peter Wollen, *Paris Hollywood: Writings on Film* (London: Verso, 2002), chapter 15, "The Canon," is a masterful study, using lists from the National Film Archive in London, *Cahiers du cinéma*, *Sight and Sound*, and others to show how film canons have to be understood as historical negotiations among institutions, aesthetics standards, and taste.

3. Ibid., 218.

4. Rick Altman, *Film/Genre* (London: British Film Institute, 1999), 12.

5. Ibid., 91.

6. Again, this raises interesting points of comparison with Keating's discussion of Gabriel Figuera. See Patrick Keating, "The Volcano and the Barren Hill: Gabriel Figueroa and the Space of Art Cinema," in *Global Art Cinema: New Theories and Histories*, ed. Rosalind Galt and Karl Schoonover (New York: Oxford Univ. Press, 2010), 201–217.

7. "MEDIA, is the support programme for the European audiovisual industry . . . ," http://ec.europa.eu/culture/media/index_en.htm (accessed September 13, 2010).

8. Bill Nichols, "Discovering Form, Inferring Meaning: New Cinemas and the Film Festival Circuit," *Film Quarterly* 47, no. 3 (spring 1994): 17–18.

9. See Mansor Bin Puteh's Web site at http://voize.my/events/arts-culture/how-has-cannes-berlin-and-venice-destroyed-world-cinema/.

10. David Bordwell, "The Art Cinema as a Mode of Film Practice," *Film Criticism* 4, no. 1 (fall 1979): 1–8; David Bordwell, *Poetics of Cinema* (London: Routledge, 2008); Steve Neale, *Genre* (London: British Film Institute, 1980); Steve Neale, "Art Cinema and the Question of Independent Film," in *The New Social Function of Cinema*, ed. Rod Stoneman (London: British Film Institute, 1981); Rosalind Galt and Karl Schoonover, eds., *Global Art Cinema: New Theories and Histories* (New York: Oxford Univ. Press, 2010).

11. Mark Betz, *Beyond the Subtitle: Remapping European Art Cinema* (Minneapolis: Univ. of Minnesota Press, 2009), 28; Andras Balint Kovacs, *Screening Modernism: European Art Cinema, 1950–1980* (Chicago: Univ. of Chicago Press, 2007).

12. A more detailed discussion of post-revolutionary Iranian cinema will be given in chapter 5.

13. Kristen Thompson has suggested that the lack of tight institutional strength, like that of Hollywood, may explain the development of the varied European avant-garde in the 1920s and 1930s. See Kristen Thompson, "The International Exploration of Cinematic Expressivity," in *The Silent Cinema Reader*, ed. Lee Grieveson and Peter Kramer, 254–270 (New York: Routledge, 2004).

14. Peter Brunette, *The Films of Michelangelo Antonioni* (Cambridge: Cambridge Univ. Press, 1998), 22.

15. Ibid.

16. Pierre Sorlin. *Italian National Cinema 1896–1996* (London: Routledge, 1996), 199–201.

17. Penelope Houston, "L'Avventura," *Sight and Sound* 30, no. 1 (winter 1960–1961): 11–12.

18. "The centre is widely known in Iran as Kanun, meaning 'center' or 'institute'" (Alberto Elena, *The Cinema of Abbas Kiarostami* [London: Saqi, in Association with the Iran Heritage Foundation, 2005], 17).

19. Elena, *The Cinema of Abbas Kiarostami*, 40.

20. Azadeh Farahmand, "Perspectives in Recent (International Acclaim for) Iranian Cinema," in *The New Iranian Cinema Politics, Representation and Identity*, ed. Richard Tapper, 93–95 (London: I. B. Tauris, 2002).

21. Cannes, "Press Statistics Chart, 1966–2009," http://www.festival-cannes.com/assets/File/Web/about/enchiffres/2009/En%20chiffres-Medias-2009-VA.pdf (accessed October 17, 2009).

22. Bosley Crowther, "Italian Film Wins Cannes Top Prize," *New York Times*, May 21, 1960.

23. Robert F. Hawkins, "Focus on an Unimpressive Cannes Film Fete," *New York Times*, May 29, 1960.

24. J. Hoberman, "Seeing and Nothingness: A Must-See Retrospective Celebrates the Works of a Modernist Master," *Village Voice*, May 30, 2006, http://www.villagevoice.com/2006-05-30/film/seeing-and-nothingness/ (accessed October 20, 2009).

25. Richard Phillips, "Michelangelo Antonioni—A Flawed Legacy, Part 2," World Socialist Web Site, August 3, 2007, http://www.wsws.org/articles/2007/aug2007/ant2-a03.shtml (accessed October 20, 2009).

26. Cynthia Grenier, "Reflections on the Parisian Screen Scene," *New York Times*, November 20, 1960.

27. Philippe Roger, *The American Enemy: The History of French Anti-Americanism*, trans. Sharon Bowman (Chicago: Univ. of Chicago Press, 2005); Andrew Ross and Kristin Ross, eds., *Anti-Americanism* (New York: New York Univ. Press, 2004); Kristin Ross, *Fast Cars, Clean Bodies: Decolonization and the Reordering of French Culture* (Cambridge: MIT Press, 1995).

28. Eugene Archer, "Roman Team on an Intellectual 'Adventure,'" *New York Times*, April 2, 1961.

29. Bosley Crowther, "Screen: 'L'Avventura,'" *New York Times*, April 5, 1961.

30. Bosley Crowther, "Way Out Films: 'L'Avventura' Is a Case of Going Too Far," *New York Times*, April 9, 1961.

31. Michèle Manceaux, "An Interview with Antonioni," *Sight and Sound* 30, no. 1 (winter 1960–1961): 5–8.

32. Richard Roud, "5 Films," *Sight and Sound* 30, no. 1 (winter 1960–1961): 8–11.

33. Houston, "L'Avventura," 11–13.

34. Manceaux, "An Interview with Antonioni," 6.

35. Roud, "5 Films."

36. Ibid., 9.

37. Ibid., 9.

38. Ibid., 11.

39. Houston, "L'Avventura," 12.

40. Ibid., 12.

41. Ibid., 13.

42. Robert F. Hawkins, "Active Italians: Antonioni Films a Roman 'Eclipse'—Veteran Scenarist Has New Vogue," *Variety*, August 27, 1961. Morgan was a British author who had died in 1958; he was known for his serious tone and had gained a large following in France.

43. For a comprehensive bibliography on Antonioni, please consult: http://www.lib.berkeley.edu/MRC/antonioni.html.

44. Brunette, *The Films of Michelangelo Antonioni*, 11.

45. William Arrowsmith, *Antonioni: The Poet of Images*, ed. with an introduction and notes by Ted Perry (New York: Oxford Univ. Press, 1995), 36.

46. Seymour Chatman, *Michelangelo Antonioni: The Investigation, 1912–2007* (Koln: Taschen, 2008).

47. Ibid., 39.

48. Goeff Brown, "Sometimes, We Get It Right: Locarno Film Festival," *The Times* (London), August 21, 1989, http://www.lexisnexis.com (accessed May 8, 2010).

49. Jacques Siclier, "Un écolier Iranien: 'Où est la maison de mon ami,' du cinéaste Abbas Kiarostami, est un produit du nouveau cinéma Iranien," *Le Monde*, April 3, 1990.

50. In Elena, *The Cinema of Abbas Kiarostami*, 93.

51. Agence France Presse, "Iran Bans Kiarostami from Cannes," April 24, 1997.

52. Todd McCarthy, "Cannes-Troversial: China, Iran Playing Hardball with Directors," *Variety*, April 25, 1997.

53. Todd McCarthy, "Iran Relents, Clear 'Cherry,'" *Daily Variety*, May 7, 1997.

54. Joan Dupont, "Abbas Kioarostami: Parables, Not Protest," *International Herald Tribune*, May 20, 1997.

55. John Follain, "Cannes Rewards Film Victims," *The Australian*, May 20, 1997.

56. "Rétrospective Abbas Kiarostami: Cinq courts métrages et sept longs métrages du grand cinéaste Iranien," *Le Monde*, July 25, 1997.

57. Steve Erickson, "Taste of Cherry by Abbas Kiarostami," *Film Quarterly* 52, no. 3 (spring 1999): 52–54, 54.

58. Ibid., 53.

59. Ibid.

60. Ibid., 54.

61. Ibid.

62. Joan Dupont, "Abbas Kiarostami: Parables, Not Protests; 50TH CANNES FESTIVAL," *International Herald Tribune*, May 20, 1997, http://www.lexisnexis.com (accessed September 11, 2009).

63. Jonathan Rosenbaum, *Movie Wars: How Hollywood and the Media Limit What Films We Can See* (London: Wallflower Press, 2000), 158.

64. John Berra, "DVD Review Syndromes and a Century," *Film International* 8, no. 1 (2010): 73–74.

65. Laura Mulvey, "Kiarostami's Uncertainty Principle," *Sight and Sound* 8, no. 6 (June 1998): 24–27.

66. Ibid.

67. Ibid.

68. Ibid.

69. Ibid., 64.

70. Mehrnaz Saeed-Vefa and Jonathan Rosenbaum, *Abbas Kiarostami* (Urbana: Univ. of Illinois Press, 2003), 50.

71. Elena, *The Cinema of Abbas Kiarostami*.

72. Ibid., 186.

73. Manohla Dargis, "In Films at Cannes, Rumblings of Real and Often Devastating Events," *New York Times*, May 21, 2010, C1.

74. Rob Nelson, "Certified Copy," *Daily Variety*, May 19, 2010.

75. Ibid.

76. Robert Chazal, in Jean-Claude Romer and Jeanne Moreau, *Cannes Memories 1939–2002: La grande histoire du Festival* (Montreuil: Media Business and Partners, 2002), 55.

77. Gene Siskel Film Center, http://www.artic.edu/webspaces/siskelfilmcenter/2007/july/1.html (accessed October 20, 2009).

78. Richard Von Busack, "The Affluent Angst of Antonioni," http://www.metroactive.com/papers/sfmetro/01.18.99/antonioni-9902.html (accessed October 20, 2009).

79. "Modernist Master: Michelangelo Antonioni," http://www.bampfa.berkeley.edu/filmseries/antonioni (accessed October 20, 2009).

80. Michelangelo Antonioni Retrospective, http://www.nationalmuseum.sg/michelangelo_antonioni_retrospective.pdf (accessed October 20, 2009).

81. For a list of their publications, please go to: http://osiris22.pi-consult.de/view.php3?show=5870734.

82. A. R. Duckworth, "Michelangelo Antonioni's Cannes Statement for L'Avventura (1960)," *The Motley View* (October 15, 2009), http://ardfilmjournal.wordpress.com/2009/10/15/michelangelo-antonionis-cannes-statement-for-lavventura-1960/.

83. Michelangelo Antonioni, *The Architecture of Vision: Writings and Interviews on Cinema*, ed. Carlo di Carlo and Giorgio Tinazzi, American edition by Marga Cotinno-Jones (Chicago: Univ. of Chicago Press, 2007), 78.

84. Archer, "Roman Team on an Intellectual 'Adventure.'"

85. I located the document at the MOMA Film Library, under Abbas Kiarostami.

86. Saeed-Vafa and Rosenbaum, *Abbas Kiarostami*, 28–29.

87. Janet Maslin, "Iranian Film Makes It Past Censors to Cannes," *New York Times*, May 17, 1997.

88. "Conférence de presse: 'Copie Conforme' de Abbas Kiarostami," http://www.festival-cannes.fr/en/mediaPlayer/10614.html.

CHAPTER 4 — FILM FESTIVALS AND FILM INDUSTRIES

1. See discussions of authors in Richard Porton, ed., *Dekalog 3: On Film Festivals* (London: Wallflower Press, 2009), for example.

2. Roger Ebert, *Two Weeks in the Midday Sun: A Cannes Notebook* (Kansas City: Andrews and McNeel 1987), 6.

3. Fipresci, "Karlovy Vary 2008," Festival Report, http://www.fipresci.org/festivals/archive/2008/karlovy_vary/kvvary_08_ndx.htm (accessed October 11, 2008).

4. Dina Iordanova, *Cinema of the Other Europe* (London: Wallflower Press, 2003), 30; Dina Iordanova, "Showdown of the Festivals: Clashing Entrepreneurship and Post-Communist Management of Culture," *Film International* 4, no. 23 (October 2006): 25–38.

5. Robert Chazal, "Retrospective—1939," in Jean-Claude Romer and Jeanne Moreau, *Cannes Memories 1939–2002: La grande histoire du Festival* (Montreuil: Media Business and Partners, 2002), 3.

6. Vanessa Schwartz, "The Cannes Film Festival and the Marketing of Cosmopolitanism," in *It's So French! Hollywood, Paris, and the Making of Cosmopolitan Film Culture* (Chicago: Univ. of Chicago Press, 2007), 56–101.

7. Hollywood did not invest in this film, but it was later distributed by United Artists.

8. Steve Pond, "Cannes Wants Americans . . . But Not in Competition," *The Wrap*, April 15, 2010, http://www.thewrap.com/movies/column-post/cannes-wants-americans-not-competition-16343.

9. Peter Biskind, *Down and Dirty Pictures: Miramax, Sundance, and the Rise of Independent Film* (New York: Simon and Schuster, 2004).

10. Ebert, *Two Weeks in the Midday Sun,* 16. Cannon Films would go into decline in the late 1980s, and after separations and scandal it would terminate officially in 1993.

11. Cannes, press statistics chart, http://www.festival-cannes.com/assets/File/Web/about/enchiffres/2010/En%20chiffres-Medias-2010-VA.pdf (accessed July 9, 2008).

12. Louise Jury, "Last Stand of Star Wars Expects to Be Box Office Blast," *Independent,* May 16, 2005.

13. Video clips, Cannes Inside Scene, Coen Brothers, http://media.amctv.com/video/video_smso_cannes.html (accessed May 29, 2007).

14. Romer and Moreau, *Cannes Memories,* 239.

15. Marijke de Valck, *Film Festivals: From European Geopolitics to Global Cinephilia* (Amsterdam: Amsterdam Univ. Press, 2007), 95–96.

16. Ebert, *Two Weeks in the Midday Sun,* 15.

17. Kenneth Turan, "Festival Has Many Looks," *LA Times,* March 17, 2006, http://www.chicagotribune.com/topic/env-et-cannes17may172,0,839271.story (accessed July 15, 2008).

18. Ron Holloway, "Cannes 2005 Report," http://www.kinema.uwaterloo.ca/article.php?id=267&feature (accessed June 12, 2010). This dichotomy is a constant concern in collections such as Dina Iordanova with Ragan Rhyne, eds., *Film Festival Yearbook 1: The Festival Circuit* (St. Andrews: St. Andrews Film Studies, 2009), or Porton, ed., *Dekalog 3.*

19. On the fringes of Europe, Thessaloniki hosts a fairly big market, the Agora, in November. It specializes in promoting films from southeastern Europe and the eastern Mediterranean. On its Web site, it underscores the goal of developing "a film market with a focused geographic interest." Across the former Iron Curtain, meanwhile, Karlovy Vary does not have a market, but a film industry office. In 2006, 592 buyers and industrial representatives visited the festival. People from the industry can attend industry screenings, which include both films shown in competitions as well as new films

from the region and works in progress. In 2008, one of its programs was "Interfacing with Hollywood, Production and Marketing of Your Movies," where Hollywood insiders were invited to speak to the regional delegates. Even post-socialist regional film festival markets want some kind of connections to Hollywood and big cinema business.

20. John Anderson, *Sundancing: Hanging Out and Listening In at America's Most Important Film Festival* (New York: Avon, 2000), 150.

21. Manohla Dargis, "In the Big Picture, Big Screen Hopes," *New York Times*, December 18, 2008.

22. In Christine Vachon, with David Edelstein, *Shooting to Kill: How an Independent Producer Blasts through Barriers to Make Movies That Matter* (New York: Quill, 1998), 287.

23. Ibid.

24. Patrick Frater, "Autumn Film Festivals: Big Changes Require New Survival Techniques," *Variety*, August 24, 2007, http://www.variety.com/index.asp?layout=print_story&articleid=VR1117970822&categoryid=13 (accessed July 12, 2008).

25. AFI Film Festival was launched in 1987 when it took over Filmex in Los Angeles.

26. Stephen Teo, "Asian Film Festivals and Their Diminishing Glitter Domes: An Appraisal of PIFF, SIFF and HKIFF," in *Dekalog 3: On Film Festivals*, ed. Richard Porton, 109–121 (London: Wallflower Press, 2009).

27. Wendy Kan, "Fest Adds Sales Event: Hong Kong-Asia Screenings to Feature Networking, Market," *Variety*, April 1, 2002, http://www.variety.com/index.asp?layout=festivals&jump=story&id=1061&articleid=VR1117864685&cs=1&query=film+market (accessed July 3, 2008).

28. Patrick Frater and Marcus Lim, "Asian Film Market Ends with a Whimper," *Variety*, October 7, 2008, http://www.variety.com/index.asp?layout=festivals&jump=pusan&query=asian+film+market+ends+with+a+whimper (accessed Oct 22, 2010). See Teo, "Asian Film Festivals and Their Diminishing Glitter Domes."

29. Arthur Jones, "Shanghai Film Fest Now an Industry Event: Chinese Studios Swell Festivals' Market Launch," *Variety*, June 8, 2007, http://www.variety.com/article/VR1117966536.html?categoryid=2594&cs=1 (accessed July 3, 2008).

30. Michael Jones, "Rising Film Festival Stress: Glut of Events Creates High-Stakes Rivalries," *Variety*, December 7, 2007, http://www.variety.com/index.asp?layout=festivals&jump=story&id=1061&articleid=VR11179 77355 (accessed July 7, 2008).

31. http://www.sis.gov.eg/VR/cinema/english/6n22.htm (accessed January 10, 2010). Nick Roddick, "Coming to a Server Near You: The Film Festival in the Age of Digital Reproduction," in *Film Festival Yearbook 1: The Festival Circuit*, ed. Dina Iordanova with Ragan Rhyne, 116–135 (St. Andrews: St. Andrews Film Studies, 2009), concurs that "Cairo's A status is the scandal of the Festival circuit—and one that everyone seems too scared to address" (165).

32. Lindiwe Dovey, "Director's Cut: In Defense of African Film Festivals Outside Africa," in *Film Festival Yearbook 2: Film Festivals and Imagined Communities*, ed. Dina Iordanova and Ruby Cheung, 45–73 (St. Andrews: St. Andrews Film Studies, 2010).

33. Wendy Kan, "Fest Adds Sales Event: Hong Kong-Asia Screenings to Feature Networking, Market," *Variety*, April 1, 2002, http://www.variety.com/index.asp?layout=festivals&jump=story&id=1061&articleid=VR1117864685&cs=1&query=film+market (accessed July 3, 2008).

34. Vachon, with Edelstein, *Shooting to Kill*, 285.

35. Fabien Lemercier, "Cannes According to Wild Bunch," http://www.cineuropa.org/interview.aspx?lang=en&documentID=76775.

36. Ibid.

37. Anderson, *Sundancing*, 102

38. Ibid., 253.

39. Information obtained from Berlin's European Film Market, http://www.berlinale.de/en/das_festival/festivalprofil/berlinale_in_zahlen/index.html (accessed January 11, 2011).

40. Frater, "Autumn Film Festivals."

41. Ibid.

42. *Variety*, "Berlin: Probst Drinks to the Market," http://www.variety.com/blog/1390000339/post/120021412.html?&query=film+market (accessed July 3, 2008).

43. Ibid.

44. Frater, "Autumn Film Festivals."

45. In chapter 2, I talk about the distributors' importance in influencing the lineup of a festival's competition.

46. Personal correspondence, April 2007, Hong Kong.

47. See Geoffrey Macnab, "The Match-Makers—New Co-Production Markets," *Screen Daily*, October 12, 2007, http://www.screendaily.com/ScreenDailyArticle.aspx?intStoryID=35208.

48. Thomas Elsaesser has discusses this parallel phenomenon from a slightly different perspective in *European Cinema: Face to Face with Hollywood* (Amsterdam: Amsterdam Univ. Press, 2005), 88.

49. Randall Halle, "Offering Tales They Want to Hear: Transnational European Film Funding as Neo-Orientalism," in *Global Art Cinema: New Theories and Histories*, ed. Rosalind Galt and Karl Schoonover, 303–319 (New York: Oxford Univ. Press, 2010).

50. Gianni Canova, "New Film Movements and New Departures," The Nineties and the Third Millennium, Festival History, Film Festival Locarno, http://www.pardo.ch/jahia/Jahia/home/Festival/History/The-90s-and-the-third-Millenium/lang/en.

51. "What Is the Berlinale Talent Campus?" http://www.berlinale.de/en/das_festival/berlinale_talent_campus/index.html (accessed March 30, 2007).

52. Eurimages Web site, http://www.coe.int/t/dg4/Eurimages/About/default_en.asp, in Halle, "Offering Tales They Want to Hear," 304.

53. Halle, "Offering Tales They Want to Hear," 313–314.

54. Press kit for *Waiting for the Clouds*, www.silkroadproduction.com/pdfs/presskit.pdf (accessed May 25, 2010).

55. Halle, "Offering Tales They Want to Hear," 314.

56. "Hong Kong-Asia Film Financing Forum (HAF) Presents Asian Filmmakers with Awards," HAF, www.haf.org.hk/haf/release1.htm.

57. "CineMart." http://www.filmfestivalrotterdam.com/en/about/cinemart/.

58. "HBF Categories." http://www.filmfestivalrotterdam.com/professionals/hubert_bals_fund/hbf_plus/.

59. "Nov 09, 2004: Berlinale Jury for the *World Cinema Fund*," http://www.berlinale.de/en/archiv/jahresarchive/2005/08_pressemitteilungen_2005/08_Pressemitteilungen_2005-Detail_1533.html.

60. "World Cinema Fund," 2, http://www.berlinale.de/media/pdf_word/world_cinema_fund/generelle_information_pdf/WCF_Flyer.pdf.

61. Sonja Heinen, "Passion, Pragmatism, Efficient Co-operation and Limits: The Existence of a Small Film Fund," WCF Booklet, February 2007, 6, http://www.berlinale.de/media/pdf_word/world_cinema_fund/WCF-Booklet_2007.pdf.

62. Again, see Halle, "Offering Tales They Want to Hear," for an analysis of ideological questions in German coproductions.

63. "Selection Completed for Open Doors 2006—11 Projects from Southeast Asia Invited to Locarno," press release, June 22, 2006, http://www.pardo.ch/jahia/Jahia/home/2007/cache/offonce/lang/en/pid/19?cnid=802.

64. Euromed Audiovisual, "Locarno's Open Doors Chief Vincenzo Bugno Announces His Pick of Film Projects from the Mashrek," http://www.euromedaudiovisuel.net/newsdetail.aspx?treeID=74&lang=en&documentID=8215.

65. "New Cinema Network: An Introduction," *Screen Daily*, September 20, 2007, http://www.screendaily.com/new-cinema-network-an-introduction/4034744.article.

66. For more information on 2010 PPP, go to http://www.finecut.co.kr/renew/news/news_view.asp?num=85.

67. See Liz Shackleton and Jean Noh, "Pusan Cements Regional Role," *Screen Daily*, October 19, 2007, http://www.screendaily.com/ScreenDailyArticle.aspx?IntStoryID=35354.

68. J-pitch is a Japanese initiative to promote Japan film industries in the direction of coproduction. It is affiliated with the Tokyo International Film Festival.

69. CineMart Partners, http://www.filmfestivalrotterdam.com/nl-partners/cinemart_partners/.

70. "Cape Town World Cinema Festival Jury Announces Winning Films," press release, http://www.sithengi.co.za/festival/festival_news/stories/cape_town_world_cinema_festival_jury_announces_winning_films?section=/festival/festival_news (accessed November 7, 2007).

71. "'Grbavica' by Jasmila Zbanic FILMFONDS-WIEN + FILMFÖRDERUNG BADEN-WÜRTTEMBERG," http://www.cine-regio.org/co-production/case-studies/grbavica/ (accessed Jan 9, 2011).

72. Halle, "Offering Tales They Want to Hear," 314.

73. Kitano Film is a Japanese production company formed by Takashi Kitano, a famous local Japanese actor/director as well as a festival regular and director and actor of Hana-bi.

74. At the time of writing, this project is in production.

75. "Jia Zhangke's New Movie 'Banned,'" Sing tao Daily (US), C 10, June 18, 2010.

76. "Premier of 'I Wish I Know,' Jia Zhangke emphasized biographical and sensitive issues," http://ent.163.com/10/0701/23/6AHU83Q6000300B1.html (accessed July 1, 2010).

77. Ibid.

78. Bill Nichols, "Discovering Form, Inferring Meaning: New Cinemas and the Film Festival Circuit," Film Quarterly 47, no. 3 (spring 1994): 16–30, 27.

79. NEH, NEA, and local Arts Councils support some American filmmakers. Universities also have resources that support equipment and venue rental. American universities have also begun to support their own film festivals as well through screening exchanges.

80. Heinen, "Passion, Pragmatism, Efficient Co-operation and Limits," 6.

81. Vincenzo Bugno, "About WCF, A Work in Progress, Film, Content, and Strategies: Exploring New Directions," WCF Booklet (February 2007), 9, http://www.berlinale.de/media/pdf_word/world_cinema_fund/WCF-Booklet_2007.pdf (accessed January 15, 2008).

82. Halle, "Offering Tales They Want to Hear," 312. See Frantz Fanon, The Wretched of the Earth (New York: Grove Press, 1961).

CHAPTER 5 — FESTIVALS AS PUBLIC SPHERES

1. Here, we intersect with the politicization of imagined communities envisioned by Benedict Anderson in his classic work, Imagined Communities: Reflections on the Rise of Nationalism (London: Verso, 1991).

2. Jürgen Habermas, The Structural Transformation of the Public Sphere: An Inquiry into a Category of Bourgeois Society, trans. Thomas Burger, with the assistance of Frederick Lawrence (Cambridge: MIT Press, 1989).

3. Craig Calhoun, ed., *Habermas and the Public Sphere* (Cambridge: MIT Press, 1992); Miriam Hansen, *Babel and Babylon: Spectatorship in American Silent Film* (Cambridge: Harvard Univ. Press, 1991); Miriam Hansen, "Early Cinema, Late Cinema: Transformations of the Public Sphere," in *Viewing Positions: Ways of Seeing Film*, ed. Linda Williams, 134–154 (New Brunswick: Rutgers Univ. Press, 1995); Michael Warner, *Publics and Counterpublics* (New York: Zone Books, 2002); Oscar Negt and Alexander Kluge, *Public Sphere and Experience* (Minneapolis: Univ. of Minnesota Press, 1993); Nancy Fraser, "Rethinking the Public Sphere: A Contribution to the Critique of Actually Existing Democracy," *Social Text*, no. 25/26 (1990): 56–80; Nancy Fraser, "Politics, Culture, and the Public Sphere: Toward a Postmodern Conception," in *Social Postmodernism: Beyond Identity Politics*, ed. Linda Nicholson and Steven Seidman, 287–315 (New York: Cambridge Univ. Press, 1995); Nancy Fraser, "Transnationalizing the Public Sphere" in *Globalizing Critical Theory*, ed. Max Pensky, 46–61 (Lanham, Md.: Rowman and Littlefield, 2005); Nancy Fraser, *Scales of Justice: Reimagining Political Space in a Globalizing World* (New York: Columbia Univ. Press, 2009); Pauline Johnson, *Habermas: Rescuing the Public Sphere* (London: Routledge, 2006).

4. Fraser, "Rethinking the Public Sphere," 56.

5. Ibid., 57

6. Kay Armatage, "Material Effects: Fashions in Feminist Programming," in *There She Goes: Feminist Filmmaking and Beyond*, ed. Corinn Columpar and Sophie Mayer, 92–104 (Detroit: Wayne State Univ. Press, 2009).

7. Roland Barthes, *Mythologies* (Paris: Editions du Seuil, 1957).

8. American Film Renaissance Institute, "Film Festival: Our History of Film Festivals," http://www.afrfilmfestival.com/content.cfm?sid=filmfe.

9. Geoff Eley in Nancy Fraser, "Rethinking the Public Sphere," 56–80.

10. Amy Gutmann, "Introduction," in Michael Ignatieff, *Human Rights as Politics and Idolatry*, ed. Amy Gutmann (Princeton: Princeton Univ. Press, 2001), xvii.

11. Lindiwe Dovey raises some crosscutting issues of this geography in "Director's Cut: In Defense of African Film Festivals Outside Africa," in *Film Festival Yearbook 2: Film Festivals and Imagined Communities*, ed. Dina Iordanova and Ruby Cheung, 45–73 (St. Andrews: St. Andrews Film Studies, 2010).

12. Fraser, "Rethinking the Public Sphere," 65–70; see Fraser, *Scales of Justice*.

13. Dina Iordanova and Ruby Cheung, eds., *Film Festival Yearbook 2: Film Festivals and Imagined Communities* (St. Andrews: St. Andrews Film Studies, 2010).

14. Habermas, *Structural Transformation*. See chapter 9 on Hong Kong, an especially important case given the divorce of colonial governance and civil society which precluded an active parliamentary/bourgeois public sphere.

15. Bodo Blüthner et al., "The Oberhausen Manifesto" (1962) in *German Essays on Film*, ed. Richard McCormick and Alison Guenther-Pal, 202 (New York: Continuum, 2004).

16. Elizabetta Povoledo, "Critical Cannes Film Angers Italian Official," *New York Times*, May 13, 2010, A6.

17. Mark Brown, "Hundreds Protest as 'Anti-French' as Outside the Law Was Screened," *Guardian*, May 21, 2010, http://www.guardian.co.uk/film/2010/may/21/rachid-bouchareb-outside-the-law-protests.

18. Robert Marquand, "Cannes Film Festival's 'Hors la Loi': How Well Does France Face Its Past in Algeria?" *Christian Science Monitor* online, June 1, 2010, http://www.csmonitor.com/World/Europe/2010/0601/Cannes-Film-Festival-s-Hors-la-Loi-How-well-does-France-face-its-past-in-Algeria.

19. Rebecca Meckelburg, "Queer Films Banned in Tasmania," *GreenLeft*, March 29, 1995, http://www.greenleft.org.au/node/9594 (accessed May 22, 2010).

20. Anand Patwardhan, "Festival in Contrast," *The Hindu*, January 18, 2004, http://www.hinduonnet.com/mag/2004/01/18/stories/2004011800120500.htm (accessed August 12, 2010).

21. Anand Patwardhan, "India and Pakistan, Film Festivals in Contrast," December 23, 2003, http://www.patwardhan.com/writings/press/Fest%20contrast.htm (accessed April 12, 2010).

22. Ramola Talwar Badam, "Censor Board Bans Film on One of India's Worst Religious Riots," AP Wire, August 6, 2004, http://www.lexisnexis.com (accessed May 22, 2010).

23. Fraser, *Scales of Justice*.

24. Wolfgang Jacobsen, *50 Years Berlinale* (Berlin: Filmmuseum, 2000), 361.

25. "An Interview with Adriano Apra, Director of Pesaro Film Festival," *International Film—A Cross Cultural Review* 3, no. 3 (summer 1995, Tehran): 9–10.

26. Ibid., 2.

27. Michael Slackman, "Defying Censors and Threats, Iranian Filmmakers Keep Focus on the Turmoil," *New York Times*, January 4, 2010, A4.

28. A. O. Scott, "No One Knows about Persian Cats," *New York Times*, April 16, 2010, http://movies.nytimes.com/2010/04/16/movies/16noone.html.

29. Kayzan Farzeneh, "Iran's Home Movies," *Foreign Policy*, April 20, 2010, http://www.foreignpolicy.com/articles/2010/04/20/interview_bahman_ghobadi.

30. Medhi Abdollahzadeh, "Fajr Film Festival's 30-Year Span since the Islamic Revolution: A Look at the Roots of the Festival Boycott," *Gozaar* (February 16, 2010), http://www.gozaar.org/template1.php?id=1438&language=english (accessed March 13, 2010).

31. Slackman, "Defying Censors and Threats, Iranian Filmmakers Keep Focus on the Turmoil."

32. Scott Tobias, "Iranian Filmmaker Jafar Panahi Arrested (Again)," A. V. Club, March 2, 2010, http://www.avclub.com/articles/iranian-filmmaker-jafar-panahi-arrested-again,38716/ (accessed March 2, 2010).

33. Xan Brooks, "Film-Maker Jafar Panahi Arrested in Iran," *Guardian*, March 2, 2010, http://www.guardian.co.uk/film/2010/mar/02/jafar-panahi-arrested-in-iran (accessed March 2, 2010).

34. Agence France Presse, "Iranian Director Panahi Protested Innocence from Jail," May 15, 2010, http://www.lexisnexis.com.

35. Agence France Presse, "Juliette Binoche: I hope Jafar Panahi will be here next year," May 24, 2010, http://www.lexisnexis.com.

36. Human Rights Watch, "About IFF," http://www.hrw.org/en/iff/about (accessed December 8, 2009).

37. Bill Nichols, *Representing Reality: Issues and Concepts in Documentary* (Bloomington: Indiana Univ. Press, 1992).

38. "China Blue," http://www.bullfrogfilms.com/catalog/china.html (accessed February 8, 2010).

39. For example, Cairo Human Rights Film Festival, http://www.cairofilm.org/, Seoul Human Rights Watch Festival, http://sarangbang.or.kr/hrfilm/index.php?option=com_content&task=view&id=19&Itemid=79&1ang=en, Tri-Continental Film Festival in South Africa, http://www.3continentsfestival.co.za/, the Stalker International Film Festival in Russia, http://www.stalkerfest.org/ (accessed February 1, 2010).

40. The Nobel Peace Prize in 1997 was awarded to the International Campaign to Ban Landmines. Human Rights Watch was one of the six founding members of this campaign.

41. For example, see James Kidd, "How to Put the World to Shame; London," *South China Morning Post*, March 9, 2008, http://www.lexisnexis.com (accessed January 5, 2010).

42. In order to remain free from government interference, HRW does not accept any government money or grants.

43. Please refer to: Stacy Long, "Adobe Youth Voices Featured at Human Rights Watch International Film Festival," Adobe featured blog, http://blogs.adobe.com/conversations/2010/06/adobe_youth_voices_featured_at.html (accessed January 11, 2010).

44. Derek Elley, "Eden Is West," *Variety*, February 16, 2009, http://variety.com/review/VE111793968o.html?categoryid=31&cs=1 (accessed February 8, 2010).

45. For more information, please refer to the network website: http://www.humanrightsfilmnetwork.org/.

46. Human Rights Film Network, "HRFN Programmers Choose Winners of International Human Rights Film Award 2008," http://www.humanrightsfilmnetwork.org/index.php?option=com_content&view=category&layout=blog&id=2&Itemid=2 (accessed January 11, 2011).

47. Ibid.

48. The 2009 HRWFF films: *Eden Is West*—Greek immigrant in Paris; *Reckoning*—Congo warlords; *The Yes Men Fix the World*—U.S.; *Afghan Star; The Age of Stupid*—West; *Back Home Tomorrow*—Darfur, Kabul; *Crude*—Ecuador Chevron; *Good Fortune*—Africa; *In the Holy Fire of Revolution*—Russia; *Kabuli Kid*—Kabul; *Look into My Eyes*—anti-Semitism in Europe; *My Neighbor, My Killer*—Rwanda; *Born into Brothels*—Calcutta; *Ford Transit*—Ramallah; *Iraq in Fragments*—Iraq; *Jung (War) in the Land of the Mujaheddin*—Afghan; *Regret to Inform*—Vietnam War; *Mrs. Goundo's Daughter*—West African women fight for asylum in the U.S.; *Remnants of a War*—Lebanon; *Snow*—postwar Bosnia; and *Tapologo*—South Africa.

49. See Dovey, "Director's Cut."

50. Fraser, *Scales of Justice*, 98.

51. I primarily use the term "queer" to describe most of these festivals because of the perceived inclusiveness of this term, with the full understanding that this term has a complex history.

52. Harry Benshoff and Sean Griffin, *Queer Images* (Lanham, Md.: Rowman and Littlefield, 2006), 172–173.

53. "Frameline 33, Films/Programs, Closing Night," http://www.frameline.org/festival/film/programdetail.aspx?FID=45&PID=32 (accessed December 13, 2009).

54. Ibid.

55. 2010 Qfest Catalog, http://www.qfest.com/film-details.cfm?c=236&id=9487.

56. See Warner, *Publics and Counterpublics;* Fraser, "Rethinking the Public Sphere."

57. Patricia White, Ruby Rich, Eric Clarke, and Richard Fung, "Queer Publicity: A Dossier on Lesbian and Gay Film Festivals," *GLJ* 5, no. 1 (1999): 73–93.

58. Ibid., 82.

59. Ibid., 82.

60. "About GAZE Film Festival," http://www.gaze.ie/about.aspx.

61. Jeremy Goldkorn, "Beijing International Gay and Lesbian Film Festival," Danwei: Chinese Media, Advertising, and Urban Life, April 21, 2005, http://www.danwei.org/film/beijing_international_gay_and.php.

62. Tina Tran, "Gays in China: Beijing Queer Film Festival Goes Off without a Hitch," www.HuffingtonPost.com, June 18, 2009, http://www.huffingtonpost.com/2009/06/18/gays-in-china-beijing-que_n_217486.html.

63. Shane Engstrom, "A (Brief) History of the Connecticut Gay and Lesbian Film Festival," http://www.ctglff.org/history.htm (accessed February 9, 2010).

64. "Damron, the First Name and the Last Word in Lesbian and Gay Travel," https://damron.com/film_festivals.php (accessed February 22, 2010).

65. "Cannes Film Festival to Get First Gay Award," May 6, 2010, http://www.pinknews.co.uk/2010/05/06/cannes-film-festival-to-get-first-gay-award/.

66. See also Benshoff and Griffin, *Queer Images*, 219–240.

67. Kevin Thomas, "*Mala Noche*, Film with Gay Theme Airs on KCET," *LA Times*, June 23, 1989, http://articles.latimes.com/1989-06-23/entertainment/ca-2604_1_ray-monge-walt-curtis-portland-s-skid-row (accessed February 12, 2010).

68. Mix NYC: The New York Queer Experimental Film Festival, http://www.nyc-arts.org/organizations/1801/mix-nyc-the-new-york-queer-experimental-film-festival (accessed January 11, 2011).

69. White, Rich, Clarke, and Fung, "Queer Publicity."

70. Barrett et al., "Queer Film and Video Festival Forum, Take One: Curators Speak Out," *GLQ: A Journal of Lesbian and Gay Studies* 11, no. 4 (2005): 596.

71. Ibid., 596.

72. Ibid., 597.

73. Roya Rastegar, "The De-Fusion of Good Intentions, Outfest's Fusion Film Festival," *GLQ* 15, no. 3 (May 2009): 481.

74. Ibid., 483.

75. Ibid., 483.

76. Joshua Gamson, "The Organizational Shaping of Collective Identity: The Case of Lesbian and Gay Film Festivals in New York," *Sociological Forum* 11, no. 2 (June 1996): 231–261.

77. Personal interview with Sarah Schulman, June 18, 2008.

78. MIX 2009 letter to donors, July 31, 2009, www.mixnyc.org/downloadables/MIX-appeal.pdf.

79. Ibid.

80. Gamson, "The Organizational Shaping of Collective Identity."

81. NewFest, "Mission," http://newfest.org/wordpress/mission/ (accessed February 22, 2010).

82. Gamson, "The Organizational Shaping of Collective Identity," 249.

83. White, Rich, Clarke, and Fung, "Queer Publicity."

CHAPTER 6 — THE HONG KONG INTERNATIONAL
FILM FESTIVAL AS CULTURAL EVENT

1. E.g. Cindy Wong, "Cities, Cultures and Cassettes: Hong Kong Cinema and Transnational Audiences," *Spectator* 22, no. 1 (2002): 46–64; Cindy Wong and Gary McDonogh, "Consuming Cinema: Reflections on Movies and Market-places in Contemporary Hong Kong," in *Consuming Hong Kong*, ed. Gordon Mathews and Tai-lok

Lui, 81–116 (Hong Kong: Hong Kong Univ. Press, 2001); Gary McDonogh and Cindy Wong, "The Mediated Metropolis: Anthropological Issues in Cities and Mass Communication," *American Anthropologist* 103, no. 1 (2001): 96–111; Gary McDonogh and Cindy Wong, *Global Hong Kong* (London: Routledge, 2005).

2. See Steven Teo, "Asian Film Festivals and Their Diminishing Glitter Domes: An Appraisal of PIFF, SIFF and HKIFF," in *Dekalog 3: On Film Festivals*, ed. Richard Porton, 109–121 (London: Wallflower Press, 2009), and Ruby Cheung, "Corporatising a Film Festival: Hong Kong," in *Film Festival Yearbook 1: The Festival Circuit*, edited by Dina Iordanova with Ragan Rhyne, 99–116 (St. Andrews: St. Andrews Film Studies, 2009).

3. Claims of barrenness as well as sovereignty have been disputed by subsequent scholars and citizens. See McDonogh and Wong, *Global Hong Kong*.

4. For background on Hong Kong history, see McDonogh and Wong, *Global Hong Kong*; Jung-Fang Tsai, *Hong Kong in Chinese History* (New York: Columbia Univ. Press, 1993); Steve Tsang, *A Modern History of Hong Kong* (London: I. B. Tauris, 2004); Leo Lee, *City between Worlds: My Hong Kong* (Cambridge: Harvard Univ. Press, 2008).

5. Poshek Fu, *Between Shanghai and Hong Kong: The Politics of Chinese Cinemas* (Stanford, Calif.: Stanford Univ. Press, 2003), 67–69.

6. John Woo was born and raised in this neighborhood. See Alan Smart, *The Shep Kip Mei Myth* (Hong Kong: Hong Kong Univ. Press, 2006).

7. *Under the Lion Rock* is a television series produced by the governmental Radio Television Hong Kong (RTHK). It started in the mid-1970s and was very popular, with its emphasis on lives of everyday working-class people in a public housing estate. Its production was continued until the 1980s; however, new series were still produced as late as 2006.

8. *Hong Kong Report 1955* (Hong Kong: Government Printing, 1956): 176–177.

9. Charles Allen, *Communication Patterns in Hong Kong* (Hong Kong: Chinese Univ. Press, 1978); I. C. Jarvie, *Window on Hong Kong: A Sociological Study of the Hong Kong Film Industry and Its Audience* (Hong Kong: Centre of Asian Studies, Hong Kong University, 1978); McDonogh and Wong, "The Mediated Metropolis," 96–111.

10. See Matthew Turner and Irene Ngan, *Hong Kong 60s/90s: Designing Identity* (Hong Kong: Performing Arts Centre, 1996); McDonogh and Wong, *Global Hong Kong*, 2005

11. Richard Hughes, *Borrowed Place, Borrowed Time* (London: Deutsch, 1968).

12. Yueng, Yue-man, ed., *The First Decade* (Hong Kong: Chinese Univ. Press, 2007); Xu Xi, ed., *Fifty/Fifty: New Hong Kong Writing* (Hong Kong: Haven Books, 2008).

13. Documents from the Public Record Office of Hong Kong—correspondence from the British Council, 1952.

14. They later became film critics.

15. Rumors also floated around Hong Kong that U.S. money was involved, since it was published by Union Press, funded by the Asian Society from the United States, within the warming climate of U.S. anticommunism.

16. Personal interview with Law Kar, June 6, 2007.

17. The author took production classes there. Many years later, in conversation with Fruit Chan, she found out that he was in those classes with her in the late 1970s.

18. Webpage of Baptist University School of Communication, Department of Cinema and Television, http://www.comm.hkbu.edu.hk/ (accessed June 16, 2008).

19. David Bordwell, *Planet Hong Kong: Popular Cinema and the Art of Entertainment* (Cambridge: Harvard Univ. Press, 2000).

20. Besides cultural activities, the Urban Council is also responsible for the collection of trash and other duties related to sanitation.

21. Ching Ling Kwok and Emily Lo, "Interview with Paul Yeung: The Birth of HKIFF," in *20th Anniversary of the Hong Kong International Film Festival*, 33 (Hong Kong: Hong Kong Urban Council, 1996).

22. Personal interview, Hong Kong, June 2007.

23. Kwok and Lo, "Interview with Paul Yeung: The Birth of HKIFF," 26.

24. Nina Kwong and Emily Lo, "Interview with Freddie Wong: The Fighter," in *20th Anniversary of the Hong Kong International Film Festival*, 47–48. (Hong Kong: Hong Kong Urban Council, 1996).

25. Ching Ling Kwok, "Interview with Leong Mo-Ling: The Cloud Capped Star," in *20th Anniversary of the Hong Kong International Film Festival*, 53–54 (Hong Kong: Hong Kong Urban Council, 1996). She bought Gerardo de Leon's *Dyesebel* and *Sanda Wong* for the 1985 festival.

26. Nina Kwong, and Emily Lo, "Interview with Li Cheuk-Yo: There for the Long Run," in *20th Anniversary of the Hong Kong International Film Festival*, 75–77. (Hong Kong: Hong Kong Urban Council, 1996).

27. List of Hong Kong Cinema Retrospective Catalogues:

1978   *Cantonese Cinema Retrospective (1950–1959)*.

1979   *Hong Kong Cinema Survey (1946–1968)*.

1980   *A Study of the Hong Kong Martial Arts Film*.

1981   *A Study of the Hong Kong Swordplay Film (1945–1980)*.

1982   *Cantonese Cinema Retrospective (1960–1969)*, rev. ed., 1996.

1983   *A Comparative Study of Postwar Mandarin and Cantonese Cinema: The Film of Zhu Shilin, Qin Jian, and Other Directors*.

1984   *A Study of Hong Kong Cinema in the Seventies (1970–1979)*.

1985   *The Traditions of Hong Kong Comedy*.

1986   *Cantonese Melodrama (1950–1969)*.

1987   *Cantonese Opera Film Retrospective*, rev. ed., 1996.

1988   *Changes in Hong Kong Society Through Cinema.*

1989   *Phantoms of the Hong Kong Cinema.*

1990   *The China Factor in Hong Kong Cinema.*

1991   *Hong Kong Cinema in the Eighties.*

1992   *Overseas Chinese Figures in Cinema.*

1993   *Mandarin Films and Popular Songs: 40's to 60's.*

1994   *Cinema of Two Cities: Hong Kong—Shanghai.*

1995   *Early Images of Hong Kong and China.*

1996   *The Restless Creed: Cantonese Stars of the Sixties.*

1997   *Fifty Years of Electric Shadows.*

1998   *Transcending the Times: King Hu and Eileen Chang.*

1999   *Hong Kong New Wave: Twenty Years After.*

2000   *Border Crossings in Hong Kong Cinema.*

28. Frank Bren, "A Century of Chinese Cinema: The 25th Hong Kong International Film Festival And Beyond," *Senses of Cinema*, April 6–21, 2001, http://www.sensesofcinema.com/contents/festivals/01/14/hongkonged.html (accessed June 5, 2008).

29. Ibid.

30. Bordwell, *Planet Hong Kong,* 4

31. Jeff Reichert, "On the Move: An Interview with Olivier Assayas," in *Reverse Shot,* no. 21 (2007), http://www.reverseshot.com/article/interview_olivier_assayas (accessed June 4, 2008).

32. Serge Daney, ed., *Cahiers du cinéma,* número speciale, *Made in Hong Kong,* no. 362–363 (September 1984): 1.

33. Ibid.

34. Ibid., 8, 42, 64, 74, 94, 118.

35. McDonogh and Wong, *Global Hong Kong;* Tsang, *A Modern History of Hong Kong.*

36. Chris Berry, "Translator Note," in *Memoirs from the Beijing Film Academy: Genesis of China's Fifth Generation,* by Ni Zhen, vii–viii (Durham: Duke Univ. Press, 2002).

37. Edward Gargan, "A Chinese Studio Becomes a Haven for Innovators," *New York Times,* December 27, 1987.

38. Hong Kong Urban Council, *20th Anniversary of the Hong Kong International Film Festival* (Hong Kong: Hong Kong Urban Council, 1996), 27.

39. "Absent Friends," *The Economist,* April 25, 1992, 101.

40. "Extraordinary Event," *Ta Kung Pao,* short commentary, April 3 1992.

41. "Chinese Crackers: Hong Kong Film Festival," *The Economist,* April 9, 1994, 95–95.

42. Marie Cambon, "Hong Kong Worries over Film Festival Flap," *Asian Wall Street Journal,* April 4, 1994.

43. Edward Gargan, "China Cultural Crackdown," *New York Times,* July 12, 1987.

44. "Beijing Gives Reasons for Withdrawing Hong Kong Film Festival Entries," BBC Summary of World Broadcast, April 4, 1994.

45. Ibid.

46. Ibid.

47. "Red Lined," *The Economist*, April 22, 1995, 89.

48. Rhonda Lam Wan, "Festival's Film Snub to Beijing," *South China Morning Post*, November 25, 1995.

49. "Under the Gun," *The Economist*, April 13, 1996, 80.

50. Quinton Chan, "China Films Recall 'Threat' to the Arts," *South China Morning Post* March 26, 1996.

51. Fionnuala Halligan, "Cinematic Celebration Cloaked in Uncertainty," *South China Morning Post*, March 2, 1997.

52. Wong and McDonogh, "Consuming Cinema."

53. Turner and Ngan, *Hong Kong 60s/90s*.

54. Mike Archibald, "An Interview with Tony Rayns," *Offscreen* 11, no. 1 (January 31, 2007), http://www.offscreen.com/biblio/phile/essays/tony_rayns/P1/.

55. Putonghua and Mandarin are the same language; it is called Potonghua in the PRC and Mandarin/Guoyu in Taiwan.

56. Erik Davis, "Berlinale Review: Lost in Beijing," *Moviefone*, February 18, 2007, http://blog.moviefone.com/2007/02/18/berlinale-review-lost-in-beijing   (accessed January 10, 2011).

57. Jonathan Landreth, "Producer: 'Beijing' to Open HK Fest," *Hollywood Reporter*, February 8, 2007, http://www.allbusiness.com/services/motion-pictures/4769137-1.html (accessed June 17, 2008).

58. Joel Martinsen, "Lost in Beijing Finally Gets Killed," http://www.danwei.org/media_regulation/lost_in_beijing_finally_gets_k.php (accessed June 17, 2008).

59. "Hong Kong Film Fest Entries Stir Up Controversy," *CBS News*, March 27, 2008, http://www.lexisnexis.com.

60. Ironically, festival films, including Chinese films, shown in the Shanghai International Festival do not need to go through the Chinese censor. Yet the Shanghai festival, for many years, did not screen many local films.

61. "Hong Kong Film Fest Entries Stir Up Controversy."

62. "The Other Kurasawa," *The Economist*, April 24, 1999, 83–84.

63. Lisa Roosen-Runge, "The 25th Hong Kong International Film Festival," *Senses of Cinema* (June 2001), http://archive.sensesofcinema.com/contents/festivals/01/14/hkiff_report_lisa.html (accessed June 10, 2008).

64. Personal interview with Peter Tsi, June 5, 2007. See Cheung, "Corporatising a Film Festival."

65. Hong Kong Arts Development Council, "HKIFF to Form New Company," press release, September 7, 2002, http://www.hkadc.org.hk/en/infocentre/press/press_20020907 (accessed June 16, 2008).

66. Personal interview with Peter Tsi, June 5, 2007.

67. Hong Kong Arts Development Council, "The 26th Hong Kong International Film Festival," press release, February 28, 2002, http://www.hkadc.org.hk/en/infocentre/press/press_20020228 (accessed June 11, 2008).

68. SARS stands for Severe Acute Respiratory Syndrome. In 2003, the virus killed 299 people in Hong Kong in less than half a year. For further information, read McDonogh and Wong, Global Hong Kong, 2–6.

69. Michaela Boland, "Australia Launches Pan-Asian Film Awards," Variety, April 18, 2007, http://www.varietyasiaonline.com/content/view/1195/53/ (accessed June 26, 2008).

70. Ibid.

71. Jacob Hing-Cheung Wong, "Our Cinema, Our Times, 23 Days of Torture and Rebirth," Ming Pao, April 15, 2007, 23, http://ol.mingpao.com/cfm/Archive1.cfm?File=20070415/sta13/vzk3.txt (accessed June 16, 2008).

72. The filmmaker himself describes Autohystoria as a collection of digitalized memories of both reality and dreams (from http://www.filmfestivalrotterdam.com/en/films/autohystoria/ [accessed June 20, 2008]).

73. Jacob Hing-Cheung Wong, "Our Cinema, Our Times, 23 Days of Torture and Rebirth," Ming Pao, April 15, 2007, http://ol.mingpao.com/cfm/Archive1.cfm?File=20070415/sta13/vzk3.txt (accessed June 16, 2008), author's translation from Chinese.

74. Li Cheuk To, "Our Cinema, Our Time: An Open and Diversified Festival," Ming Pao, April 8, 2007, http://ol.mingpao.com/cfm/Archive1.cfm?File=20070408/sta13/vzm1h.txt (accessed June 20, 2008).

75. Ibid., author's translation from Chinese.

CONCLUSION

1. Scott Roxborough, "Movienet Takes 'Uncle Boonmee' for Germany," Hollywood Reporter, June 9, 2010, http://www.hollywoodreporter.com/hr/content_display/asia/news/e3i773194c18528fcf7e4639c91b75db5c9 (accessed June 15, 2010).

2. Mike Hale, "Festival Moves to Fancier Base but Keeps Its Genre-Bending Fare," New York Times, June 4, 2010, C6.

3. Nick Roddick, "Coming to a Server Near You: The Film Festival in the Age of Digital Reproduction," in Film Festival Yearbook 1: The Festival Circuit, ed. Dina Iordanova with Ragan Rhyne, 160 (St. Andrews: St. Andrews Film Studies, 2009).

4. See "Part 2 Festival Case Studies," in *Film Festival Yearbook 1: The Festival Circuit*, ed. Dina Iordanova with Ragan Rhyne, eds., 49–154 (St. Andrews: St. Andrews Film Studies, 2009).

5. Ferdinand de Saussure, *Course in General Linguisics*, ed. Charles Bally and Albert Sechehaye, trans. Roy Harris (Lasalle, Ill.: Open Court, 1983).

6. Nancy Tartaglione-Violatte, "Without the Auteurs There Wouldn't Be a Festival," *Screen International*, May 18, 2007, http://www.screendaily.com/without-the-auteurs-there-wouldnt-be-a-festival/4032535.article.

7. Roddick, "Coming to a Server Near You," 166.

8. Caroline Marvin, *When Old Technologies Were New: Thinking about Electric Communication in the Late Nineteenth Century* (New York: Oxford Univ. Press, 1990).

9. Gary McDonogh and Cindy Wong, "The Mediated Metropolis: Anthropological Issues in Cities and Mass Communication," *American Anthropologist* 103, no. 1 (March 2001): 96–111.

10. Noël Burch, *To the Distant Observer: Form and Meaning in the Japanese Cinema* (Berkeley: Univ. of California Press, 1979).

11. Derek Elley, "Director Envisions Next Millennium of Fest," *Variety Special Supplement, Cannes at 50*, March 24–30, 1997, 6.

Bibliography

Aaron, Michele. *New Queer Cinema: A Critical Reader.* New Brunswick: Rutgers Univ. Press, 2004.

Abdollahzadeh, Medhi. "Fajr Film Festival's 30-Year Span since the Islamic Revolution: A Look at the Roots of the Festival Boycott." *Gozaar,* February 16, 2010, http://www .gozaar.org/template1.php?id=1438&language=english (accessed March 13, 2010).

Abel, Richard. *The Ciné Goes to Town: French Cinema, 1896–1914.* Berkeley: Univ. of California Press, 1994.

———. *French Cinema: The First Wave, 1915–1929.* Princeton: Princeton Univ. Press, 1984.

———. "The Perils of Pathé, or the Americanization of the American Cinema." In *Cinema and the Invention of Modern Life,* edited by Leo Charney and Vanessa Schwartz, 183–225. Berkeley: Univ. of California Press. 1995.

———, ed. *Silent Film.* New Brunswick: Rutgers Univ. Press, 1996.

"Absent Friends." *The Economist,* April 25, 1992, 101.

Agence France Presse. "'Growing Sympathy' for Romania Secured Cannes Prize: Director." May 31, 2007, http://www.lexisnexis.com (accessed May 18, 2010).

———. "Iran Bans Kiarostami from Cannes." April 24, 1997.

———. "Iranian Director Panahi Protested Innocence from Jail." May 15, 2010. http://www.lexisnexis.com.

———. "Juliette Binoche: I hope Jafar Panahi will be here next year." May 24, 2010. http://www.lexisnexis.com.

Ahn SooJeong. "The Pusan International Film Festival 1996–2005: South Korean Cinema in Local, Regional, and Global Context." Ph.D. diss, University of Nottingham, 2008. http://etheses.nottingham.ac.uk/archive/00000513/ (accessed October 15, 2008).

Allen, Charles. *Communication Patterns in Hong Kong.* Hong Kong: Chinese Univ. Press, 1978.

Althusser, Louis. "Ideology and Ideological State Apparatuses (Notes towards an Investigation)." In *Mapping Ideology,* edited by Slavoj _i_ek, 100–140. London: Verso, 1994.

Altman, Rick. *Film/Genre.* London: British Film Institute, 1999.

Ambrosioni, Dalmazio. *Locarno: città del cinema i cinquant'anni del festival internazionale del film.* Locarno: Armando Dadò, 1998.

Anderson, Benedict. *Imagined Communities: Reflections on the Origin and Spread of Nationalism*. London: Verso, 1991.

Anderson, John. *Sundancing: Hanging Out and Listening In at America's Most Important Film Festival*. New York: Avon, 2000.

Andrew, Dudley. "Foreword." In *Global Art Cinema: New Theories and Histories*, edited by Rosalind Galt and Karl Schoonover, v–xi. New York: Oxford Univ. Press, 2010.

———. *Mists of Regret: Culture and Sensibility in Classic French Film*. Princeton: Princeton Univ. Press, 1995.

———. "The 'Three Ages' of Cinema Studies and the Age to Come." *PMLA* 115, no. 3 (May 2000): 341–351.

———. *What Cinema Is—Bazin's Quest and Its Charge*. Malden, Mass.: Blackwell, 2010.

Andrew, Jeff. "Abbas Kiarostami: Interview." *Time Out London*. http://www.timeout .com/film/features/show-feature/7995/abbas-kiarostami-interview.html (accessed May 22, 2010).

Andrews, David. "Toward an Inclusive, Exclusive Approach to Art Cinema." In *Global Art Cinema: New Theories and Histories*, edited by Rosalind Galt and Karl Schoonover, 63–74. New York: Oxford Univ. Press, 2010.

Antonioni, Michelangelo. *The Architecture of Vision: Writings and Interviews on Cinema*. Edited by Carlo di Carlo and Giorgio Tinazzi; American edition by Marga Cotinno-Jones. Chicago: Univ. of Chicago Press, 2007.

Archer, Eugene. "Roman Team on an Intellectual 'Adventure.'" *New York Times*, April 2, 1961.

Archibald, Mike. "An Interview with Tony Rayns." *Offscreen* 11, no. 1 (January 31, 2007). http://www.offscreen.com/biblio/phile/essays/tony_rayns/P1/.

Armatage, Kay. "Material Effects: Fashions in Feminist Programming." In *There She Goes: Feminist Filmmaking and Beyond*, edited by Corinn Columpar and Sophie Mayer, 92–104. Detroit: Wayne State Univ. Press, 2009.

———. "Toronto Women and Film International 1973." *Film Festival Yearbook 1: The Festival Circuit*, edited by Dina Iordanova with Ragan Rhyne, 82–98. St. Andrews: St. Andrews Film Studies, 2009.

Arrowsmith, William. *Antonioni: The Poet of Images*. Edited, with an Introduction and Notes by Ted Perry. New York: Oxford Univ. Press, 1995.

Auty, Martyn, and Gillian Hartnoll, eds. *Water Under the Bridge: 25 Years of the London Film Festival*. London: British Film Institute, 1981.

Bachman, Gregg, and Thomas J. Slater, eds. *American Silent Film: Discovering Marginalized Voices*. Carbondale: Southern Illinois Univ. Press, 2002.

Badam, Ramola Talwar. "Censor Board Bans Film on One of India's Worst Religious Riots." *AP Wire*, August 6, 2004. http://www.lexisnexis.com.

Baecque, Antonie de, and Serge Toubiana. *Truffaut: A Biography*. Berkeley: Univ. of California Press, 2000. Originally published in France as *François Truffaut* by Editions Gallimard, 1996.

Bangré, Sambolgo. "African Cinema in the Tempest of Minor Festivals." In *African Experiences in Cinema*, edited by Imruh Bakari and Mbye Cham, 157–161. London: British Film Institute, 1996.

Barnouw, Erik. *Documentary: A History of Non-Fiction Film*. Oxford: Oxford Univ. Press, 1993.

Barrett, Michael, et al. "Queer Film and Video Festival Forum, Take One: Curators Speak Out." *GLQ: A Journal of Lesbian and Gay Studies* 11, no. 4 (2005): 579–603.

Barthes, Roland. *Mythologies*. Paris: Editions du Seuil. 1957.

Bartyzel, Monical. "Girls on Film: The Estrogen-Free Cannes Competition." *Cinematical*, April 19, 2010. http://www.cinematical.com/2010/04/19/girls-on-film-theestrogen-free-cannes-competition.

Bates, Robin. "Audience on the Verge of a Fascist Breakdown: Male Anxieties and Late 1930s French Film." *Cinema Journal* 36, no. 3 (spring 1997): 25–55.

Baumann, Shyon. "Intellectualization and Art World Development: Film in the United States." *American Sociological Review* 66, no. 3 (June 2001): 404–426.

Bazin, André. "The Festival Viewed as a Religious Order." In *Dekalog 3: On Film Festivals*, edited by Richard Porton, 1–10. London: Wallflower Press, 2009.

———. *What Is Cinema? Essays Selected and Transcribed by Hugh Gray*. Berkeley: Univ. of California Press, 2005.

Beauchamp, Cari, and Henri Béhar. *Hollywood on the Riviera*. New York: William Morrow, 1992.

Becker, Howard. *Art Worlds*. Berkeley: Univ. of California Press, 1982.

"Beijing Gives Reasons for Withdrawing Hong Kong Film Festival Entries." BBC Summary of World Broadcast, April 4, 1994.

Benjamin, Walter. "The Work of Art in an Age of Mechanical Reproduction." In *Art in Modern Culture: An Anthology of Critical Texts*, edited by Francis Frascina and Jonathan Harris, 297–308. New York: HarperCollins, 1992. Originally published as "Das Kunstwerk im Zeitalter seiner technischen Reproduzierbarkeit," 1935.

Benshoff, Harry, and Sean Griffin. *Queer Images*. Lanham, Md.: Rowman and Littlefield, 2006.

Berra, John. "DVD Review Syndromes and a Century." *Film International* 8, no. 1 (2010): 73–74.

Berry, Chris. "*East Palace, West Palace*: Staging Gay Life in China." *Jump Cut*, no. 42 (December 1998): 84–89.

———. "From National Cinema to Cinema and the National Chinese-Language Cinema and Hou Hsiao-hsien's 'Taiwan Trilogy.'" In *Theorising National Cinema,* edited by Valentina Vitali and Paul Willemen, 148–157. London: British Film Institute, 2006.

———. "Introducing 'Mr. Monster': Kim Ki-young and the Critical Economy of the Globalized Art-House Cinema." In *Post-Colonial Classics of Korean Cinema,* edited by C. Choi, 39–47. Irvine, Calif.: Korean Film Festival Committee at University of California, 1998.

———, ed. *Perspectives on Chinese Cinema.* London: British Film Institute, 1991.

———. "Translator Note." In *Memoirs from the Beijing Film Academy: Genesis of China's Fifth Generation,* by Ni Zhen, vii–viii. Durham: Duke Univ. Press, 2002.

Bertelli, Gian Carlo, et al., eds. *Festival internazionale del film Locarno 40 ans: chronique et filmographie.* Locarno: Festival internazionale del film dé Locarno, 1987.

Betz, Mark. *Beyond the Subtitle: Remapping European Art Cinema.* Minneapolis: Univ. of Minnesota Press, 2009.

Biskind, Peter. *Down and Dirty Pictures: Miramax, Sundance, and the Rise of Independent Film.* New York: Simon and Schuster, 2004.

Blüthner, Bodo, et al. "The Oberhausen Manifesto" (1962), in *German Essays on Film,* edited by Richard McCormick and Alison Guenther-Pal. New York: Continuum, 2004.

Boland, Michaela. "Australia Launches Pan-Asian Film Awards." *Variety,* April 18, 2007. http://www.varietyasiaonline.com/content/view/1195/53/ (accessed June 26, 2008).

Bordwell, David. "The Art Cinema as a Mode of Film Practice." *Film Criticism* 4, no. 1 (fall 1979): 56–64.

———. *Planet Hong Kong: Popular Cinema and the Art of Entertainment.* Cambridge: Harvard Univ. Press, 2000.

———. *Poetics of Cinema.* London: Routledge, 2008.

———. *The Way Hollywood Tells It: Story and Style in Modern Movies.* Berkeley: Univ. of California Press, 2006.

Bowser, Pearl, Jane Gaines, and Charles Musser, eds. and curators. *Oscar Micheaux and His Circle: African-American Filmmaking and Race Cinema of the Silent Era.* Bloomington: Indiana Univ. Press, 2001.

Bourdieu, Pierre. *Distinction.* Cambridge: Harvard Univ. Press, 1984.

———. *The Field of Cultural Production.* Edited by R. Johnson. New York: Columbia Univ. Press, 1993.

———. *The Rules of Art: Genesis and Structure of the Literary Field.* Cambridge: Polity Press, 1996.

Bren, Frank. "A Century of Chinese Cinema: The 25th Hong Kong International Film Festival. And Beyond." *Senses of Cinema*, April 6–21, 2001. http://www.sensesofcinema .com/contents/festivals/01/14/hongkonged.html (accessed June 5, 2008).

Brooker, Will, ed. *The Audience Studies Reader*. New York: Routledge, 2002.

Brooks, Xan. "Film-Maker Jafar Panahi Arrested in Iran." *Guardian*, March 2, 2010. http://www.guardian.co.uk/film/2010/mar/02/jafar-panahi-arrested-in-iran (accessed March 2, 2010).

Brown, Goeff. "Sometimes, We Get It Right: Locarno Film Festival." *The Times* (London), August 21, 1989.

Brown, Mark. "Hundreds Protest as 'Anti-French' as Outside the Law was Screened." *Guardian*, May 21, 2010. http://www.guardian.co.uk/film/2010/may/21/rachid-bouchareb-outside-the-law-protests.

Brunette, Peter. *The Films of Michelangelo Antonioni*. Cambridge: Cambridge Univ. Press, 1998.

Budd, Michael. "Authorship as a Commodity: The Art Cinema and *The Cabinet of Dr Caligari*." In *Auteurs and Authorship: A Film Reader*, edited by Barry Keith Grant, 249–254. Oxford: Blackwell, 2008.

———, ed. *The Cabinet of Dr. Caligari: Texts, Contexts, Histories*. New Brunswick: Rutgers Univ. Press, 1990.

Burch, Noël. *The Silent Revolution Volume 2—She! Denmark (1902–1914)*. 2000.

———. *To the Distant Observer: Form and Meaning in the Japanese Cinema*. Berkeley: Univ. of California Press, 1979.

Calhoun, Craig, ed. *Habermas and the Public Sphere*. Cambridge: MIT Press, 1992.

Cambon, Marie. "Hong Kong Worries over Film Festival Flap." *Asian Wall Street Journal*, April 4, 1994.

Canova, Gianni. "New Film Movements and New Departures." The Nineties and the Third Millennium, Festival History, Film Festival Locarno. http://www.pardo.ch/jahia/Jahia/home/Festival/History/The-90s-and-the-third-Millenium/lang/en.

Castells, Manuel. *The Rise of the Network Society*. Oxford: Blackwell, 1996.

Celli, Carlo, and Marca Cottino-Jones. *A New Guide to Italian Cinema*. New York: Palgrave Macmillan, 2007.

Chan, Quinton. "China Films Recall 'Threat' to the Arts." *South China Morning Post*, March 26, 1996.

Charney, Leo, and Vanessar R. Schwartz, eds. *Cinema and the Invention of Modern Life*. Berkeley: Univ. of California Press, 1995.

Chatman, Seymour. *Michelangelo Antonioni: The Investigation, 1912–2007*. Koln: Taschen, 2008.

Chen Kuan-Hsing. "Taiwan New Cinema, or a Global Nativism?" In *Theorising National Cinema*, ed. Valentina Vitali and Paul Willemen, 138–147. London: British Film Institute, 2006.

Chen, Tina Mai. "International Film Circuits and Global Imaginaries in the People's Republic of China, 1949–57." *Journal of Chinese Cinemas* 3, no. 2 (June 2009), 149–161.

Cheung, Ruby. "Corporatising a Film Festival: Hong Kong." In *Film Festival Yearbook 1: The Festival Circuit*, edited by Dina Iordanova with Ragan Rhyne, 99–116. St. Andrews: St. Andrews Film Studies, 2009.

———. "Funding Models of Themed Film Festivals." In *Film Festival Yearbook 2: Film Festivals and Imagined Communities*, edited by Dina Iordanova and Ruby Cheung, 74–106. St. Andrews: St. Andrews Film Studies, 2010.

Chin, Faryl, and Larry Qualls. "Try to Remember: Cinematic Year in Review 2002." *A Journal of Performance and Art* 25, no. 2 (May 2003): 48–64.

"Chinese Crackers: Hong Kong Film Festival." *The Economist*, April 9, 1994, 95.

Cohn, Lawrence. "Scorsese Leads Tribute to Filmmaker Antonioni." *Daily Variety*, October 20, 1992. http://www.lexisnexis.com (accessed May 15, 2010).

Cook, David. "'We're in the Money!' A Brief History of Market Power Concentration and Risk Aversion in the American Film Industry from the Edison Trust to the Rise of the Transnational Media Conglomerates." In *Theorising National Cinema*, edited by Valentina Vitali and Paul Willemen, 158–171. London: British Film Institute, 2006.

Corless, Kieron, and Chris Darke. *Cannes: Inside the World's Premier Film Festival*. London: Faber and Faber 2007.

Corliss, Richard, and Mary Corliss. "Haneke's *The White Ribbon* Wins Cannes Palme d'Or." *Time*, May 24, 2009. http://www.time.com/time/arts/article/0,8599,1900754,00.html (accessed July 15, 2009).

Cosandey, Roland, et al., eds. *Chronique et filmographie*. Locarno: Festival internazionale del film di Locarno, 1988–1997.

Cottino-Jones, Marga, ed. *Michelangelo Antonioni: The Architecture of Vision: Writings and Interviews on Cinema*. Chicago: Univ. of Chicago Press, 1996.

Cowie, Peter. "Memories of Late-but-Not-Always-Lamented Fests." In *The Variety Guide to Film Festivals: The Ultimate Insider's Guide to Film Festivals around the World*, edited by Steven Gaydos. New York: Berkley, 1998.

Crowther, Bosley. "Italian Film Wins Cannes Top Prize." *New York Times*, May 21, 1960.

———. "Screen: 'L'Avventura.'" *New York Times*, April 5, 1961.

———. "WAY-OUT FILMS: 'L'Avventura' Is a Case Of Going Too Far, WAY OUT FILMS 'L'Avventura' Contras With British Drama," *New York Times*, April 9, 1961, X1.

Czach, Liz. "Film Festivals, Programming, and the Building of a National Cinema." *Moving Image* 4, no. 1 (2004): 76–88.

Dabashi, Hamid. *Close Up: Iranian Cinema, Past, Present and Future.* London, New York: Verso, 2001.

Dai Qing. "Raise Eyebrows for *Raise the Red Lantern.*" *Public Culture* 5 (1993): 333–336.

Daney, Serge, ed. *Cahiers du cinéma.* Número speciale: *Made in Hong Kong,* no. 362–363 (September 1984).

———. "Journal de Hong-Kong." *Cahiers du cinéma,* no. 320 (1981): 26–42.

Dargis, Manohla. "In Films at Cannes, Rumblings of Real and Often Devastating Events." *New York Times,* May 21, 2010, C1.

———. "In the Big Picture, Big Screen Hopes." *New York Times,* December 18, 2008.

Davis, Darrell William. "Reigniting Japanese Tradition with Hana-Bi." *Cinema Journal* 40, no. 4 (summer 2001): 55–80.

Davis, Erik. "Berlinale Review: Lost in Beijing." *Moviefone,* February 18, 2007. http://blog .moviefone.com/2007/02/18/berlinale-review-lost-in-beijing. Accessed Jan 10, 2011.

Dayan, Daniel. "Looking for Sundance: The Social Construction of a Film Festival." In *Moving Images, Culture, and the Mind,* edited by Ib Bondebjerg, 43–52. Luton: Univ. of Luton Press, 2003.

Deleau, Pierre-Henri. *La Quinzaine des réalisateurs à Cannes: Cinéma en liberté: 1969–1993.* Paris: Editions de La Martinière, 1993.

De Valck, Marijke. *Film Festivals: From European Geopolitics to Global Cinephilia.* Amsterdam: Amsterdam Univ. Press, 2007.

De Valck, Marijke, and Malte Hagener. *Cinephilia: Movies, Love and Memory* (Film Culture in Transition). Amsterdam: Amsterdam Univ. Press, 2005.

Donald, James, Anne Friedberg, and Laura Marcus, eds. *Close Up, 1927–1933: Cinema and Modernism.* London: Cassell, 1998.

Dovey, Lindiwe. "Director's Cut: In Defense of African Film Festivals Outside Africa." In *Film Festival Yearbook 2: Film Festivals and Imagined Communities,* edited by Dina Iordanova and Ruby Cheung, 45–73. St. Andrews: St. Andrews Film Studies, 2010.

Duckworth, A. R. "Michelangelo Antonioni's Cannes Statement for L'Avventura (1960)." *The Motley View* (October 15, 2009). http://ardfilmjournal.wordpress.com/2009/10/15/michelangelo-antonionis-cannes-statement-for-lavventura-1960/.

Dudley, Andrew. "Waves of New Waves and the International Film Festival." *Asia/Cinema/Network: Industries, Technology and Film Culture. The 20th Pusan International Film Festival Symposium Programme Booklet.* Pusan: 10th PIFF, 2005. 225–265.

Dupont, Joan. "Abbas Kiarostami: Parables, Not Protests; 50th Cannes Festival." *International Herald Tribune,* May 20, 1997.

Dwyer, Michael. "Cannes Jury Gives Its Heart to Works of Graphic Darkness." *Irish Times,* May 25, 2009. http://www.irishtimes.com/newspaper/world/2009/0525/1224247325203.html?digest=1 (accessed September 26, 2009).

Ebert, Roger. "The Leopard." *This Great Movie Review*, September 14, 2003. http://rogerebert.suntimes.com/apps/pbcs.dll/article?AID=%2F20030914%2FREVIEWS08%2F309140302%2F1023&AID1=&AID2=%2F20030914%2FREVIEWS08%2F309140302%2F1023 (accessed May 15, 2010).

———. *Two Weeks in the Midday Sun: A Cannes Notebook*. Kansas City: Andrews and McMeel, 1989.

Elena, Alberto. *The Cinema of Abbas Kiarostami*. London: Saqi, in Association with the Iran Heritage Foundation, 2005.

Elizondo, Jon, et al., eds. *56 Festival Catalog de San Sebastián/Donostia Zinemaldia*. San Sebastián: Donostia-San Sebastián Festival Internationale de Cine de Donostia-San Sebastián, 2008.

Elley, Derek. "Auteurs Today: To Do Is to Be." *Variety*, May 6–12, 1996.

———. "Director Envisions Next Millennium of Fest." *Variety Special Supplement, Cannes at 50*. March 24–30, 1997.

———. "Eden Is West." *Variety*, February 16, 2009. http://variety.com/review/VE1117939680.html?categoryid=31&cs=1. Accessed February 8, 2010.

———. "Fest Helmer's Focus, Projecting into the Next Millennium." In *Cannes, Fifty Years of Sun, Sex, and Celluloid: Behind the Scenes at the World's Most Famous Film Festival*, edited by Peter Bart and the editors of *Variety*, 95–96. New York: Hyperion, 1997.

Elsaesser, Thomas. *The BFI Companion to German Cinema*. London: British Film Institute, 1999.

———. *European Cinema: Face to Face with Hollywood*. Amsterdam: Amsterdam Univ. Press, 2005.

———. *Weimar Cinema and After: Germany's Historical Imaginary*. London: Routledge, 2000.

Engstrom, Shane. "A (Brief) History of the Connecticut Gay and Lesbian Film Festival." http://www.ctglff.org/history.htm (accessed February 9, 2010).

Erickson, Steve. "Taste of Cherry by Abbas Kiarostami." *Film Quarterly* 52, no. 3 (spring 1999): 52–54.

Ethis, Emmanuel, ed. *Au Marches du Palais: Le festival de Cannes sous le regard des sciences sociales*. Paris: Documentation Française, 2004.

Evans, Owen. "Border Exchanges: The Role of the European Film Festival." *Journal of Contemporary European Studies* 15, no. 1 (2007): 23–33.

"Extraordinary Event." *Ta Kung Pao*. Short commentary, Hong Kong, April 3, 1992.

Fanon, Frantz. *The Wretched of the Earth*. New York, Grove Press, 1961.

Farahmand, Azadeh. "At the Crossroads: International Film Festivals and the Constitution of the New Iranian Cinema." Ph.D. diss., University of California,

Los Angeles, 2006. http://proquest.umi.com/pqdweb?did=1317311961&sid=1&Fmt=2&clientId=79356&RQT=309&VName=PQD (accessed January 8, 2009).

———. "Disentangling the International Festival Circuit: Genre and Iranian Cinema." In *Global Art Cinema*, edited by Rosalind Galt and Karl Schoonover, 263–284. New York: Oxford Univ. Press, 2010.

———. "Perspectives in Recent (International Acclaim for) Iranian Cinema." In *The New Iranian Cinema Politics, Representation and Identity*, edited by Richard Tapper, 93–95. London: I. B. Tauris, 2002.

Farmer, Brett. "Apichatpong Weerasethakul, Transnational Poet of the New Thai Cinema: Blissfully Yours." *Senses of Cinema* 38 (January–March 2006): www.sensesofcinema.com/2006/cteq/blissfully_yours/.

Farzeneh, Kayzan. "Iran's Home Movies." *Foreign Policy*, April 20, 2010. http://www.foreignpolicy.com/articles/2010/04/20/interview_bahman_ghobadi (accessed January 25, 2011).

Fehrenbach, Heide. *Cinema in Democratizing Germany: Reconstructing National Identity After Hilter*. Chapel Hill: Univ. of North Carolina Press, 1995.

Fipresci. "Karlovy Vary 2008." Festival Report. http://www.fipresci.org/festivals/archive/2008/karlovy_vary/kvvary_08_ndx.htm (accessed October 11, 2008).

Florida, Richard. *Cities and the Creative Class*. New York: Routledge, 2004.

Follain, John. "Cannes Rewards Film Victims." *The Australian*, May 20, 1997.

Ford, Hamish. "Antonioni's L'avventura and Deleuza's Time-Image." *Senses of Cinema* 28 (June 2003). http://archive.sensesofcinema.com/contents/03/28/1_avventura_deleuze.html (accessed April 28, 2010).

Fraser, Nancy. "Politics, Culture, and the Public Sphere: Toward a Postmodern Conception." In *Social Postmodernism: Beyond Identity Politics*, edited by Linda Nicholson and Steven Seidman, 287–231. New York: Cambridge Univ. Press, 1995.

———. "Rethinking the Public Sphere: A Contribution to the Critique of Actually Existing Democracy" *Social Text*, no. 25/26 (1990): 56–80.

———. *Scales of Justice: Reimagining Political Space in a Globalizing World*. New York: Columbia Univ. Press, 2009.

———. "Transnationalizing the Public Sphere." In *Globalizing Critical Theory*, edited by Max Pensky, 46–61. Lanham, Md.: Rowman and Littlefield, 2005.

Frater, Patrick. "Autumn Film Festivals: Big Changes Require New Survival Techniques." *Variety*, August 24, 2007.

Frater, Patrick, and Marcus Lim. "Asian Film Market Ends with a Whimper." *Variety*, October 7, 2008. http://www.variety.com/index.asp?layout=festivals&jump=pusan&query=asian+film+market+ends+with+a+whimper (accessed Oct 22, 2010).

Frosch, Jon. "Eclectic Cannes Line Up Mixes Veterans and New Blood." http://www
.france24.com/en/20100415–eclectic-globe-spanning-cannes-festival-line-up-mixes-
veterans-new-blood-cinema (accessed April 29, 2010).

Fu, Poshek. *Between Shanghai and Hong Kong: The Politics of Chinese Cinemas*. Stanford,
Calif.: Stanford Univ. Press, 2003.

Fusion Conference. *Ignite the Fuse: Queer People of Color in Film, TV, and Video*. 2007.
http://www.outfest.org/fusion/itf2008.html (accessed May 1, 2009).

Galt, Rosalind, and Karl Schoonover, eds. *Global Art Cinema: New Theories and Histories*.
New York: Oxford Univ. Press, 2010.

Gamson, Joshua. "The Organizational Shaping of Collective Identity: The Case of
Lesbian and Gay Film Festivals in New York." *Sociological Forum* 11, no. 2 (June 1996):
231–261.

Garcia, Roger, ed. *Out of the Shadows: Asians in American Cinema*. Festival Internazionale
del Film Locarno. Milan: Olivares, 2001.

Gargan, Edward. "China Cultural Crackdown." *New York Times*, July 12, 1987.

———. "A Chinese Studio Becomes a Haven for Innovators." *New York Times*,
December 27, 1987.

Gaydos, Steven, ed. *The Variety Guide to Film Festivals: The Ultimate Insider's Guide to Film
Festivals around the World*. A Variety Book. New York: Berkley, 1998.

Germain, David. "Ken Loach Goes to War with Route Irish." Associated Press, May 21,
2010. www.azcentral.com/thingstodo/movies/articles/2010/05/21/20100521ken-loach-
goes-war-cannes-drama-route-irish.html.

Gerow, Aaron. *Visions of Japanese Modernity: Articulations of Cinema, Nation, and
Spectatorship, 1895–1925*. Berkeley: Univ. of California Press, 2010.

Gerstner, David, and Janet Staiger. *Authorship and Film*. New York: Routledge, 2003.

Gillespie, David. *Russian Film*. New York: Longman, 2003.

Gitten, David. "Venice Film Festival Reviews." *Sunday Telegraph*. September 3, 2007.
http://www.telegraph.co.uk/culture/film/starsandstories/3667676/Venice-Film-
Festival-reviews-Michael-Clayton-In-the-Valley-of-Elah-Its-a-Free-World . . . -and-
Cassandras-Dream.html.

Goldman, William. *Hype and Glory*. New York: Villard Books, 1990.

Grant, Barry Keith. *Auteurs and Authorship: A Film Reader*. Malden, Mass.; Oxford:
Blackwell, 2008.

Grenier, Cynthia. "Reflections on the Parisian Screen Scene." *New York Times*,
November 20, 1960.

Guerín, Frances. *A Culture of Light: Cinema and Technology in 1920s Germany*. Minneapolis:
Univ. of Minnesota Press, 2005.

Guillén, Michael. "Diasporas by the Bay: Two Asian Film Festivals in San Francisco." In *Film Festival Yearbook 2: Film Festivals and Imagined Communities*, edited by Dina Iordanova and Ruby Cheung, 151–170. St. Andrews: St. Andrews Film Studies, 2010.

Gündoğdu, Mustafa. "Film Festivals in the Diaspora: Impetus to the Development of Kurdish Cinema?" In *Film Festival Yearbook 2: Film Festivals and Imagined Communities*, edited by Dina Iordanova and Ruby Cheung, 188–197. St. Andrews: St. Andrews Film Studies, 2010.

Gupta, Dipti, and Janine Marchessault. "Film Festivals as Urban Encounter and Cultural Traffic." In *Urban Enigmas: Montreal, Toronto, and the Problem of Comparing Cities*, edited by Johanne Sloan, 239–254. Montreal: McGill-Queen's Univ. Press, 2007.

Gutman, Amy. "Introduction." In Michael Ignatieff, *Human Rights as Politics and Idolatry*, edited by Amy Gutman. Princeton: Princeton Univ. Press, 2001.

Habermas, Jürgen. *The Structural Transformation of the Public Sphere: An Inquiry into a Category of Bourgeois Society*. Translated by Thomas Burger, with the assistance of Frederick Lawrence. Cambridge: MIT Press, 1989.

Hale, Mike. "Festival Moves to Fancier Base but Keeps Its Genre-Bending Fare." *New York Times*, June 4, 2010, C6.

Halle, Randall. "Offering Tales They Want to Hear: Transnational European Film Funding as Neo-Orientalism." In *Global Art Cinema: New Theories and Histories*, edited by Rosalind Galt and Karl Schoonover, 303–319. New York: Oxford Univ. Press, 2010.

Halligan, Fionnuala. "Cinematic Celebration Cloaked in Uncertainty." *South China Morning Post*, March 2, 1997.

Hamid, Rahul. "From Urban Bohemia to Euro Glamour: The Establishment and Early Years of the New York Film Festival." In *Film Festival Yearbook 1: The Festival Circuit*, edited by Dina Iordanova with Ragan Rhyne, 67–82. St. Andrews: St. Andrews Film Studies, 2009.

Hansen, Miriam. "America, Paris, the Alps: Kracauer (and Benjamin) on Cinema and Modernity." In *Cinema and the Invention of Modern Life*, edited by Leo Charney and Vanessa R. Schwartz, 362–402. Berkeley: Univ. of California Press, 1995.

———. *Babel and Babylon: Spectatorship in American Silent Film*. Cambridge: Harvard Univ. Press, 1991.

———. "Early Cinema, Late Cinema: Transformations of the Public Sphere." In *Viewing Positions: Ways of Seeing Film*, edited by Linda Williams. New Brunswick: Rutgers Univ. Press, 1995.

Harbord, Janet. *Film Cultures*. Thousand Oaks, Calif.: Sage, 2002.

———. "Film Festivals-Time-Event." In *Film Festival Yearbook 1: The Festival Circuit*, edited by Dina Iordanova with Ragan Rhyne, 40–48. St. Andrews: St. Andrews Film Studies, 2009.

Hardy, Forsyth. "The Edinburgh Film Festival." *Hollywood Quarterly* 5, no. 1 (autumn 1950): 33–40.

Hawkins, Robert F. "Active Italians: Antonioni Films a Roman 'Eclipse' Veteran Scenarist Has New Vogue." *Variety*, August 27, 1961.

———. "Focus on an Unimpressive Cannes Film Fete." *New York Times*, May 29, 1960.

Heise, Tatiana, and Andrew Tudor. "Constructing (Film) Art: Bourdieu's Field Model in a Comparative Context." *Cultural Sociology* 1 (2007): 165–187.

Hernandez, Eugene. "SPC v. IFC." *IndieWIRE*. September 8, 2009. http://www .indiewire.com/article/eugene_hernandez_spc_v._ifc/ (accessed April 16, 2010).

Hjort, Mette, and Duncan Petrie, eds. *The Cinema of Small Nations*. Bloomington: Indiana Univ. Press, 2007.

Hoberman, J. "Seeing and Nothingness: A Must-See Retrospective Celebrates the Works of a Modernist Master." *Village Voice*, May 30, 2006. http://www .villagevoice.com/2006–05-30/film/seeing-and-nothingness/ (accessed October 20, 2009).

Holden, Stephen. "12 Days, 132 Films, 38 Countries." *New York Times*, April 15, 2010.

Holloway, Ron. "Cannes Report 2004." *Kinema* (2008). http://www.kinema.uwaterloo .ca/article.php?id=428&feature (accessed May 10, 2010).

———. "Cannes 2005 Report." http://www.kinema.uwaterloo.ca/article.php?id= 267&feature (accessed June 12, 2010).

Homer, Sean. "Retrieving Emir Kusturica's *Underground* as a Critique of Ethnic Nationalism." *Jump Cut*, no. 51 (spring 2009). http://www.ejumpcut.org/archive/ jc51.2009/Kusterica/index.html.

Hong Kong Arts Development Council. "The 26th Hong Kong International Film Festival." Press release, February 28, 2002.

———. "HKIFF to Form New Company." Press release, September 7, 2002.

"Hong Kong Film Fest Entries Stir Up Controversy." *CBS News*, March 27, 2008. http://www.lexisnexis.com.

Hong Kong International Film Festival. *Border Crossings in Hong Kong Cinema*. Hong Kong: HKIFF, 2000.

———. *Cantonese Cinema Retrospective (1950–1959)*. Hong Kong: HKIFF, 1978.

———. *Cantonese Cinema Retrospective (1960–1969)*. Revised edition, 1996. Hong Kong: HKIFF, 1982.

———. *Cantonese Melodrama (1950–1969)*. Hong Kong: HKIFF, 1986.

———. *Cantonese Opera Film Retrospective*, rev. ed. Hong Kong: HKIFF, 1996.

———. *Changes in Hong Kong Society Through Cinema*. Hong Kong: HKIFF, 1988.

———. *The China Factor in Hong Kong Cinema*. Hong Kong: HKIFF, 1990.

———. *Cinema of Two Cities: Hong Kong—Shanghai*. Hong Kong: HKIFF, 1994.

———. *A Comparative Study of Postwar Mandarin and Cantonese Cinema: The Film of Zhu Shilin, Qin Jian, and Other Directors*. Hong Kong: HKIFF, 1983.

———. *Early Images of Hong Kong and China*. Hong Kong: HKIFF, 1995.

———. *Fifty Years of Electric Shadows*. Hong Kong: HKIFF, 1997.

———. *Hong Kong Cinema in the Eighties*. Hong Kong: HKIFF, 1991.

———. *Hong Kong Cinema Survey (1946–1968)*. Hong Kong: HKIFF, 1979.

———. *Hong Kong New Wave: Twenty Years After*. Hong Kong: HKIFF, 1999.

———. *Mandarin Films and Popular Songs: 40's to 60's*. Hong Kong: HKIFF, 1993.

———. *Overseas Chinese Figures in Cinema*. Hong Kong: HKIFF, 1992.

———. *Phantoms of the Hong Kong Cinema*. Hong Kong: HKIFF, 1989.

———. *The Restless Creed: Cantonese Stars of the Sixties*. Hong Kong: HKIFF, 1996.

———. *A Study of Hong Kong Cinema in the Seventies (1970–1979)*. Hong Kong: HKIFF, 1984.

———. *A Study of the Hong Kong Martial Arts Film*. Hong Kong: HKIFF, 1980.

———. *A Study of the Hong Kong Swordplay Film (1945–1980)*. Hong Kong: HKIFF, 1981.

———. *The Traditions of Hong Kong Comedy*. Hong Kong: HKIFF, 1985.

———. *Transcending the Times: King Hu and Eileen Chang*. Hong Kong: HKIFF, 1998.

Hong Kong Report 1955. Hong Kong: Government Printing, 1956.

Hong Kong Urban Council. *20th Anniversary of the Hong Kong International Film Festival*. Hong Kong: Hong Kong Urban Council, 1996.

Hossein Ghazian. "Perspectives on Recent (International Acclaim for) Iranian Cinema." In *The New Iranian Cinema: Politics, Representation and Identity*, edited by Richard Tapper. London: I. B. Tauris, 2002.

Houston, Penelope. "L'Avventura." *Sight and Sound* 30, no. 1 (winter 1960–1961): 11–12.

Hughes, Richard. *Borrowed Place, Borrowed Time*. London: Deutsch, 1968.

Human Rights Film Network. "HRFN Programmers Choose Winners of International Human Rights Film Award 2008." http://www.humanrightsfilmnetwork.org/ index.php?option=com_content&view=category&layout=blog&id=2&Itemid=2 (accessed January 11, 2011).

Human Rights Watch. "About IFF." http://www.hrw.org/en/iff/about (accessed December 8, 2009).

Iordanova, Dina. *Cinema of the Other Europe*. London: Wallflower Press, 2003.

———. "The Film Festival Circuit." In *Film Festival Yearbook 1: The Festival Circuit*, edited by Dina Iordanova with Ragan Rhyne, 23–39. St. Andrews: St. Andrews Film Studies, 2009.

———. "Mediating Diaspora: Film Festivals and 'Imagined Communities.'" In *Film Festival Yearbook 2: Film Festivals and Imagined Communities*, edited by Dina Iordanova and Ruby Cheung, 12–44. St. Andrews: St. Andrews Film Studies, 2010.

———. "Showdown of the Festivals: Clashing Entrepreneurship and Post-Communist Management of Culture." *Film International* 4, no. 23 (October 2006): 25–38.

Iordanova, Dina, and Ruby Cheung, eds. *Film Festival Yearbook 2: Film Festivals and Imagined Communities*. St. Andrews: St. Andrews Film Studies.2010.

Iordanova, Dina, with Ragan Rhyne, eds. *Film Festival Yearbook 1: The Festival Circuit*. St. Andrews: St. Andrews Film Studies, 2009.

Jacobsen, Wolfgang. *50 Years Berlinale*. Berlin: Filmmuseum, 2000.

Jarvie, I. C. *Window on Hong Kong: A Sociological Study of the Hong Kong Film Industry and Its Audience*. Hong Kong: Centre of Asian Studies, Hong Kong University, 1978.

Johnson, Pauline. *Habermas: Rescuing the Public Sphere*. London: Routledge, 2006.

Jones, Arthur. "Shanghai Film Fest Now an Industry Event: Chinese Studios Swell Festivals' Market Launch." *Variety*, June 8, 2007. http://www.variety.com/article/VR1117966536.html?categoryid=2594&cs=1 (accessed July 3, 2008).

Jones, Michael. "Rising Film Festival Stress: Glut of Events Creates High-Stakes Rivalries." *Variety*, December 7, 2007. http://www.variety.com/index.asp?layout=festivals&jump=story&id=1061&articleid=VR1117977355 (accessed July 7, 2008).

Jury, Louise. "Last Stand of Star Wars Expects to Be Box Office Blast." *Independent*, May 16, 2005.

Kan, Wendy. "Fest Adds Sales Event: Hong Kong-Asia Screenings to Feature Networking, Market." *Variety*, April 1, 2002. http://www.variety.com/index.asp?layout=festivals&jump=story&id=1061&articleid=VR1117864685&cs=1&query=film+market (accessed July 3, 2008).

Kaufman, Anthony. "Sundance vs. Rotterdam; Differing Styles Bring Forth New International Cinema." *IndieWIRE*. January 14, 2004. http://www.indiewire.com/article/sundance_vs._rotterdam_differing_styles_bring_forth_new_international_cinem/ (accessed June 22, 2009).

Kaufman, Anthony. "Why the Iranian Filmmakers are in Limbo." *IndieWIRE*, February 9, 2011. http://www.indiewire.com/article/why_the_iranian_filmmakers_are_in_limbo/(accessed February 9, 2011.)

Keating, Patrick. "The Volcano and the Barren Hill: Gabriel Figueroa and the Space of Art Cinema." In *Global Art Cinema: New Theories and Histories*, edited by Rosalind Galt and Karl Schoonover, 201–217. New York: Oxford Univ. Press, 2010.

Keathley, Christian. *Cinephilia and History, or the Wind in the Trees*. Bloomington: Indiana Univ. Press, 2005.

Kelly, Richard. *The Name of this Book Is Dogme95*. London: Faber and Faber, 2000.

Kessler, Frank, and Nanna Verhoeff, eds. *Networks of Entertainment: Early Film Distribution, 1895–1915*. Eastleigh: John Libbey, 2007.

Kidd, James. "How to Put the World to Shame; London." *South China Morning Post*, March 9, 2008. http://www.lexisnexis.com.

Kim Jihoon. "Between Auditorium and Gallery: Perception in Apichatpong Weerasethakul's Films and Installations." In *Global Art Cinema: New Theories and Histories*, edited by Rosalind Galt and Karl Schoonover, 124–139. New York: Oxford Univ. Press, 2010.

Kim Soyoung. "'Cine Mania' or Cinephilia: Film Festivals and the Identity Question." In *New Korean Cinema*, edited by Chi-Yun Shin and Julian Stringer, 79–91. Edinburgh: Edinburgh Univ. Press, 2005.

King, Rob. "Made for the Masses with an Appeal to the Classes: The Triangle Film Corporation and the Failure of Highbrow Film Culture." *Cinema Journal* 44, no. 2 (winter 2005): 3–33.

Klingmann, Anna. *Brandscapes: Architecture in the Experience Economy*. Cambridge: MIT Press, 2007.

Koch, Gertrud. "On Pornographic Cinema: The Body's Shadow Realm." *Jump Cut* 35 (April 1990): 17–29.

Koehler, Robert. "Cinephilia and Film Festivals." In *Dekalog 3: On Film Festivals*, edited by Richard Porton, 81–97. London: Wallflower Press, 2009.

Kohn, Eric. "Tribeca's Image Problem: Wrapping Up the 2010 Fest." *IndieWIRE*, May 3, 2010. http://www.indiewire.com/article/tribecas_image_problem (accessed June 20, 2010).

Kovacs, Andras Balint. *Screening Modernism: European Art Cinema, 1950–1980*. Chicago: Univ. of Chicago Press, 2007.

Kreimeier, Klaus. *The UFA Story: A History of Germany's Greatest Film Company, 1918–1945*. Translated by Robert Kimber and Rita Kimber. Berkeley: Univ. of California Press, 1999.

Kwok Ching Ling. "Interview with Leong Mo-Ling, the Cloud Capped Star." In *20th Anniversary of the Hong Kong International Film Festival*, 53–54. Hong Kong: Hong Kong Urban Council, 1996.

Kwok Ching Ling and Emily Lo. "Interview with Paul Yeung, the Birth of HKIFF." In *20th Anniversary of the Hong Kong International Film Festival*, 33. Hong Kong: Hong Kong Urban Council, 1996.

Kwong, Nina, and Emily Lo. "Interview with Freddie Wong: The 'Fighter.'" In *20th Anniversary of the Hong Kong International Film Festival*, 47–48. Hong Kong: Hong Kong Urban Council, 1996.

———. "Interview with Li Cheuk-Yo: There for the Long Run." In *20th Anniversary of the Hong Kong International Film Festival*, 75–77. Hong Kong: Hong Kong Urban Council, 1996.

Lam Wan, Rhonda. "Festival's Film Snub to Beijing." *South China Morning Post,* November 25, 1995.

Landreth, Jonathan. "Producer: 'Beijing' to Open HK Fest." *Hollywood Reporter,* February 8, 2007. http://www.allbusiness.com/services/motion-pictures/4769137-1.html (accessed June 17, 2008).

Lasica, Tom. "Tarkovsky's Choice." *Sight and Sound* 3, no. 3 (March 1993). http://www.acs.ucalgary.ca/~tstronds/nostalghia.com/TheTopics/Tarkovsky-TopTen.html (accessed June 15, 2009).

Lau, Jenny Kwok Wah. "*Farewell My Concubine:* History, Melodrama, and Ideology in Contemporary Pan-Chinese Cinema." *Film Quarterly* 49, no. 1 (autumn 1995): 16–27.

Lee, Leo. *City between Worlds: My Hong Kong.* Cambridge: Harvard Univ. Press, 2008.

Lemercier, Fabien. "Cannes According to Wild Bunch." http://www.cineuropa.org/interview.aspx?lang = en&documentID = 76775.

Li Cheuk To. "Our Cinema, Our Time: An Open and Diversified Festival." *Ming Pao,* April 8, 2007. http://ol.mingpao.com/cfm/Archive1.cfm?File=20070408/sta13/vzm1h.txt (accessed June 20, 2008).

Lim, Dennis. "Cannes, Lars von Trier Vigorously Defend Antichrist's Genital Mutilation." *New York Magazine,* May 18, 2009. http://nymag.com/daily/entertainment/2009/05/cannes_lars_von_trier_vigorous.html (accessed September 25, 2009).

Loist, Skadi, and Marijke de Valck. "Film Festival/Film Festival Research: Thematic, Annotated Bibliography," 2nd ed.: Film Festival Research Network, 2010. http://www1.uni-hamburg.de/Medien/berichte/arbeiten/0091_08.html (accessed May 25, 2010).

Long, Stacy. "Adobe Youth Voices Featured at Human Rights Watch International Film Festival." *Adobe featured blog.* http://blogs.adobe.com/conversations/2010/06/adobe_youth_voices_featured_at.html (accessed January 11, 2010).

Lopez, Ana M. "Early Cinema and Modernity in Latin America." In *Theorising National Cinema,* edited by Valentina Vitali and Paul Willemen, 209–225. London: British Film Institute, 2006.

Ma Ran. "Rethinking Festival Film: Urban Generation Chinese Cinema on the Festival Circuit." In *Film Festival Yearbook 1: The Festival Circuit,* edited by Dina Iordanova with Ragan Rhyne, 116–135. St. Andrews: St. Andrews Film Studies, 2009.

Maltby, Richard. *Hollywood Cinema.* Malden, Mass.: Blackwell, 2003.

Manceaux, Michèle. "An Interview with Antonioni." *Sight and Sound* 30, no. 1 (winter 1960–1961): 5–8.

Mandelberger, Sandy. "Cinemart: US Indies Come to Rotterdam." www.filmfestivals.com, February 2, 2001. http://www.filmfestivals.com/servlet/JSCRun?obj=

ShowNewsRotterdam&CfgPath=ffs/filinfo&Cfg=news.cfg&news=bizz&text_id= 16371 (accessed June 22, 2009).

Marchetti, Gina, "Chinese Film Criticism." *Jump Cut* 46 (2003). http://www.ejumpcut .org/archive/jc46.2003/marchetti.dai/text.html (accessed October 24, 2008).

Marcus, Laura. *The Tenth Muse: Writing About Cinema in the Modernist Period.* New York: Oxford Univ. Press, 2007.

Marquand, Robert. "Cannes Film Festival's 'Hors la Loi': How Well Does France Face Its Past in Algeria?" *Christian Science Monitor* online, June 1, 2010. http://www .csmonitor.com/World/Europe/2010/0601/Cannes-Film-Festival-s-Hors-la-Loi-Howwell-does-France-face-its-past-in-Algeria.

Martinsen, Joel. "Lost in Beijing Finally Gets Killed." http://www.danwei.org/ media_regulation/lost_in_beijing_finally_gets_k.php (accessed June 17, 2008).

Marvin, Caroline, *When Old Technologies Were New: Thinking about Electric Communication in the Late Nineteenth Century.* New York: Oxford Univ. Press, 1990.

Maslin, Janet. "Iranian Film Makes It Past Censors to Cannes." *New York Times,* May 17, 1997.

McCarthy, Todd. "Cannes-Troversial: China, Iran Playing Hardball with Directors." *Variety,* April 25, 1997.

———. "Iran Relents, Clear 'Cherry.'" *Daily Variety,* May 7, 1997.

McDonogh, Gary, and Cindy Wong. *Global Hong Kong.* London: Routledge, 2005.

———. "The Mediated Metropolis: Anthropological Issues in Cities and Mass Communication." *American Anthropologist* 103, no. 1 (March 2001): 96–111.

McGilligan, Patrick. *Oscar Micheaux, the Great and Only: The Life of America's First Black Filmmaker.* New York: HarperCollins, 2007.

McGreal, Chris. "U.S. Actor Jane Fonda Backs Away from Israel Row at Toronto Film Festival." *The Guardian,* September 16, 2009.

Meckelburg, Rebecca. "Queer Films Banned in Tasmania." *GreenLeft,* March 29, 1995. http://www.greenleft.org.au/node/9594 (accessed May 22, 2010).

MIX NYC: The New York Queer Experimental Film Festival. http://www.nyc-arts.org/organizations/1801/mix-nyc-the-new-york-queer-experimental-film-festival (accessed January 11, 2011).

Moreck, Curt. *Sittengeschichte des Kinos.* Dresden, 1956. www.buchfriend.de/ Sittengeschichte-des-Kinos-Moreck-Curt-eigentl-Kurt-Haemmerling,29064253-buch (accessed July 1, 2010).

Mottram, James. *The Sundance Kids: How the Mavericks Took Back Hollywood.* New York: Faber and Faber, 2006.

Mulvey, Laura. "Kiarostami's Uncertainty Principle." *Sight and Sound* 8, no. 6 (June 1998): 24–27.

Nada, Hisashi. "The Little Cinema Movement in the 1920s and the Introduction of Avant-Garde Cinema in Japan." *ICONICS* 3 (1994): 43.

Naficy, Hamid. *An Accented Cinema*. Princeton: Princeton Univ. Press, 2001.

Neale, Steve. "Art Cinema and the Question of Independent Film." In *The New Social Function of Cinema*, edited by Rod Stoneman. London: British Film Institute, 1981.

————. *Genre*. London: British Film Institute, 1980.

Negt, Oscar, and Alexander Kluge. *Public Sphere and Experience*. Minneapolis: Univ. of Minnesota Press, 1993.

Nelson, Rob. "Certified Copy." *Daily Variety*, May 19, 2010.

Ni Zhen. *Memoirs from the Beijing Film Academy: The Genesis of China's Fifth Generation*. Translated by Chris Berry. Durham: Duke Univ. Press, 2002.

Nichols, Bill. "Discovering Form, Inferring Meaning: New Cinemas and the Film Festival Circuit." *Film Quarterly* 47, no. 3 (spring 1994): 16–30.

————. *Representing Reality: Issues and Concepts in Documentary*. Bloomington: Indiana Univ. Press, 1992.

Nygren, Scott. *Time Frames: Japanese Cinema and the Unfolding of History*. Minneapolis: Univ. of Minnesota Press, 2007.

"The Other Kurasawa." *The Economist*, April 24, 1999, 83–84.

Patwardhan, Anand. "Festival in Contrast." *The Hindu*, Jan 18, 2004. http://www.hinduonnet.com/mag/2004/01/18/stories/2004011800120500.htm (accessed August 12, 2010).

————. "India and Pakistan, Film Festivals in Contrast." www.patwardhan.com, December 23, 2003. http://www.patwardhan.com/writings/press/Fest%20contrast.htm (accessed April 12, 2010).

Pearson, Roberta. *Eloquent Gestures: The Transformation of Performance Style in the Griffith Biograph Films*. Berkeley: Univ. of California Press, 1992.

Peranson, Mark. "First You Get the Power, Then You Get the Money: Two Models of Film Festivals." *Cineaste* 33, no. 3 (2008): 37–43.

Phillips, Richard. "Michelangelo Antonioni—A Flawed Legacy, Part 2." World Socialist Web Site, August 3, 2007. http://www.wsws.org/articles/2007/aug2007/ant2–7a03.shtml (accessed October 20, 2009).

Polan, Dana. "The Beginnings of American Film Study." In *Looking Past the Screen: Case Studies in American Film History and Method*, edited by Jon Lewis and Eric Smoodin, 37–60. Durham: Duke Univ. Press, 2007.

Pond, Steve. "Cannes Wants Americans . . . But Not in Competition." *The Wrap*, April 15, 2010. http://www.thewrap.com/movies/column-post/cannes-wants-americans-not-competition-16343.

Porton, Richard, ed. *Dekalog 3: On Film Festivals*. London: Wallflower Press, 2009.

————. "A Director on the Festival Circuit: An Interview with Atom Egoyan." In *Dekalog 3: On Film Festivals*, edited by Richard Porton, 169–182. London: Wallflower Press, 2009.

Povoledo, Elizabetta. "Critical Cannes Film Angers Italian Official." *New York Times*, May 13, 2010, A6.

Pugh, Carol. "East Block Filmmakers Lack Ideas and Money since Communism Fell." Associated Press, February 9, 1990.

Pulver, Andrew. "Review: Shirin." *Guardian*, August 29, 2008. http://www.guardian.co.uk/film/2008/aug/29/shirin.venicefilmfestival (accessed June 25, 2009).

Quandt, James. "The Sandwich Process: Simon Field Talks about Polemics and Poetry at Film Festivals." In *Dekalog 3: On Film Festivals*, edited by Richard Porton, 53–80. London: Wallflower Press, 2009.

Rastegar, Roya. "The De-Fusion of Good Intentions: Outfest's Fusion Film Festival." *GLQ* 15, no. 3 (May 2009): 481–497.

Rayns, Tony. "Interview." http://www.offscreen.com/biblio/phile/essays/tony_rayns/P1/.

Reader, Keith. *Robert Bresson*. Manchester, UK: Manchester Univ. Press, 2000.

"Red Lined." *The Economist*, April 22, 1995, 89.

Reichert, Jeff. "On the Move: An Interview with Olivier Assayas." *Reverse Shot*, no. 21 (2007). http://www.reverseshot.com/article/interview_olivier_assayas (accessed June 4, 2008).

"Rétrospective Abbas Kiarostami: Cinq courts métrages et sept longs métrages du grand cinéaste Iranien." *Le Monde*, July 25, 1997.

Rhyne, Ragan. "Film Festival Circuits and Stakeholders." In *Film Festival Yearbook 1: The Festival Circuit*, edited by Dina Iordanova with Ragan Rhyne, 9–22. St. Andrews: St. Andrews Film Studies, 2009.

————. "The Global Economy of Gay and Lesbian Film Festivals." *GLQ: A Journal of Lesbian and Gay Studies* 12, no. 4 (2006): 617–619.

Richardson, Michael. *Surrealism and Film*. New York: Berg, 2006.

Rithdee, Kong. "The Sad Case of the Bangkok Film Festival." In *Dekalog 3: On Film Festivals*, edited by Richard Porton, 122–130. London: Wallflower Press, 2009.

Roddick, Nick. "Coming to a Server Near You: The Film Festival in the Age of Digital Reproduction." In *Film Festival Yearbook 1: The Festival Circuit*, edited by Dina Iordanova with Ragan Rhyne, 116–135. St. Andrews: St. Andrews Film Studies, 2009.

Roger, Philippe. *The American Enemy: The History of French Anti-Americanism*. Translated by Sharon Bowman. Chicago: Univ. of Chicago Press, 2005.

Romer, Jean-Claude, and Jeanne Moreau. *Cannes Memories 1939–2002: La grande histoire du Festival*. Montreuil: Media Business and Partners, 2002.

Roof, Maria. "African and Latin American Cinemas: Contexts and Contact." In *Focus on African Films*, edited by Françoise Pfaff, 240–270. Bloomington: Indiana Univ. Press, 2004.

Roosen-Runge, Lisa. "The 25th Hong Kong International Film Festival." *Senses of Cinema* 14 (June 2001). http://www.sensesofcinema.com/contents/festivals/01/14/hkiff_report_lisa.html (accessed June 10, 2008).

Rosen, Philip. "History, Textuality, Nation: Kracauer, Burch, and Some Problems in the Study of National Cinemas." In *Theorising National Cinema*, ed. Valentina Vitali and Paul Willemen, 17–28. London: British Film Institute. 2006.

———. "Notes on Art Cinema and the Emergence of Sub-Saharan Film." In *Global Art Cinema: New Theories and Histories*, edited by Rosalind Galt and Karl Schoonover, 252–263. New York: Oxford Univ. Press, 2010.

Rosenbaum, Jonathan. *Movie Wars: How Hollywood and the Media Limit What Films We Can See*. London: Wallflower Press, 2000.

Ross, Andrew, and Kristin Ross, eds. *Anti-Americanism*. New York: New York Univ. Press, 2004.

Ross, Kristin. *Fast Cars, Clean Bodies: Decolonization and the Reordering of French Culture*. Cambridge: MIT Press, 1995.

Ross, Miriam. "Film Festivals and the Ibero-American Sphere." In *Film Festival Yearbook 2: Film Festivals and Imagined Communities*, edited by Dina Iordanova and Ruby Cheung, 171–187. St. Andrews: St. Andrews Film Studies, 2010.

Ross, Steven. *Working-Class Hollywood: Silent Film and the Shaping of Class in America*. Princeton: Princeton Univ. Press, 1998.

Roud, Richard. "5 Films." *Sight and Sound* 30, no. 1 (winter 1960–1961): 8–11.

———. *A Passion for Films: Henri Langlois and the Cinémathèque Française*. 1983. Reprint, Baltimore: Johns Hopkins Univ. Press, 1999.

Roxborough, Scott. "Movienet Takes 'Uncle Boonmee' for Germany." *Hollywood Reporter*, June 9, 2010. http://www.hollywoodreporter.com/hr/content_display/asia/news/e3i773194c18528fcf7e463 9c91b75db5c9 (accessed June 15, 2010).

Rüling, Charles-Clemens. "Festivals as Filed Configuring Events: The Annecy International Animated Film Festival and Market." In *Film Festival Yearbook 1: The Festival Circuit*, edited by Dina Iordanova with Ragan Rhyne, 49–66. St. Andrews: St. Andrews Film Studies, 2009.

Saeed-Vafa, Mehrnaz, and Jonathan Rosenbaum. *Abbas Kiarostami*. Urbana: Univ. of Illinois Press, 2003.

Sandels, Alexandra, and Ramin Mostaghim. "Iran: Annual Film Festival to Kick Off Amid Opposition Calls for Boycott." *LATimesblogs*, January 2010. http://latimesblogs.latimes.com/babylonbeyond/2010/01/iran-1.html (accessed March 12, 2010).

Sarris, Andrew. "Notes on the Auteur Theory in 1962." In *Auteurs and Authorship: A Film Reader*, edited by Barry Keith Grant, 35–45. Oxford: Blackwell, 2008.

Saussure, Ferdinand de. *Course in General Linguistics*. Edited by Charles Bally and Albert Sechehaye. Translated by Roy Harris. Lasalle, Ill.: Open Court, 1983.

Scheib, Ronnie. "Festival Review, Shirin." *Variety*, August 28, 2008. http://www.variety.com/index.asp?layout=festivals&jump=review&id=2559&reviewid=VE 1117938104 (accessed June 25, 2009).

Schwartz, Vanessa. "The Cannes Film Festival and the Marketing of Cosmopolitanism." In *It's So French! Hollywood, Paris, and the Making of Cosmopolitan Film Culture*, 56–101. Chicago: Univ. of Chicago Press, 2007.

———. "Cinematic Spectatorship before the Apparatus: The Public Taste for Reality in Fin-de-Siècle Paris." In *Cinema and the Invention of Modern Life*, edited by Leo Charney and Vanessa R. Schwartz, 297–319. Berkeley: Univ. of California Press, 1995.

Scott, A. O. "A Film Festival with a Penchant for Making Taste, Not Deals." *New York Times*, September 24, 2010, C4.

———. "Jiggers: Take Out the Dictionary." *New York Times*, June 22, 2010.

———. "New Wave on the Black Sea." *New York Times*, January 20, 2008.

———. "No One Knows about Persian Cats." *New York Times*, April 16, 2010. http://movies.nytimes.com/2010/04/16/movies/16noone.html.

Shea, Daniel. "Small and Mighty: Telluride Has Become the Place for Little Films to Build Big Reputations." *W*, November 2008, 214–215.

Shiel, Mark. *Italian Neorealism: Rebuilding the Cinematic City*. London: Wallflower Press, 2006.

Siclier, Jacques. "Un écolier Iranien: 'Où est la maison de mon ami,' du cinéaste Abbas Kiarostami, est un produit du nouveau cinéma Iranien." *Le Monde*, April 3, 1990.

Slackman, Michael. "Defying Censors and Threats, Iranian Filmmakers Keep Focus on the Turmoil." *New York Times*, January 4, 2010, A4.

Slide, Anthony. *Nitrate Won't Wait: A History of Film Preservation in the United States*. Jefferson, N.C.: McFarland, 1992.

Slocum, J. David. "Film and/as Culture: The Uses of Cultural Discourses at Two African Film Festivals." In *Film Festival Yearbook 1: The Festival Circuit*, edited by Dina Iordanova with Ragan Rhyne, 136–154. St. Andrews: St. Andrews Film Studies, 2009.

Smart, Alan. *The Shep Kip Mei Myth*. Hong Kong: Hong Kong Univ. Press, 2006.

Smith, Lory. *Party in a Box: The Story of the Sundance Film Festival*. Salt Lake City: Gibbs Smith, 1999.

Sorlin, Pierre. *Italian National Cinema 1896–1996*. London: Routledge. 1996.

Spoto, Donald. *The Dark Side of Genius: The Life of Alfred Hitchcock*. London: Da Capo Press. 1999.

Staiger, Janet. *Perverse Spectators*. New York: New York Univ. Press, 2000.

———. "The Politics of Film Canons." *Cinema Journal* 24, no. 3 (spring 1985): 4–23.

Stelter, Brian. "Cablevision Unit Buys Sundance Channel." *New York Times*, May 8, 2008.

Stone, Marla. "The Last Film Festival: The Venice Biennale Goes to War." In *Re-viewing Fascism*, edited by Jacqueline Reich and Piero Garofalo, 293–314. Bloomington: Indiana Univ. Press, 2002.

Stringer, Julian. "Global Cities and the International Film Festival Economy." In *Cinema and the City: Film and Urban Societies in a Global Context*, edited by Mark Shiel and Tony Fitzmaurice, 134–146. Oxford: Blackwell, 2001.

Tartaglione-Violatte, Nancy. "Without the Auteurs There Wouldn't Be a Festival." *Screen International*, May 18, 2007. http://www.screendaily.com/without-the-auteurs-there-wouldnt-be-a-festival/4032535.article.

Teo, Stephen. "Asian Film Festivals and Their Diminishing Glitter Domes: An Appraisal of PIFF, SIFF and HKIFF." In *Dekalog 3: On Film Festivals*, edited by Richard Porton, 109–121. London: Wallflower Press, 2009.

———. *Hong Kong Cinema: The Extra Dimensions*. London: British Film Institute, 1997.

Tesson, Charles, and Marco Mueller. "Calligraphie et simulacres." *Cahiers du cinéma* 362/363 (1984): 20–24.

Thomas, Dana. "Romanian Films: From Ban to Boom." *Washington Post*, September 16, 1990, Sunday Show, G3.

Thomas, Kevin. "*Mala Noche*, Film with Gay Theme Airs on KCET." *LA Times*, June 23, 1989. http://articles.latimes.com/1989–06–23/entertainment/ca-2604_1_ray-monge-walt-curtis-portland-s-skid-row (accessed February 12, 2010).

Thompson, Kristen. "The International Exploration of Cinematic Expressivity." In *The Silent Cinema Reader*, edited by Lee Grieveson and Peter Kramer, 254–270. New York: Routledge, 2004.

Thomson, David. "Berlin's History Steeped in Film." *Variety*, February 14, 2010. http://www.variety.com/article/VR1118014712?RefCatId=3934 (accessed June 20, 2010).

Tobias, Scott. "Iranian Filmmaker Jafar Panahi Arrested (Again)." *A. V. Club*, March 2, 2010. http://www.avclub.com/articles/iranian-filmmaker-jafar-panahi-arrested-again,38716/ (accessed March 2, 2010).

Tran, Tina. "Gays in China: Beijing Queer Film Festival Goes Off without a Hitch." www.HuffingtonPost.com, June 18, 2009. http://www.huffingtonpost.com/2009/06/18/gays-in-china-beijing-que_n_217486.html.

Tsai, Jung-Fang. *Hong Kong in Chinese History*. New York: Columbia Univ. Press, 1993.

Tsang, Steve. *A Modern History of Hong Kong*. London: I. B. Tauris, 2004.

Tudor, A. "The Rise and Fall of the Art (House) Movie." In *The Sociology of Art*, edited by David Inglis and John Hughson, 125–138. New York: Macmillan, 2005.

Turan, Kenneth. *From Sundance to Sarajevo: Film Festivals and the World They Made.* Berkeley: Univ. of California Press, 2003.

———. "Festival Has Many Looks." *LA Times,* March 17, 2006. http://www .chicagotribune.com/topic/env-et-cannes17may172,0,839271.story (accessed July 15, 2008).

Turner, Graeme. *Film as Social Practice,* 4th ed. London: Routledge, 2006.

Turner, Matthew, and Irene Ngan. *Hong Kong 60s/90s: Designing Identity.* Hong Kong: Performing Arts Centre, 1996.

Uncle Boonmee Who Can Recall His Past Lives. Press Release. http://www.festival-cannes .com/assets/Image/Direct/033783.pdf (accessed May 22, 2010).

"Under the Gun." *The Economist,* April 13, 1996, 80.

Vachon, Christine, with David Edelstein. *Shooting to Kill: How an Independent Producer Blasts through Barriers to Make Movies That Matter.* New York: Quill, 1998.

Variety editors. *Cannes, Fifty Years of Sun, Sex and Celluloid: Behind the Scenes at the World's Most Famous Film Festival.* New York: Hyperion, 1997.

Vivarelli, Nick. "Rome Film Festival Budget Slashed: Funds Cut from $24 Million to $15 Million." *Variety,* December 18, 2008. http://www.variety.com/article/VR1117997592 .html?categoryid=1061&cs=1.

Wang Jing and Tani E. Barlow. *Cinema and Desire: Feminist Marxism and Cultural Politics in the Work of Dai Jinhua.* London: Verso, 2002.

Wang Ning. "Orientalism versus Occidentalism?" *New Literary History* 28, no. 1, Cultural Studies: China and the West (winter 1997): 57–67.

Warner, Michael. *Publics and Counterpublics.* New York: Zone Books, 2002.

Wasson, Haidee. *Museum Movies: The Museum of Modern Art and the Birth of Art Cinema.* Berkeley: Univ. of California Press, 2005.

———. "The Woman Film Critic: Newspaper, Cinema, and Iris Barry." *Film History* 18 (2006): 154–162.

Weissberg, Jay. "Report on the 22nd Pordenone Silent Film Festival." *Senses of Cinema.* http://archive.sensesofcinema.com/contents/festivals/03/29/22nd_pordenone .html (accessed April 22, 2010).

Wexman, Virginia Wright. "The Critic as Consumer: Film Study in the University, *Vertigo,* and the Film Canon." *Film Quarterly* 39, no. 3 (spring 1986): 32–41.

———, ed. *Film and Authorship.* New Brunswick: Rutgers Univ. Press, 2003.

White, Patricia, Ruby Rich, Eric Clarke, and Richard Fung. "Queer Publicity: A Dossier on Lesbian and Gay Film Festivals." *GLJ* 5, no. 1 (1999): 73–93.

Wollen, Peter. "An Alphabet of Cinema: 26 Responses to a Self-Interview." *Point of Contact* 5, no. 1 (1997): 5–17.

———. "The Auteur Theory (1969) (excerpt)." In *Auteurs and Authorship: A Film Reader*, edited by Barry Keith Grant, 55–64. Oxford: Blackwell, 2008.

———. *Paris Hollywood: Writings on Film*. London: Verso. 2002.

Wong, Cindy. "Cities, Cultures, and Cassettes: Hong Kong Cinema and Transnational Audiences." *Spectator* 22, no. 1 (2002): 46–64.

———. "Distant Screens: Film Festivals and the Global Projection of HK Cinema." In *Hong Kong Films, Hollywood, and the New Global Cinema*, edited by Gina Marchetti and See Kam Tan, 177–192. London: Routledge, 2006.

Wong, Cindy, and Gary McDonogh. "Consuming Cinema: Reflections on Movies and Market-places in Contemporary Hong Kong." In *Consuming Hong Kong*, edited by Tai-lok Lei and Gordon Mathews, 81–116. Hong Kong: Hong Kong Univ. Press, 2001.

Wong, Jacob Hing-Cheung. "Our Cinema, Our Times, 23 Days of Torture and Rebirth." *Ming Pao*, April 15, 2007. http://ol.mingpao.com/cfm/Archive1.cfm?File= 20070415/sta13/vzk3.txt (accessed June 16, 2008).

Xu Xi, ed. *Fifty/Fifty: New Hong Kong Writing*. Hong Kong: Haven Books, 2008.

Yueng, Yue-man, ed. *The First Decade*. Hong Kong: Chinese Univ. Press, 2007.

Zeller, Shay. "Telluride by the Sea, Bill Pence." *Front Porch*. NHPR–New Hampshire Public Radio, September 15, 2005. http://www.nhpr.org/node/9641 (accessed April 11, 2010).

Filmography

4 Months, 3 Weeks, and 2 Days (4 luni, 3 saptamâni, si 2 zile). 2007. Cristian Mungiu.

8¹/₂. 1963. Federico Fellini.

The 11th Hour. 2007. Leila Conners and Nadia Conners.

12 registi pera 12 città. (Rome segment) 1989. Michelangelo Antonioni.

12:08 East of Bucharest (A fost sau n-a fost?). 2006. Corneliu Porumboiu.

24 City (Er shi si cheng ji). 2008. Jia Zhangke.

The 400 Blows (Le Quatre cent coups). 1959. François Truffaut.

Across the Pacific. 1942. John Huston.

Across the Universe. 2007. Julie Taymor.

Afghan Star. 2009. Havana Marking.

L'Age d'Or. 1930. Luis Buñuel.

The Age of Stupid. 2009. Franny Armstrong.

Ah Ying (Boon bin yen). 1983. Allen Fong.

Alexandra. 2007. Andre Sakurov.

Ali-G Indahouse. 2002. Mark Mylod.

All About Eve. 1950. Joseph Mankiewicz.

All That Jazz. 1979. Bob Fosse.

Alphaville (Alphavilla, une étrange aventure de Lemmy Caution). 1965. Jean-Luc Godard.

And Then There Were None. 1945. René Clair.

Angels of the Street (Les Anges du péché). 1943. Robert Bresson.

Anger (La rabia). 2006. Oscar Cardenas Navarro.

Anna Karenina. 1935. Clarence Brown.

Antichrist. 2009. Lars von Trier.

Apocalypse Now. 1979. Francis Ford Coppola.

Around the World in Eighty Days. 1956. Michael Anderson.

Around the World in 80 Days. 2004. Frank Coraci.

Arthur and the Invisibles (Arthur et les Minimoys). 2006. Luc Bresson.

Assassins: A Film Concerning Rimbaud. 1985. Todd Haynes.

L'Atalante. 1934. Jean Vigo.

L'avventura (The Adventure). 1960. Michelangelo Antonioni.

Autohystoria. 2007. Raya Martin.

Babel. 2006. Alejandro González Iñárritu.

Back Home Tomorrow (Domani torno a case). 2008. Fabrizio Lazzaretti and Paolo Santolini.

Barfly. 1987. Barbet Schroeder.

The Basilisks, the Lizards (I basilischi). 1963. Lina Wertmuller.

Bathing Beauty. 1944. George Sidney.

The Battle of Algiers (La battaglia di Algeri). 1966. Gillo Pontecorvo.

The Battle of Chile (La batalla de Chile). 1975–1979. Patricio Guzman.

Beijing Bastards (Beijing za zhong). 1993. Zhang Yuan.

Ben-Hur. 1959. William Wyler.

The Best Years of Our Lives. 1946. William Wyler.

Betelnut (Binglang). 2006. Heng Yang.

Beyond the Clouds (Al di là della nuvole). 1995. Michelangelo Antonioni and Wim Wenders.

The Big Parade (Da yue bing). 1986. Chen Kaige.

The Birds. 1963. Alfred Hitchcock.

Blackboards (Takhté siah). 2000. Samira Makhmalbaf.

The Blair Witch Project. 1999. Daniel Myrick and Eduardo Sánchez.

Blissfully Yours (Sud Sanaeha). 2002. Apichatpong Weerasethakul.

Bloody Morning (Xuese Qingchen). 1992. Shaohong Li.

Bloody Sunday. 2002. Paul Greengrass.

Born into Brothels. 2004. Zana Briski and Ross Kauffman.

Blow-Up. 1966. Michelangelo Antonioni.

Boat People (Tau ban non hoi). 1982. Ann Hui.

The Bread and Alley (Nan va Koutcheh). 1970. Abbas Kiarostami.

Breathless (A bout de souffle). 1960. Jean-Luc Godard.

Brokeback Mountain. 2005. Ang Lee.

Buffalo Bill and the Indians, or Sitting Bull's History Lesson. 1976. Robert Altman.

The Cabinet of Dr. Caligari (Das cabinet des Dr. Caligari). 1920. Robert Wiene.

Cabiria. 1914. Giovanni Pastrone.

California Dreaming (Nesfarsit). 2007. Cristian Nemescu.

Campaign. 2007. Kazuhiro Soda.

Carmen Jones. 1954. Otto Preminger.

The Case of Lena Smith. 1929. Josef von Sternberg.

Castaway on the Moon (Kimssi pyoryugi). 2009. Lee Hae-Jun.

Certified Copy (Copie conforme). 2010. Abbas Kiarostami.

Chacun son cinéma. (To Each His Own). 2007. Multiple directors.

The Changeling. 2008. Clint Eastwood.

Charlotte Bronte's Jane Eyre. 1996. Franco Zeffirelli.

The Chaser (Chugyeogja). 2008. Hong-jin Na.

Che, Part I. 2008. Steven Soderbergh.

Che, Part II. 2008. Steven Soderbergh.

Un chien andalou. 1929. Luis Buñuel.

China (Chung kuo–Cina). 1972. Michelangelo Antonioni.

China Behind (Zai jian Zhongguo). 1975. Shu Shuen Tong.

China Is Far Away—Antonioni and China. 2008. Liu Haiping.

Chronicle of the Burning Years (Chronique des années de braise). 1975. Mohammed Lakhdar-Hamina.

Chungking Express (Chung hing sam lam). 1994. Wong Kar Wai.

City of Sadness (Bei qing cheng shi). 1989. Hou Hsiao-hsien.

The Class (Entre les murs). 2008. Laurent Cantet.

Clean. 2004. Olivier Assayas.

Close-Up (Nema-ye Nazdik). 1990. Abbas Kiarostami.

The Color of Life (Vermilion Pleasure Night). 2002. Yoshimasa Ishibashi.

Colossal Youth (Juventude en marcha). 2006. Pedro Costa.

Coming Out Under Fire. 1994. Arthur Dong.

Compassion in Exile: The Life of the 14th Dalai Lama. 1993. Mickey Lemle.

Confessions (Kokuhaku). 2010. Tetsuya Nakashima.

The Cow (Gaav). 1969. Dariush Mehrjui.

Cría cuervos. 1975. Carlos Saura.

The Crucified Lovers (Chikamatsu monogatari). 1954. Kenji Mizoguchi.

Crude. 2009. Joe Berlinger.

The Cry (Il grido). 1957. Michelangelo Antonioni.

Cup of Glory. 2006. Musekiwa Samuriwo.

Dangerous Liaisons. 1988. Stephen Frears.

Daughters, Wives, and a Mother (Musume tsuma haha). 1960. Mikio Naruse.

The Days (Dongchun de rizi). 1993. Wang Xiaoshuai.

Days of Glory (Indigènes). 2006. Rachid Bouchareb.

The Death of Mr. Lazarescu (Moartea Domnului Lazarescu). 2005. Cristi Puiu.

Death Wish 4: The Crackdown. 1987. J. Lee Thompson.

A Decade of Love (Sup fun chung ching). 2008. Bryan Chang and Wing-Chiu Chan.

The Deer Hunter. 1978. Michale Cimino.

Dersu Uzala. 1975. Akira Kurosawa.

Detective Story. 1951. William Wyler.

Diary of a Country Priest (Journal d'un curé de campagne). 1951. Robert Bresson.

The Diary of Anne Frank. 1959. George Stevens.

Dirt (Tou fa luan le). 1994. Guan Hu.

Disgrace. 2008. Steve Jacobs.

Doctor Zhivago. 1965. David Lean.

Dogville. 2003. Lars von Trier.

La dolce vita. 1960. Federico Fellini.

Do the Right Thing. 1989. Spike Lee.

Double Indemnity. 1944. Billy Wilder.

Do You Remember Dolly Bell? (Sjecas li se Dolly Bell?). 1981. Emir Kusturica.

Draquila: Italy Trembles. 2010. Sabina Guzzanti.

Dream (Bi-mong). 2008. Ki-duk Kim.

Drugstore Cowboy. 1989. Gus Van Sant.

Dumbo. 1941. Samuel Armstrong, Norman Ferguson, Wilfred Jackson, Jack Kinney, Bill Roberts, and Ben Sharpsteen.

Durian Durian (Liulian piao piao). 2000. Fruit Chan.

Dyesebel. 1953. Gerardo de Leon.

East Palace, West Palace (Dong gong xi gong). 1996. Zhang Yuan.

Echoes of the Rainbow (Sue yuet san tau). 2010. Alex Law.

The Eclipse (L'eclisse). 1962. Michelangelo Antonioni.

Eden Is West (Eden a l'ouest). 2009. Costa-Gavras.

The Eel (Unagi). 1997. Shohei Imamura.

Elephant. 2002. Gus Van Sant.

The Elevator (El ascensor). 1978. Tomás Muñoz.

Emmanuelle Goes to Cannes. 1980. Jean-Marie Pallardy.

Enemies of Happiness (Vores lykkes fjender). 2006. Eva Mulvad.

The Equation of Love and Death (Li mi de caixiang). 2008. Cao Baoping.

Eros. 2004. Michelangelo Antonioni, Steven Sonderbergh, and Wong Kar Wai.

Eternity and a Day (Mia aioniotita kai mia mera). 1998. Theodoros Angeloupolos.

The Execution of P (Kinatay) 2009. Brillante Mendoza.

Exodus. 1960. Otto Preminger.

Ezra. 2007. Newton Aduaka.

Fahrenheit 9/11. 2004. Michael Moore.

The Fall of the Roman Empire. 1964. Anthony Mann.

Fantastic Mr. Fox. 2009. Wes Anderson.

Farewell My Concubine (Ba wang bie ji). 1993. Chen Kaige.

Fast, Fast (Deprisa, deprisa). 1981. Carlos Saura.

Father and Son (Foo ji ching). 1981. Allen Fong.

Father and Son (Otets i syn). 2003. Aleksandr Sokurov.

Final Solution. 2003. Rakesh Sharma.

Finding Forrester. 2000. Gus Van Sant.

Find Me Guilty. 2006. Sidney Lumet.

Five Dedicated to Ozu. 2003. Abbas Kiarostami.

Five Ways to Kill Yourself. 1987. Gus Van Sant.

Flight of the Red Balloon (Le voyage du ballon rouge). 2007. Hou Hsiao-hsien.

Ford Transit. 2002. Hany Abu-Assad.

Friendly Persuasion. 1956. William Wyler.

From Here to Eternity. 1953. Fred Zinnemann.

Frozen River. 2008. Courtney Hunt.

Il gabbiano. 1977. Marco Bellocchio.

Gaslight. 1944. George Cukor.

Gate of Hell (Jigokumon). 1953. Teinosuke Kinugasa.

Gerry. 2002. Gus Van Sant.

Ghost Town (Fei cheng). 2009. Zhao Dayong.

Gigantic. 2008. Matt Aselton.

Gilda. 1946. Charles Vidor.

The Girlfriends (Le amiche). 1955. Michelangelo Antonioni.

Godzilla. 1998. Roland Emmerich.

Go Fish. 1994. Guinevere Turner and Rose Troche.

The Good German. 2006. Steven Soderbergh.

Good Fortune. 2009. Landon Van Soest.

The Good Shepherd. 2006. Robert De Niro.

Good Will Hunting. 1997. Gus Van Sant.

Grand Illusion (La Grande Illusion). 1937. Jean Renoir.

Grbavica. 2006. Jasmile Zbanich.

Hannah Free. 2009. Wendy Jo Carlton.

The Hive (La colmena). 1983. Mario Camus.

Hobson's Choice. 1954. David Lean.

The Hole (Dong). 1998. Tsai Ming-ling.

The Holy Girl (La niña santa). 2004. Lucrecia Martel.

Homework (Mashgh-e shab). 1989. Abbas Kiarostami.

The Host. 2006. Joon-Ho Bong.

House of Strangers. 1949. Joseph Mankiewicz.

Human Imperfections (Tinimbang ka ngunit kulang). 1974. Lino Brocka.

Human Pork Chop (Bat sin fan dim ji yan yuk cha siu bau). 1993. Herman Yau.

The Hunchback of Notre Dame. 1939. William Dieterle.

I Am a Cyborg, But That's OK (Saibogujiman kwenchana). 2006. Park Il-Sun.

Ichi the Killer (Koroshiya 1). 2001. Takashi Miike.

Identification of a Woman (Identificazione di una donna). 1982. Michelangelo Antonioni.

If I Want to Whistle, I Whistle (Eu cand vreau sa fluier, fluier). 2010. Florin Serban.

The Imaginarium of Dr. Parnassus. 2009. Terry Gillman.

Indiana Jones and the Kingdom of Crystal Skull. 2008. Steven Spielberg.

In Expectation (Wu shan yan yu). 1996. Zhang Ming.

Inglourious Basterds. 2009. Quentin Tarantino.

In Good Company. 2004. Paul Weitz.

In Harm's Way. 1965. Otto Preminger.

Inner Senses (Yee do hung gaan). 2002. Law Chi Leung.

In the Holy Fire of Revolution. 2008. Masha Novikova.

In the Name of the Father. 1993. Jim Sheridan.

In the Valley of Elah. 2007. Paul Haggis.

Iraq in Fragments. 2006. James Longley.

Italy: Year One. 1974. Roberto Rossellini.

Ivan the Terrible (Ivan Groznyy). 1944. Sergei Eisenstein.

I Wish I Knew (Hai shang chuan qi). 2010. Jia Zhangke.

Joe's Bed-Stuy Barbershop: We Cut Heads. 1983. Spike Lee.

Journey to the Sun (Günese yolculuk). 1999. Yesim Ustaoglu.

Ju Dou. 1990. Zhang Yimou.

Jung (War) in the Land of the Mujaheddin. 2001. Fabrizio Lazzaretti.

Juno. 2007. Jason Reitman.

Kabuli Kid. 2008. Barmak Akram.

Kagemusha. 1980. Akira Kurosawa.

Keep Cool (You hua hao hai shuo). 1997. Zhang Yimou.

The Kids Are All Right. 2010. Lisa Cholodenko.

King of Children (Hai zi wang). 1987. Chen Kaige.

The King of Comedy. 1982. Martin Scorsese.

The King of Masks (Bian lian). 1996. Tian Ming Wu.

Komaneko—The Curious Cat. 2006. Tsuneo Goda.

Kung Fu Chefs (Gung fu chu shen). 2009. Wing Kin Yip.

Kung-fu Master! (Le petit amour). 1988. Agnès Varda.

Ladies of the Bois de Boulogne (Les dames du Bois de Boulogne). 1945. Robert Bresson.

The Lady from Shanghai. 1947. Orson Welles.

The Land of the Wandering Souls (La terre des âmes errantes). 2000. Rithy Panh.

Last Days. 2005. Gus Van Sant.

The Last House on the Left. 1972. Wes Craven.

Last Tango in Paris (Ultimo tango in Parigi). 1972. Bernardo Bettolucci.

Lemon Popsicle. 1978. Boaz Davidson.

The Leopard (Il gattopardo). 1963. Luchino Visconti.

Liberated China (New China). 1951. Sergei Gerasimov.

Life, and Nothing More . . . (Zendegi va digar hich). 1992. Abbas Kiarostami.

Little Miss Sunshine. 2006. Jonathan Dayton and Valerie Faris.

Look Into My Eyes. 2008. Naftaly Gliksberg.

Lost in Beijing (Ping guo). 2007. Li Yu.

Lost Indulgence (Mi guo). 2008. Zhang Yibai.

Love and Death. 1975. Woody Allen.

Luciano Serra, pilota. 1938. Goffredo Alessandrini.

Lumière and Company (Lumière et compagnie). 1995. 40 directors.

Lust, Caution (Se, jie). 2007. Ang Lee.

The Magdalene Sisters. 2002. Peter Mullan.

Magnolia. 1999. Paul Thomas Anderson.

Mala Noche. 1985. Gus Van Sant.

Mao's Last Dancer. 2009. Bruce Beresford.

Marie Antoinette. 2006. Sofia Coppola.

Marty. 1955. Delbert Mann.

Mary Poppins. 1964. Robert Stevenson.

M*A*S*H. 1970. Robert Altman.

Men of Israel. 2009. Michael Lucas.

Merry Christmas Mr. Lawrence. 1983. Nagisa Ôshima.

Michael Collins. 1996. Neil Jordan.

A Mighty Heart. 2007. Michael Winterbottom.

Milk. 2008. Gus Van Sant.

Missing. 1982. Costa-Gavras.

Money (L'argent). 1983. Robert Bresson.

Mother and Son (Mat i syn). 1997. Aleksandr Sokurov.

Mouchette. 1967. Robert Bresson.

Mrs. Goundo's Daughter. 2009. Barbara Attie and Janet Goldwater.

La mujer sin cabeza (The Headless Woman). 2008. Lucrecia Martel.

My Blueberry Nights. 2007. Wong Kar Wai.

My Brother's Sin. 2008. Jide Bello.

My Neighbor, My Killer. 2009. Anne Aghion.

My Own Private Idaho. 1991. Gus Van Sant.

The Mystery of Oberwald (Il misteri di Oberwald). 1981. Michelangelo Antonioni.

Nanking. 2007. Bill Guttentag and Dan Sturman.

Next Stop Paradise (Terminus paradis). 1998. Lucian Pintilie.

No. 16, Barkhor South Street. 1997. Duan Jinchuan.

No Country for Old Men. 2007. Ethan and Joel Coen.

No Man's Land. 2001. Danis Tanovic.

No One Knows about Persian Cats (Kasi az gorbehaye irani khabar nadareh). 2009. Bahman Ghobadi.

Notorious. 1946. Alfred Hitchcock.

La notte. 1961. Michelangelo Antonioni.

O Brother, Where Art Thou? 2000. Ethan and Joel Coen.

Occident. 2002. Cristian Mungiu.

Of Gods and Men (Des hommes et des dieux). 2010. Xavier Beauvois.

Olympia Part One: Festival of the Nations (Olympia 1: Teil—Fest der Volker). 1938. Leni Riefenstahl.

One Day You'll Understand (Plus tard tu comprendras). 2008. Amos Gitai.

Open City (Roma città aperta). 1945. Roberto Rossellini.

Opera Jawa. 2006. Garin Nugroho.

Othello. 1952. Orson Welles.

Outside the Law (Hors-la-loi). 2010. Rachid Bouchareb.

Oxhide (Niu pi). 2005. Liu Jiayin.

Padre nuestro/Sangre de mi sangre. 2007. Richard Zalia.

Pandora's Box (Pandoranin kutusu). 2008. Yesim Ustaoglu.

The Paper Will Be Blue (Hîrtia va fi albastră). 2006. Radu Muntean.

Paranoid Park. 2007. Gus Van Sant.

The Passenger (Professione: reporter). 1975. Michelangelo Antonioni.

Pather panchali. 1955. Satyajit Ray.

People of the Po Valley (Gente del Po). 1947. Michelangelo Antonioni.

Peppermint Frappé. 1967. Carlos Saura.

Persepolis. 2007. Vincent Paronnaud and Marjane Satrapi.

Persona. 1966. Ingmar Bergman.

Philadelphia. 1993. Jonathan Demme.

The Piano. 1993. Jane Campion.

The Piano Teacher (La pianiste). 2001. Michael Haneke.

Pickpocket. 1959. Robert Bresson.

Pickpocket (Xiao Wu). 1997. Jia Zhangke.

A Pilot Returns (Un pilota ritorna). 1942. Roberto Rossellini.

Platform (Zhantai). 2000. Jia Zhangke.

Police, Adjective (Politist, adjectiv). 2009. Corneliu Porumboiu.

Postman. 1995. He Jianjun.

Potemkin (Bronenosets Potyomkin). 1925. Sergei Eisenstein.

A Prairie Home Companion. 2006. Robert Altman.

Precious. 2009. Lee Daniels.

Prince of Persia: The Sands of Time. 2010. Mike Newell.

A Prophet (Un prophète). 2009. Jacques Audiard.

Pulp Fiction. 1994. Quentin Tarantino.

Queer Sarajevo Festival 2008. 2009. Cazim Dervisevic and Masa Hilcisin.

Quinceañera. 2006. Richard Glatzer and Wash Westmoreland.

Raining in the Mountain (Kong shan ling yu). 1979. King Hu.

Rashômon. 1950. Akira Kurosawa.

Rebecca. 1940. Alfred Hitchcock.

The Reckoning. 2009. Pamela Yates.

Red Beads (Xuan lian). 1993. He Jianjun.

Red Desert (Il deserto rosso). 1964. Michelangelo Antonioni.

Red Sorghum (Hong gao liang). 1987. Zhang Yimou.

Regret to Inform. 1998. Barbara Sonneborn.

Remnants of a War. 2009. Jawad Metni.

The Report (Gozaresh). 1977. Abbas Kiarostami.

The Road to Guantanamo. 2006. Matt Whitecross and Michael Winterbottom. .

Robin Hood. 2010. Ridley Scott.

Roma città libera. 1946. Marcello Pagliero.

Rosetta. 1999. Jean-Pierre Dardenne and Luc Dardenne.

The Rules of the Game (La règle du jeu). 1939. Jean Renoir.

The Runner (Davandeh). 1985. Amir Naderi.

La sagrada familia (The Sacred Family). 2005. Sebastian Campos.

Sanda Wong. 1955. Gerardo de Leon.

Scipio Africanus: The Defeat of Hannibal (Scipione l'Africano). 1937. Carmine Gallone.

Sex and the City 2. 2010. Michael Patrick King.

Sex Lies and Videotape. 1989. Steven Soderbergh.

Shine. 1996. Scott Hicks.

Shirin. 2008. Abbas Kiarostami.

Shrek. 2001. Adam Adamson and Vicky Jensen.

Shrek Forever After. 2010. Mike McDowell.

Shy People. 1987. Andrey Konchalovskiy.

Signal Left, Turn Right (Da zuo deng xiang). 1996. Jianxin Huang Yazhou Yang.

The Silent Revolution, vol. 2—She! (Denmark 1902–1914) / The Enemy Below (France 1904–1912) (VHS). 1987. Noël Burch.

The Sky, the Earth, and the Rain (El cielo, la tierra y la lluvia). 2008. Jose Luis Torres.

Snow (Snijeg). 2008. Aida Begić.

The So-Called Friend (Ge er men). 2001. Chin-hua Lien and Tai-Lung Tai.

Somewhere. 2010. Sofia Coppola.

The Son (Le fils). 2002. Jean-Pierre Dardenne and Luc Dardenne.

The Song of Bernadette. 1943. Henry King.

The Son's Room (La stanza del figlio). 2001. Nanni Moretti.

The Southerner. 1945. Jean Renoir.

The Spanish Apartment (L'auberge espagnole). 2001. Cédric Klapsich.

Spirited Away (Sen to chihiro no kamikakushi). 2001. Hayao Miyazaki.

Spring Fever (Chun feng chen zui de ye wan). 2009. Lou Ye.

Lo squadrone bianco. 1936. Augusto Genina.

The Square (Guang chang). 1994. Zhang Yuan and Duan Jinchuan.

Star Wars. 1977. George Lucas.

State of Siege. 1972. Costa-Gavras.

Still Life (Sanxia haoren). 2006. Jia Zhang Ke.

Story of a Love Affair (Cronaca di un amore). 1950. Michelangelo Antonioni.

The Story of Wang Laobai (Wang Lobai de gushi). 1996. Lu Wangping.

Strictly Ballroom. 1992. Baz Luhrmann.

The Strike (Siréna). 1947. Karel Steklý.

Stuff and Dough (Marfa şi banii). 2001. Cristi Puiu.

Sudden Rain (Shû u). 1956. Mikio Naruse.

Summer at Grandpa's (Dong dong de jia qi). 1984. Hous Hsiao-Hsien.

Summer Palace (Xihe yuan). 2006. Lou Ye.

Superman IV. 1987. Sidney J. Furie.

The Swamp (La ciénaga). 2001. Lucrecia Martel.

Sweetgrass. 2009. Ilisa Barbash and Lucien Castaing-Taylor.

Sweet Rush. 2009. Andrzej Wajda.

Swordsman II (Xiao ao jiang hu zhi: Dong Fang Bu Bai). 1992. Siu-Tung Ching and Stanley Tong.

Syndromes and a Century (Sang sattawat). 2006. Apichatpong Weerasethakul.

The Tale of Genji (Genji monogatari). 1951. Kozaburo Yoshimura.

Tales from the Golden Age (Amintiri din epoca de aur). 2009. Cristian Mungiu.

Tapologo. 2008. Gabriela Gutiérrez Dewar and Sally Gutiérrez Dewar.

Taste of Cherry (Ta'm-e guilass). 1997. Abbas Kiarostami.

Taxi Driver. 1976. Martin Scorsese.

Tell Me Lies. 1968. Peter Brook.

Temptation of a Monk (You seng). 1993. Clara Law.

Ten. 2002. Abbas Kiarostami.

The Terrorizer (Kong bu fen zi). 1986. Edward Yang.

Thirst (Bakjwi). 2009. Park Chan-Wook.

The Three Caballeros. 1944. Norman Ferguson.

Three Colors: Blue (Trois couleurs: Bleu). 1993. Krzysztof Kieslowski.

Three Colors: Red (Trois couleurs: Rouge). 1994. Krzysztof Kieslowski.

Three Colors: White (Trzy kolory: Bialy). 1993. Krzysztof Kieslowski.

Through the Olive Trees. 1994. Abbas Kiarostami.

Thundercrack. 1975. Curt McDowell.

Tickets. 2005. Ken Loach, Ernammo Olmi, and Abbas Kiarostami.

Tilai. 1990. Idrissa Oedraogo.

A Touch of Zen (Xia nu). 1974. King Hu.

Tough Guys Don't Dance. 1987. Norman Mailer.

Triage. 2009. Danis Tanovic.

The Trial of Joan of Arc (Procès de Jeanne d'Arc). 1962. Robert Bresson.

Tropical Malady (Sud pralad). 2004. Apichatpong Weerasethakul.

Tropic Thunder. 2008. Ben Stiller.

The Trouts (Las truchas). 1978. José Luis García Sánchex.

The True-Hearted (Xin xiang). 1992. Zhou Sun.

Tuya's Marriage (Tuya de hun shi). 2006. Wang Quanan.

Twilight. 2008. Catherine Hardwicke.

Two Cents' Worth of Hope (Due soldi di speranza). 1952. Renato Castellani.

Typical Pictures of Swiss Life. 1946. Profilm.

U-Carmen e-Khayelitsha. 2005. Mark Dornford-May.

Ulysses' Gaze (To vlemma tou Odyssea). 1995. Theo Angelopoulos.

Uncle Boonmee Who Can Recall His Past Lives (Loong Boonmee raleuk chat). 2010. Apichatpong Weerasethakul.

Underground. 1995. Emir Kusturica.

Unknown Pleasure (Ren xiao yao). 2002. Jia Zhangke.

Up. 2009. Pete Docter and Bob Peterson.

Useless (Wuyong). 2007. Jia Zhangke.

Vagabond (Sans toit ni loi). 1985. Agnès Varda.

Vengeance (Fuk sau). 2009. Johnnie To Kei Fung.

Vincere. 2009. Marco Bellocchio.

I vinti. 1953. Michelangelo Antonioni.

Viridiana. 1961. Luis Buñuel.

Viva Zapata. 1952. Elia Kazan.

Volver. 2006. Pedro Almodóvar.

Waiting for the Clouds (Bulutlari beklerken). 2003. Yesim Ustaoglu.

Walking on the Wild Side (Lai xiao zi). 2006. Han Jie.

Warrior Lanling (Lanlinmg wan). 1995. Sherwood Hu.

What Max Said (Las palabras de Max). 1978. Emilio Martinez Lázaro.

When Father Was Away on Business (Otac na sluzbenom putu). 1985. Emir Kusturica.

Where Is the Friend's Home? (Khane-ye doust kodjast?). 1987. Abbas Kiarostami.

Whispers and Moans (Sing kung chok tse sup yut tam). 2007. Herman Yau.

The White Ribbon (Das weisse band—Eine Deutsche kindergeschichte). 2009. Michael Haneke.

Wicked City (Yiu sau duo si). 1992. Tai Kit Mak.

Wild Strawberries (Smultronstället). 1957. Ingmar Bergman.

The Willow Tree (Beed-e majnoun). 2005. Majid Majidi.

Wind from the East (Le vent d'est). 1970. Groupe Dziga Vertov.

The Wind That Shakes the Barley. 2006. Ken Loach.

Winds of September (Jiu jiang feng han yan). 2008. Tom Lin.

The Wind Will Carry Us (Bad ma ra khahad bord). 1999. Abbas Kiarostami.

The Wizard of Oz. 1939. Victor Fleming.

A Woman, a Gun and a Noodle Shop (San qiang pai an jing qi). 2009. Zhang Yimou.

Woman as Property. 2008. Norie Taniguci.

The World (Shijie). 2004. Jia Zhangke.

The World of Suzie Wong. 1960. Richard Quine.

The Wrestler. 2008. Darran Aronofsky.

Xiao Shan Goes Home (Xiao Shan hui Jia). Jia Zhangke.

Yellow Earth (Huang tu di). 1985. Chen Kaige.

The Yes Men Fix the World. 2009. Andy Bichlbaum, Mika Bonanno, and Kurt Engfehr.

Yol. 1982. Serif Goren and Yilmaz Guney.

Yuen Ling-yuk. 1992. Stanley Kwan.

Z. 1969. Costa-Gavras.

Zabriskie Point. 1970. Michelangelo Antonioni.

Zhangzhi Tests His Wife. 1913. Li Minwei.

Ziegfeld Follies. 1945. Lemuel Ayers, Roy del Ruth, Robert Lewis, Vincente Minnelli, Merrill Pye, George Sidney, and Charles Walters.

Index

About the Author

Cindy Hing-Yuk Wong chairs the Department of Media Cultures at the College of Staten Island, City University of New York. In addition to her work on film festivals worldwide, she has drawn on her global background in communications, film, and anthropology to examine grassroots cinema in Philadelphia, transnational diasporic Chinese media, and cultural formation and media practices in Hong Kong. She is the coauthor of *Global Hong Kong* (2005) and coeditor of the *Encyclopedia of Contemporary American Culture* (2000). She holds a Ph.D. in communication from the Annenberg School of Communication at the University of Pennsylvania.